A Fascist Century

A Fascist Century

Essays by Roger Griffin

Edited by

Matthew Feldman

with Preface by Stanley G. Payne

First published 2008 by
PALGRAVE MACMILLAN
Houndmills, Basingstoke, Hampshire RG21 6XS and
175 Fifth Avenue, New York, N.Y. 10010
Companies and representatives throughout the world

PALGRAVE MACMILLAN is the global academic imprint of the Palgrave
Macmillan division of St. Martin's Press, LLC and of Palgrave Macmillan Ltd.
Macmillan® is a registered trademark in the United States, United Kingdom
and other countries. Palgrave is a registered trademark in the European
Union and other countries.

ISBN-13: 978–0–230–20518–5 hardback
ISBN-10: 0–230–20518–6 hardback
ISBN-13: 978–0–230–22089–8 paperback
ISBN-10: 0–230–22089–4 paperback

This book is printed on paper suitable for recycling and made from fully
managed and sustained forest sources. Logging, pulping and manufacturing
processes are expected to conform to the environmental regulations of the
country of origin.

A catalogue record for this book is available from the British Library.

Library of Congress Cataloging-in-Publication Data
Griffin, Roger.
  A fascist century / essays by Roger Griffin ; edited by Matthew
  Feldman ; with preface by Stanley Payne.
      p.   cm.
  Includes bibliographical references and index.
  ISBN 0–230–20518–6
  1. Fascism.   I. Feldman, Matthew.   II. Title.
  JC481.G695 2008
  320.53′3—dc22   2008020981

10   9   8   7   6   5   4   3   2   1
17   16   15   14   13   12   11   10   09   08

Printed and bound in Great Britain by
CPI Antony Rowe, Chippenham and Eastbourne

For Mariella and Vincent
with a love that outlasts the centuries

We have every reason to believe that this is the century of authority, a century tending to the 'right', a fascist century.

Benito Mussolini *The Doctrine of Fascism* (1932)

Contents

Editorial Acknowledgements

Many hands have touched, improved, and then totally overhauled *A Fascist Century*. Moreover, the collaborative nature of such an undertaking as this one makes it impossible to properly thank all those helping to prepare this volume – ranging from helpful anonymous readers to publishers of journals around the world. In the first place, publisher, author, and editor gratefully acknowledge permission to reproduce several of Roger Griffin's essays; the initial place of publication is cited in the first footnote in each of the eight chapters presented here.

Above and beyond the help received from various library, publishing, editing, and academic quarters, however, five names stand out. Nicolle Robinson was of great assistance in earlier stages of this project, as was Tudor Georgescu's incalculable insight and help in later preparation of the manuscript for publication; the latter also helpfully compiled the extensive bibliography. Gracious thanks are also due to Paula Bowles for her magnificent help with proofs; to Professor Stanley Payne for his support of this project; and to the excellent Michael Strang at Palgrave Macmillan. Yet were Roger Griffin not a groundbreaking scholar, not insatiable in his curiosity about dynamics of 'extreme' ideologies in the modern world, and not an inspirational teacher, this volume would never have seen the light of day. Finally, this book is also intended as a tribute to Kathy and Craig Orange, an honourable and loving pair.

Matthew Feldman
Oxford, January 2008

Roger Griffin, Fascistologist: A Preface by Stanley G. Payne

In the 17 years since *The Nature of Fascism* was published in 1991, Roger Griffin has moved to the very forefront of contemporary 'fascistologists'. His achievements have rivalled those of Ernst Nolte's original decade of specialisation in the history of fascism, and at the present time he stands unequalled among his currently active peers. His Oxford reader *Fascism* (1995) gave us the best single collection of fascist texts available in a single volume in any language, while the subsequent *International Fascism* (1998) provided the most sophisticated and up-to-date collection of studies and arguments on the interpretation of fascism. Subsequently the monumental five-volume *Fascism: Critical Concepts in Political Science* (2004), co-edited with Matthew Feldman, simply lapped the field, in its sweeping and inclusive presentation of the widest possible range of studies and interpretations from the 1920s to the present. More recently his *magnum opus, Modernism and Fascism: The Sense of a Beginning under Mussolini and Hitler* (2007), promises to be the most important book to appear on the history of fascism in a decade or more, accomplishing a sort of 'paradigm shift' in Fascist Studies which fully integrates fascism not just within cultural and political modernity, but within modernism itself. In short, Roger Griffin has given us a commitment otherwise shown only by A. James Gregor at the University of California-Berkeley: a scholar in his prime who has devoted many years unremittingly to the study and analysis of fascism, both in its classic historic manifestations and in its *sequelae*, as well.

Some of Griffin's best work has appeared in his scattered shorter pieces, so that the publication of the present volume constitutes another important contribution for scholars and students. These articles range widely from considering the temporal dimension of fascism's revolutionary assault on the *status quo*, to the analysis of Nazism, the exploration of the post-war evolution fascism (a topic traditionally neglected by historians of interwar Europe), and the theory of fascism as a twentieth-century phenomenon and a fully fledged revolutionary ideology in its own right. None of them have been printed in Anglophone academic publications till now, and several have only been available in translation (Chapters 3, 5, and 6), so keen collectors of Griffinalia are in for a treat.

A number of these pieces touch on the central issue of fascism's relationship to modernity. This question has been one of the major battlegrounds in the evolution of the interpretation of fascism, and has required a long struggle. The interpretation of fascism as a product not merely of a modern crisis or set of problems, but as the bearer of its own kind of modernity was generally long rejected. As the tendency towards a limited 'new consensus' developed among specialists during the 1990s, it eventually began to make headway. Symptomatic was the change of position by George Mosse. Since 1991 Griffin has been in the forefront of this specific controversy, and in this volume several of the chapters, but most especially 'Modernity under the New Order', deal convincingly with the problem, defining well the technocratic tendencies in fascism.

Another important dimension is the millennial – the cultural revolution and the creation of the new man. This theme is taken up in a number of the articles in quite an original way, approaching the problem from the concept of time and beginning anew, a feature common to all the fully revolutionary movements, and to both transcendent and political religions. In terms of the appeal of fascism, 'Fatal Attraction' is a useful corrective to rational-choice approaches. The latter are useful up to a point, but are inadequate to lay bare the broader appeal to true believers.

The fertility of Griffin's mind is always expressed by new analytical approaches, and none of the chapters in this volume brings more of the crucial themes together in a new analytical framework than 'Exploding the Continuum of History'. This is a most instructive study, for, to my mind, it does a better job than any of the preceding literature in analysing the fascist revolutionary thrust from the frame of the major modern revolutionary paradigm, Marxism. With regard to the left-collectivist revolutionary movements, fascism always functioned as a counterrevolutionary force, an obvious fact that opened the way for the Marxist interpretation of fascism as reactionary, and so on. What is always forgotten is the dictum of Joseph de Maistre: 'La contre-révolution n'est pas l'opposé d'une revolution; c'est une révolution opposée'. As a true reactionary, De Maistre was opposed to counter-revolution, but this was fundamental to fascist revolutionism, not merely in terms of finding an opportunity and generating support, but also in terms of being certain of its own emphases, even though its autonomous core doctrines stood alone. Fascism developed strength in Hungary and Romania as a primary revolution, but counter-punching in terms of tactics and programme was quite significant in the other four countries where it became important. Failure, or at least frustration, of the classic leftist revolution was a crucial feature of the classic 'fascist situation', in which fascism could exert a 'fatal attraction' that was holistic, not merely a return to a discredited past, but an alternative revolution of modernity against a Marxist revolution that was either rejected or stagnating.

These articles also provide extensive and lucid study of neo-fascism and the radical right, though this also may be the area on which the book enters slippery ground. To a degree even greater than that of historical fascism, neo-fascism is in the eye of the beholder, and here one must be careful not to inflate, or conflate, the subject matter. At one point Griffin cites my position to the effect that fascism is a continuing phenomenon not limited to interwar Europe, a correct reference, but one which should be qualified with the stipulation that all its significant manifestations were strictly historical. The cultural, intellectual, social, and political changes in the Western world preclude any significant revival. Movements with some of the significant features of fascism have emerged in the non-Western world, but there too contemporary conditions are such that the new candidates cannot assume the full characteristics of fascism. The more significant phenomena of this sort in the Western world do not have, or have been forced to abandon, strictly fascist characteristics, whereas the many small genuinely neo-fascist grouplets are condemned to insignificance. Moreover, the dominant new Western ideology – multi-cultural political correctness – though in one sense an easy enough target for a genuine neo-fascist movement, is slippery to deal with and is more repressive than classical liberal democracy.

Despite this caveat, taken together, these studies – illuminated by an interview between editor and author glittering with insights both personal and methodological into Griffin's constantly evolving engagement with his subject – help to advance the analysis of fascism in its interwar and post-war incarnations one step more. This volume should take not merely a useful but even an honoured place in a very large literature.

Editorial Introduction By Matthew Feldman

> Theories are like nets: he who casts will catch.
>
> – Novalis

> The longer you're here, the more things you understand, so the fewer monsters you see. Because, in the end, 'monster' is just a name for something you do not understand.
>
> –Adrian Shine, leader of the 2006 Loch Ness Project.[1]

Soundings in (an academic) Loch Ness?

'Fascism is a genus of political ideology whose mythic core in its various permutations is a palingenetic form of populist ultra-nationalism.'[2] Nearly one generation and one hundred publications of varying lengths and registers have passed since this single-sentence definition – first advanced in the groundbreaking text, *The Nature of Fascism* – heralded a groundbreaking attempt to 'catch' fascist ideology. In terms of Roger Griffin's theoretical 'net' of 1991 and the various manifestations of fascism (in this volume the small case always refers to generic fascism as opposed to Italian Fascism) hauled in, both the reception of that monograph and those ideas exemplified the major historiographical ripples and (often *ad hominem*) hostility so often associated with big-game fishing in academic waters. By way of an ongoing intellectual response, much of Griffin's time between then and now has been spent amending and, in places, jettisoning – tightening, in short – the initial casting used to trawl for the elusive, so-called 'fascist minimum'. One instance from this process may be observed in the 2004 publication of a five-volume anthology for Routledge, entitled *Fascism: Critical Concepts*. While the same materials employed in Griffin's initial approach to fascism are evident, these are also unmistakeably refined, allowing him to (re-)define fascism as a

> revolutionary form of nationalism bent on mobilizing all 'healthy' social and political energies to resist the onslaught of 'decadence' so as to achieve the goal of national rebirth, a project that involves the regeneration (palingenesis) of both the political culture and the social and ethical culture underpinning it.[3]

For Griffin, the intervening years between these two quotations included the throwing back of 'fishy' aspects in his earliest definition (in particular, historically specific characteristics which are not generic, but are intrinsic to fascist paradigms established during in the interwar period, like uniformed paramilitary marches and charismatic leadership), and their replacement with new emphases, new evidence, and vitally, new trends in scholarship on fascism. By way of contribution to this fluid area of research, the essays collected in *A Fascist Century*, taken together, cover precisely this period of refinement and suturing in what will be considered presently as an important interpretative aide in approaching fascist ideology: a 'Griffinite theory of fascism'.

But first, a few words on the more general relevance, scope, and methodology of this volume are in order. As to the first, without doubt, Griffin has been at the forefront of central academic disputes over the nature of fascist ideology during the last 15 years. Notably, in 1998, he rather prematurely asserted that a 'new consensus' was emergent amongst scholars on fascism, who 'are finally in a position to treat fascism like any other political ideology rather than as a 'special case' in which its negations or the apparatus and style of exercising power when it is implemented become paramount'.[4] If only in terms of further generating debate regarding points of (especially) divergence, Griffin's putative convergence in the late 1990s itself proved to be something of a self-fulfilling prophecy – notwithstanding a fair amount of intemperate criticism raised at the time, of which more below. Alongside the question of scholarly agreement (or otherwise) in academic conceptions of fascism, Griffin's contributions to several further historiographical debates are also evident in every section of the book. These are, respectively, particularly engaged in coverage of generic (or comparative) fascist ideology; its relevance to German National Socialism and, after 1933, the Third Reich; and finally, in Part III, the persistence of fascism after 1945 in several variably tailored guises of sheep's clothing. In consequence, the developments in Griffin's theoretical approach to 'palingenetic ultra-nationalism' over the last generation, so evident between *The Nature of Fascism* and the concluding interview here – indeed, lengthily dwelled upon in the latter text rounding out this volume – relates directly and substantially to the growing sophistication of studies into this most modern of ideological specimens.

A Fascist Century's relevance is thus, in fact, at least twofold. As suggested earlier, one reason for this book is obvious: the increasing currency of Griffin's view of generic fascism, not to mention that view's demonstrable utility to a range of twentieth century case studies. As such, individual chapters here present specific interventions into central, continuing debates on what fascism 'is', in addition to how scholars and students might, in turn, profitably understand and apply 'it' (the all-important quotation marks shall be expanded upon below). Inversely, the evolution of Griffin's own approach to fascist ideology, in many ways, also parallels the evolution of recent scholarship on fascism as whole, increasingly willing to conceive of fascist ideology not only as recognisable *in and of itself*, but more specifically, as a comprehensive doctrine for the regeneration of ethnic and/or national communities. Yet as the chapters here make clear, this is but a doorway to a more 'maximalist' reading forming an ever-larger portion of Griffin's research; one that encompasses not merely ideology but faith and action, aesthetics and culture, society, and indeed (however chillingly, as in the case of Nazi genocide) ethics.

Parenthetically, such a view, of course, is not to bestow a system of values *upon* Nazism (or for that matter, any other fascist movement), but an attempt to historically contextualise fascism; that is, an attempt to understand fascists as they understood, and continue to understand, themselves and their mission. This is an attempt to discern the values fascists themselves held, and how these were translated into practice. As Griffin has repeatedly stressed in his writings, such a reading derives from a tradition inherited from the late and great historian of fascism, George Mosse: 'methodological empathy'. Yet this is not simply abstract theorising without relation to the Real World (although it is too often ignored that theories can only ever be *pictures* of the world, not essentialist, or perfectly imitative, reproductions of the world *itself*). This neglected point has been recently emphasised by a renowned empirical historian of Nazism, Karl Dietrich Bracher:

> The formation of historico-political concepts, as the argument surrounding the concepts of Fascism and totalitarianism of the last two decades has shown, is of greatest significance – and this not only for the formation of political consciousness, but for the research and portrayal of historical contexts themselves; for the latter is always based upon the selection and incorporation of the event, its tradition and its recollection.[5]

Secondly, in terms of relevance, the very course and direction of the eight chapters in this book – most of which are printed here in English for the very first time and which vary so strikingly in tone, remit, and, here and there, sophistication[6] – represent a kind of academic *Gestalt*; that is, this volume may collectively offer more insight than the sum of its individual texts. For the progressive refinement of approach, alongside the various examples of international fascism covered here, are but different keys playing a now-familiar melody, even if Griffin's theoretical piano has been noticeably re-tuned in the light of recent scholarship and criticism. In short, the theories and case studies presented in *A Fascist Century* as a whole may be seen to offer a window onto the ongoing refinement of an academic theory on fascist ideology, and latterly, in fact, the maturation of a nascent discipline: Fascist Studies.

Likewise, the scope of this collection of essays reflects both Griffin's own range of enquiry – greatly aided by his fluency in Italian, French, and German – yet also, significantly, the sharp edge of disagreement about how fascist ideology can be extended to the fascist practices. By way of initiation to these debates, the reader may actually find it helpful to start reading back to front; that is, one might usefully start with the concluding interview. This is due to the sharp variations in language and composition date separating individual texts here, a central consideration in editorial attempts to effectively represent the very scope of Griffin's register, development, and areas of coverage. This means, in effect, that some chapters are much shorter and easier to read than others, while still different texts respond to contemporaneous historical events in the last 15 years (such as the end of the Cold War forming the backdrop to Chapter 7). The reasons for such an idiosyncratic remit is addressed in the final interview, which is both discursive in tone and sequential in its reflection upon the circumstances shaping each of the preceding eight chapters. And as such, it is there, rather than here, that a chapter-by-chapter summary and synoptic overview for *A Fascist Century* may be consulted. The final interview is thus envisioned as both a reflection on earlier chapters, as well as a snapshot of current debates in Fascist Studies.

Another general feature related to the scope traversed by *A Fascist Century* actually concerns the work of Griffin's colleagues in the field. Situated within a tradition of scholarship as he is, a number of features initially neglected in *The Nature of Fascism* are developed in the ensuing chapters. These include a close engagement with Emilio Gentile's reading of sacralised politics; employment of Stanley Payne's well-known taxonomy for interwar fascist regimes; and more recently, a turn towards Victor Turner's sociological work on 'revitalisation movements', and Zygmunt Bauman's take on totalitarian regimes (the USSR, Nazi Germany, and Fascist Italy in particular) as 'gardening states' on account of their cultivation of desirable elements and ruthless weeding out of others.[7] All of the above, to varying degrees, come to bear upon the essays to follow, and have significantly contributed to the broadening of Griffin's own remit in exploring fascism. Inclusion of political religion and totalitarianism theories, 'biopolitics', and so on, moreover, illustrates the manner in which Griffin's approach is intended to serve as a 'heuristic' aide, of which more momentarily.

Yet these theoretical modifications since 1991 are revealing in and of themselves. They give further proof that no theory is definitive; and in Griffin's case, an extended scope of coverage is due to his learning from, and collaboration with, academics working in the same area. Derivatively, this has led Griffin to see the 'clustering' of overlapping concepts to add depth to his own analysis of fascist ideology. For example, while Nazism may be viewed as a form of generic fascism, the latter may itself be subsumed into the larger concept of political religions (applicable to left- and right-wing totalitarian regimes). In turn, all of these can be understood as an enforced harnessing of 'modernity', a condition progressively brought about by the various revolutions and industrial developments in post-feudal Europe. This process is particularly evident in several of the essays from the 1990s – notably the first two chapters in this volume, which focus on themes given short shrift in *The Nature of Fascism*. The point is that this collaborative clustering of theories, so evident over the course of these essays, is indicative of a larger working method: by embracing the abutting work of colleagues, the scope of Griffin's own theoretical starting-point is substantially augmented.

In respect of this theoretical point of departure, a final few words at the out-set covering Griffin's methodology are necessary. As the contents in *A Fascist Century* shows, engagement with concepts such as 'modernity', 'temporality', 'ultra-nationalism', and 'palingenesis' suffuse Griffin's scholarship, and all are consistently employed here. Yet these terms' patrimony is much indebted to the conceptual modelling undertaken by Max Weber, especially as mediated by Thomas Burger's important work on the subject. Griffin has made use of both scholars for his own 'ideal type' on fascism, as the practice of 'idealising abstraction' in search of an ineliminable or definitional core of an ideology necessitates the use of theories to group together and explain a sequence of unique events. One recognisable ideal type are the events collectively known as 'World War Two' – usually understood as the global conflict between September 1939 and August 1945 – which, in most theories of the Second World War (even if the accounts claim not to use 'theory'), excludes the Sino-Japanese War from 1931. Ideal types are fashioned for use: were the exceptions to dis-prove the rule, the ideal type would not stand up to empirical verification. As Burger makes clear, the suitability (or otherwise) of any Weberian point of departure to historical events is predicated on usefulness; that is, the *heuristic* value of a given theory: 'general concepts do not describe the elements [...] a class of phenomena have in common in the empirical world, but the elements which they have in common in an imaginary world, a utopia'.[8] By heuristically approaching fascist ideology in this way, Griffin's methodology is explicitly open-ended and predicated on perceived features of commonality across move-ments, countries, and regimes, as a passage from Chapter 8 (pages 183–184) shows:

> The result of idealising abstraction is a conceptually pure, artificially tidy model which does not correspond exactly to any concrete manifestation of the generic phenomenon being investigated, since 'in reality' these are always inextricably mixed up with features, attributes, and surface details that are inherently unique, and which are not considered definitional to that example of it. The basic question to be asked about any definition of 'fascism', therefore, is not whether it is true, but whether it is heuristically useful. Vitally, for the study of generic fascism, this entails heuristically gathering common features from a large body of independent phenomenon in interwar Europe and beyond.

Perhaps the most significant methodological revision Griffin's engagement with ideal types has brought about is the trial-and-error separation of ineliminable components of fascism from their attendant features and specific manifestations. Griffin's distinction between the 'core' and 'adjacencies' of an ideology also post-date *The Nature of Fascism*, and owe much to Michael Freeden's research on 'ideological morphology'.[9] This understanding has been a great boon to Griffin's evolving methodology. For an engagement with Freeden's scholarship over the 1990s better allowed Griffin to differentiate between ideologically decisive elements of fascism – those concepts that *cannot* be excluded from the definition, like revolutionary renewal and the perceived crisis of modernity – notably the endlessly malleable way in which these can be interpreted and implemented. That interwar fascism relied on flag-waving paramilitaries and charismatic leadership does not mean that all permutations of fascism need do so. Since 1945, as Griffin makes clear in Part III, a basic premise amongst fascist ideologues is to abandon 'classic' fascist characteristics as a necessary survival strategy. Thus, anti-fascists looking only for jackbooted marches through town centres might believe that fascism is dead.

As a consequence, if one concedes that fascism has an ideology, and accepts that ideologies have a morphological nature – they change with the times, just as American liberalism outlived American slavery – the face of fascist ideology is not simply the face of Hitler or Mussolini, nor the millions they inspired. Nor, as Griffin has recognised since *The Nature of Fascism*, are anti-Bolshevism, expectations of a post-liberal order, or the imminent expectation of national rebirth – even fascism's strictly 'national' dimensions, as evidenced by the 'Pan-European fascism' spouted by the likes of Per Engdahl during the Cold War – defining parts of fascist ideology. These were certainly inextricable from the 'fascist era' between 1919 and 1945, as were expansionist para/militarism and, often, overt anti-Semitism. But none of these are inseparable from fascist ideology *as such*; all are ideological traits no less definitional than a first-past-the-post system is the signature of British liberalism, for instance, while German liberalism favours proportional representation. The latter examples are simply national permutations of a generic ideology; they are manifestations of an ineliminable core intrinsic to liberalism: democratic participation. As regards the ineliminable core of fascism, any Griffinite theory of fascism must start from precisely this methodological basis. And it is this ideal type and its heuristic applicability now meriting further discussion.

A Griffinite theory of fascism

Whereas two of Griffin's own characterisations of fascism are given above, it is important to note that these single-sentence definitions are *always* punctuated with the proviso that such descriptions must be subsequently 'unpacked'; that is, qualified, extended, and delimited at length. Naturally enough, no concise definition can do appropriate justice to the ideological syncretism and challengingly diverse manifestations fascism has assumed since its inception. In consequence and by way of introductory example, the rest of this essay will be taken up with discussing the following summary of what a Griffinite theory of fascism might (currently!) look like.

> Since it first emerged in the wake of World War One, fascism can be profitably conceptualised as *a specifically modern form of secular 'millenarianism' constructed culturally and politically, not religiously, as a revolutionary movement centring upon the 'renaissance' of a given people (whether perceived nationally, ethnically, culturally, or religiously) through the total reordering of all perceivedly 'pure' collective energies towards a realisable utopia;* an ideological core implacably hostile to democratic representation and socialist materialism, equality and individualism, in addition to any specific enemies viewed as alien or oppositional to such a programme.

Although specific expressions of 'palingenetic ultra-nationalism' have ranged from culturally metapolitical movements to actively genocidal regimes, both fascist ideology and its attendant tactics are advanced by fascists themselves in the interests of a revolutionary socio-political praxis; that is, a fusion of mind and body, of word and deed. Ideas buttressing the rise of fascism in the interwar period were, in the first instance, taken from a number of counter-cultural thinkers from the late nineteenth century and since (Friedrich Nietzsche, Georges Sorel, Vilfredo Pareto, Houston Stewart Chamberlain, and Charles Maurras, e.g., are frequently cited in this 'proto-fascist' connection). Like Hitler, Mussolini, Mosley, and millions of other demobilised soldiers after 1918 – many of whom were to become, like the first three, revolutionary nationalists forming the spine of most interwar fascist movements – little attention was paid to whether the intellectual currency of these new ideas had derived from the 'left' or 'right'. Largely on this account (but also due to the rhetoric of many fascist ideologues), it has been frequently noted that fascist movements attempted to forge a 'third way' between communism and liberalism; one touted as a more spiritual alternative to these competing, supposedly materialistic ideological systems.

Also critical to the early development of fascism were utopian myths of a 'regenerated' community, almost always an existing nation-state in the generation between 1919 and 1939. This 'new' nation was to be forcibly insulated against the unwanted trappings of the modern world – multi-culturalism, democracy and liberalism, Marxism and communism, individualism, internationalism, capitalism, 'undesirables' (typically Jews, but certainly other marginalised groups as well), and so on – alongside recourse to violence (often perpetrated by paramilitary formations), xenophobia and racism, and an accompanying intellectual bid for 'right-wing hegemony' through engagement with art and culture. These aspects were to form a mythic, utopian alternative to the chaotic conditions existing across Europe, at the heart of which lay the goal of achieving a new source of collective 'health' within a 'sick' or decadent community. The cover image celebrating Nazi labour on May Day 1937 invokes many of these themes: the equation of all things German with Nazism; an idealised 'people's community' finding no place for 'community aliens'; and not least, the propagation of these mythic ideas via art – in this case, through a modernist, panoramic Nazi painting.

Prominent too in my characterisation of fascism is, in Griffin's phrase, the 'fascist minimum' (given in italics above); that is, components which are indispensable to fascist ideology, with peripheral features conditioning and individuating fascist practices revolving around this core, giving fascist movements their undeniable uniqueness. Just as British and American liberalism remain cousins rather than twins, and just as Communist China and the Soviet Union maintained their own – oftentimes bitterly opposed – versions of Marxism, so too with specific permutations of fascism. In sum, all three political doctrines (and institutional systems) may be defined and understood ideologically; though it must, again, be stressed that theories are invariably less messy than reality (especially if they are useful ones). While the specific values championed by, for example, Léon Degrelle's Belgian *Rex* [Christ the King] appear far removed from those of Vidkun Quisling's Norwegian *Nasjonal Samling* [National Rally] – instanced by the Roman Catholicism of the former and the Protestantism of the latter – or similarly, the valorisation of the peasantry in the Iron Guard's understanding of the Romanian nation as opposed to the small shopkeepers heavily featured in the British Union of Fascists' [BUF] propaganda; specific fascist movements are, as a rule, both generically identifiable and individually unique.

Moreover, the Janus-face presented by a generic ideology and the particular manifestations of it remain applicable after the defeat of European fascist movements in 1945. The post-war, militant defence of the 'white race' by Louis Beam's Aryan Nations in America, as opposed to the 'neo-populist' attacks on multi-culturalism by Jean-Marie Le Pen's *Front National*, exemplifies this. Programmes and methods frequently vary (often markedly); nevertheless, all of the above movements may be heuristically grouped together through the lens of Griffin's approach to fascist ideology.

How, then, would such a Griffinite theory of fascism take shape in practice? In the first instance, modernity – a condition as ambiguous and restless as its definition – is, as is made clear by the term's increasing relevance in chapters here, the point of departure for Griffin's approach to fascism. In Griffin's work, modernisation and modernity have progressively stepped from behind the interpretative curtain to be viewed as the driving dynamic that under-pins fascism's bid to create a new world through an 'alternative modernity' than that envisioned by democratic and communist societies. For 'the modern world' is the Petri dish in which all ideologies grow; none more so than the twentieth-century birth and rapid maturation of fascism.

Like all the terms Griffin employs, analysis of 'the modern' is 'ideal-typical'; that is, the concept's utility is directly tied to the way in which it is explained (or 'defined'), understood (or 'explicated'), and incorporated (or 'applied'). Such concepts 'exist' only insofar as they are useful. Thus, when considering words with a variety of meanings, or ways of generally broaching the concept repre-sented by a given word – for example, 'fascism' means fundamentally different things to Marxists and liberals, let alone to fascists themselves – it is salutary to bear in mind that all 'ideal types' are academically constructed to better describe parts of the world, not to seek or determine their essence. 'The nature of fascism' is thus an idea of a different order from an existing person or thing, like 'the nature of Adolf Hitler'. Hence, the nebulous term 'modernity' is, for Griffin, much less akin to a mathematical problem with one solution, than to various types of reading glasses, the criteria of which is not a question of the right or wrong prescription, but instead focus. This point is amplified by the anthropologist Clifford Geertz, another influential scholar whose work Griffin draws upon: 'cultural analysis is intrinsically incomplete [. . . .] Anthropology is a science whose progress is marked less by perfection of consensus than by a refinement of debate.'[10]

Griffin's use of the term 'modern', a principal subject of his recent mono-graph, *Modernism and Fascism*,[11] in effect recognises the totalising scope and effects of modernity from the nineteenth century in the industrialising world. This does not merely refer to the increasing mechanisation of commerce, trans-port, and production, but also embraces the codification of secular authority (especially through the European nation-state), the rise of capitalism, bureau-cracy, and professionalisation (as in the human, social, and medical sciences); and underpinning all of these, the very fragmenting of the world into con-flicting cosmologies registered by artists like Charles Baudelaire, philosophers like Oswald Spengler, scientists like Herbert Spencer, or even theosophists like Madame Blavatsky. In short, challenges to the stability of the 'old world' drowned the individual in urban centres, economic rationalisation, and com-peting world-views, both sacred and secular. Against the rising tides of *anomie* and doubt, fascists flatly asserted that a new collective was needed to recreate a sense of belonging and certainty.

With Europe already at a crossroads of value, the militarisation and nation-alism of the masses contesting the First World War acted as an ideological accelerator – to use Chalmers Johnson's important understanding of the term[12] – of unprecedented proportions. 'A God at last!' decreed the German poet Rainer Maria Rilke in 1914. On the other side of the world – and indeed a world apart in terms of how the Great War was received – the Australian author Frederic Manning's semi-autobiographical Great War novel from 1929, *The Middle Parts of Fortune*, revealed the extent of demoralisation brought about by the wartime conditions of the Western Front:

> 'C'est la guerre,' they would say, with resignation that was almost apathy: for all sensible people know that war is one of the blind forces in nature, which can neither be foreseen nor controlled. Their attitude, in all its simplicity, was sane. There is nothing in war which is not in human nature; but the violence and passions of men become, in the aggregate, an impersonal and incalculable force, a blind and irrational movement of the collective will, which one cannot control, which one cannot understand, which one can only endure as these peasants, in their bitterness and resignation, endured it. *C'est la guerre.*

While many, like the Italian Futurists, valorised war and urged their nations to rush forward; others too, like Ludwig Meidner, had an inkling of what the reality would be like, as evidenced by his famous apocalyptic landscapes on the eve of the First World War. Moreover, after the war and the unsatisfactory settlement for all concerned – especially the losing nations and a particularly disappointed Italy – groups like the *Freikorps* in Germany and the *Squadristi* in Italy were proving that the 'war to end all wars' had already become a myth by 1919. In the ensuing revolutionary period, fewer and fewer voices like Manning's embraced pacifism as the only possible alternative: 'War is waged by men; not by beasts, or by gods. It is a peculiarly human activity [. . . .] Perhaps some future attempt to provide a solution for it may prove to be even more astonishing than the last'.[13] Paramilitary uniforms trumped pacifism in this era of discord, uncomfortably separating two global wars sparked off in Europe. But whatever the response during the interwar period, the First World War undoubtedly acted as a fundamental *caesura* with the preceding *belle époque*, changing lives in a hitherto unprecedented fashion, and igniting both the glorification of warfare, the diffusion of various myths (such as the 'stab in the back' in Germany), and the extensive intervention of the state in civil and social affairs. All of these were to have disastrous ramifications in the hands of fascists across Europe after 1919.

In Griffin's account of the appeal of fascism in the interwar period, this confluence of long-term and short-term upheavals in Europe remains decisive – both objectively (such as the 1929 Wall Street Crash) and subjectively (such as Germany's imposed 'war guilt clause' in the Treaty of Versailles). Riven with ideological conflict (not least because of the 'materialist' and 'atheist' revolution under Bolshevism resulting in the creation of the Soviet Union after 1917), the legacies of unprecedented violence, pervasive adhesive of nationalism, and economic uncertainties punctuated by crises – all of these contributed to what Gerald Platt has described as 'a sense-making crisis' in interwar Europe.[14] This approach has taken Griffin from the confines of history towards the history of ideas, political sciences, and even anthropology. For the interwar period cannot merely be accounted for with dates and statistics. Promises of a comprehensive renewal ('palingenesis') from the decadent face of modernism, anomic longings for a new (political) religion, a cause worthy of sacrifice and one able to give a collective value to the apparent senselessness of the world, surely formed a large part of the European attraction to fascism. This movement, again, is not understood by Griffin as merely an Italian phenomenon, but a generic political ideology embracing both ideas and practice; one that was comparable insofar as it spread across Europe (and also emerged in a handful of places outside Europe), but became highly variegated as each national community looked to its own traditions and characteristics for the catch-all answer to the problems faced.

By flourishing in societies facing 'sense-making' crises, the interwar period was an ideal incubator for a wide range of fascist movements. Consequently, the empowerment of fascism in Italy and Germany were thus an expression for currents much larger than just these two regimes. For Griffin, Fascism and Nazism were modern, revolutionary movements predicated on wholly revising any pre-existing social contract in Europe: the rights of individuals were value-less against the 'will' of the collective; propaganda was to shape the community's outlook (in the original, etymological sense of 'propagating the faith'), while state terror was to crush any who disagreed or did not fit in. For this was to be an *alternative modernity* to those already under construction in the Soviet Union and America, to name but two. For the intended majority of the community under the two fascist regimes, this meant a total resolution of modernity's ambiguities of modernity through an enforced national renaissance, like a staged act of faith (i.e. 'political religion'). This secular devotion was to be expressed everywhere, from road-building to eugenically driven natalism, and aimed at nothing less than the recreation of state and people in a consciously mythic, aesthetic, yet deadly serious totalitarian project intended to 'save' the nation's socio-cultural values from expressions of 'decadence' (variously defined as Judaism, liberalism, modern art, feminism, Marxism, and so on – this list is by no means exhaustive). In expressing this new value-system, both regimes restarted the Judeo-Christian calendar: 1922 thus became Year 1 in Italy, while some buildings erected before the 1936 Olympics in Germany bore the inscription Year III.

Yet a Griffinite theory of fascism embraces a larger point in a temporal and geographical sense too. If it follows that fascism is a distinctively modern political ideology aimed at forcefully recreating comprehensive, utopian meaning for self-defined communities in a world of competing values and systems, then there is no reason that this should be limited either to regimes in Germany and Italy, let alone to the 'fascist epoch' of 1919 to 1945. The very range of abortive (i.e. never governing) fascist movements – each with distinctive characteristics, but each conforming to the ideological features set out above – by no means limited to Europe alone,[15] demonstrates just how seductive a vision of comprehensive national redemption can be. From the small yet programmatic [BUF] to the large yet amorphous Hungarian Arrow Cross, fascism spread across interwar Europe rapidly and forcefully – accompanied nearly always by handmade uniforms, collective violence, and fire-and-brimstone leaders.

To Griffin's thinking, however, none of the latter characteristics are defining components of fascist ideology. After 1945, on account of the very destruction wreaked by fascist movements across Europe, let alone the new historical paradigm that created the hegemonic Russian and American superpowers during the Cold War, fascism, above all, needed to re-brand itself. Whereas the interwar period was generally one of nationalist militarism for fascists, the postwar era – albeit still inscribed with the comprehensive rebirth of a championed community, though no longer imminently expected – was to witness substantial alterations to fascism's language and organisation.[16] Thus, for example, ideologues like Mosley and Francis Parker Yockey advocated a pan-European fascist movement in the initial years of the Cold War;[17] William Pierce's subsequent emphasis on race, as well as Louis Beam's more recent Aryan Nations, envisioned a unity of all 'whites' (including Caucasian Americans, Australians, etc.).[18] More recently, 'neo-fascism' has also cloaked itself under the rubric of populism, in the form of parties like Nick Griffin's British National Party (BNP) or under the guise of metapolitical think-tanks like Alain de Benoist's GRECE [*Le Groupement de Recherche et d'Études pour la Civilisation Européenne*].[19] Finally, in the past decade, the diffusion of White Noise punk music as well as 'groupuscules' enjoying an almost-exclusively online existence (such as Aleksandr Dugin's *Arctogaia* website; or more marginally, Michael Walker's 'third way' journal, *The Scorpion*) shows that global reach can belie the often miniscule membership of these 'virtual' fascist movements.[20] Of course, this does not exclude either 'classic' fascist paramilitary groups like the English Combat-18 or the American Neo-Nazis, let alone 'lone wolf' fascists committing individual acts of terrorism like the Soho nail-bomber David Copeland.[21] But together, the heterogeneity of fascist phenomena evinces both the clear perseverance and necessary mutation of fascist ideology since 1945. As Part III in this volume demonstrates, this wider understanding of fascism – beyond Europe, and in particular, beyond the 'fascist era' – suggests an underlying continuation of fascism from its interwar inception to the present day, making this ideology less a subject of purely historical research than one tracked by journalists and political scientists as well.[22]

Although the above makes no claim to conclusively 'netting' Griffin's approach to fascist ideology and movements, it does hopefully place the reader in a position to consider the arguments advanced over the ensuing chapters. But just as importantly, it should also help to clarify what Griffin's theory of fascism is not. This is particularly important for two reasons. First, exploring generic fascism in its own terms means dealing with violence and hatred without trivialising its intellectual roots, of suspending moral judgements on both individual fascists and movements from a perspective that retains a practicing liberalism detesting such an exclusionary ideology. Yet navigation between the Scylla of dispassionate understanding and the Charybdis of humanistic opposition to fascist ideology is a familiar problem faced by, for example, scholars of the Holocaust. Simply consider the following quotation by Field Marshal von Reichenau during the onset of Nazi genocide in Eastern Europe:

> Hereby tasks develop for the troops, which go beyond conventional one-sided soldiering. The soldier in the Eastern territories is not merely a fighter according to the rules of the art of war, but also bearer of a ruthless national idea and the avenger of all the bestialities, which have been inflicted upon German and racially related people.[23]

Finding this document nauseating in a human capacity is easy and clear enough in the following chapters – a point bearing further emphasis momentarily – yet the Mossean 'methodological empathy' intrinsic to Griffin's theory of fascism attempts to *comprehend* (rather than simply analyse) the doctrinal underpinnings of this 'ruthless national idea' as well as the mindsets inculcated by it. That is to say, taking the above 'seriously' as something more than propaganda or false consciousness is not to endorse its validity, but instead is to academically examine its basis as a specific manifestation of generic fascist ideology.

Some working in the same area, it must be noted, fail to recognise this vital distinction in Griffin's writings, resulting in a few rather less than collegial responses. A recent example is found in the introduction to Michael Mann's sociological study, *Fascists*. 'Griffin's idealism is nothing to be proud of. It is a major defect', writes Mann, who continues, 'Griffin also sanitizes fascism, remaining silent on its distinctly brutal violence and paramilitarism'.[25] Two quotations by Griffin, neither in this collection of essays, must suffice to patently refute such a 'defect': 'This book has ascribed the horrific human consequences of fascism, when put into practice, to its mythic core of a palingenetic vision, a vision which encourages, not a creative interaction and healthy integration with the external world, but a total and perverse identification with only a narrow part of it'. And secondly:

> The racial nationalisms considered in this volume never became the basis of state policy; however, the practical implementations of enacting them were demonstrated in all their blood-chilling horror by the Third Reich. The mass production of torture and murder in which science, medicine, and technology became so deeply implicated under the Nazis underlines the disturbing ambivalence of the instinctual human desire to grow mysterious trees of utopianism where they perceive a wasteland.

To be sure, neither quotation is hidden: the former is contained in the two-paragraph postscript to Griffin's 1991 monograph, while the latter forms much of the conclusion to a 2006 text on scientific racism and nationalism in South-Central Europe, c. 1900–1940.[24] As the reader may judge from the chapters to follow, these comments, separated by 15 years of scholarship, hardly bookend an 'idealising' or sanitising approach to fascism in Griffin's *oeuvre*. Further-more, neither quotation, at any stretch, may be said to constitute 'silence' on the human wreckage left behind in fascism's destructive wake, and – regrettable though it may be to have to point this out in an academic intro-duction – the reader will encounter several similar statements in the course of the following chapters which reveal such charges to be unfounded, perverse even.

Also unfounded, despite recurrent focus on Weberian 'ideal type' theory and the frequent marshalling of terms like 'heuristic', 'non-essentialist', and so forth, are charges that Griffin somehow reifies fascism, meaning that his approach sets out to be a kind of mathematical equation able to quantitatively solve the question of which movements or individuals 'were actually' fascists. Far from it: as the reworkings of Griffin's own approach makes clear – not to mention some of the false starts and dead-ends evident in the chapters herein – charac-terising fascism is much more akin to chaos theory than Euclidean geometry. Question marks are preferred to exclamation points throughout. This is befit-ting such an intrinsically contested term like fascism, whose only 'essence' is that ascribed to it by others, not the Kantian thing-in-itself. Indeed, already in *The Nature of Fascism* Griffin defended himself against charges of essen-tialism, perhaps in anticipation of those castigating the basic principles of this 'idealising abstraction': 'fascism has been demonised quite enough into a suprahuman force already at the level of popular mythology without the waters being muddied even further by an academic work with "essentialist" implications'.[26]

Finally, one of the more valuable aspects of Griffin's theory of fascism evident here is that it allows the evolution of fascism to be tracked over the course of the twentieth century; that is, not only before the watershed year 1945, but in the twenty-first century as well. For it is after 1945 – sometimes called the 'era of postfascism' in order to contrast with the 'fascist epoch' – when fascist ideology necessarily assumes a new identity (and often an alias), as with the case of the European New Right. Such a view thus is especially in keeping with the view of Taguieff, Pierre-André with respect to the neo-fascist credentials of Alain de Benoist's GRECE: 'If vigilance was only a game of recognising something already well-known, then it would only be a question of remembering'.[27] Without doubt, it is in the contribution to developing an evermore historiographically refined consideration of fascism's attempt to literally 'begin time anew', as well as to undertake an historically informed ability to monitor the contemporary permutations of the fascism, that much of the importance of these essays ultimately rests.

Here Primo Levi's sentiments, more fully reprinted in the epilogue to Griffin's *Fascism: A Reader* as 'The Deadly Trunk of Fascism', are apposite.[28] As Griffin's last chapter in this collection argues, fascism's 'facelessness' in the post-war era does not make it any less real or acceptable – whether as 'leaderless' terrorism or 'metapolitical' assaults on the existing order. Homosexual targets of neo-Nazi David Copeland's bombing in London's Soho, or Jewish families having to erase swastikas from the gravestones of relatives in French cemeteries, appreciate this only too well. To be sure, the lack of a 25-Point Programme does not preclude neo-fascist activism or the continuing generation of fascist ideas, sometimes with frightening sophistication. Griffin encourages both historians and political scientists to relate fascism's ideology to its practice, as well as to engage with fascism's remarkable power to mutate from its interwar form and to adapt to new lochs.

Only through a keen interest in the morphology of fascism – its capacity for metamorphosis not unlike other contemporary political ideologies – can the human sciences appropriately fulfil their 'watching brief' advocated by Levi, who saw it as his duty to bear autobiographical witness to the realities of his torture in Auschwitz. For as long as the exclusivist temptations of fascist ideology remain amongst us, proudly marching or advancing stealthily incognito, methodological understanding is surely needed in equal measure to moral condemnation. Primo Levi's written testimony and prophetic warnings – his brilliantly stark ability to look forwards and backwards simultaneously – remain both a reminder of interwar fascism's attempt to induce national rebirth through mass murder, as well as a mandate to stay forever vigilant against the temptations of exclusivist utopias:

A new Fascism, with its trail of intolerance, of abuse, and of servitude, can be born outside a country and imported into it, walking on tiptoe and calling itself by other names, or it can loose itself from within with such violence that it routes all defences. At that point, wise counsel no longer serves, and one must find the strength to resist. Even in this contingency, the memory of what happened in the heart of Europe, not very long ago, can serve as support and warning.[29]

Part I
Fascism's Temporal Revolution

1

'I am no longer human. I am a Titan. A god!'

The Fascist Quest to Regenerate Time*

The 'revolutionary festival'

Some two decades ago, Mona Ozouf's *Festivals and the French Revolution*[1] pro-vided impressive testimony to the centrality of myth and ritual in the dynamics of even a 'modern', 'rational' revolution purportedly carried out in the name of Enlightenment principles. Now that, at long last, some scholars are taking seriously the proposition that Fascism[2] as well as Nazism[3] attempted to create a new type of culture, it seems an appropriate moment to consider whether the conspicuously ritualised, theatrical component of both Fascism and generic fascism can be illuminated by the concept of 'the revolutionary festival'. As we shall see, applying such a concept has a particular heuristic value when applied to fascist ideology and practice, despite the radical differences which clearly sep-arate the largely spontaneous explosion of populist mythic energies unleashed by the French Revolution from those deliberately engineered in ordinary cit-izens by Fascist and Nazi elites. By the time he wrote *Mein Kampf* Hitler was already aware of the need to emulate the power of the mass demonstrations held by communists which

> burned into the small wretched individual the proud conviction that, pal-try worm as he was, he was nevertheless part of a great dragon, beneath whose burning breath the heated bourgeois world would one day go up in fire and flame and the proletarian dictatorship would celebrate its ultimate final victory.[4]

---

* This chapter is based on a talk given for a postgraduate seminar series on Fascism held at University College London in 1997, which was then written up as a paper to appear in 1998 on the newly created *Electronic Seminars in History* (see http://www. history.ac.uk/seminars) published by the Institute of Historical Research at the University of London, and is reproduced here with their kind permission.

The notion that there can be qualitatively different experiences of time is pivotal to such an investigation. The issue of subjective 'times' is clearly one of enormous psychological and anthropological complexity, and is by its nature susceptible to any number of conceptual schemes. Yet it is significant that not only countless poets[5] but also several major Western intellectuals have suggested that a dichotomy between 'ordinary' time and 'special' time persists in the age of modernity. Émile Durkheim, for example, not only distinguished between 'sacred' and 'profane' time,[6] but devoted considerable attention to 'effervescent assemblies' in which individual, anomic time gives way to a collective sense of belonging and temporal purpose. Similarly, one of the effects which Max Weber attributed to the progressive 'rationalisation' of all aspects of modern existence was 'disenchantment' (*Entzauberung*), the erosion by secularisation of the religious, magic dimension of reality that bound together pre-modern communities, though he recognised that it might re-emerge capriciously and spasmodically in the form of collective charismatic energies to temporarily release human beings from their iron cage of reason.[7] More anthropologically oriented cultural commentators such as Joseph Campbell, building on Carl Jung's pioneering studies of the 'archetypal unconscious', have explored how mythic consciousness still provides the substratum of 'modern' human experience, lifting individuals out of ordinary time whenever their lives intersect with primordial patterns of cosmological ('mythopoeic') and ritual consciousness.[8] One of the most influential figures in the investigation of the distinction between profane and sacred time is Mircea Eliade, who, in a stream of writings, has documented the constant recourse by human beings to myth and ritual in order to stave off the 'terror of history', the invasion of life by the all-consuming *chronos* of meaningless clock-time.[9]

Seen from such a perspective, the cultural rebellion against the Enlightenment project which gathered such strength from the 1880s onwards in Europe – generally known today as 'the revolt against positivism'[10] – can be seen as the appearance of a number of highly idiosyncratic quests to put an end to 'decadence' (i.e. a 'fallen', disenchanted, entropic, private, 'old' time) and inaugurate a 'rebirth' (i.e. enter a 'higher', magic, regenerative, collective, ' "new" time').[11] If confined to the experiential sphere of individuals or small groups, this might involve no more than the cultivation of visionary, mystic states of consciousness, or the quest for sources of knowledge and insight neglected by mainstream Western culture to the point of causing the cults of Carl Jung, William Blake, and Carlos Castaneda during the counter-cultural 'revolt' of the 1960s. However, so widespread was the disaffection with the official cult of material, liberal progress in linear time that intellectuals and artists all over Europe were attracted to the idea that their own bid to break free from a stultifying 'normality' was part of a wider impulse, a sea change in history. They were convinced they were living through a watershed in the evolution of Western civilisation. In individual experiences, this was often existentially characterised by a qualitative change in time itself, from the personally meaningless to the collectively significant. Leading personalities in the occult revival, and many pioneers of artistic modernism, fit this pattern. Thus, figures like Helena Blavatsky, Rudolf Steiner, William Butler Yeats, Richard Wagner, Igor Stravinsky, Wassily Kandinsky, Pablo Picasso, Vincent Van Gogh, and Rainer Maria Rilke, and artists from such disparate movements as Expressionism, Cubism, and Surrealism were, in their very different ways, concerned both with the achievement of 'ecstasy' (states which allowed them to 'stand outside' ordinary time) and with acting as a catalyst for the diffusion of new forms of consciousness to 'save' the West from what they saw as a process of spiritual atrophy. For some, the very notion of the 'modern' was infused with a sense of cultural regeneration, the birth of a new age.[12] For example, Hermann Bahr wrote in 1890:

> It may be that we are at the end, at the death of exhausted mankind, and that we are experiencing mankind's last spasms. It may be that we are at the beginning, at the birth of a new humanity and that we are experiencing only the avalanches of spring. We are rising to the divine or plunging, plunging into night and destruction – but there is no standing still.
>
> The creed of *Die Moderne* is that salvation will arise from pain and grace from despair, that a dawn will come after this horrific darkness and that art will hold communion with man, that there will be a glorious, blessed resurrection.[13]

An investigation of the late nineteenth century European *avant-garde* on the basis of its philosophy of time and history would show how deeply associated both are with the passionate belief that routinised, sclerotic ways of feeling and seeing – associated with the age of materialism and philistinism – can be transfigured individually or collectively through the awakening of visionary faculty better attuned to a 'higher' time. Indeed, this could well prove to be the main, if not the only, common denominator which underlies the rich profusion of so many conflicting aesthetics and nuanced visions of reality that are embraced by the terms 'modernism' and 'avant-garde'.

Nevertheless, occultism and visionary art were not the only channels through which such longings could be expressed in the '*fin de siècle*' – the very concept of which implied not only that a whole era of values and sensibility was closing, but that another might be opening. Other figures attempted to contribute to the inauguration of a new time through philosophy and social theory, Friedrich Nietzsche and Georges Sorel being outstanding examples here. Both thinkers specifically looked to (differently conceived) mythic energies rather than Enlightenment reason as the basis for of the regeneration of European society. The extraordinary resonance which their works found amongst their contemporaries can be best explained by the fact that European culture was pervaded by an unfulfilled palingenetic expectancy which demanded articulation. Unlike Nietzsche, Sorel trespassed from 'pure' cultural and philosophical speculation into uncharted territory for another major outlet for palingenetic aspirations, namely revolutionary politics. This revolutionary approach, by definition, attempted to create a new time by advancing the utopian idea of a better society so underpinning its affective driving force, no matter how systematically such politics may be rationalised by doctrines and theories.[14]

The origins of Fascism in projects to inaugurate a new experience of time

Locating Fascism's genesis within the context of a European culture saturated with longings to recapture a 'magic' or 'epic' sense of time throws into relief the fact that the *Partito Nazionale Fascista* [PNF] is not reducible to an arbitrary and ideologically vacuous decision made by Mussolini in the spring of 1919 for reasons of personal ambition.[15] Instead, Italian Fascism may be more profitably comprehended though a wave of intense politico-cultural speculation and activism which flooded Italy between 1900 and 1915, much of which centred on the project of national renewal. An example bearing heavily on the present topic is an article published on the eve of the outbreak of the First World War under the title 'La democrazia e la festa'. It claims that the fundamental problem of modern life

> was the lack of public festivals, rituals and theatrical elements that could restore an aura of grand spectacle to an increasingly impersonal and individualistic world. Modern people had ceased to believe in Catholicism, but had yet to find appropriate secular substitutes for its festivals. Without religious and seasonal festivals the world had become sad.[16]

Conventional historians have largely ignored the hard documentary evidence that Mussolini was part of this subculture long before he became a Fascist. Indeed, it was one particular current of palingenetic agitation, the Florentine avant-garde associated with Giovanni Papini and the periodicals *Il Regno* [The Kingdom (of Italy)], *Leonardo*, and *La Voce* [The Voice], which exerted a decisive influence on Mussolini's own sense of revolutionary vocation several years *before* the First World War.[17] In 1935, Mussolini declared to his biographer Yvon De Begnac, 'I first had the feeling of being called to announce a new era when I started corresponding with the *Voce* circle.'[18] The writings of some Syndicalists – theorising the desired Marxist revolution in terms of myth, voluntarism, and the nation rather than socio-economics, determinism, and the Communist International – had also helped convert him from an internationalist to a national socialist well in time for Mussolini to become an interventionist in the spring of 1915.[19]

But of all the tributaries of ideological energy which influenced the young Mussolini, and subsequently flowed into Fascism in its formative period unto 1925, that of Futurism was undoubtedly the most extreme, both in its rejection of the past and in its belief in the imminence of a renewal envisioned to contain both an international as well as a strictly national dimension.[20] Futurists consciously conceived their revolution as a metamorphosis in the experience of space and time. Indeed, in the very first of many Futurist manifestos Filippo Marinetti had proclaimed:

> We stand on the last promontory of the centuries! [...] Why should we look back, when what we want is to break down the mysterious doors of the Impossible? Time and Space died yesterday. We already live in the absolute, because we have created eternal, omnipresent speed.[21]

Mussolini, the national revolutionary, obsessed with the idea that a new historical cycle in the life of the nation and indeed the Western world impended, was thus very much a child of his age, the product of a cultural climate pervaded with longings for a new society; a new experience of time.[22] He owed his 'charisma' to his instinctive ability to recycle, synthesise, and re-present myths of the nation's imminent renewal; and thus to embody, crystallise, and give organisational form to the mood of national palingenesis which was 'in the air' breathed by Italy's intelligentsia even before 1915, thereafter to be dramatically popularised and radicalised as a result of Italian intervention in the First World War. The veterans who were to form the backbone of the *Fasci* and the paramilitary 'action squads' were men who had returned from the trenches with the conviction that the war marked a turning point from an old Italy governed by a spineless gerontocracy to a new one led by a youthful, courageous ruling elite; a 'trenchocracy'. They nurtured heady fantasies of forming the vanguard of a national renewal, inspired by the terrible sacrifices which they – and their less fortunate comrades who had not survived – had made to defend and advance the honour of their country.[23]

The need to explain the rise of Fascism in terms of mythic currents and ideological structures, rather than the personal ambitions of Mussolini or the machinations of capitalism, is underlined by the profound impact on the popular imagination made quite independently by the ageing poet Gabriele D'Annunzio, who established his Regency in Fiume as the expression of his own, essentially aesthetic, palingenetic vision of Italy's destiny. For D'Annunzio and his supporters, Fiume signalled the country's entry into a new, epic cycle of greatness and heroism, one which would put an end to the pusillanimous age of mediocrity suffusing the Giolittian era.[24] Once the threatened 'March on Rome' had persuaded the King to appoint Mussolini head of state, both the Nationalists and Giovanni Gentile as well as lesser-known Futurists and Dannunzians were able to project their own schemes for the nation's renewal onto Fascism, ensuring that new currents of palingenetic myth – not to mention the policies to achieve them – intensified the momentum of the movement. By the time Mussolini set about creating a totalitarian regime in 1925, the *littorio* or 'lictor's rods and axe' could be seen to symbolise the radical shift from the leftist rhetoric of San Sepolcro Fascism to an authoritarian, rightist force in which the myth of a reborn Rome now played the dominant role. But such a confluence also represented the nature of Fascist ideology itself: a loose alliance of different, and often contradictory, strands of revolutionary nationalism held together in a single-party state prepared to use violence to crush any opposition. The force which held them together was the common belief in the imminence of a new age.

Yet if Mussolini was able to dominate this alliance, it was partly because he had few scruples about the ideological compromises and contradictions wrought by such wanton syncretism. The core of his own revolutionary drive between 1909 – when his profound attraction to *La Voce*'s call for cultural renewal can be first documented[25] – and the formation of the first *Fasci* in March 1919 was little more than the nebulous myth of a new Italy brought about through the agency of '*homines novi*' ('new men'). For Mussolini, the significance of the war rested upon its phoenix-like creation of a new elite to provide the mass base for such a movement of renewal.[26] The tablets of the old law were crumbling and the new ones had yet to be written. He saw the period leading up to the establishment of the Fascist regime as a time not only for programmes and doctrines, but for action.[27] His conspicuous lack of interest in providing a definitive doctrine and a cogent set of policies to 'rationalise' Fascism before the early 1930s was not just tactically necessary in order to guarantee the new regime as wide a support base as possible. This reticence also reflected his own deep-seated reluctance to commit himself to a particular version of the palingenetic myth. In a way, then, it was the vision of renewal itself which became the adhesive linchpin for fascist ideology, rather than any particular set of policies or clearly conceived theory of state.[28]

This vision was deeply bound up with Mussolini's recurrent stress on Fascism's epochal significance in history. The regime was living proof that 'Italy did not exhaust herself in creating its first and second civilisation, but [was] already creating a third.'[29] The core of this revolution was not institutional but ethical: Fascist vitalism would lift the apathetic, cynical individual of the Giolittian age into a new spiritual orbit.

> 'I don't give a damn' (*me ne frego*) [...] sums up a doctrine which is not merely political: it is evidence of a fighting spirit which accepts all risks.

It signifies a new style of Italian life. The Fascist accepts and loves life; he rejects and despises suicide as cowardly. Life as he understands it means duty, elevation, conquest; life must be lofty and full, it must be lived for oneself but above all for others, both nearby and far off, present and future.[30]

In different permutations, the belief that Fascism's creation of a new type of state was the materialisation and externalisation of a subjective revolution in values and national character was a recurrent *topos* in Fascist thought. To cite just two examples, a chapter on 'Fascism and the Future of Culture' in a 1928 tome entitled *Fascist Civilisation* affirms that the significance of the Fascist revolution was not just evident in the creation of a new regime, but an entirely new cosmology:

> When we affirm the divinity of our beautiful Italian nation, we mean by that we are announcing a religious idea in the true sense of the word, capable of creating a whole new development in culture, practical and theoretical via which we can arrive at new conceptions of God, cosmic reality, and human destiny, at a new way of ordering our interior life and external social life.[31]

Similarly, on 19 December 1925, Giovanni Gentile devoted his inaugural speech to the National Institute of Fascist Culture on this new force 'which, despite the obstacles in its path, which at times seemed to block its effects, has gradually regimented the whole nation' and 'infused it with a single sentiment: the passion for greatness at any price, at the cost of any sacrifice'.

> What has come over us to endow us with this sensibility, the sign that new spiritual needs and new directions are being taken by life and thought? [...] It is a religious sentiment [...] one which takes life seriously: really seriously [...] and no longer separates doing from talking, deed from thought, literature from life, reality from programmes, life and death from the triumph of ideals which we have faithfully served: this is the new spiritual value which Fascism has planted in the Italian soul: it is to these heights that we are now trying to raise national culture.[32]

The temporal implications of this 'religious' conception of Fascism are made clear in Gentile's subsequent definition (my emphasis) for the *Enciclopedia Italiana*:

> The world seen through Fascism is not this material world which appears on the surface, in which man is an individual separated from all others and standing by himself, and in which he is governed by a natural law that makes him instinctively live a life of selfish and momentary pleasure. The man of

Fascism is an individual who is nation and fatherland, which is a moral law, binding together individuals and the generations into a tradition and a mission, suppressing the instinct for life enclosed within the brief round of pleasure in order to restore within duty *a higher life free from the limits of time and space*.[33]

The Fascist bid to regenerate time through social engineering

In concrete terms, the reordering of 'the interior and exterior social life' to create a 'new style of Italian life' led to the ritual style of politics striking generations of scholars as the outstanding feature of life under Fascism. One of the first academics to draw attention to this aspect of the new Italy was an American, Herbert Schneider, who, during his study of the regime carried out between 1926 and 1927, recognised the existence of a 'Fascist religion'. Presciently, he commented on the fact that 'less subtle and more generally effective' than Gentile's school reforms for winning over youth to the regime was 'the new Fascist art of secular celebrations':

> It is not for nothing that Fascism is so ritualistic. The marches, salutes, yells, songs, uniforms, badges, and what not, are giving a new focus to the imagination of the Italian youth, are linking their social life to political organisations and are filling their minds with political – I will not say ideas, but political – feelings. This is perhaps the greatest of the fascist revolutions. Good Italian youths still go to mass and participate in religious festivities, but their sentiments, their imaginations, their moral ideals are centred elsewhere.[34]

Schneider also notes how the Italian calendar was 'assuming a secular structure', citing as examples the way the regime had given certain dates a twofold mythic significance. Thus March 23, Youth Day, commemorated the founding of the *Fasci*; April 21, Labour Day, the founding of Rome; May 24, Empire Day, the entry of Italy into the First World War; September 20, Italian Unity, the incorporation of Rome into the Kingdom of Italy; and October 28, the Fascist Revolution, the March on Rome.[35] In 1931, the regime even introduced a 'Fascist Epiphany' which, in Milan, included a 'Christmas Day's distribution of gifts in the name of the *Duce*, to be known as "the *Duce*'s Christmas"'.[36] In this way, ordinary Italians were encouraged to experience the unfolding of the Fascist Revolution in secular time as a phenomenon with a transcendental core on a par with the metaphysical reality underlaying Christianity, which also intercalated working days with 'giorni festivi' (also known simply as 'feste', i.e. not just holidays but holy-days or feast days).

The outstanding example of this attempt to appropriate a religious concept of time, and to make it an integral part of the experience of the new Italy, was the superimposition of a specifically Fascist calendar on the Gregorian one. The year 1922 thus became 'Year One' of the Fascist era, and most publications were dated in terms of both *Anno Domini* and the time which had passed since the March on Rome. In this way, Italians were encouraged to feel that Mussolini's conquest of power signified the inauguration of a new dispensation in the history of an 'eternal, Italian civilisation'.

Some six decades passed before scholarship moved beyond Schneider's insights, especially regarding the centrality to the Fascist Revolution of the deliberate staging of events designed to create a collective sense of sacred time. Emilio Gentile's ground-breaking *Il Culto del Littorio* (translated as The Sacraliza-tion of Politics in Fascist Italy) meticulously documented the concerted efforts by the Fascist regime to create a state religion. By inventing an elaborate politi-cal liturgy and symbology Italian Fascism sought to create a civic and political religion to 'realise a "metanoia" in human nature, whence a "new man" would emerge, regenerated and totally integrated into the community'.[37] Though Gen-tile does not explicitly focus upon the meaning of 'political religion' for the fascist experience of time, the primary evidence he adduces clearly demon-strates that some Fascists consciously conceived their movement as a temporal revolution. Thus Dario Lupi wrote in July 1923:

> He who joins us either becomes one of us in body and soul, in mind and flesh, or he will inexorably be cut off. For we know and feel ourselves in possession of the truth; for of all the ideologies, past and present [...] we know and feel ourselves to be part of the only movement in marvellous harmony with the historic time in which we live.[38]

Gentile's insights are extensively corroborated by Simonetta Falasca-Zamponi's study of 'the aesthetics of power in Mussolini's Italy', which documents the way in which the fabric of daily life under the regime reflected how it

> strove to produce cultic values and hailed spiritual principles as the basis for the regeneration and renewal of Italian society. Born as a countermovement to the 'lifeless' politics of liberal government, fascism claimed its will to create a new world on the premises of a Nietzschean return to the ideal.[39]

The profound temporal implications of such a project are implicit in her exten-sive treatment of the central role played by myth in the socio-political life of the regime. Occasionally, Falasca-Zamponi alludes to operant myths directly, as when she comments on the Futurist concept of war which had such a major influence on Mussolini's thinking (my emphasis):

> Because the futurists stressed action and glorified the future, only war could respond to the ideal of a never-ending movement. War embodied

the perennial necessity of fighting: *it was a festival* in which the expenditure of energies, almost in an ethnological sense, emphasised life's fullness. As the 'only hygiene of the world', war granted the expansion of human potentialities. It was a purifying bath from which a new person, who perceived the world through categories of action speed, and confrontation, would be born. War would thus clean Italy from *passatismo* and open the way to future renewal.[40]

Another contemporary scholar, Jeffrey Schnapp, has also fully grasped that the deeper significance of Fascism's ritualised and aesthetic style of politics lies in its attempt to mass-produce a qualitatively different experience of reality. Schnapp's fascinating analysis of the 1932 Exhibition of the Fascist Revolution shows how the regime deliberately manipulated the aesthetics of architecture, exhibitions, symbols, space, and song to contrive for the visitor an experience of passing from the chaos of the immediate post-war years to the sublime harmony of the Fascist era. The last room, the climax of the entire exhibit, simulated a Fascist rally. Yet this was no ordinary rally, but instead 'a rally of the living dead, a rally taking place in some indeterminate secular otherworld, "immortal" yet of this world, where history's victims are forever present to each other'.[41] The exhibition did not serve as a state memorial to the March on Rome, but was intended as

a *living* monument capable of serving as the focal point for mass happenings that would mobilise the Italian nation as a whole, from the highest government offices to the factory floor. To this end, the exhibition set out to be revolutionary: new, ultramodern, audacious, free from the melancholy and mourning that usually accompany the remembrance of things past. Instead of simply embalming the movement's origins, it strove to [...] present fascism's 'heroic era' with such shocking intensity and immediacy that it would almost literally be brought back to life [...] No sense of loss or discontinuity would divide the past from the present.[42]

If the Exhibition of the Fascist Revolution is taken as the epitome of the regime's calculated bid to transform the nation as a whole, then it becomes clear that at the heart of its 'totalitarianism' lay neither Mussolini's 'will to power' nor the obsession of conservative or capitalist elites to maintain their grip on the levers of power. Its driving force was instead the urge to lift Italians out of the anomic experience of time under liberalism by reconnecting them with the epic life of the nation. Fascism was the medium through which they would be reconciled and reunited with the living organism of the Italian state. The *Risorgimento* would be completed, the task of 'making Italians' finally fulfilled. Ordinary citizens would, for the first time since the Roman era, once more be able to participate mystically in Italy and hence, in its imminent destiny, to become once again the focal point of world civilisation and progress – yet another manifestation of the 'eternal genius' of the race producing the Roman Empire, the Catholic Church, and the Renaissance. In the context of such a vision the 'monumental' – such a major feature of Fascist (and all totalitarian) art – acquires specific connotations. It refers to a cult of remembering practised not in a conservative spirit, but in a revolutionary one: the past is to be remembered in order to regenerate the present and transform the future. This paradox is best expressed in the slogan of the post-war *Movimento Sociale Italiano* (the direct descendant of the PNF), 'Nostalgia for the Future'.[43]

The academic best illuminating the specifically temporal aspect of this enterprise is Mabel Berezin. She identifies the central drive of Fascism as a political ideology that attempts 'to fuse public and private self' in a new 'community of feeling'.[44] Berezin goes on to demonstrate the vital role played by ritual in enabling ordinary Italians to imagine that they belonged to a 'new political community', then – crucially for our thesis – she devotes a whole chapter to the Fascist bid to 'colonise time'. Using Verona as a case study, Berezin documents the extraordinary lengths to which the regime went to reshape the experience of time and history itself through a combination of official events which she classifies as celebrations, symposia, commemorations, demonstrations, and inaugurations. In just 20 years (1922–1942) the citizens of Verona could participate in 727 such events: an average of 36 per year, or one every ten days!

The ultimate purpose of such a systematic subsuming of private time by regime time was the obliteration of the old self, and the making of a Fascist self. The underlying palingenetic thrust thus emerges clearly from a May 1926 speech made by Augusto Turati, National Secretary of the Fascist Party. He told listeners in Verona that the Fascist 'crowd of a million arms, legs and faces' had a 'single soul, a single song, and a single hope: Italy in every heart, Italy above every heart'. The *Patria* [or 'fatherland'] was 'a living thing [...] something truly inside us [...] If the Patria is the memory of the Dead, then the Patria lies in the will to rebirth and transformation.'[45]

Nazi correlatives to the Fascist bid to transcend anomic personal time

Given that Nazism shares Fascism's mythic core of palingenetic ultra-nationalism, also constituting a permutation of generic fascism, it is not surprising to find constant allusions in its ideology to regeneration and rebirth.[46] In a spirit directly paralleling the Fascist conception of a temporal (and political) revolution, the Nazis set out to inaugurate a new era by reattaching Germans to what Schnapp called the 'intermediate otherworld', one constituted by an epic sense of national history. One of Hitler's earliest biographers records that he was obsessed with 'the concept of a great turning point in the history of the world. A new age was beginning; history was once more setting the mighty wheel in motion and apportioning lots anew'.[47]

Though Nazism's racial, eugenic, and scientistic concept of the national community meant that this vision was conveyed through discourses far different from the ones used by Fascism, the premise that the new regime was carrying out a total, and hence totalitarian, cultural revolution, through which the individual would transcend anomic time, is common to both. Thus Hitler's speech on art, in his address to the Seventh Nuremberg Rally in September 1935, has striking parallels with Giovanni Gentile's inaugural address cited earlier:

When the poor human soul, oppressed with cares and troubles and inwardly distracted, has no longer a clear and definite belief in the greatness and the future of the nation to which it belongs, that is the time to stimulate its regard for the indisputable evidences of those eternal racial values which cannot be affected in their essence by a temporary phase of political or economic distress. The more the natural and legitimate demands of a nation are ignored or suppressed, or even simply denied, the more important it is that these vital demands should take on the appeal of a higher and nobler right by giving tangible proof of the great cultural values incorporated in the nation. Such visible demonstration of the higher qualities of a people, as the experience of history proves, will remain for thousands of years as an unquestionable testimony not only to the greatness of a people but also to their moral right to existence.

Hitler went on to ask,

What would the Egyptians be without their pyramids and their temples and the artistic decorations that surround their daily lives? What would the Greeks be without Athens and the Acropolis? What would the Romans be without their mighty buildings and engineering works? What would the German emperors of the Middle Ages be without their cathedrals and their imperial palaces? And what would the Middle Ages itself be without its town halls and guild halls etc.? What would religion be without its churches? That there was once such a people as the Mayas we should not know at all, or else be unconcerned about them, had they not left for the admiration of our time those mighty ruins of cities that bear witness to the extraordinary epic qualities of that people, such ruins as have arrested the attention of the modern world and are still a fascinating object of study for our scholars. A people cannot live longer than the works which are the testimony of its culture.[48]

As in Fascism, the corollary of this project to recreate the 'epic' sense of time felt to be the hallmark of all 'great civilisations' was the creation of an all-pervasive political liturgy, its effects reinforced by the extensive use of propaganda, social control, and terror. As a result, the everyday life of Germans – at least of those who were not deemed to incarnate biological or moral degeneracy – was infiltrated by the ethos of the Third Reich to the point that it became an act of heroic resistance to keep a firm grip on alternative values, let alone assert them publicly; even the path into 'inner emigration' was far from easy.

One major contribution aiming to comprehend this cultic dimension of Nazism – paralleling what Gentile's *Culto del littorio* has done for Fascism, is *Magie und Manipulation: Ideologischer Kult und politische Religion des National-sozialismus* [Magic and Manipulation: The Ideological Cult and Political Religion under Nazism].[49] Here, Klaus Vondung records the intense efforts of the regime to develop a political liturgy in order to bring about a subjective revolution in the Germans' experience of time itself. A striking example is the elaborate ceremony, or *Heldnischer Feier* (Heroic Celebration), designed by Gerhard Schumann for the 'memorial day for the fallen of the movement'. It was designed to be performed on the steps of the Feldherrnhalle in Munich's Odeonplatz, built to commemorate the martyrs of the failed November putsch in 1923, thus reviving them as national heroes, and semiotically recoding the square and the hall itself into a temple to Nazism and the religion of the reborn German race. Vondung analyses in detail the texts and ritual choreography of the ceremony, showing how it, like countless other examples of Nazi liturgy, was calculated to generate 'the collective feeling of participation in the permanent revolutionary process of fermentation and in the transcending of individual death through an ill-defined "after-life" within this continuous revolution'.[50] As a result,

> 9 November 1923 is interpreted within National Socialist myth as a turning-point at which the old era finished and something totally new began. The verse by Boehme [...] makes this clear: 'The earth died with your death, with your glory our lives begin'. 'The beginning of life' means here the beginning of a transformed, new, essential life, means a quite specific change in the structure of human life, a metamorphosis of the human condition. The vision or prophecy of a process of transformation from an incomplete to a complete existence is a *topos* of historical speculation. Eric Voegelin calls this phenomenon 'metastatic faith'.[51]

What Vondung's impressively scholarly investigation demonstrates is that Nazism cannot be fully understood if we ignore its efforts to bring about a sense of 'metastasis', or rebirth, subjectively experienced as moving from a mere 'existence' of *anomie* and isolation into a qualitatively different time in which individual life and death itself is transcended by becoming merged with the eternity of the nation and race.

The concern over breaking out of 'ordinary time' and into a collective 'magic time' presumably predisposed some future Nazis – notably Hitler in his Vienna days before the First World War as well as Heinrich Himmler – to flirt with occultist ideas about the origins of civilisation and the imminent rebirth of the Aryan super-race.[52] Certainly, the testimony which Hermann Rauschning provides of his conversations with Hitler suggests not only that the latter, like Mussolini, harboured notions that he had been called upon to inaugurate a new era, but that for him the forces which would bring it about were of an awesome, almost supernatural power:

> We had come to a turning-point in world history – that was his constant theme [...] He saw himself as chosen for superhuman tasks, as the prophet of the rebirth of man in a new form. Humanity, he proclaimed, was in the throes of a vast metamorphosis [...] The coming age was revealing itself in the first great human figures of a new type.[53]

Yet such a passage does not suggest that the Third Reich was such an eruption of occultist energies, however much this notion might appeal to those whose historical imaginations have been corrupted by an *X-Files* perspective to the point that they mistake sensationalist bestsellers (such as *The Dawn of the Magicians*) for serious history.[54] In fact Hitler went to some length to dissociate Nazism from occultism.[55] What Rauschning does corroborate is the important realisation that all dialects of Nazism, whether 'blood-and-soil', militaristic, cultural, or technocratic, together shared the belief that there was a higher spiritual and temporal reality bound up with the history and destiny of the race that remained hidden to decadent, 'non-Aryan', minds.

When the individual experienced the moment of union with this sublime plane of reality, it could produce a sense of ecstatic rebirth, one whose psychological implications have been explored in such forensic psychoanalytical detail by Klaus Theweleit's *Male Fantasies*.[56] One primary source for his analysis is Joseph Goebbels' semi-autobiographic novel *Michael: Ein deutsches Schicksal in Tagebuchblättern*[57] [Michael: The Diary of a German Destiny], which traces the transformation of the central character's *ennui* into a sense of collective belonging. Commenting on the way the conflict between despair and hope is resolved, Theweleit notes (my emphasis):

> At the end of the book, Michael joins the ranks of the 'workers'; he begins to work in a mine. This offers him an opportunity to invoke the intensities of work as a form of *intoxication*, which, like the blackouts and intoxications

of the drill, guarantees 'redemption': 'I have no wish to be a mere inheritor'. The purpose of 'work' instead is to allow Michael to become a new and self-born man within an apparatus which strips him of his ego boundaries. '*I am no longer human. I am a Titan. A god!*' [...] 'If we are strong enough to form the life of our era, it is our own lives that must first be mastered. A new law is approaching – the law of a labour realised in battle and of the spirit that is labour. The synthesis of these three will be internally and externally liberating; labour will become battle and spirit labour. Herein lies redemption.[58]

Goebbels' novel expresses the subjective dimension within the concept of the 'new man'; the *homo fascistus* which Mussolini and Giovanni Gentile describe from the outside. To become a Nazi is to be stripped of ego-boundaries, and thus become ready for absorption into a regenerated national community which will one day become synonymous with the state itself. The moment of conversion to Nazism (which is also described in *Michael* in ecstatic terms) is one of intoxication, of rebirth, of redemption – a transcending of the old self and the decadent age that produced it.

The core experiences which the Nazi manipulation of society, in all its aspects, sought to induce was that of being reborn from meaningless individual time into the epic communal time of the *Volksgemeinschaft* – a consideration fully borne out by scholars working on the minutiae of culture under the Third Reich. Iain Boyd Whyte's reconstruction of the May Day festival held in Berlin in 1936, for example, shows how the entire event was deliberately staged through the creation of liturgical space, choreography of the crowds, and the enactment of a ritual invented for the occasion in order to superimpose onto a spring festival of seasonal regeneration a Nazi concept of national renewal.[59] For this to happen, ancient pagan customs had to be reshaped into what the art historian Hans Weigert, in 1934, called 'the deepest maternal foundations of blood and soil'.[60] The Nazis' act of mythic appropriation and subversion is epitomised by the huge swastika crowning the maypole. The painting subsequently recording the festival completed the transfiguration of a stage-managed piece of political propaganda transformed into the icon of a transcendental moment in the history of the reborn *Volk*.

Further examples of the deliberate manipulation of time in Nazi culture are provided by Linda Schulte-Sass' *Entertaining the Third Reich: Illusions of Wholeness in Nazi Cinema*.[61] In her study of the film *Hitlerjunge Quex* [Hitler Youth Member Quex], for example, she shows the way in which the scene when Heini is drawn away from the Communist camp and towards the Hitler Youth camp 'is the film's first encoding of birth or passage into a new world'. The climax of the film, in which Heini is killed by Communists, is shot in such a way as to imply that his death is 'his third and final stage of "rebirth" ' into what Jeffrey Schnapp called in the context of Fascism a supra-individual, quasi-religious 'indeterminate secular otherworld', an 'ill-defined after-life':

> The film's final montage sequence that follows Heini's death is again of feet, this time masses of feet multiplying Heini's spirit hundredfold, marching towards the spectator, as if to march right off the screen and into life (and death!), depicting retroactively the geographical and spiritual reappropriation of 'home', not only for an individual but for a collective.[62]

Another Nazi film, *Wunschkonzert* [Request Concert], traced the story of a pair of lovers, Inge and Herbert, whom fate thrusts together at the Berlin Olympics and then wrenches apart when Herbert is called up to fight in the Spanish Civil War. Herbert is able to signal to Inge that he has never forgotten her by having a radio show play the music they heard at the Olympics when they fell in love. This emphatically supports Schulte-Sass' central thesis that the Nazi cinema aesthetically engineers an alternative temporality to that of Hollywood or liberal democracies. The love-story of two individuals is framed first within the vast physical community forged by the Olympics which not only had unleashed a flood of nationalistic pride, but in the film comes to represent 'a timeless, unsurpassable experience of wholeness, of life as a dream or work of art, that National Socialism constantly aspires to achieve'. It is then played out as a disembodied bonding of two individuals who form part of the imagined community of Germans listening to the record requests, thus 'synthesising the timeless interpellation of music with a timely mystification of the radio's transcendence of time and space'.[63] By constantly evoking images of supra-individual wholeness in this way, the Nazi cinema not only aestheticised the Third Reich, but presented reality to the film-goers in such a way that they were encouraged to feel their own lives had been transfigured and subsumed into the epic destiny of a truly imagined (identically and ultimately mythic) community, the *Volksgemeinschaft*.

Such examples of Nazism's manipulation of time could be easily multiplied. It would be fascinating, for instance – especially given recent anthropological work on the significance of Stonehenge as a site for shamanic rituals designed to mediate between natural, human time and the supernatural world of the spirits – to investigate the function of the vast ritual spaces that Albert Speer created for the Third Reich, specifically for rallies and parades. There would surely be some mileage in analysing the Zeppelinfeld, the vast parade ground constructed by Albert Speer to stage the Party congresses in Nuremberg as a ritual space deliberately created as a generator of ancient shamanic energies within a modern context. Here the swirling swastika replaced the archetypal vortex[64] as the symbol of access to a higher reality, while Hitler acted as chief shaman, attended by lesser medicine-men to induce a collective trance state in the choreographed masses. In establishing the difference between the genuinely metaphysical concept of reality underlying shamanism and the pseudo-supernatural dimension of 'national destiny', scholars could sharpen the distinction between the connotations of sacred time immanent in authentic religious traditions and experiences, and its grotesque travesty in 'political religions'.

In short, there is ample evidence to suggest that Nazism conspired to create a sense of festival time, of 'party-time'. Tragically for humanity, the party generating it was the type associated not with the coloured costumes of the Brazilian Carnival, but with the brown shirted thuggery of the NSDAP. The contrast between the dance and the march, between the samba and the strains of the *Horst Wessel Lied*, points to the gulf separating a life-asserting community from a community which exists only by creating a demonised other.

The cult of sacred time in neo-fascism

While 1945 may have signalled the end of Fascism and Nazism as regimes, the palingenetic longings which fuelled them have proven remarkably persistent and adaptable in a post-war climate which, at least in liberal democracies, has remained profoundly inhospitable to revolutionary ideologies of either left or right. Since the concept of 'festival time' is so entrenched in fascism's myth of national regeneration, we should not be surprised if it continues to recur in various guises as part of its crusade against the Enlightenment concept of history.

One of fascism's most influential ideologues in Italy, for example, has been Julius Evola. His impact is largely attributable to the way his occultist theory of reality and arcane philosophy of history satisfy the need experienced by post-war fascists for a comprehensive 'vision of the world' – one catering to the subjective sense of access to 'sacred' time.[65] This same need also explains the extraordinary way a number of 'fantasy' writers, notably John Tolkien, have become part of the staple diet for neo-fascists.[66] Sometimes the call for 'festival time' becomes explicit. One of the contributors to a 1981 conference organised by the extreme right, Franco Cardini spoke about the need to create a new culture for the transmission of fascist ideas. His lecture was entitled 'A quest for the roots of a conception of the world to come. The community is recreating itself: myth, ritual, liturgy, play, festival [festa]).' Cardini went on to assert that

> To restore 'la festa' means opposing the omnipotence of the capitalist-technological system; it means rediscovering an 'extraordinariness' which acts as a qualifying limit to the everyday, and hence recreating the foundations of everyday reality itself so as to resist the temptation to conceive

time as a homogeneous entity and hence life as waiting for inevitable and irreversible destruction, as an anguish which can only be escaped through oblivion. Rediscovering festival time means rediscovering the non-primacy of economism and productionism, it means rediscovering the whole man.[67]

There are curious echoes of this theme in a brilliant essay on fascism under the title 'Between festival and revolution'. This text was written by Marco Tarchi, editor of *Diorama letterario* – one of the foremost organs behind the rethinking of neo-fascist ideology in the 1970s and 1980s – and author of a major study of the role of a crisis in 'collective identities' in the fascist seizure of power in Italy and Germany.[68] Tarchi concludes by suggesting the attempt to bring about a temporal revolution through creating a national community is the definitional feature of generic fascism:

> The choice of the qualitative and organic community [...] is a constant of fascist movements transcending the level of historic contingencies to find articulation in the realm of cultural expression in the full sense of the term, namely in political philosophy and doctrine: the myth of the 'community of destiny', the moment of supreme collective identification, and the pivotal concept of the 'new politics' intuited by Mosse and buried by the catastrophe of the Second World War, is both its emblem and its culmination.[69]

But north of the Alps too, neo-fascism is profoundly preoccupied with break-ing out of 'profane time'. One of the most important books in the renewal of fascist thought in Germany, France, and Italy is *The Conservative Revolu-tion: A Handbook*. According to Armin Mohler's analysis within it, the central concern of the interwar German artists and authors he identifies was the end-ing of a decadent cycle in an *Umschlag* (sudden metamorphosis) and rebirth. Such an event and temporal shift would finally close the 'interregnum' into which history had decayed since the end of the Second Reich.[70] In the 1970s and 1980s, many ideologues of the New Right, notably Alain de Benoist in France and Marco Tarchi in Italy, adopted either the Conservative Revolution-ary, Nietzschean, 'nominalist' concept of cyclic time advanced by Mohler, or instead Julius Evola's mythic, metaphysical alternative to it.[71] More recently, the international New Right (which now includes Russia) has become increasingly interested in 'Indo-European' concepts of the 'sacred', another symptom of the same palingenetic longings to escape the 'decadent' time now identified with the globalisation of time and space under the hegemony of the 'American way of life'.

The implications for Fascist Studies: The centrality of a sacred time to fascist ideology

Undoubtedly a neglected area of Fascist Studies concerns the attempts by Fascism and Nazism to engineer a subjective revolution in the experience of time as an integral part of their project to regenerate the nation. It is suggested here that while much scholarship exists on the fascist project to create a national community – and some scholarly attention is at last being paid to fascist culture – the temporal aspects of both topics have received scant attention. This is no doubt partly because most academics are heirs to the Enlightenment rationalist tradition, and perhaps because the nature of their work means that they tend to operate conceptually from within the subjective confines of individual, profane, normal time, rather than collective, ecstatic, festive, holiday time. As a result, an 'outside in' approach has characterised most studies of fascism to date, rather than stray into forbidden territories of psychology and anthropology to shore up the findings of 'methodological empathy' with fascists as historical subjects.

An instance of this neglect is the way Walter Benjamin has been introduced into studies of fascist culture. References to 'the aestheticisation of politics' are *de rigueur* in such studies. But I have yet to see a single reference to his 'Theses on the Philosophy of History' concerning the French Revolution despite its considerable bearing on fascism. Part of Benjamin's argument (written while persecuted by the Nazis) reads as follows:

> History is the subject of a structure whose site is not homogeneous, empty time, but time filled by the presence of the now (*'Jetztzeit'*). Thus, to Robespierre ancient Rome was a past charged with the time of the now which he blasted out of the continuum of history. The French Revolution viewed itself as Rome incarnate.

In other words, a revolution is a moment when a mythically charged 'now' creates a qualitative change in the continuum of history, a change that fundamentally opposes undifferentiated 'clock' time, the invisible medium in which all events 'happen'. Benjamin continues (my italics),

> The awareness that they are about to make the continuum of history explode is characteristic of the revolutionary classes at the moment of their action. The great revolution introduced a new calendar. The initial day of a calendar serves as a historical time-lapse camera. And, basically, it is the same day that keeps recurring in the guise of holidays, which are days of remembrance. Thus the calendars do not measure time as clocks do; they are monuments of a historical consciousness *of which not the slightest trace has been apparent*

in Europe in the last hundred years. In the July Revolution an incident occurred which showed this consciousness was still alive. On the first evening of fighting it turned out that the clocks in towers were being fired on simultaneously and independently from several places in Paris.[72]

Given our discussion on fascism thus far, this is an extraordinary statement. Benjamin is writing in 1940. Two European regimes have gone to elaborate lengths to break entire nations out of a chaotic experience of time widely felt to be mythically discharged and degenerating. One was activating the myth of Rome, the other a myth of Aryan blood. Both introduced a new calendar,[73] and made it a central goal to fill their subjects' lives with a sense of ritual 'nowness'. So why is Benjamin, who actually lived through the rise of Nazism until he was forced into exile in 1933, so blind to the fascist bid to shoot down the clocks of liberal time taking place in front of his eyes?

The answer lies, surely, in the way his Marxism paradoxically both enabled him to arrive at his brilliant conception of the aestheticisation of politics and limited his grasp of its applicability to historical events. Fascism was not the attempt by capitalists to mystify their retention of power by coating the state apparatus – modern technology, work, the regimentation and exploitation of the masses, and war itself – with an artificial 'aura' of magic and aesthetic significance. Nor was fascism a pseudo-revolution cynically staged in order to stave off a 'genuine' revolution. For believers in national regeneration, fascism was a genuine bid to use the unprecedented resources of the modern state to recreate the 'auratic', the 'magic', and the 'numinous', which they sensed was not just draining away from works of art, but from the texture of historical time itself. Thus fascism was an attempted revolution, both aesthetic and temporal: a bid to create a new total culture in the sense that the Romans and the Mayans were a total culture; a bid to inaugurate a new era. Had Benjamin realised that the 'aura' fascists wanted to recreate was of the same stuff as that of the mythic 'nowness' comprising the French Revolution, that the aestheticisation of politics under fascism was profoundly linked to the explosion of festival time in the French Revolution, then he would have provided himself with a powerful heuristic device to unlock its secrets as a political phenomenon. Instead, the aestheticisation of politics merely implied a film-set reality, which is all that most students of fascism have seen since.

This chapter contends that if we do not treat the fascist attempt to retool the experience of time seriously, the logic underlying the fascist revolution and its terrifying human consequences will remain elusive. Fascism's concepts of society, human nature, history, and culture were all so perverted by nationalism, militarism, racism, and male chauvinism that the bid to realise their socio-political dream was bound to lead to disaster. Nevertheless, the failure of fascism and the catastrophes it led to – and would lead to again if it ever seized power[74] – should not blind us to the deadly earnestness with which its most fervent supporters sought to carry out its revolutionary mission. We should thus be prepared to devote proper scholarly attention to the fascist *jihad* against the secular time of liberalism, one undertaken in an attempt to banish 'the terror of history' with a fortress of mythic energies. To build such a fortress, two regimes forged a formidable alliance between the modern state's powerful arsenal for social engineering and the primordial force of ethnic nationalism and the myth of collective rebirth. The result was the mass-production of 'History', which was only crushed by the conventional forces of history at the expense of some 55 million lives.

The Italian scholar Giorgio Galli has rightly observed

> There is need for a historical reconstruction of the magic and esoteric component of 'historical fascisms', albeit carried out with the caution stressed by Furio Jesi in his *Cultura di destra* in which he criticises the approach adopted in *The Dawn of the Magicians*, but without the habitual diffidence shown to the topic by traditional historiography.[75]

While this is a worthwhile enterprise, what would contribute even more to the historiography of fascism is a thorough investigation of the 'secular otherworld' at the centre of its imaginings as well as the 'revolutionary festivals' they led to. Hopefully, this chapter has at least highlighted the relevance and scope of such an undertaking, even if it has also demonstrated how much still remains to be done.

2
Modernity Under the New Order
The Fascist Project for Managing the Future*

> Future organisation is a matter for technicians with the ring kept free
> for the operation of science and organisation by the universal authority
> of an organised and disciplined movement . . . Thus can be achieved the
> great necessity of steadily and systematically increasing the power to
> consume as science and rationalisation increase the power to produce.
>
> Oswald Mosley, *The Greater Britain* 1932[1]

The problematic relationship between fascism and the modern

Any attempt to conceptualise the relationship of fascism and modernity means
operating with two terms which are semantic mine-fields in their own right
and about whose definition a formidable literature has grown up. What makes
matters worse is that even some of the most perceptive scholarly attempts to
establish a relationship between the two have been marred by the intrinsic nebulousness of the two concepts so that there is little in the way of authoritative
monographs or articles to build on. For this necessarily overcondensed bid to
suggest a new conceptual framework appropriate to the subject, I thus propose
to return to basics.

A foretaste of the debate is to be found in *The Menace of Fascism* by John
Strachey who, in the year Hitler achieved power, went to some lengths to expose
the fallacy underlying the thesis of a certain Professor Scott Nearing, according
to whom the spread of fascism would lead to the 'slow destruction of world trade

* This chapter was first published by the Oxford Brookes School of Business as part of a
series of papers on modernity given in 1993, and appeared as a Thamesman Publication
with the Oxford Brookes School of Business imprint, 1994. It was based on a talk given for
a seminar on Nazism and modernity held by Ian Kershaw at the University of Sheffield
the same year. It contains the kernel of ideas fully elaborated in Griffin's *Modernism and
Fascism. The Sense of a Beginning under Mussolini and Hitler*. London: Palgrave Macmillan,
2007.

and modern mass production by the conscious policy of extreme economic self-sufficiency'. Instead, Strachey asserts that fascism 'will actually foster the highest forms of modern technique in the short term in preparation of a new war'.[2] Yet it was some 20 years after the Second World War, when 'modernisation theory' became a staple product within the social sciences industry, that a spate of texts started appearing which claimed in markedly contrasting ways, to illuminate the relationship between fascism and 'the modern', some of which have the status of classics for scholars trying to speed-read their way into the current debate.

Included here are Barrington Moore[3] who offered a theory of global patterns of development, claiming that fascism (exemplified for him in Nazi Germany and more problematically Imperial Japan) emerged as a form of 'conservative modernisation' in an attempt to make an essentially reactionary political system populist. Similarly, A. F. K. Organski[4] asked for fascism (as illustrated by Mussolinian Italy and also problematically Peronist Argentina) to be seen as 'part of the process of transition from a limited participation to a 'mass system', and as 'a last-ditch stand by the élites, both modern and traditional, to prevent the expansion of the system over which they exercised hegemony'. In contrast, Henry Turner Jnr[5] proposed that the key to generic fascism lies in its 'utopian anti-modernism', its pursuit of a mythicised past, albeit using the fruits of modern technology. A counter-position to Turner is evident in James Gregor[6] who stresses the centrality of productivism to Fascism, arguing that Italy reached economic maturity under Mussolini, so that generic fascism is to be seen as a transitional form of 'modernising dictatorship' with parallels in Stalinism, Maoism, Castroism, and post-colonial African national socialist states. Yet another position is that of Arnold Hughes and Martin Kolinsky,[7] who reversed Gregor's central thesis by claiming that Fascism was a mixture of conservative, reformist, and revolutionary impulses, and that its modernising impulses lay not at the core of the regime: they were marginalised by such anti-modern features as the leader cult, the worship of force and violence, the goal of autarky, and the notion of new Roman Empire.[8]

By far the most fertile source of contributions to the debate over fascism's relationship to modernisation, especially in recent years, has been the controversy that raged over the nature of Nazism particularly among German academics (i.e. if it is accepted that Nazism is a form of fascism: even this is contentious). Here again a lack of consensus is the characteristic feature of the debate, and the various positions which have been adopted can be broadly divided into five groups: (1) those who in one way or another see Nazism as anti-modern, though its 'anti-modernism' may be interpreted as 'resistance to transcendence'[9] or as 'millenarianism'. A passing reference in an edited work entitled *Sociology Responds to Fascism* centres upon the response of sociology to fascism to 'the backward-looking and romantic aims of National Socialist ideology', a position that persists even though Carsten Klingemann's essay considers how Third

Reich sociologists were a caste that worked on behalf of 'the rationalisation and modernisation of social conditions';[10] (2) those who see the Third Reich as an episode in unintended modernisation, which presents Nazism as exploding the traditional bonds of social hierarchy and authority; (3) those viewing Nazism as essentially reactionary, but as a movement that could take forms which embraced technological modernity;[11] (4) those holding that Nazism contained a central modernising thrust in areas of social policy, technology, and planning;[12] and finally, (5) the sceptics, who read, at best, scholarly ingenuousness and, at worst, questionable apologetic motives into attempts to present the Third Reich as an episode in modernisation, while playing down the massive scale of systemic inhumanity which was the direct and planned social cost of the 'new order'.[13]

Thus a tangled – and sometimes heated – debate has grown up regarding fascism's relationship to modernisation, modernity, and the modern. The confusion is epitomised in the sleeve notes to Ze'ev Sternhell's *The Birth of Fascist Ideology*,[14] which tell us that Fascism's proponents 'wished to preserve all the achievements of modern technology and the advantages of the market economy' while completely denying 'the intellectual and moral heritage of modernity'. It is the task of this chapter to suggest a way of refocusing this contended conceptual framework of fascism and modernity, one which places more emphasis on what fascists themselves claimed concerning such issues.

Some basic definitions

In the first instance, my 1991 monograph suggests a new approach to resolving the continuing debate on the minimum definition of generic fascism. *The Nature of Fascism* presents fascism as an ideology whose core myth centres on the imminent rebirth (palingenesis) of an existing nation-state from decadence and dissolution prevailing within a post-liberal (and decidedly anti-Marxist) new order, a concept summed up in the (binomial) expression 'palingenetic ultra-nationalism'. When applied to concrete movements and regimes, this definition produces a taxonomy very close to Stanley Payne's, but differs in terms of the stress placed on the revolutionary thrust of fascism; that is, its bid to create a new type of socio-political order as the essential component of fascism from which all aspects of its negations, style, and organisation derive. Stress upon the quest for national rebirth as the mobilising myth of fascism is not to deny, of course, the role played by conservatives and anti-modernists in helping both Nazism and Fascism to achieve and maintain power, or the appeal fascism could exert on middle class elements with essentially reactionary attitudes to socialist (and liberal) progress. What *The Nature of Fascism* does question is the usefulness of definitions which see such elements as forming the backbone of fascism rather than a part of a tactical alliance, rejecting views conceiving Nazism as an intrinsically reactionary, anti-modern 'counter-revolution'. The relationship of fascism's innovative, regenerative dynamic with its frequent invocation of a mythicised past is a point to which we will return.

Once the semantic focus shifts from 'anti-modernism' to 'modernisation', it does not take long to realise how apt the judgement of the *Social Science Encyclopedia* appears in understanding the latter term as one that 'slips and slides, alludes and obtrudes'. Fascist Studies also bears out the comment that the topics to which the term has been applied have tended to be 'more mis-understood than understood'.[15] The basic problem is that 'modern' can cover any number of forces which threaten to overturn or modify 'traditional' society (which is itself a far from monolithic or unproblematic concept), evidenced by sociological theorists both great (e.g. Karl Marx, Émile Durkheim, Max Weber, and Anthony Giddens) and small who have produced varying models of this process. It also tends to be laden with value-judgements and teleological conno-tations which imply that the destruction of traditional society by a certain form of modernisation, whether capitalist or socialist, is an essentially good; and indeed inevitable process (Francis Fukuyama's much-hyped 'End of History' thesis is the latest in a long line of such positions). Nevertheless, it is fairly uncontentious to argue that modernisation covers a nexus of forces which stem from the working out, on a potentially global scale, of the Enlightenment project of 'emancipating' humankind from the perceived strictures and irrationalities of traditional society. In practise, these conceptions tend towards the creation of a world under 'rational' human control, in close conjunction with the forces of technology and capitalism (whether corporatist or 'free') as well as the growth of centralised state power (whether liberal, military, right-wing or left-wing authoritarian).

'Modernisation' thus refers to the cumulative impact on traditional society by some of the following (this list makes no claim to completeness and any attempt to produce a hierarchy, or a causal map, of how these elements interconnect would be highly problematic): (i) *ideological changes*: the spread of Enlighten-ment humanism, secular reason in addition to the 'progress' myth, the cult of science, technology, and capitalism as liberating forces, in addition to the rise of materialism and consumerism, and the advance of instrumental rationality; (ii) *technical changes*: the industrialisation of production, the growth of ratio-nalised bureaucracy, technologised communications, the industrial – military complex, and the professionalisation of war; (iii) *political changes*: the entry of the masses into the political arena, the emergence of the nation-state as part of a world system, the bureaucratisation of power, the establishment of the notion of the planned society and economy, and the growth of state-employed military violence, social engineering, and coercion; (iv) *social changes*: urban-isation, demographic growth, democratisation in various forms, the spread of education and literacy, the growth of social mobility and the division of labour, massification (e.g. department stores), the rise of individualism, the breakdown of the extended family, changes in gender roles, and the replacement of community by society; (v) *economic changes*: the dominance of capitalism, laissez-faire individualism, and the progressive commodification of existence; and (vi) *cultural and psychological changes*: the pervasive impact of the mass media, the rise of secular ideologies, the growing sense of secular time, the dis-embedding of the individual from traditional communities and shared rituals as well as myths and cosmologies, the growing awareness of pluralism and of the existence of other cultures and values, the sense of the transience, imper-manence, the malleability of history, of linear time careening towards unseen possibilities, and the encroachment of isolation and *anomie*.

A dramatic image for 'modernisation', when approached from the perspective of its generally devastating impact on traditional society, was offered by Walter Benjamin. In one of his 'Theses on the Philosophy of History', Benjamin depicts the experience of progress from the point of view of the Angel of History:

> Where we perceive a chain of events, he sees one single catastrophe which keeps piling wreckage upon wreckage and hurls it in front of his feet. The angel would like to stay, awaken the dead, and make whole what has been smashed. But a storm is blowing from Paradise; it has got caught in his wings with such violence that the angel can no longer close them. This storm irresistibly propels him into the future to which his back is turned, while the pile of debris before him grows skyward. This storm is what we call progress.[16]

Modernisation revisited

One way of cutting through the intricate Gordian knot tied by successive attempts to conceptualise fascism's relationship to 'the modern' is to delib-erately create an artificial distinction between 'modernisation' and 'modernity'. I suggest that any concrete example of 'modernity' represents the product of a complex and ongoing interaction between a particular form of traditional soci-ety and particular forces of modernisation. Thus all modern societies represent a fusion of global, tradition-eroding forces with those maintaining the cohesion of the pre-existing culture with its own language(s), religion(s), rituals, customs, and local economy and technology. To offer a linguistic metaphor, the Celtic, Graeco-Latin, Germanic and Slavonic languages are all derived from fusions between forms of a primordial language known as 'Indo-European', and lan-guages which were already spoken regionally. In a similar way, as global forces of modernisation spread, they create highly specific local dialects of moder-nity according to their impact (whether gradually from within, as in Europe and the United States, or dramatically from without, as in large parts of Africa and Asia), and the particular reaction of a given traditional society. Whereas modernisation is a broadly uniform process, modernity thus assumes many different, constantly evolving forms.

Approached from such an angle, it becomes a central feature of modernisation that, wherever it impinges on a traditional culture, it will provoke a counter-reaction to its corrosive effects on the highly specific sense of ritual, rootedness, and identity traditionally provided. Traditional societies may sometimes be wiped out by modernisation, but in the main they survive, albeit radically transformed, sometimes out of all recognition. Their rear-guard action expresses itself in the constant generation or maintenance of myths which counteract a sense of ephemerality and *anomie*. These myths may operate within a purely personal sphere, as the commitment to particular forms of religious or spiritual belief, or in a cultic relationship to particular types of consumerism and display, such as car- or fashion-mania. In the sphere of socio-political thought, it produces ideologies at whose core lies a utopian vision of an ideal society, many of which lead to the 'invention of traditions'[17] to create a sense of the future's continuity with the past. Such mythic reactions will generally draw upon the specific tradition which is under threat. In psychological terms, their effect is to help re-anchor individuals in a contemporary history which would otherwise be unintelligible and threatening.

The validity of this perspective is corroborated by Shmuel Eisenstadt, an academic who pays considerable attention to the complex repercussions of modernisation, and to the need to consider – without ethnocentric prejudice – what should be construed as 'normal' development; that is, the unique permutation of modernity which will arise wherever it has impacted on tradition. In his editorial preface to a volume of collected essays dealing with the theme of non-Western forms of modernity, Eisenstadt outlines the main components of change subsumed within the term, and then observes:

> It is out of these processes that there have been continuously crystallising in different societies and civilisations different modes of incorporation and reinterpretation of the premises of modernity; of the different symbolic reactions to it; as well as the development of various modern institutional patterns and dynamics, or conversely, different modes of reinterpretation of the premises and historical traditions of the civilisation.[18]

In the light of such an approach, the world can be seen to abound with the essentially mongrel phenomena brought about by the interaction of ongoing modernisation with traditional forces. On closer inspection, every modern state reveals itself as a hybrid of global 'modern' and particular traditional elements. Just to take forms of state, the British constitutional monarchy represents (in Weberian terms) a fusion of traditional authority rooted in England's feudal and aristocratic system, with a parliamentary structure incorporating a rational, legalistic type of authority. A more flagrant example is how, in the twentieth century, Japan modernised under traditional authority and social structures, culminating in the imperialist regime which fought the Second World War.[19] Similarly, an analysis of the contemporary Iranian state, Ba'athist Iraq, contemporary China, or any of the Pacific Rim countries, would doubtlessly reveal each as a complex fusion of the global with the local; the modern with the traditional.

The collapse of the Soviet Empire has provided academics with a rich variety of case studies illuminating the process of cultural formation under the aegis of modernisation. Now that Communist Russia can no longer impose a particular form of modern society and state on the partially modernised nations of Eastern Europe, each of them is forced to forge (in both senses of the term) its own synthesis of global aspects of modernisation (capitalism, technology, consumerism, mass media, individual freedom, and sum) with tradition. This may well account for the regional intensification of nationalist sentiment and the fabrication of 'instant' rituals and a sense of historical roots whose function is to anchor people in what would otherwise be experienced as a whirlwind of potentially anarchic change. An example is the Ukrainian Republic, where in 1993, the new government staged a mass rally at night, complete with fireworks and national songs, to enact their new national identity. At its zenith a Uniat Bishop, exiled for nationalist agitation by the Soviet regime (Uniat Catholicism had become a signifier for Ukrainian nationalism, along with the indigenous language and a highly edited narrative of national history) solemnly kissed the Ukrainian flag and handed it to an officer of the new national army, with President Krouchek looking on benignly. It is precisely this (often shotgun) marriage of new and old, secular and religious, modern and traditional which so characterises 'modernity'. Thus, even if Fukuyama is right and Western modernity proves to outlive all the others, it would be wrong-headed to see a regime such as the one installed by Pol Pot in the 1970s as 'anti-modern', despite its enforced re-ruralisation of Cambodia. It used modern weapons and communications, modern techniques of social control and state terror to carry out its gruesome experiment in social engineering geared to bringing about an alternative modernity.

As for socio-political ideologies, the variants of liberal democracy and capitalism which originated in the 'West' and spread throughout the 'North' are clearly to be seen, not as the quintessence of modernity, but as one contingent form of it. *Khmer Rouge* ideology, for example, is a strange and terrible blend of 'traditional' Buddhism with Marxism and nationalism. It is but one symptom of the proliferation of nationalist, ethnic, or racist myths throughout the world containing a wide range of relationships to liberalism, all of which play the role of encouraging groups of populations (or minorities within them) to re-root, or re-embed, themselves so as to counteract the tradition-eroding force of modernisation: they are thus an expression of modernity, not its rejection or negation. This also applies to fundamentalist Islam, Christianity (as in the Bible Belt of the

United States), or Hinduism (as with the *Bharatiya Janata Party* [BJP] in India) just as much as in more secular varieties (e.g. the Communist nationalism of China or Ceaucescu's Romania). Even the familiar political discourses of liberalism, socialism, and conservatism are expressions of attempts to establish bulwarks of 'inalienable' rights and 'imprescriptible' values to offset the collapse into the total relativism and anarchy which modernisation perpetually threatens to disseminate.

As for the profusion of conflicting philosophical and aesthetic positions characterising Western culture over the last two centuries, some (such as those elaborated by Baudelaire, Tolstoy, and Nietzsche) seem markedly anti-modern when compared to the familiar varieties of 'modernism' (e.g. Futurism) or 'postmodernism' that proclaim themselves to be pro-modern. Yet at bottom, they are all different ways of asserting meaning and counteracting *anomie*. In a sense, then, *every* ideological and spiritual product of a society affected by modernisation cannot help but be a manifestation of modernity: they are not to be seen as 'pro-' or 'anti-modern', but as resulting from the interaction of specific forces of modernity with specific forms of traditional society within a unique and dynamically changing configuration of historical forces.

The implications for fascism

Seen in this way, fascism represents one response to modernisation within a protracted, complex, and unpredictable evolution of particular nation-states away from traditional society. Its core myth of national palingenesis, through the creation of a new socio-political and ethical order, means that it always portrays itself as a radical alternative to existing ideology and as the pioneer of a new path to modernity made necessary by the bankruptcy or decadence of (all) existing alternatives.

This position fully endorses that adopted by one of the foremost contemporary experts on both Italian and generic fascism, Emilio Gentile. Gentile fully accepts that 'if we identify modernity with liberalism in its widest sense, it seems automatic to exclude fascism from modern phenomena'. But he goes on to ask

Is it true that modernity and liberalism coincide? Is it true that traditional and modern society are two totally opposed realities so that where there is tradition modernity cannot be involved? Where there is ruralism modernity cannot be involved? Where there are political myths and political religion modernity cannot be involved?

Gentile then refers to those experts on modernisation theory who stress that there is currently a 'crisis in the Western-rationalist-liberal model of modernity and the process of modernisation which sees it as an effective, radical replacement of traditional society with a modern society, entirely based on rationality, industrialisation, on what Max Weber called "disenchantment"'. This leads him to conclude that 'intense processes of modernisation have taken place under the aegis of traditionalist myths and symbols. The crisis of the rationalist, progressive, Enlightenment model, if we want to call it that, has caused us to realise that modernity is not at all incompatible with authoritarianism, irrationalism or fascism'.

Alive to the danger that such an argument could be used in a revisionist spirit, to somehow euphemise or vindicate the fascist project, Gentile stresses that,

> All this is not an invitation to celebrate the modern aspects of authoritarianism present in fascism, but to reflect on the non-incompatibility of authoritarianism and modernity. If modernity is mass society, mass mobilisation, and the exultation of political myths, fascism is thoroughly modern. [. . .] (T)here are forms of authoritarianism which are not a reaction to modernity or a resistance to modernity, but are born of modernity itself, from the contradictions of modern society, and hence are to be studied as such.[20]

To expand on this argument, fascism as an *ideology* and *movement* can be seen as proposing a radical alternative to liberal and socialist visions of modernity. It represents an uncompromising rejection both of thorough-going liberalism and of extreme 'modernism', whose logical culmination the latter sees as relativism, *anomie*, subjectivism, and the loss of definitive meaning and 'eternal' values. It is thus an attempt to re-anchor modern human beings within that highly modern phenomenon, the totalitarian state (a term used positively by Italian Fascism) through consciously manipulated historical, national, and racist myths (all deeply modern ideological constructs). As a *regime* (mercifully exemplified in the only regimes which fascism was able to create, Fascist Italy and the Third Reich) fascist ideology set out to provide a new basis for participatory democracy and for the legitimacy of the modern nation-state, involving the transformation of ultra-nationalism into a 'secular religion' and the exaltation of the supremacy of the national community over individualism, through aggressive permutations of social control and social engineering. The fascist regimes actually installed constitute two of the many permutations of the tendentially absolutist power which the modern state can deploy against the inhabitant of modern society.

As for the recurrent tendency of fascists to invoke idealisations of the past as central parts in its 'political liturgy' (e.g. the Fascist myth of Romanità, the Nazi Aryan myth, the BUF's celebration of the Elizabethan age), the approach recommended here suggests that it is unhelpful to see this as the symptom of fascism's anti-modernity postulated by Henry Turner (1972). The most succinct corrective to such a view may be found in *The 18th Brumaire of Louis Bonaparte* where, having observed the readiness of Napoleon's III's regime to use myths based on the past to enlist popular support for the Second Empire, Marx asks rhetorically: 'Why did the revolutionaries themselves anxiously conjure up the spirits of the past to their service and borrow from them names, battle cries, and costumes in order to present the new scene of world history in this time honoured disguise and borrowed language?' His answer is that the 'awakening of the dead in bourgeois revolutions served the purpose of glorifying the new struggles, not parodying the old; of magnifying the given task in imagination, not fleeing from its solution in reality; of finding once more the spirit of revolution, not making a ghost walk around again'.

Marx believed that, unlike 'bourgeois ideologies', socialism was not to 'draw its poetry from the past';[21] that is, it could do without myth and the aestheticisation of politics – though in practice it could not do without them, as all the regimes of 'actually existing socialism' have demonstrated. By contrast, fascism celebrated precisely such forces as the way to recreate a sense of reality, meaning, and subjective revolution. This can be seen in the title of Alfred Rosenberg's *The Myth of the Twentieth Century*, or Mussolini's declaration in his 'Naples speech' of 24 October 1922, only hours before the March on Rome, that

> we have created our myth. The myth is a faith, a passion. It is not necessary for it to be a reality. It is a reality in the sense that it is a stimulus, is hope, is faith, is courage. Our myth is the nation, our myth is the greatness of the nation.[22]

On close inspection, whether it was the myth of Aryan blood or the myth of the past glories of Rome, all fascist celebrations of the past are in fact future-oriented, and an integral part of fascists' quest to find a Third Way out of the cul-de-sac of Western history which they felt liberalism and Marxism represented.

At the heart of this Third Way lies the myth of the regenerated national community (in German, *Volksgemeinschaft*), whose realisation is conceived by fascists as providing a solution to several basic problems characteristic of liberal-capitalist; modern society, notably (i) the troubled relationship between the 'masses' and the state; (ii) the crisis of morality, identity, and authority posed by life exposed to modernisation; and (iii) the tensions between the individual's private existence and ethnicity, culture, society, nationality, and history in the civic realm. However, the nebulousness of the core fascist myth of (ultra-)nationalist regeneration and the fact that each fascism will necessarily be nation-specific allows it, in principle, to embrace a wide range of responses to modernisation. In particular, it can be both *modernist* (as when Italian Futurists celebrated the urban, technological, tradition-destroying thrust of the contemporary age) and *anti-modernist*, as when the 'blood and soil' current of Nazism called for a new aristocracy based on the peasantry. However, all its ideological, organisational, and (potentially) institutional manifestations are products of modernity, no matter how reactionary or retrogressive they might seem when confronted with an alternative vision of modernity (which will always contain its own anti-anomic myths to act as a palliative to the crisis of meaning and social cohesion bred by modernisation).

Examples of fascist modernity

Italian fascisms

Once fascism is approached as a movement driven by a core palingenetic myth, and bent on pioneering an alternative form of modernity based on a new kind of authoritarian state, then D'Annunzio's occupation of Fiume between September 1919 and January 1921 assumes a fresh significance. It is common to regard the year-long regency by the former decadent poet turned war hero, by then well into his 50s, simply as a precursor to Mussolini's 'aesthetic style of politics', the most durable image being his melodramatic harangues from the balcony to the crowd. What is obscured, however, is the extent to which the Fiume 'Regency' presaged Fascism, and also generic fascism, in another important respect, namely by pioneering a charismatic form of populist nationalism with a distinctively modern thrust. Symptomatic of this aspect of D'Annunzio's new order is the adoption of the *Carta del Carnaro* [the syndicalism-inspired 'Carnaro Charter'] as its constitutional basis, a document which the anarcho-syndicalist, De Ambris, had a major role in drawing up. Of the constitution's three basic principles – communalism, corporatism, and participatory citizenship – the first two may seem archaic and the third unexceptional. However, as Mario Sznajder has shown in some detail, all three 'were now imbued with a new meaning, and adapted to the changed realities of modern industrial society. The aim was to fashion a new political structure which might answer the new needs resulting from industrialisation, urbanisation and the politicisation of the masses'.[23] He concludes that, by attempting to bring about a 'social revolution within a national integrative framework', the Carta becomes 'a document of political modernisation'.[24]

What of Fascism itself? When eyes are focused on the revolutionary, modernising zeal as opposed to reactionary, anti-modern animus, the symptoms are everywhere. The main currents of political culture which flowed first into interventionism, and then into early Fascism were Futurism, a nationalist version of syndicalism, and the brand of nationalism spawned by the *Associazione Nazionalista Italiana* [ANI]. Futurism was one of the most fanatically pro-modernist movements ever to exist, disparaging anything to do with the past as 'pastist' and celebrating the material and psychological fruits of the industrial and scientific revolution. It aspired to bring about, through ultra-modernist art and through cultural propaganda, an Italy liberated of the onerous burden of the past and transformed into a country of youth, dynamism, and heroic energy both at home and abroad.[25] National syndicalism was an offshoot – and some might say a perversion – of socialist syndicalism which came to the conclusion that the prerequisite for a proletarian revolution was for Italy to become not only a modern industrialised country (which had a certain logic), but a major power on the European scene as well. By 1914, this scenario included participation in the First World War, which would not only catapult Italy into the twentieth century, but create the heroic generation needed to transform Italy.[26] The ANI Nationalists were also modernisers. Concerned at the all-pervasive weakness of Italian liberalism, they looked forward to the country being swept into a new era on a groundswell of patriotism able to replace Giolitti's weak and corrupt liberal system with a corporate state under strong and hierarchical leadership. The new state would not only save the nation from socialism but oversee the country's transformation into a modern industrial and colonial power, one able to hold its head up high in the company of Britain, France, or Germany.[27]

The fact that Fascism in power was an alliance of these different strands of revolutionism with Mussolinian socialism – itself a modernising myth akin to both syndicalism and Futurism – helps explain why the theme of modernisation ran through every sphere of policy-making. Italian corporatism was not conceived as the return to medieval conceptions of the economy (which some Catholic theorists might have hankered after), but was seen in both its more proletarian-syndicalist and more statist-Nationalist versions as a Third Way between laissez-faire economics and the Bolshevik planned society. After the Wall Street Crash, liberal economics could quite plausibly be presented as having failed to meet the needs of modern society, while socialist totalitarianism and materialism destroyed in the name of an abstract 'humanity' the national identity and sense of the spiritual fundamental to human existence. In the early 1930s the Fascist experiment in pioneering a corporatist economy was seen by many non-fascist foreign observers[28] as a new synthesis; a role model for the future evolution of capitalism within a modern industrial state.

As for Fascism's relationship to technocracy, there can hardly have been a regime in history so keen to associate itself with the dynamism of the industrial revolution than the 'Third Rome'. The creation of motorways, the opening of hydro-electric power stations, the draining of the Pontine Marshes, the wonders of radio (Guglielmo Marconi became an Italian folk-hero), the launch of the new FIAT car, the exploits of Italo Balbo's spectacular flying 'cruises' to the United States: at every turn Fascist rhetoric sought to forge the link in the public's mind between dynamism, technology, the *Duce*, and the New Italy. Nor was this mere propaganda. Fascism set up a number of institutions to oversee the country's modernisation (e.g. *Consigli Tecnici, Gruppi di Competenza, Confederazione Generale dell'Industria Italiana, Istituto per la Ricostruzione Industriale*), and one of its most ardent and competent 'hierarchs', Giuseppe Bottai, enthusiastically used his roles as Minister of Corporations, Minister of Education, and editor of

Critica Fascista to promote the technocratic, modernising strand underpinning the New Italy.

In contrast to Germany, there was a large measure of convergence between the technological modernism of the Fascist state and its policy on art. Instead of regarding aesthetic modernism as 'decadent', the regime hosted various currents of modern art; in painting, graphic design, photography, and architecture. These included 'second Futurism', abstraction, and movements such as *Novecento* ['20th Century'] and *Stracittà* ['hyper-city'], all of which, in one way or another, celebrated the break with classical precepts and traditional forms of Italian culture. Of course, exceptions to this can be found. One of the art currents which prospered under Mussolini's laissez-faire art policy of 'hegemonic pluralism'[29] was *Strapaese*, which, as its name implies ['hyper-country'] promoted idyllic images of rural life as the image of the regenerated Italy. However, even the ruralism and racism of *Strapaese* represents a reaction to modernisation which looked to a modern state apparatus, not anarchic local communes, to provide the framework for a harmonious national community; in that sense, it may be seen as attempting to create a new synthesis of new and old – a new form of modernity rather than literally to restore an idyllic past. In the main, it was the ethos of modernism which prevailed in the abortive Fascist projects for an alternative modernity. Nor is this to be dismissed as a piece of opportunism on the part of the regime. Walter Adamson has demonstrated how deeply early Fascism was rooted in the pre-1914 avant-garde which, in the hands of art critics such as the *Vociani* Giovanni Papini and Giuseppe Prezzolini, fused the call for Italy's regeneration from decadence with the dynamism of the movement from now outmoded aesthetic norms. He argues that 'the modernists, a minority within the fascist movement, were disproportionately influential in legitimating it'.[30]

As has already been stressed, fascist ideology is by its nature opposed to all those aspects of modernity which are associated with decadence; namely, cultural pluralism, liberalism, and materialism. Yet this does not preclude fascists from experiencing a deep awe at the transforming power of technology once purged of these aspects. This can be seen clearly in Fascism's ambivalent attitude to the United States. Emilio Gentile's investigation of this topic concludes with the observation that,

> as a descendant of early twentieth-century modernist nationalism, fascism does not identify with anti-modernism, but in its own way, as we can see from 'fascist Americanism', it had a certain passion for modernity not inconsistent with its harking back to the traditions of the past [...] The fascists saw themselves as the modern 'Romans'. [...] In this way *romanità* became compatible with the myth of the future and with fascism's ambition of revising modernity in order to leave its mark on the new civilisation in the age of the masses.[31]

This last observation contains a vital point to be borne in mind when considering those aspects of Fascist and (generic) fascist utopianism which seem to be uncompromisingly reactionary and past-oriented. As a palingenetic creed, generic fascism is always future-oriented. When it does invoke myths of the nation's cultural achievements in the historical or mythic past, it does so in order to enlist slumbering nationalist forces in the battle for a *new* civilisation. It is obvious that *Scipio of Africa* (partially made in the ultra-modern film studios of Cinecittà outside Rome) was intended to legitimate the notion that the conquest of Ethiopia was the *renewal* of the spirit which created the Roman Empire, and that Mussolini was *emulating* the leadership qualities of the Caesars. It was not an attempt to encourage Italians to wear togas and speak in Latin. Marx's remarks on the French Second Empire's attempts to 'rewaken the dead' are again relevant here.

In short, everything points to Fascism being a movement, not of utopian anti-modernism, but towards a utopian modernity, a point on which much scholarship agrees.[32] Emilio Gentile captures the tone of all their conclusions on the subject when he states,

> The Fascists maintained that their rituals were celebrations projected into the future, rituals which marked the stages and victories in a 'continuous revolution' which was laying the foundations of a 'new civilisation': Fascism was not 'bent on commemorating the past like the old democracies' but continued to march 'with an eye turned to what was to come': 'All around an old individualist and libertarian civilisation is collapsing and Italy is called upon to give new life principles to nations who want to save themselves'.[33]

British and French fascisms

In the light of what we have seen in the case of Fascism, it should come as no surprise to see pronounced pro-technological components in other national expressions of fascism. A major theme of Mosley's BUF was the need to restore Britain's greatness by a thorough programme of modernisation. Symptomatic of this was a 1938 BUF pamphlet, called *Motorways for Britain* which looked enviously at the road networks in Italy and Germany, finishing in a rhetorical flourish which is hardly anti-modern: 'Let our Motorways of the future be an example of engineering skills to the world, and let us adopt of a method of government which will break financial restrictions and release the unbounding energies of the British people'.[34]

Consistent with this was Mosley's faith that Britain could still find a way out of the terminal decline he saw perpetuated by the parliamentary system and laissez-faire capitalist economy. Under his leadership, a movement of the most patriotic and productive elements of the population would blend the genius of the Elizabethan age (the monarchy would be retained) with a British version of the corporate state in order to create a new type of socio-economic order which would lead to the Empire being revitalised alongside the mother country. Typical of the revolutionary tenor of *The Greater Britain* (1932), in which Mosely expounded his fascist vision, is the chapter 'Finance, Industry and Science'. Here he proposes a close link between the National Investment Board and scientific research in terms which would not be entirely unfamiliar to Britain's Council for the Advancement of Science:

> for the first time, science would be properly supported, not only by official discrimination between the genuine and the bogus, but also by financial machinery to support the genuine discovery, and to translate it into industrial achievement. *We must call for the new world of science to redress the balance of the old world of industry.*[35]

The technocratic, modernising fervour of the whole book is epitomised in the quote which serves as the epigraph for this chapter.

Similar pleas emanate from many fascist defenders of corporatism, both within the BUF and abroad. For example, a recent political biography of Marcel Déat, founder of the collaborationist and (as opposed to the Vichy regime) decidedly fascist *Rassemblement National Populaire*, reveals a central concern with the modernisation of French productive capacity, in addition to attempts to bring it in line with the Nazi industrial machine.[36] This technocratic vision was typical of the French fascist and radical as a whole in the interwar period,[37] underlining yet again the inappropriateness of Turner's ideal type of 'utopian anti-modernism' as a key to understanding generic fascism.

Post-war fascisms: the New Right

Post-war fascism has spawned new varieties, notably the deeply anti-liberal European New Right, an international current of cultural criticism launched by Alain de Benoist's sustained attacks on 'ethno-pluralism' and egalitarianism in the late 1970s. Significantly enough, this is a form of palingenetic ultra-nationalism which is neither paramilitary in orientation (because it has appropriated the Gramscian theory of the primacy of cultural hegemony over the political, indeed calling itself 'Right-wing Gramscism'), nor narrowly nationalist (because it sees Europe as a culturally homogeneous territory made up of many ethnic nations, or *ethnies*). Through a feat of perverse logic it claims that it is liberal society which is racist, on account of its encouragement of racial mixing – both ethnically and culturally – it shows it is bent on destroying racial integrity, the only sound basis of a healthy and meaningful existence. A recurrent theme of the New Right is that Europe can overcome the decadence of the present by revitalising its Indo-European (i.e. Aryan) heritage. In this new

Europe technology will play a crucial role, but only once it becomes the servant of human beings rather than its master:

> European civilisation is not in danger because of technical progress, but because the egalitarian utopia which seems to be winning out nowadays is proving to be in contradiction with the needs of modern society, born, among other things, of this very technological progress. It is the egalitarian technology which undermines the will of man to affirm his *sovereignty over what he has created*. The end of the 'domination of the machine' does not reside in its destruction, but in the will of man to *transform* himself in order to remain the master of his 'productions'.[38]

The major spokesperson for this type of 'metapolitical' fascism in Germany is the Frenchman Pierre Krebs, founder of the Thule Seminar (whose very name alludes to the Thule Society, out of which the NSDAP grew at the end of the First World War). In his pamphlet *Die europäische Wiedergeburt* [*The Rebirth of Europe*], Krebs claims the New Right is pioneering an authentic 'core modernity' based on an organic concept of society, in glaring contrast to the pseudo-modernity which is ultimately no more than a form of fashion or snobbism. As Friedrich Hölderlin, Ezra Pound, Gottfried Benn, and Martin Heidegger have shown, 'organic modernity' draws on the possibilities latent in the organic roots of a people (*Volk*), and arises from the interaction of the forces of transformation with those of cultural heritage. Permutations of modernity without these organic roots is 'doomed to decay'.[39]

Significantly, the most scholarly overview of the whole subject of fascism's relationship with modernity to date has been provided not by Marxist scholars (generally too preoccupied with its capitalist dynamic) or liberal critics (generally too concerned with its 'pathology'), but by intellectuals of neo-fascist persuasion themselves. In 1985, *Diorama Letterario* [*Literary Panorama*], a major periodical of the Italian Radical Right, devoted a series of issues to the Conservative Revolution. The first of these was entitled simply 'Modernity'. The issue contains an introduction by Marco Tarchi, one of Italy's foremost ideologues of right-wing culture ('cultura di destra'), in addition to essays on the concept of technological society found in the writings of Ernst Jünger, Arthur Moeller van den Bruck, and Oswald Spengler. The most revealing piece is entitled 'The "Conservative Revolution" and Modernity'.

The article, written with an exemplary scholarly technique by Louis Dupeux, reveals the sustained impact on the New Right of Armin Mohler's efforts to establish the Conservative Revolutionaries as the 'Trotskyites of the German Revolution' (Hitler being its 'Stalin') immediately after the Second World War. Dupeux also points to a profound acquaintance with major pre-1945 German writers including Theodor Fritsch (prolific and rabid anti-Semite), Arthur Moeller van den Bruck, Oswald Spengler, Carl Schmitt, Thomas Mann (often cited in these contexts by the right), Friedrich Nietzsche, Ernst Niekisch, and Ernst Jünger. Dupeux argues that the central preoccupation of the Conservative Revolutionaries is with decadence and degeneration, but the hallmark of their response to it is not cultural pessimism, but the belief in 'Resurrection [*Wiedergeburt, Auferstehung*]'. 'In contrast to "Cultural Pessimists", "Conservative Revolutionaries" do not feel prisoners of a hated century. They seem themselves at a historical "turning point" [*Zeitwende*]. Their attitude expresses itself in affirmation [*Bejahung*]'.[40] Going on to argue that an essential ingredient of this cultural optimism (or palingenetic myth) is the embrace of technology 'as an essential means of *power*', Dupeux cannot understand why the major German historian of the anti-liberal ideas current in right-wing circles under the Weimar Republic, Kurt Sontheimer, can talk of their passionate rejection of technological civilisation 'when proof of the contrary abounds'. He stresses the central role played by technocratic assumptions to Conservative Revolutionary thinking to the point where rapid industrial progress was seen as an integral component of the imminent national rebirth on condition that it could be made healthy by becoming a means to the realisation of a higher national destiny, and not as an end in itself.[41]

Dupeux concludes by suggesting that Hitler himself fits this pattern (contrary to Henry Turner's insistence on Hitler's animus against technology); *Mein Kampf* being replete not just with reflections on 'decadence' and 'the general collapse of our civilisation', but also with allusions to a fascination with modern technology – to the point of comparing his party with 'a great industrial concern'. Dupeux's final sentence, furthermore, is unambiguous: that 'the study of the problem of modernity is the key to understanding the Conservative Revolution and, if we can cautiously extend the topic, to what, rightly or wrongly, is generally defined "fascism"'.[42]

Such claims by fascists to be the harnessers – not the enemies of – technology and modernity are nothing new. In 1931, Major J. S. Barnes, one-time director of the Centre for International Fascist Studies in Lausanne, was reassuring the readers of his volume in the Home University Library Series, *Fascism*, that it would

> reject nothing *a priori* of the result of modern 'progress', claiming only that what vitiated the value of so much that has been accomplished since culture ceased to have its roots in revealed religion was its materialistic and super-individualistic basis; that to remove this bias, to substitute for it a spiritual, dualistic outlook on life will enable the gold to be separated rapidly from the dross and cause every modern conquest of value to fall into its proper place in a new cultural synthesis such as the world has not known since the height of the middle ages.[43]

Nazism

We are now in a position to return to the thorny issue of Nazism's relationship to modernity. Seen through the lens applied above, its thrust towards an alternative, uniquely German modernity can be seen at work everywhere. Even in the most apparently reactionary currents within Nazism, such as Darré's 'Blood and Soil' movement, the regeneration of the peasantry and the restoration of the bond between Germans and the land, is the precondition for the creation of a healthy, imperial, and technologically advanced 'new' Germany (hardly 'green' in the ecological sense). There is no intention to carry out the coercive de-urbanisation of Germany as Pol Pot was to do half a century later (and, as we suggested earlier, even here the catastrophic human consequences of palingenetic myth were at work to create a *new* Cambodia, not literally to restore the medieval Khmer Empire).

Away from this ultimately marginalised mode of Nazism, the Third Reich was saturated with technocratic values. A consideration of *Todt Organisation*, which turned the motorway into a symbol of the New Germany;[44] the Four Year Plan for 1935–1939;[45] the activities of the *Amt Schönheit der Arbeit* [The Beauty of Work Office],[46] *Kraft durch Freude*, [Strength through Joy] and *Deutsche Arbeitsfront* [German Work Front]; the productivism of Albert Speer;[47] the quest to develop a German physics and the related programme to build the Atom Bomb;[48] and technophile Nazi ideologues[49] – all point in the same direction. The V2 rocket bomb could hardly have been developed by an anti-technological culture. Nazism was not anti-modern, but celebrated technology as the externalisation of the Faustian drive and Aryan creativity of the German people which – unlike the 'decadent' Jews, British, and Americans – instinctively combined inner and outer, brawn and brain. Liberated from the 'artificiality' of liberal society and the threat of Bolshevism, Germans were free to pursue technological mastery, not in the spirit of materialism or individualism, but as servants to the regeneration of the national community (*Volksgemeinschaft*). Under Adolf Hitler, they would finally gain their rightful place in the vanguard of history.

Even the famed anti-modernism of Nazi art policy should be treated cautiously. The Nazis believed they were engaged in a battle against cultural decadence embodied in demonised Jews and Communists (*Kulturbolschewismus*). In the early years of the regime Goebbels favoured the idea that Expressionism, a highly modernist artistic idiom, should be considered a fruit of the Aryan creative drive, but he was overruled by Hitler, who had a taste for neoclassicism and the Baroque. The result was an outpouring of lifeless neoclassical or kitschified vernacular painting and megalomaniacal architectural projects. Yet even these were produced as exemplifications of the healthy spirit which was to inform the new Reich, not just as nostalgic references to the past; indeed, some of the painting had decidedly modern themes, such as the building of an Autobahn bridge. Every new artistic product was meant to demonstrate that the Aryan, the promethean creator of civilisation, was at work.

Thus the orgy of destruction which accompanied the rise of the Third Reich was not wanton nihilism. It was what Armin Mohler, the hagiographer of the Conservative Revolution, has called 'German nihilism', the will to destroy in order to build, to create ashes if necessary so that a Phoenix may rise again. Even the Holocaust may be seen as the fruit of this perverted logic, one preceded in the euthanasia programme, in which some 100,000 ethnic Germans were killed in the name of creating a healthy, athletic German race. In short, the recurrent stress on the *völkisch* dimension of Nazism, on its function as a 'religion'[50] or as a millenarian cult,[51] is misleading. Nazism embraced conflicting attitudes to rural life, urbanisation, and the past, but the celebration of technology and industry were vital to the main thrust of its ethos and policies. Nazis fought a crusade against what they perceived as decadent aspects of industrial society (the cult of progress, the espousal of materialism, the pursuit of technocracy for its own sake), not modernity as such. In this sense, it was no counter-revolution, but a revolution in its own right.[52]

This is not to be taken as unqualified endorsement of the view that Hitler was a conscious moderniser, which has been argued by some scholars.[53] His basic obsession was not with modernising Germany, but with eradicating the nexus of forces to which he attributed its collapse (*Zusammenbruch*) and dissolution (*Zersetzung*). While he admired American technology, he loathed the multi-racial liberalism and materialism it embodied, and strove to turn Germany into the heart of a European empire based on crude racist and Social Darwinist principles for the triumph of the fittest. But while Ian Kershaw is right to criticise Zitelmann's thesis,[54] it is still appropriate to see Hitler's vision as an alternative, and (no matter how perverse and unrealisable) a revolutionary version of modernity, rather than the expression of anti-modernity or 'reactionary modernism'. It is a palingenetic utopia (indissociable in retrospect from the horrendous dystopian implications of its actualisation) which reverberates in Hitler's words on the occasions where he privately gave vent to his deepest convictions; 'Those who see in National Socialism nothing more than a political movement know scarcely anything of it. It is even more than a religion: it is the will to create mankind anew'.[55]

Hitler's project for the renewal of European civilisation – its transformation into a genuine *Kultur* – under German hegemony involved a wholesale rejection of many aspects of the modern (indeed when he used the term it was with negative connotations). However, not only was this project entirely reliant for its realisation on all aspects of modernisation able to be co-ordinated with Hitler's larger palingenetic aim, but the aim itself was inconceivable without such quintessentially modern forces as massification, social engineering, bureaucratisation, rationalisation, the technologisation of warfare, Social Darwinism, nationalism, racism, and charismatic power. Furthermore, its focus was the quintessentially modern form of power assumed by the nation-state. The Third Reich was a permutation of modernity.

Such a conclusion makes no claim to originality. Nor should it be exploited to euphemise Nazism's atrocities in a spirit of 'historical revisionism'. Both are underlined by a study of Zygmunt Bauman's brilliant *Modernity and the Holocaust* (1989), which reveals at length how the Final Solution was run by bureaucracies and technocracies, rationalised by science, and subjected to the logic of accountancy. Moreover, it was only made possible by the awesome power of a modern state capable of operating largely beyond control of the international community. In other words, the Holocaust could only occur conceptually, organisationally, legally, and technically in a country at an advanced stage of modernity. With modernity violence becomes a technique, acted out through a division of labour turning personal responsibility into technocratic responsibility: Bauman cites the efforts of German engineers to increase the efficiency of the gassing-van used in the early stages of the extermination programme which was reduced to a question of logistics and technical efficiency. At the root of the Holocaust was the state-led drive for a fully designed, fully controlled social world, of a society lovingly tended and ruthlessly pruned by the 'gardening state'. So far the forces of pluralism at work in modern society have conspired to prevent such biopolitical projects from being carried out on a grand scale. But when this countervailing moment is overridden by authoritarianism there is little to stop wholesale social engineering and the terror state this creates: the electoral victory of Nazism in 1933 ensured that its totalitarian scheme of utopian society could be implemented to a terrifying degree.

To study Nazism is, on one level, to study the awesome potential of modernisation to create ephemeral and abortive (but to their victims terrifyingly real and definitive) symbioses between the traditional and the modern, to produce a form of modernity deliberately attempting to crush the Enlightenment humanist tradition. To grasp this fact destroys any comforting equation between modernity and humanism, modernity and civilisation, modernity and progress, modernity and the good. There is a famous line at the end of Brecht *The Resistible Rise of Arturo Ui*, namely 'The womb that gave birth to Nazism is fertile still'. I suggest this metaphor applies more aptly to modernisation than to capitalism.

Conclusion

One inference from the line of enquiry suggested above is that studying the link between modernity and fascism casts direct light on the contemporary resurgence of racism and ultra-nationalism. The retrenchment within a sense of ethnic or national identity is a global process of increasing intensity, the break-up of Yugoslavia being only the most dramatic example from a Eurocentric (media) point of view. Ultra-nationalism offers its believers a solution to the modern crisis of identity, an instant 'grand narrative' within which to locate the trajectory of the self, a panacea to *anomie*. Without succumbing to the temptation to vindicate such anti-human ideologies, scholars should at least take to heart their indictment of the failure of mainstream liberal-capitalist society to provide an adequate sense of identity and purpose in times of crisis. In doing so they would be forced to show more understanding towards alternative schemes of modernity, no matter how utopian or perverse, because they represent the *faulty* diagnosis of a *genuine* malfunction, and register the translation into mythic discourse of *real* social and psychic needs.

There is, however, an even more fundamental conclusion to be drawn, namely that researchers into the history of fascism need to shed the mind of any preconception about the most desirable or valid form of modernity when grappling with schemes for an ideal society that diverge radically from their own. This means repressing any culturally induced temptation to associate 'modern' with something intrinsically good or positive. It is this misconception which lies at the heart of the perverse or deliberately apologetic view that fascism's attempt to pioneer an alternative form of modernity somehow mitigates its crimes against humanity, crimes which themselves were essentially, though not quintessentially, modern. It also means abandoning all forms of ethnocentrism or teleological thinking, especially those which in Fukuyamian manner assert the progress of the 'Western idea' as one which will eventually eliminate all rival forces. Only thus can various 'Third Ways', no matter how abortive or unsustainable, be understood intelligently. To underline this point I would refer to the growing symptoms even within mainstream society that the world is facing an ecological crisis of awesome proportions. To take just one statistic, conservative, scientific estimate: there will be *no more rain forest left* on the planet by the year 2025. The most superficial familiarity with the scientific debate about the need for sustainable development to replace unsustainable growth calls into question the viability of the Western historical project as radically as any Spenglerian: actually *more* so, since Spengler had no scientific data to go on for his sense of decline, merely intuition and mythopoiea. In contrast, modern science and technology ensures that the legion threats to the ecosystem are being exhaustively documented. Yet, at present the impact of the mode of modernity which makes this monitoring possible also ensures that the annihilation of the biosphere is proceeding at an ever quickening pace.

In the context of such considerations, 'modern', 'anti-modern', and 'post-modern' turn out to be highly fuzzy concepts. Are dark greens 'anti-modern' if conventional technocratic myth guarantees there will be no 'modern' at all in a handful of generations time, while they are fighting to assure the survival of humanity on the basis of an *alternative* notion of progress (based on such fundamental components as energy sources which do not run out or destroy the ecosystem)? When an eminent Cambridge professor of sociology[56] argues that only a sustainable, post-scarcity society would be post-modern, since the forms of modernity which exist today doom the world to self-destruction, is *he* being a 'cultural pessimist', 'reactionary', or 'anti-modern'? Or is this better applied to those contemporary Panglosses who believe that we already live in the best of all possible worlds, and dismiss green thought as neo-Luddite nonsense?

3
Exploding the Continuum of History
A Non-Marxist's Marxist Model of Fascism's Revolutionary Dynamics*

The awareness that they are about to make the continuum of history explode is characteristic of the revolutionary classes at the moment of their action. The great revolution introduced a new calendar. The initial day of a calendar serves as a historical time-lapse camera. And, basically, it is the same day that keeps recurring in the guise of holidays, which are days of remembrance. Thus the calendars do not measure time as clocks do; they are monuments of a historical consciousness of which not the slightest trace has been apparent in Europe in the past hundred years.

Walter Benjamin, 'Theses on the Philosophy of History', 1940

The philosophy of nature evolved by occasional leaps and bounds alternating with delusional pursuits, *culs-de-sac*, regressions, periods of blindness and amnesia. The great discoveries which determined its

---

* This article was first published in Italian translation in the socialist journal *Mondoperaio* 3, May-June (2008) under the title *'Fascismo: la lettura marxista di un non marxista'*. It grew out of another originally written for the Copsey, Nigel and Renton, David (eds). *British Fascism, the Labour Movement and the State*. London: Palgrave Macmillan, 2005, and rejected as inappropriate for that volume on the grounds that its subtext was too critical of the traditional Marxist analysis of fascism and its scholarship shaky on some key aspects of Marxist thinking. If it is a little more cogent (but no less contentious) now it is thanks to a number of academics for transforming the polemic of the original version into a hopefully more scholarly 'thesis', even if I obviously must take final responsibility for the argument in its final form: Nigel Copsey, Alfred Schobert, Peter Osborne, Joe Yannielli, Erik van Ree, Martin Durham, Walter Adamson, and John Stewart. Particular thanks go to David Renton, author of the most important restatement of a Marxist approach to the historiography and analysis of fascism, who, despite some fundamental disagreements, was very helpful at least in placing some limits on the scope for this piece to go astray. It should be pointed out that 'non-Marxist Marxist' is an allusion to (the Marxist) Isaac Deutscher's autobiography, *The Non-Jewish Jew*. London: The Merlin Press, 1981: a title ingeniously suggested by David Renton himself.

course were sometimes the by-products of a chase after quite different hares. At other times, the process of discovery consisted merely in the clearing away of rubbish that blocked the path, or in the rearranging of existing items of knowledge in a different pattern.

Arthur Koestler, Epilogue, The Sleepwalkers, 1959

Blindspots and dialogues of the deaf

Walter Benjamin's insight into the temporal dimension of revolution is contained within one of what became known as his 'Theses on the Philosophy of History', a series of illuminations formulated during his personal 'moment of danger'[1] – exile in Paris from the Third Reich, just months before his suicide on the Spanish border in September 1940. The idiosyncratic form of analogical thinking he developed for exploring the nature of history in the thrall of modernity (which itself can be considered emblematic of modernism),[2] enabled him to recognise the powerful ideological energy that can be unleashed by the mythopoeic power of collective associative memory during a period of social and political ferment. He saw that the act of forging an allegorical link between the present and a mythically shaped and largely imagined episode from the past can result in an epic temporal trigonometry, producing a line of sight towards an alternative future. With it is born a revolutionary vision capable of blasting the space for a new political and social order out of the seemingly monolithic *status quo*. Suddenly the barren present becomes pregnant with the anticipation of rebirth, thereby transforming as if by a conjuring trick the endless temporal continuum which Benjamin equates with the 'historicist' concept of time. 'Historicism' as he presents it is reminiscent of the 'ever-expanding, grey future' in which Franz Kafka once imagined a tawdry circus act taking place *ad infinitum* until one member of the audience finally bursts into the ring and shouts 'stop!'.[3]

Benjamin's 'Theses' are a compelling synthesis of political theory, historical explanation, philosophy, metaphysical speculation, and programmatic radicalism. Yet what strikes the non-Marxist about the passage cited in the epigraph is how adamantly Benjamin refuses even to contemplate the possibility that the fission energy generated by mixing myth with history could be detected in the very ideology whose human vectors were eventually to hound him to death. Nor is he alone in this. His contemporary Ernst Bloch, who stands alongside Benjamin and Gramsci as one of the most creative Marxist cultural and political theorists of the twentieth century, dedicated nine years of his life in exile from the Third Reich to exploring the power of the 'Not-Yet-Conscious' which he sees as the wellspring of myriad utopian projects detectable in every sphere of human activity, and as the driving-force behind cultural and political change throughout human history. Yet his mind remained closed to the presence of hope and future-oriented projects of liberation at the heart of the

Nazi movement itself. Instead, he perpetuated the crude 'agent theory' of orthodox Marxism that axiomatically denied Nazism any autonomous, trans-class,
revolutionary dynamic:

> Hitler rose out of the Night of the Long Knives, he was called by the masters
> out of the dream of this night when he became useful to them. [. . .] The mob
> can be bought, is absurdly dangerous, and consequently it can be blinded
> and used by those who have a real vested interest in the fascist pogroms. The
> instigator, the essence of the Nights of Knives was, of course, big business,
> but the raving petit bourgeois was the astonishing, the horribly seducible
> manifestation of the essence.[4]

Post-war (post-)Marxists have also, whatever their sophistication as political
thinkers, shown little inclination to move beyond interpretations of fascism as
the expression of bourgeois reaction and the vested interests of capital, seemingly blinded by their ideological preconceptions in the very act of seeing. Thus
in *The Society of the Spectacle*, Guy Debord's panopticon of the central role played
by theatrical display and liturgy in the 'totalitarian management of the conditions of existence', could only offer a blinkered perspective on fascism, despite
the wealth of case studies in his topic offered by the lavish theatrical politics of
both Fascist and Nazi regimes:

> Fascism was an extremist defence of the bourgeois economy threatened
> by crisis and by proletarian subversion. Fascism is a *state of siege* in cap-
> italist society, by means of which this society saves itself and gives itself
> stop-gap rationalisation by making the State intervene massively in its
> management.[5] [original emphasis]

A similar set of axiomatic assumptions informs Andrew Hewitt's *Fascist Modernism*, which displays impressive fluency in the arcane discourse evolved within
the long left-wing tradition of engagement with Benjamin's concept of the 'aestheticisation of politics', further enriched by the impact of the 'linguistic turn'
in the human sciences. Yet the light on fascism that passes through the carefully wrought hermeneutic prism it offers has itself undergone no significant
deflection since Benjamin first formulated his theory. Hewitt proceeds on the
unquestioned premise that an inherent paradox exists in the dangerous liaison
with the 'reactionary' forces of fascism entered into by such avant-garde artists
as Hanns Johst, Wyndham Lewis, Ezra Pound, and Filippo Marinetti. He seeks to
resolve this by focusing on the contradictions of capitalism arising through the
'bourgeois construction of the public sphere' operating within 'the paradigm
of imperialism', an approach which leads to the conclusion that 'a deep-seated

theatricality' lurks beneath the 'traditionally antispecular' ideology of the capitalist classes 'to which fascism merely gives expression'.[6] The possibility of
a spontaneous and authentic synergy between modernism and fascism is not
even contemplated.

Behind enemy lines

Meanwhile non-Marxist Fascist Studies seem to have been carried out in a parallel universe, either blissfully or wilfully ignorant of Max Horkheimer's 1939
injunction that 'whoever is not prepared to talk about capitalism should also
remain silent about fascism'. As early as March 1921, over a year before Mussolini's March on Rome, Antonio Gramsci was already seeking to identify the
essential traits of fascism 'on an international scale', which he saw as 'the
attempt to resolve the problems of production and exchange with machine
guns and pistol-shots'.[7] By contrast, it was not till the 1960s that the first serious
attempts were made by non-Marxist academics to identify the nature of fascism
as a generic force. Until then, it was routinely considered to have been driven
by energies so irrational, barbaric, nihilistic, pathological, or charismatic that it
defied rational analysis as a coherent ideological or political phenomenon, an
assumption which severely compromised its heuristic value as a generic concept.
Typical of this remarkably unproductive phase in comparative Fascist Studies is
Hugh Trevor-Roper's 1968 essay 'The Phenomenon of Fascism' which, having
dismissed Nazism as a 'vast system of bestial Nordic nonsense', fails to deliver
any cogent definition of the phenomenon under investigation.[8] Certainly 'capitalism', and much besides, tends to be passed over in silence within non-Marxist
Fascist Studies, and accounts stressing the role played in the rise of fascism by
the (lower) 'middle classes' usually portrayed them as driven into fascism's
arms by the nebulous *Angst* induced by the disembedding forces of modernity,
rather than by the material threat to their livelihoods and political hegemony
posed by revolutionary socialism. As long as fascism was widely regarded as
a 'conundrum', the pragmatic solution adopted by most practising historians
was to focus empirical analysis on the development of individual movements or
regimes and ignore the increasingly tangled and inconsequential 'nomothetic'
debate among political scientists about the term's generic semantics.

Over the last decade, however, just when Marxist Fascist Studies seemed to
have lost their momentum, becoming radically impoverished in conceptual
incision compared to their interwar heyday, a sea-change has come about in the
way liberal academia now approaches the concept of fascism (one that has yet
to affect its usage in the 'bourgeois public sphere' in general). Though consensus
in the sense of total unanimity is as far off (and indeed both unrealisable and
undesirable) as in any heated taxonomic debate within the human sciences,

there is at least a growing meeting of minds on the following propositions, or what I have (provocatively) called 'the new consensus':[9]

a) no matter how much conservatives and reactionaries of all kinds were drawn to specific fascist movements (or attempted to use it for their own ends), and how far capitalists colluded with them in pursuit of reactionary ends, fascism itself was *in its own terms* an autonomous revolutionary force which could exert a genuine trans-class popular appeal in the exceptional crisis conditions of inter-war Europe;

b) although the specific impact of short-term (but not terminal) crises in the capitalist economic system following the First World War was a vital prerequisite for the emergence of fascism as an alternative to authoritarian conservatism, liberal democracy, and Soviet communism, neither the preservation of capitalism from the onslaught of socialism nor the destruction of the working class movement were central to fascism's main goal;

c) this goal, instead, was the total – and totalitarian[10] – transformation of the political, moral and aesthetic culture of the nation to produce a new type of national community and a new type of 'man': a social, political, cultural, and anthropological revolution subsumed in the vision of imminent national rebirth (palingenesis);

d) local historical conditions, and the specific terms in which the nation was conceived, dictated whether the rebirth from decadence that a fascist movement tried to implement was translated into an aggressive foreign policy, expansionist imperial ambitions, or programmes of racial persecution, ethnic cleansing, and even genocide, none of which are definitional traits of fascism as such;

e) where fascist movements acted in this way such policies, and the violence and destruction they produced – or would have led to had the given movement seized power – were conceived by fascists themselves as integral to the process of national regeneration rather than as ends in themselves, and are not to be seen as the manifestation of capitalism's 'true nature' as an *essentially* destructive and reactionary force;

f) the importance which fascists attached to a mythicised Golden Age in the history of the nation or race, far from being symptomatic of atavistic anti-modernism or a regressive nostalgia for lost idylls, was instead linked to the attempt to resuscitate the allegedly 'eternal' values of the nation/race that were to inspire the new order in a *future-oriented* process of renewal and regeneration, thereby pioneering an alternative modernity, one based on revolution rather than reaction.

From this perspective, capitalism and the bourgeoisie were conservative (reactionary) forces that, by colluding with fascism, were promoting an independent revolutionary movement initially seeking to overthrow the structures and values of the very liberal system that had nurtured them and guaranteed their ascendancy over the ancient régime.

Contrasting readings of fascism

To illustrate how profoundly these conflicting premises can condition the interpretation of ideological phenomena associated with (generic) fascism, let us consider an extract from the characterisation of Nazism's paradoxical relationship to modernity in Joachim Fest's *Der zerstörte Traum* [The Shattered Dream] (1991), whose subtitle is 'The End of the Utopian Age':

> The aggressive utopia that National Socialism evolved out of many a whimsical, misty-eyed, or troubled backward glance to a bygone age was not consistently projected into the past. True, its spokesmen made out that they were restoring a world-order perverted by Christianity, the Enlightenment, and the processes of industrialisation and social emancipation. This accounts for the call for a return to the values of the peasant and the soil along with a revival of all the ancient rites that were bound up with them: hence all that quirky stuff about flag-dedication ceremonies, the *Thingspiel*[11] and death cults, in a word, that longing to regress to the mists of time which had always been part of the movement. Alongside this strand, though, and constantly intertwined with it, there was a ravenous hunger for the future that took pride in sailing the biggest ships, flying the fastest planes, or providing transport for the masses, one that proclaimed the technical advance of the German nation over all others.
>
> This modern side of National Socialism has created the impression that the folksy, oldy-worldy rituals were just part of an elaborate masquerade to secure power. This was only partly true. The whole movement, including the highest ranks of leadership, was seized by a burning desire for everything that was bathed in a pre-historical twilight, but at the same time a ruthless scorn for tradition and a passion for bureaucratic efficiency in planning and execution that even today takes the breath away from anyone who studies its results.[12]

Significantly, Fest's observations make no reference to comparative Fascist Studies, and are thus typical of the long-standing tendency of non-Marxist German historians to see Nazism as a unique phenomenon, at most subsumable under the generic term 'totalitarian'. His portrait of Nazi utopianism is nevertheless consistent with the definitional criteria used to identify fascism by those working broadly within the parameters of the (highly contested) 'new consensus'. Such scholars would agree that Nazism's cult of the past was an integral part of its bid to achieve radical social renewal, one rooted in the regeneration of a nation conceived as an organic entity, and whose aim was therefore not mass deception and social control. Instead, it was the realisation of an alternative modernity to that offered by both liberalism and communism, and made possible by the collective enthusiasm for their revolution sustained by a regenerated national community.

Read through conventional Marxist lenses, however, a number of aspects of the characterisation brand Fest's account of Nazi utopianism as ideologically highly suspect: (a) his implication that the Nazi movement was driven by genuine ideological conviction; (b) the omission of any reference to the role of capitalism or the bourgeoisie whose interests Nazism was directly or indirectly serving; (c) Fest's emphasis on the Nazis' futuristic programme of modernisation rather than its reactionary war against socialism, the working class, or its political and racial enemies; (d) the way it is Nazism's 'reactionary', anti-modern obsession with reviving a mythicised past is treated as a masquerade, rather than its embrace of modernity; (e) the implication that Nazism's commitment to helping the masses (e.g. mass transport) can be taken at face value rather than as part of a populist confidence trick to conceal its real class interests. To a Marxist, then, everything about this passage points to the fact that Fest (at the time Cultural Editor of the *Frankfurter Allgemeine Zeitung* and author of the much acclaimed account of the last days of Hitler turned into the 2005 film *Der Untergang* [Downfall]) lacks a grounding in historical materialism. As a result, he has been insufficiently immunised against Nazism's beguiling rhetoric and cannot realise that the 'aestheticisation of politics' he unwittingly documents was no more than a cynical ploy to legitimise the crushing of capitalism's enemies, thereby enabling its hegemony to be perpetuated in defiance of the objective conditions signalling its demise at the hands of the proletariat.

Given this yawning gulf between the assumptions about fascism instinctively operating within the Marxist and non-Marxist traditions of Fascist Studies, it is hardly surprising if their representatives have tended to treat each other either with mutual indifference or as essentially hostile 'camps', thereby overlooking the diversity, complexity, and subtlety of at least some of the analyses of fascism generated by the (frequently demonised) 'Other'.[13] As a consequence, both sides remain largely oblivious to the potential contribution explanatory strategies employed beyond the ideological no-man's land could make to a more complete understanding of fascism.

In writing this chapter I am thus consciously offering my services as a sort of 'go-between' or 'mediator' (and thus risk being cut down by a hail of criticism from both sides!). I am offering, not an olive branch, but the rudiments of a syncretic model of fascism made up exclusively of Marxist theoretical components in the broadest sense of the term, ones deliberately selected and assembled teleologically in order to produce an interpretation of fascism congruent with the main conclusions about its ideological nature currently gaining currency in non-Marxist scholarship. I should stress that this chapter has no sinister imperialist agenda of turning Marxist Fascist Studies into a colony of the (partial and contested) 'new consensus'. Rather, it should be read as a response both to the sense of the shortcomings inherent in existing Marxist theories occasionally expressed by Marxists themselves,[14] while simultaneously serving as an invitation to 'liberal' historians to engage more actively with the rich tradition of Marxist theory and historiography in the field of comparative Fascist Studies. This reconnaissance mission 'behind enemy lines' is not a manoeuvre to open up a new front in an ideological war, but instead to call a truce in the hope of collaborative relations between the two (far from homogeneous) 'sides' which will enrich Fascist Studies for both parties.[15] Transposing Koestler's observations on the history of science to the present context, it attempts to clear away some of the rubbish that has been 'blocking the path' in *both* traditions, and to 'rearrange existing items of knowledge in a different pattern' so as to facilitate a mutual process of discovery.[16]

Four Marxist theses relating to fascism's ideological dynamics

The argument that follows is too rudimentary to serve as the foundation for an alternative Marxist theory of fascism, but at least it might serve to stake out a site within the left-wing social sciences where architects and surveyors can set to work. For the purposes of the present – necessarily highly condensed – exposition, the 'stakeout poles' will consist of four interlocking theses. The primary and secondary literature potentially relevant to each stage of the argument is vast, so for the sake of simplicity each will be associated mainly with the work of one Marxist theorist whose work is exemplified by the following theses.

Thesis 1: Ideology, though *in the last analysis* a superstructural force, may operate as a relatively autonomous factor of historical causation that transcends the sphere of economic determinism. As such it can play a critical role in enabling an anti-systemic movement to conquer power, thereby establishing a new socio-political and cultural order in defiance of 'objective' material conditions.

The key theoretician supporting this proposition is undoubtedly Antonio Gramsci.[17] Building on a rich European intellectual tradition of Marxism that had been submitting determinist readings of dialectical materialism ('economism') to radical revision since the 1880s,[18] he came to concede a considerable degree of autonomy to superstructural forces in shaping the historical process. By the early 1930s, when his imprisonment by the Mussolini regime prompted a profound reconceptualisation of the relationship between ideology and state power, he was arguing that, while in some circumstances it might be appropriate to reduce economics to politics,

> it is also distinct from it, which is why one may speak separately of economics and politics, and speak of 'political passion' as of an immediate impulse to action which is born of the 'permanent and organic' terrain of economic life but which transcends it, bringing into play emotions and aspirations in whose incandescent atmosphere even calculations involving individual human life itself obey laws different from those of individual profit.[19]

Such a forthright acknowledgment of the relative independence of both political and ideological spheres from the operation of economic forces and vested interests was closely bound up with Gramsci's recognition that the state's exercise of political power not only involved control of the 'base', but authority over the 'superstructure'. He saw this authority as dependent on the extent to which the ruling classes monopolised institutional power within the political sphere, as well as on the degree of 'cultural hegemony' the bourgeoisie secured in the realm of civil society. Indeed, in one respect cultural hegemony within civil society was more crucial to the conquest and maintenance of political power than the state institutions of social control, because, without it, power could only be exercised through force, in the form of dictatorial 'domination'. Armed with sufficient cultural power, the ruling elite could run the state on the basis of a high degree of consensus, and hence largely dispense with overt instruments of coercion.

Especially in modern capitalistic societies, a crucial role in maintaining the *status quo* within civil society is therefore played by the system's 'organic intellectuals' (its mandarin class) who ensure that society's cultural production – in its widest sense – endorses and underpins, rather than challenges and undermines, the covert dictatorship that the bourgeoisie imposes. It is only when this hegemony starts to wane or becomes effectively challenged by rival visions of the political order that should replace the present one, that the legitimising (and largely subliminal) popular consensus may break down conspicuously and dramatically, producing an *avant-garde* of intellectuals and ideologues challenging the system. At this point, even the most seemingly progressive liberal state may resort to the deployment of overtly authoritarian techniques of government in order to maintain itself in power, opting to rule through dominion rather than through hegemony.

Gramsci's deeply personal experience of Italian Fascism generated a sustained interest in the situation that can arise when the superstructural crisis is combined with an acute structural (i.e. politico-economic) one. At this point, the totality of the 'historical bloc' enters an 'organic crisis' in which a significant proportion of the public becomes psychologically detached from the policies of the leaders and from the political system which supposedly represents their interests. The four years of trench-warfare in the First World War had impressed upon him how illusory it was to assume that a modern state gripped by such a crisis can simply be swept away by a display of paramilitary violence. Putschist tactics cannot work since 'at least in the case of advanced industrial states, "civil society" has become a very complex structure and one which is resistant to the catastrophic "incursions" of the immediate economic element (crises, depressions, etc.)'; its ideological superstructures being 'like the trench-systems of modern warfare'. As a result, the revolutionary struggle is to be conceived as a protracted war of attrition in which 'only politics creates the possibility of manoeuvre and movement'.[20]

These reflections led Gramsci to distinguish between 'revolutionary explosions' like the French Revolution, in which the old ruling elite is eliminated and replaced by a new one, and a 'passive revolution' in which the feudal classes become a 'caste' with specific cultural and psychological characteristics, but without the attendant economic functions,[21] (an analysis related to Gramsci's 'Caesarist' interpretation of Fascism which draws on Marx's concept of Bonapartism).[22] He saw the period between 1815 and 1870 in Europe as one of a protracted 'war of position' or 'restoration-revolution', and the Fascist movement as the equivalent of the 'moderate and conservative liberalism in the last century' – the product of the new 'war of position' following the political 'war of movement' that lasted from March 1917 to March 1921.[23] The ensuing superstructural struggle between socialists and capitalists for cultural hegemony in Italy proved more decisive than objective economic conditions, and its outcome had been the triumph of the Fascists over the socialists. As a result, a reformist radicalism that left capitalism's economic and political hegemony largely intact had been able to keep at bay the structural change to the entire liberal system promised by communism, thereby flouting the predictions of dialectical materialism. In fact, under Fascism

> there is a passive revolution involved in the fact that – through the legislative intervention of the State, and by means of the corporative organisation – relatively far-reaching modifications are being introduced into the country's economic structure in order to accentuate the 'plan of production' element; in other words, that socialisation and co-operation in the sphere of production are being increased, without however touching individual and group appropriation of profit.[24]

Thesis 2: Interwar fascism exerted a trans-class and genuinely 'mass' appeal (however embryonic and unsustained), and contained an autonomous radical element independent of attempts by the forces of capitalist reaction and bourgeois self-interest to use it as an 'agent' in its struggle against socialism.

One of the most important post-war proponents of this interpretation of fascism is Ernesto Laclau, who saw Althusser's 'Lacanian' understanding of the dynamics of ideology to be crucial in explaining the power that fascism could exert beyond the confines of bourgeois reaction. According to Althusser, ideology is essentially 'specular', since each established socio-political order occupies 'the Centre' from which, in phenomenological terms, it calls them into being, or 'interpellates' them. In this way, the individuals constituting society are turned into subjects 'in a double mirror-connection': the state '*subjects* the subjects to the Subject', while, reciprocally, the Subject provides them with a deep sense of existential security and identity.[25] The important inference that Laclau draws from this argument is that ideology has the power to transform individuals 'who are simple bearers of structures' into 'subjects', who 'live the relation with their real conditions of existence as if they themselves were the *autonomous* principle of determination of that relation.'[26]

Once a political system enters a systemic crisis its automatic self-reproduction in the subjectivity of its citizens (subjects) breaks down and the resulting 'ideological crisis is necessarily translated into an "identity crisis" of the social agents'. As a result, each of the contending sectors 'will try and reconstitute a new ideological unity using a "system of narration" as a vehicle which disarticulates the ideological discourse of the opposing forces'. At this point, a faction may 'deny all interpellations but one, develop all the logical implications of this one interpellation and transform it into a critique of the existing system, and at the same time, into a principle of reconstruction of the entire ideological domain'.[27] A totalising revolutionary project is then born which taps deep into the psychological and existential energies of its supporters.

The close match between Laclau's analysis and Gramsci's account of the 'organic crisis' of society and its loss of 'cultural hegemony' is obvious. What adds a new dimension to Laclau's analysis, however, is his sustained critique of the type of 'class reductionism' that assumes each social class naturally has its own ideology tailor-made to express its interests, so that if elements of the working class are drawn to anything other than revolutionary socialism they, *by definition*, have been seduced by the 'wrong' ideology. Instead, he argues that the working class forms the natural constituency of support *for two competing ideologies*, the socialist struggle against capitalism, which interpellates it as part of an international proletariat, and the 'Jacobinist' struggle against traditional elites. This originates in the petty-bourgeoisie, but has a genuinely radical and popular dynamic of its own, appealing to the working class as part of a historically constituted 'people', and hence as a unique nation or race.

It is this line of argument, so much at loggerheads with both Comintern and Bonapartist theories of fascism, that leads Laclau to offer a radical revision of the Marxist orthodoxy on fascism. Far from being simply an 'invention of monopoly capitalism',[28] fascism became possible because 'the working class, both in its reformist and revolutionary sectors, had abandoned the arena of popular-democratic struggle'.[29] Behind the flawed psychohistorical theories of fascism offered by Wilhelm Reich and Erich Fromm 'lay the confused intuition that fascism was the result of processes in which ideology was playing a much more autonomous and decisive role than in other contemporary phenomena'.[30] Similarly the equally misconceived theories presenting fascism simply as a form of totalitarianism also contained a 'grain of truth', namely the realisation that 'it was not interpellations as class but interpellations as *"people"* which dominated fascist political discourse'.[31]

To substantiate this point Laclau calls on the testimony of none other than Georgi Dimitrov, whose name has been regularly taken in vain to sanction the most reductionist formulations of fascism's identity with capitalism, but who seems nonetheless to have grasped the dual nature of the 'interpellations' to which the proletarian masses were exposed. In his report to the Seventh Congress of the Comintern (1935) – which contains the famous pronouncement about the 'terroristic dictatorship of capital' under fascism – there is a passage that has been sadly neglected by orthodox Marxists. It warns of the dire consequences of continuing 'to neglect the problem of the struggle against fascist ideology', acknowledging the effectiveness of the fascists' 'rummaging through the entire history of every country' so as to 'pose as the heirs and continuators of all that was exalted and heroic in its past'. This distortion of history needed to be countered by emphasising that 'the socialist revolution will signify *the salvation of the nation* and will open up to it the road to loftier heights.'[32] The conclusion that Laclau draws from his analysis is that socialism is not to be presented as 'the opposite pole of fascism':

> Socialism is certainly a counterposition to fascism, but in the sense that, whilst fascism was a popular radical discourse, neutralised by the bourgeoisie and transformed by it into its political discourse in a period of crisis, socialism is a popular discourse whose linkages to the radical anti-capitalism of the working class permit it to develop its full revolutionary potential.[33]

For Laclau, then, fascism's ultra-nationalism is to be considered a trans-class mobilising myth rather than a reactionary middle class ideology, one which can only be imposed on the masses through propaganda and brainwashing.

Thesis 3: The cult of the past in fascism's ideology, far from being a symptom of its intrinsic reactionary conservatism, is consistent with the crucial role of remembrance and mythicising retrospection played in all revolutionary activism.

Laclau is careful to avoid attributing a fully fledged revolutionary dynamic to fascism, yet even his concession that it was a radical popular discourse to which socialism offers a 'counterposition' would be anathema to neo-Stalinists. However, his line of reasoning risks becoming even more 'heretical' once the time dimension of fascist ideology – implied by his allusion to its 'rummaging' through history – is considered in the context of Walter Benjamin's theory of the temporal dynamics of revolutionary movements encountered at the outset of this chapter. It was the fruit of a profound anti-economist and anti-Enlightenment version of historical materialism, informed by such diverse influences as the study of cinema, photography, Nietzsche, Baudelaire, Kafka, surrealism, Futurism, and a fascination with the special place that a theocratic history and ritualised memory occupied in orthodox Jewish religion. In Benjamin's *Theses* he points out that, though 'Jews were prohibited from investigating the future', they were instructed in theological and ritual techniques of remembrance. As a result, history for them could never be experienced as 'homogeneous or empty' since 'every second of time was the strait gate through which the Messiah might enter.'[34] This was contrasted with the secular or 'historicist' apprehension of time that had become hegemonic with the impact of the Enlightenment, namely a rectilinear, single-track phenomenon in which social realities are destined to unfold in an incremental, cumulative way; event after event, indefinitely, 'till the last syllable of recorded time'.[35]

By underpinning the myth of progress, making any *caesura* or quantum change in the historical process inconceivable, the hegemony of historicism sanctions the persistence of capitalism, precluding all projects (literally projections onto the future) for creating a better world. The precondition for the transformation of the present system is thus a dramatic shift in perspective or point of view that would enable the social imagination to break out of the historicism and the social system it sustains. The precondition for this is that those committed to radical change enter a special mode of temporal consciousness in which the *status quo* is illuminated through an analogy made in the historical imagination with an episode from the past, transforming the present into *Jetztzeit* ('now time' or 'presence of the now') in which linear time is shot through with 'chips of Messianic time'.

For Benjamin, the paradox that an ideologically charged recollection of things past can generate the collective sense of an imminent new epoch explains why 'the French Revolution viewed itself as Rome reincarnate', and why the Republic introduced a new calendar and new holidays, not to measure time but as 'days of remembrance' and 'monuments of historical consciousness'. Such a 'tiger's leap into the past' enables the historical materialist to recognise in a configuration of events 'pregnant with tensions [...] the sign of a Messianic cessation of happening, or put differently, a revolutionary chance in the fight for the oppressed past', and so resolve to 'blast a specific era out of the homogeneous course of history'. The 'true' historian who breaks free from the soul-numbing thrall of historicism 'stops telling the sequence of events like the beads of a rosary. Instead, he [sic] grasps the constellation which his own era has formed with a definite earlier one.'[36]

Benjamin axiomatically equated Marxist revolution with universal human emancipation and social justice. It falls to 'revolutionary *classes*' to make the continuum explode, not the *Volksgemeinschaft*. As a result, the 'true historian' could only be a socialist, and never a Giovanni Gentile, an Alfred Rosenberg, or an Alexander Raven Thompson. It is presumably for this reason that Benjamin was unable to recognise in Mussolini's speeches as *Duce* or Hitler's *Mein Kampf* contemporary examples of attempts to make 'tiger's leaps' into the future, and blast a new time and space out of the continuum of liberal-democratic history. Nevertheless, Benjamin's theses on history provide a powerful heuristic device to reveal the Fascist celebration of Romanità, the Nazi cult of the Aryan past in its classical and medieval manifestations, or the BUF's glorification of the Elizabethan era as symptoms, not of an urge to take refuge from modernity, but rather of the will to break out of its hegemonic variant and achieve an alternative modernity by exploiting the mobilising power of the 'eternal values' identified with the national community. Fascists intuitively realised that the 'storm of progress' unleashed by modernity meant that there was no going back to achieve their ideal society: the rebirth of the nation could only be achieved through a *new* birth.

Thesis 4: Though fascism promotes cults of an idealised past and utterly rejects certain aspects of modernity, its main thrust is not reactionary or conservative, but *counter-revolutionary*, pursuing the *anti-conservative* goal of realising a new order and a new era.

One of most radical challenges posed by an 'insider' to conventional Marxist wisdom about the relationship to the progressive agenda of radical socialism – and not just of fascism – but of the early twentieth century avant-garde as a whole, is contained in Peter Osborne's *The Politics of Time* (1995). The unquestioned axiom of practically all left-wing analyses of fascism is that not just its genesis, but its *raison d'être* lies in its attempt to crush the progressive forces of socialism, no matter how much it attempts to steal the clothes of socialist revolution.[37] This leads to the assumption that its 'modernity' (e.g. in the sphere of technology, industry, or communications) conceals a basic drive to 'turn back the clock' to a pre-modern utopia, and its 'radicalness' (e.g. in mobilising the masses through displays of theatrical politics) is a rhetorical ploy to counter the threat posed by progressive, revolutionary forces.

It is on the basis of such preconceptions that the open-armed embrace by Nazism – for Marxists, the archetypal manifestation of the essence of fascism – of such features of the modern world as bureaucracy, science, technology, consumerism, mass media, and the entertainment industry have come to be explained in terms of 'reactionary modernism'[38] or a 'conservative revolution'.[39] Such oxymorons imply the forced conjunction of two projects that pulled away from each other in their temporal aspect, and so generated irresolvable internal dichotomies. Thus the electrification of the railways under Mussolini, or the Third Reich's campaign to encourage the public to watch the 1936 Berlin Olympics in newly installed TV parlours, smack of a perverse hybrid between the familiar and the alien, a grotesque fusion between the sphere of modernity with the realm of myth. Following this logic, the highly public conversion to Nazism of a world-famous thinker working at the cutting edge of modern philosophy thus poses a thorny paradox whose resolution demands ingenious scholarship and elaborate analysis.

Yet Osborne's interpretation of modernity throws into relief a powerful 'elective affinity' between Martin Heidegger and the Third Reich that discloses a deep-seated logic in his enthusiastic implementation of Nazi racial policies as Rector of Freiberg University in 1933. After all, both Heidegger's philosophy and Nazi ideology were rooted in a 'diagnosis of the world-historical situation as one of crisis and decline, a nationalist definition of its political shape (conservative revolution as a *national* revolution), and hope for the future grounded in a quite particular revolutionary temporality of renewal'.[40] The First World War was seen in such a conception of the present age as a phenomenon that was 'simultaneously *nationalistic, technological* and *cultic*'. It enabled the rebirth of Germany to be imagined as a process in which, in Ernst Jünger's words, a 'new symbolic dimension' would fill technological civilisation with 'a deeper life, one superior to the purposeful life and whose essence cannot be grasped with mathematics'.[41]

In the light of such considerations, Osborne argues that binomial expressions such as 'reactionary modernism' and 'conservative revolution' are not to be understood as expressing unresolved contradictions in the relationship to historical time. Instead they refer to 'a novel, complex, but integral form of modernism in its own right':

> [A]s a counter-*revolutionary* ideology, conservative revolution is modernist in the full temporal sense of affirming the temporality of the new. Its image of the future may derive from the mythology of some lost origin or suppressed national essence, but its temporal dynamic is rigorously futural. In this respect it is the term 'conservative' which is the misnomer rather than 'revolution'.

This realisation leads him to 'revisit' the key term at the heart of so much orthodox Marxist thinking about fascism, namely 'reaction' – in the sense of the *opposite* of revolution, the *resistance* to modernity, the *flight* from futurity. Instead, he insists that:

Conservative revolution is a form of revolutionary *reaction*. It understands that what it would 'conserve' is already lost (if indeed it ever existed, which is doubtful), and hence must be created anew. The fact that the past in question is primarily imaginary is thus no impediment to its political force, but rather its very condition (myth). What Herf calls reactionary modernism is not a hybrid form (modernism plus reaction). Rather, it draws our attention to the modernistic temporality of reaction per se, once the destruction of traditional forms of social authority has gone beyond a certain point. This point seems to have been reached in the leading European societies around the time of the First World War; hence the tremendous contemporary upsurge of revolutionary ideologies of both 'reactionary' and 'progressive' types.[42]

Osborne further maintains that, within the context of the post-1918 crisis of both conservative and liberal politics in Europe, socialism and (the conservative revolutionary dimension of) fascism can thus be seen as twins – albeit warring twins – since both their projects of the future are to be seen as reactions of 'non-economic social relations' to the de-structuring, disembedding impact of capitalism. Such reflections lead him to abandon orthodox Marxism's dualistic conception of the modern age as riven by the conflict between two ideological forces locked in a Laocoon-like struggle for supremacy, namely (socialist) revolution and (capitalist) reaction in its multiple guises. Instead

> [t]here are at least three 'revolutionary' temporalities at play, quite apart from the various rearticulations of the temporality of tradition: the hegemonic temporality of the self-revolutionising process of capitalist production; the revolutionary temporality of the oppositional practice of self-transformation in the name of a new, post-capitalist (traditionally, socialist) economic form; and the counter-revolutionary temporality of a variety of reactionary modernisms. Both the second and the third of these present themselves at the cultural level as avant-garde (by virtue of their explicit political identification with radically new futures).[43]

Osborne's inference is striking in its simplicity and radicalness: 'contrary to received opinion [...] fascism is neither a relic nor an archaism, but a form of *political modernism*'[44] [original emphasis].

If this perspective is adopted, the focus of Marxist analyses of fascist reaction shifts dramatically. As long as the exclusive concern for its left-wing opponents is to demonstrate that fascism's war against revolutionary socialism was directly or indirectly the desperate 'last stand' of a beleaguered capitalism, then any phenomena symptomatic of its bid to create an alternative modernity to both liberalism and communism are lost in the blur of peripheral vision, or can only be acknowledged as epiphenomena in conflict with the essential nature of fascism, and thus rooted in irresolvable contradictions within capitalism itself. Gramsci's interpretation of fascism as the expression of a 'passive revolution', and hence a pseudo-revolution – despite the genuine appeal it exerted on the popular masses – is an outstanding example of this approach. Ultimately, Italian Fascism could never be for Gramsci anything more than one of the 'morbid phenomena' produced by the contemporary crisis of society, an 'interregnum' in which 'the old is dying and the new cannot be born'.[45]

Once fascist reaction is seen in terms of Osborne's concept of 'counter-revolution' rather than Gramsci's concept of 'restoration-revolution'[46] – or rather, once 'restoration' under the impact of modernity is attributed a radically futural dynamic – then fascism can be understood as a fully fledged revolutionary assault on the political, social, and cultural *status quo*. Where successful, this attempted revolution had a transformative impact on liberal capitalism as well, even if did not set out to replace the capitalist system as such. Seen from this perspective the contradictions between fascism's cult of the past, its attacks on 'actually existing' modernity, and its claims to be inaugurating a new historical era and a new socio-political order resolve themselves into paradoxes.

At this point, Fascism's relationship to socialism can be seen as being analogous to the one between the Counter-Reformation and the Reformation: Hitler is to Lenin what Loyola was to Luther. Those genuinely 'reactionary' conservatives, whether aristocratic or capitalist, who supported Fascism or Nazism, primarily out of fear of socialism or nostalgia for a bygone age of tradition and security, had tethered themselves to the wrong horse. Tragically for the rest of humanity, generic fascism's bid to create a new society and a new man within a regenerated national community was much more than a revolutionary façade or empty rhetoric.

The structural affinities between fascist and Marxist revolution

The main thrust of the analysis so far is that, using theories formulated by the 'organic' intellectuals of Marxism itself, fascism's relationship to socialist radicalism should be seen not in simplistic terms of an anti-modern reaction contrasted with progressive revolution. Certainly, reactionary forces attempted to use fascism as their 'agent' or 'tool' to counteract the threat of socialism. And without doubt the radicalism of Nazism and especially Fascism *as regimes* was compromised in practice by the collusion of traditional conservative elites in the exercise of state power. Nevertheless, once aggregated, the four theses we have outlined suggest that fascism had an autonomous and genuine revolutionary agenda, whose appeal and main social constituency of support was not restricted to the bourgeoisie or capitalist classes, and which was at least partially implemented by the only two regimes where fascism prevailed over the forces of conservative reaction, namely the Third Reich and Mussolini's Italy.

Although the alternative temporality that fascism offered to communism may not have been progressive in either liberal or socialist terms, it was not simply 'regressive' either, since it contained its own futural, modernist thrust towards a new society.

Marxists who have been willing to go along with the broad thrust of this argument have now been escorted to a position tantalisingly close to the 'new consensus' on fascism in liberal academia, even if an idological chasm still separates them from historians who adopt this position while feeling 'at home' within the continuum of liberal-capitalist modernity, unperturbed by longings for a 'Messianic cessation of happening'. Naturally, a major stumbling block to Marxists accepting this line of argument is the central emphasis it places on fascism's ideological goals rather than its praxis, and the loosening of linkages between these goals and either capitalism or the bourgeoisie. It also goes against the grain of much dialectical materialism by eroding the distinction between Marxist revolution and fascist 'reaction', widely considered on the left to be polar opposites.[47] Nor is the distinction restored by insisting that fascism is 'counter-revolutionary' rather than fully 'revolutionary' for, as Osborne stresses, the 'counter-' denotes not a regressive dynamic, but one which is 'rigorously futural'. Furthermore, a case could be made for seeing the Marxist revolutionary project as containing its own counter-revolutionary dynamic, to the extent that it is a response to (and *reaction* against) what Osborne terms 'the hegemonic temporality of the self-revolutionising process of capitalist production'.

An even deeper source of socialist resistance to the syncretic 'Marxist' approach to fascism proposed here may be that it implies a far closer and more uncomfortable affinity between fascism and communism *in practice* than most Marxists would like to acknowledge. As forms of political modernism, both offered totalising solutions to the problem posed by the decadence of liberal society, which were outstanding specimens of the application to socio-political engineering of the 'historical predictions' that Karl Popper identified with his concept of 'historicism'[48] – a curious reversal of the connotations given the term by Benjamin – and with the mainspring of totalitarianism. In both cases, the utopia of a new society was formulated by blending scientific and technocratic discourse with mythic thinking, thereby producing that characteristic ideological product of modernity, 'scientism'.[49] Both, when implemented, spawned an elaborate 'political religion' and, in their Nazi and Stalinist versions, provided the rationale for mass murder on an industrial scale.

A more telling objection might be that what compromises the cogency of 'my' Marxist theses is the marginality of Benjamin, Laclau, and Osborne (and in some quarters even Gramsci!) within mainstream Marxism. To take just one example, Benjamin's stress on the role played by the past in the revolutionary *imaginaire*, so crucial to the Marxist revisioning of fascism's temporality proposed here, could be considered too idiosyncratic for him to be summoned (against his will) as a witness for the defence of fascism's revolutionary credentials.[50] It is therefore worth pausing to reflect on the claim which Benjamin makes for its orthodoxy when he asserts that the 'leap in the open air is a dialectical one, which is how Marx saw revolution'.[51]

It was Marx himself who drew attention to the paradox that revolutionaries have always legitimated overthrowing the *status quo* with invocations of the past, and who directly anticipated one passage in Benjamin's *Theses* by referring to the cult of Rome that grew up among militants in the French Revolution. Perhaps the most famous declaration of *The Eighteenth Brumaire* is that 'Men make their own history, but they do not make it just as they please; they do not make it under circumstances chosen by themselves, but under circumstances directly encountered, given, and transmitted from the past'. Less familiar is the sarcastic observation about 'bourgeois' revolutions that follows:

> The tradition of all dead generations weighs like a nightmare on the brains of the living. And just as they seem to be engaged in revolutionising themselves and things, in creating something that has never yet existed, precisely in such periods of revolutionary crisis they anxiously conjure up the spirits of the past to their service and borrow from them names, battle slogans, and costumes in order to present this new scene of world history in this time-honoured disguise and this borrowed language. Thus Luther donned the mask of the Apostle Paul, the Revolution of 1789 and 1814 draped itself alternately as the Roman Republic and the Roman Empire, and the Revolution of 1848 knew nothing better to do than to parody, now 1789, now the revolutionary tradition of 1793 to 95.

Marx is at pains to stress that when revolutionaries invoke a mythicised past in this way, they do so within an imagined temporality that is entirely 'futural':

> Thus the awakening of the dead in those revolutions served the purpose of glorifying the new struggles, not of parodying the old; of magnifying the given task in the imagination, not of fleeing from its solution in reality; of finding once more the spirit of revolution, not of making its ghost walk about again.[52]

In what appears to be an unambiguous refutation of Benjamin's later claims for the intimate nexus between a mythicised past and the revolutionary future, Marx proceeds to assert that precisely what sets the socialists' revolution apart from its bourgeois travesty is that they can have no truck with either necromantic exhumations or flights into nebulous realms of remembrance:

The social revolution of the nineteenth century cannot take its poetry from the past but only from the future. It cannot begin with itself before it has stripped away all superstition about the past. The former revolutions required recollections of past world history in order to smother their own content. The revolution of the nineteenth century must let the dead bury their dead in order to arrive at its own content. There the phrase went beyond the content – here the content goes beyond the phrase.[53]

Yet, in the event, Marx's pronouncement was at least partially contradicted by the implicit place occupied in his own teleology by the highly mythicised stage of 'primitive communism' that he assumes to have existed at the dawn of human history. This primordial utopia, combined with the future utopia of the final redemption of the oppressed within a classless and stateless society, arguably performs a important function in structuring Marx's deeply teleological 'philosophy of history' in which the end-stage of civilisation recaptures some elements of a primordial harmony before the 'fall' into class-history. This suggests that his voluminous revolutionary writings are to be seen in Benjamin's terms as an attempt to lay the scientist foundations for the proletariat's collective experience of an emancipatory 'now time'. For Marx too, 'remembrance' is treated as a precondition for socialism's ability to transform into a coherent revolutionary class the exploited and alienated working masses, otherwise condemned to be trapped for ever in the inexorable continuum of capitalism.[54] On closer examination, his sustained socio-economic and political analysis is itself shot through with 'chips of Messianic time'. A scarcely concealed theology of redemption drives 'historical materialism' just as Benjamin's first thesis on the philosophy of history maintains.

Fascism, Marxism, liberalism, and the 'true' revolution

This chapter has attempted to sketch a syncretic Marxist theory of fascism that sets out to offer a more adequate heuristic framework for assessing its revolutionary credentials than those that widely employed 'on the left' to date. It should be emphasised that there is no suggestion in this exercise of endorsing fascism's aspirations, let alone of approving the practical consequence of its bid to realise them: in the language of *1066 and All That*, revolutions can be not just 'a bad thing' but 'very bad things'. Seen in this way, interwar fascism – which excludes pseudo-fascist regimes such as Franco's Spain, Dollfuss' Austria, and Antonescu's Romania – emerges as a force which, as the 'new consensus' in comparative Fascist Studies maintains, strove, on the basis of a trans-class political constituency (that could include significant segments of the proletariat), to achieve a non-communist, post-liberal 'new order' as a direct rival to and bulwark against Soviet Russia's experiment in forging an alternative modernity.

Its vision of the new type of social and political culture that this entailed was informed by allegedly 'eternal' national values located in a mythicised past. However, it simultaneously implied a fervently modernising (and modernist) futural dynamic in its radical assault on the values, historical vision ('grand narrative'), and institutions of *liberal* capitalism (its 'historicism').

Fascism's bid to install its own alternative modernity was manifested in its qualified, but generally positive, embrace of technology, and in its sustained efforts once in power in Italy and Germany to dynamite 'traditional' time and space for a new order out of the continuum of history, one not based on economic transformation and the resolution of class conflict, but on the purging of decadence from the organically conceived national community. The overriding motive behind fascism for its most fanatical believers at a lived, 'phenomenological' level (as opposed to the many 'conservative' fellow-travellers and opportunists who colluded with it and who can rightly be considered 'reactionary') was not the preservation of capitalism, or the destruction of socialism, or the elimination of racial inferiors as ends in themselves. Instead they were mobilised by deep-seated longings for a new identity, a new beginning, and a new age beyond a contemporary historical reality widely experienced as 'falling apart' and a society in the thrall of materialism, atomisation, *anomie*, and moral dissolution.

No matter how 'sketchy' the exposition of this alternative Marxist theory of fascism necessarily has been, it has hopefully made a persuasive case for a *Marxist* reading of the passage cited earlier from Fest's *The Shattered Dream*. Such a reading, instead of rejecting out of hand the whole thrust of his construction of Nazi ideology, would accept his basic observations, albeit with the important proviso that, as it currently stands, the analysis is woefully incomplete. To become more cogent it needs to be complemented first by stressing that Nazism was a manifestation of the phenomenon of generic fascism produced by the general economic, sociological, and psychological crisis of early twentieth century Europe, and second by taking into account Nazism's sociological support base, and the vested social, political, religious, and economic interests which colluded with it. Above all, a Marxist would not be content to dwell on Nazi utopianism, but on its *praxis*: namely, the concrete impact of the Third Reich's attempt to implement its utopia – for example in the sphere of imperial ambitions and racial hygiene. In doing so the analysis would bring out the systemic inhumanity that was part and parcel of Nazi modernity and the fascist revolution that underpinned it – something that Fest is in fact at pains to do elsewhere in his book. (I might take this opportunity to stress that I am deeply aware of the linkage between Nazi ideology and the human atrocities it committed in their millions, including the euthanasia campaign and the mass extermination systematically carried out on the Jews, Sinti, Roma, Poles, Russians, and other 'racial enemies'. However, I see this as the horrific by-product of the Third Reich's attempt to implement its *revolutionary* vision of a new order, in the same way that it is the attempts by states to enact communist utopias – which I have yet to see characterised by Marxists as 'reactionary' – rather than personal pathology, that ultimately accounts for the legion atrocities logged in *The Black Book of Communism*.)[55]

Though it has focused on alleged weaknesses inherent in conventional Marxist interpretations of fascism, this chapter is informed by a keen awareness of several chronic shortcomings in traditional liberal Fascist Studies which are glaringly obvious to Marxists, notably their insufficient concern with such issues as the class dynamics of fascism's ideology and policy, the crucial role played by economic factors in the genesis of its 'world-view', and the collusion of the reactionary elements of big business and the traditional ruling classes in its revolutionary 'movement'. Were both sides prepared to take the mote out of their own eyes, a fertile dialogue might at long last open up between Marxist and liberal specialists in this field. However, the immediate purpose of this analysis would be served if it simply encouraged more Marxists to reconsider the automatic equation of fascism with capitalist 'reaction', a Pavlovian reflex making it impossible to concede anything authentic whatsoever to its claims to be pioneering a new order, let alone consider Nazism as offering the vision of an alternative revolutionary modernity to Soviet communism.

Clearly they are not entirely free to do this, any more than liberals are entirely at liberty to focus on the material or sociological basis of fascism, since the history of fascism is not written 'under circumstances chosen by themselves, but under circumstances directly encountered, given, and transmitted from the past'. On the rare occasions that Marxists are prepared to grant fascism some degree of autonomous revolutionary dynamic, the instinctive way of preserving the unique validity of the Marxist revolutionary project is to present fascism as somehow less substantive, less radical, or simply less *revolutionary* than the 'real thing', namely Marxist revolution. To take the small sample of thinkers deployed in our syncretic theory: Gramsci sees it as a form of 'passive revolution' and 'restoration-revolution'; Laclau as a radical 'counterposition' that prevents the working class from developing its full revolutionary potential; and Osborne as a 'counter-revolution', and hence a 'reactionary' as opposed to a 'progressive' form of revolution. In even stronger terms, Georgi Dimitrov contrasts socialism's emancipating struggle for the 'salvation of the nation' with 'bourgeois nationalism', which he equates with '*nihilism*'.[56] As for Marx, the *Eighteenth Brumaire* displays a scarcely concealed contempt for the need of bourgeois revolutionaries to 'awaken the dead' in their drive to bring about change, implying the possibility of breathing only what William Wordsworth called 'the sweet air of futurity' as the basis of communism's 'meditated action'[57] against capitalism, air which has no need to be enriched by the artificial oxygen of remembrance.

As a 'liberal humanist' I sympathise with the need to maintain such distinctions, since to place the socialist revolution on a par with the Nazi revolution is not only grotesquely counter-intuitive, but smacks of post-modern relativism, a 'bourgeois luxury'[58] lethal to any political commitment or radical activism. Nevertheless, such distinctions are difficult to sustain at a theoretical level, since they imply the existence of objective criteria to distinguish between 'pseudo-revolution' or Ersatz revolutions and 'true' revolutions, criteria that surely are reducible to value-judgements, or rather to utopian constructs based on which alternative to the *status quo* corresponds most the personal values and hopes of the historian or political scientist.[59]

To help resolve this issue, or at least give this chapter an artificial but aesthetically pleasing sense of narrative closure, I would like to propose instead a criterion for assessing the 'authenticity' of different revolutionary projects based on the writings of an Enlightenment philosopher who has been sometimes invoked in the past by Marxists keen to provide dialectical materialism with an ethical dimension.[60] In his reflections on political revolutions, Immanuel Kant distinguished between the essentially unsustainable societies that result from 'palingenesis', and the sustainable ones that are the fruit of *metamorphosis*.[61] I would argue that the regimes produced by Fascism and Nazism, and in the long run by Soviet and Chinese communism as well, proved to be economically, politically, and, in humanistic terms, morally unsustainable, so that they can all be considered case-studies in palingenesis in this negative sense. Moreover, *pace* Francis Fukuyama, actually existing liberal capitalism in its globalised form looks increasingly unlikely to be ecologically and materially sustainable as well, leaving aside its utter indefensibility in terms of global social justice.

In short, the rival temporalities which Osborne identified as being in competition for hegemony under modernity are all more or less *palingenetic*, leaving humanity to await a genuine metamorphosis as the 'true' foundation for a less benighted epoch in human history. The main burden of my analysis in the minuscule area of academic specialism represented by Fascist Studies is to suggest the need for greater clarity about the terms 'reaction' and 'revolution', and greater attention to the contrasting temporalities they involve. In particular, by refining the criteria for evaluating the practical feasibility and sustainability of 'utopian' revolutionary projects, both Marxists and their non-Marxist colleagues may yet be able to evaluate interwar fascism's revolutionary claims on more substantive grounds than whether it simply declared itself to be a revolution, or how far it wanted to retain the economic and social structures of capitalism. If broad agreement could be achieved on this fundamental issue between Marxists and non-Marxists working in Fascist Studies, the phrase 'new consensus' would ring less hollow than it does at present in the ears of numerous academics, left and right. It may finally be possible to locate fascism's place within the unfolding of modern history with a greater sense of ideological cogency and political coherence in the 'glad light' of which Wordsworth speaks so eloquently.[62]

Part II

Nazism as a Manifestation of Generic Fascism

4

Fatal Attraction: Why Nazism Appealed to Voters*

Hitler's 'democratic' revolution

There was no Nazi 'seizure of power', or *Machtergreifung*, in the sense of an armed coup. In January 1933, Hitler was appointed Chancellor by President Hindenburg, and went on to become the absolute dictator (or *'Führer'*) of Germany by exploiting legal constitutional procedures, in a process of co-ordination (*Gleichschaltung*) between state and society. Hitler was placed in the position to do this by a decisive surge of 'people power' supporting Nazism in the previous years. In the Reichstag elections of July 1932, the NSDAP became the nation's largest political party with 13 745 800 votes, or 37.29 per cent of the total. Yet this was a party that had openly declared its hatred of parliamentary democracy, vowed to embark on a vast programme of remilitarisation and territorial expansion, break the alleged stranglehold of Jews (who numbered approximately 600 000, or less than 1 per cent of the total population of Germany) on the social and economic life of Germany, and deal ruthlessly with what it claimed were the country's political, social, and racial enemies. A moment's reflection was enough to make it obvious that these were policies that could only be pursued through dictatorship, war, and state terror. Consequentially, the Third Reich (1933–1945) led directly or indirectly to the deaths of 55 million human beings, many through the application of industrialised methods of mass murder unprecedented in human history. Countless more survived but had endured physical and psychological suffering far beyond the descriptive powers of historians.

Given what happened, it now beggars belief that people could actually vote *en masse* for Nazism. Certainly, history provides no other example of such a destructive and inhumane regime effectively achieving power through

---

* This chapter was first published in vol. 7, no. 2 (December 2001) of *New Perspective*, pp. 7–21. The journal sets out to make complex topics in history accessible to high school students. It is reproduced here with the kind permission of the publisher, Sempringham.

the ballot box. At the same time in Russia, Stalin presided over atrocities mass-produced on a parallel scale in his role as Chairman of the deeply undemocratic Communist Party created by Lenin only after a full-scale revolution had taken place in 1917. It was not the electoral strength of Fascism at the polls in Italy enabling Mussolini to 'conquer power': the mere threat of a coup enacted in the capital by his Blackshirts in October 1922 (the so-called 'March on Rome') was enough to persuade King Victor Emmanuel III to make him head of a coalition government against the wishes of parliament. This was the first step towards Mussolini becoming the infallible *Duce*, yet of dubious constitutionality. In any case, Nazism was incomparably more destructive than Fascism, and much more electorally significant.

Did Nazism's attraction to voters come from 'outside' history?

The unimaginable human catastrophe resulting from Hitler's parliamentary route to power makes it tempting to feel that ordinary history had been suspended in the final years of the Weimar Republic. Hence the abiding appeal to the general public of journalistic accounts of the Third Reich suggesting that the Nazis were less a political movement than an occultist sect, or that unearthly forces were at work in Hitler's reign of terror. So enormous was the scale and technical efficiency of genocide under the Third Reich that even Primo Levi, a Jewish scientist who survived Auschwitz to bear witness to what happened in the Holocaust, stated that Nazi hatred 'is not in us: it is outside man, a poison fruit sprung from the deadly trunk of fascism, but it is outside and beyond fascism itself'.[1] At this point, the Third Reich acquires an element of the extraterrestrial and supra-human, something better dealt with in the film *Hellraiser III* than in a student textbook. Part of the eternal fascination of Nazism is precisely the lure of dark forces inside us and outside us.

Undoubtedly, if investigations focus on individuals responsible for the death camps – such as Heinrich Himmler, the head of the SS, or Rudolf Höss, the commander of Auschwitz – then the enormity of their crimes against humanity make it all too tempting to demonise Nazism as an epidemic of evil. Yet as Ian Kershaw stresses in the preface to his second volume of the unparalleled biography of Hitler, 'evil is a theological or philosophical, rather than a historical concept. To call Hitler evil may well be true and morally satisfying. But it explains nothing'. The task for a historian, he goes on to say, is

> to understand why millions of German citizens who were mostly ordinary human beings, hardly innately evil, in general interested in the welfare and daily cares of themselves and their families, like ordinary people everywhere, and by no means wholly brainwashed or hypnotised by spellbinding propaganda or terrorised into submission by ruthless repression, would find so much of what Hitler stood for attractive.[2]

By focusing on the question 'why did Germans vote for Hitler?' it is possible to bring Nazism back within the bounds of historiography. For one thing, this question makes it necessary to consider carefully *which* Germans opted for Hitler, thus immediately spawning a number of sub-questions: How many voted at which election? From which economic, sociological, geographical, or ideological background did voters come? What was happening in Germany at the time that might 'rationally' explain their choice? Such a line of inquiry leads us away from deeply anti-historical (and even racist) generalisations about 'Germans', and enables historians to focus attention on establishing profiles of the various categories of Nazi supporter which arose in the crucial period *before* Hitler came to power (afterwards being seen to support Nazism could be a simple matter of opportunism). A small group of scholars, notably Detlef Mühlberger, William Brustein, and Jürgen Falter, have specialised in Nazism's 'political ecology' (for which they have to be experts both in German history and in psephology, the study of elections), devoting an enormous amount of painstaking archival research and statistical analysis to such issues.

Two facts stand out from amongst the deluge of data they have unearthed. First, the NSDAP was not a 'middle-class party' (a *Mittelstandspartei*), or a party supported primarily by any one type of voter. Instead, Nazism was a 'transclass party' (a *Volkspartei*) with representation in all social groupings, age-groups, and regions of Germany (though, like any party, it appealed to some types of citizen more than to others). Second, the electoral support for the NSDAP was minimal before 1929, even though by then it had built up a dynamic party organisation based on such specialist organisations as SS, SA, and NS Leagues for various teachers, students, women, and youth, and could boast a sizeable membership (over 100 000). Moreover, its activities and leader were given an obsessively high profile in the news media. In fact, in the elections of June 1928, after three years of intensive efforts to become a major force in national politics, Nazism only obtained 2.7 per cent of the vote: hardly a threat to the German interwar Republic's stability. Clearly, becoming a Nazi voter took more than just feeling a sense of national humiliation at the loss of the First World War and the terms imposed by the Versailles Treaty ten years earlier, a sense true of most Germans at the time. Nor was it enough to be anti-Semitic.

The Great Depression as a causal factor

So what happened in the four years after June 1928 to convince over a third of the German electorate to switch their allegiance to Hitler? The answer which should automatically leap into the mind of any student of the rise of Nazism is 'the Great Depression'. The causal explanation followed by most textbooks on these four vital years goes something as follows. The Weimar Republic had been deeply unpopular ever since its foundation because it was associated with the loss of the First World War, the end of the Hohenzollern dynasty (the Kaiser), the acceptance of the crushing terms of the 1919 peace settlement (which meant, among other things, reparations, the loss of entire regions of Germany, and acceptance of 'guilt' over the outbreak of the First World War), the attempt by the Communists to establish a Soviet system of rule in Germany, as well as a sustained period of socio-political chaos and economic misery. Despite all this, German democracy weathered an attempted right-wing coup (the 'Kapp Putsch') in 1920, the trauma of hyperinflation of 1923, and Hitler's attempted putsch in 1923; and thereafter, the country started to get back on its feet. But the withdrawal of American loans and the collapse of world trade as a result of the 1929 Wall Street Crash threw over six million out of work and caused a socio-economic dislocation beyond the power of the parliamentary government to solve. The pro-democratic lost their credibility; under Heinrich Brüning, Franz von Papen, and Kurt von Schleicher, 'presidential authority' and 'emergency decrees' replaced democracy; the Communists started to gain alarming support; and so the Nazi party took off as what seemed to a significant minority to be the only solution to a crisis seemingly incapable of being resolved by the Weimar system.

Now, such a line of reasoning certainly does not lack plausibility, but there is surely something missing. The standard historical accounts on the rise of Nazism confine themselves to social, economic, and political factors nevertheless skate over the crucial question: Why did mass unemployment and governmental paralysis drive over 12 million Germans, who had always spurned Nazism before, into the welcoming arms of Hitler? Why should losing one's job or one's savings suddenly lead to support for a party which was openly anti-democratic, violent, militaristic, anti-Semitic, racist, and whose foreign policies would obviously lead to war? It is not enough to stress the extraordinary efficiency of the party machine which the NSDAP had created by 1929; the effectiveness of its propaganda; the fanatical commitment of its leaders and local organisers; the impressiveness of its uniforms, marches, and rallies; the way it created an image of dynamism and youth; or the tactical astuteness of its leader Adolf Hitler. The awkward fact is that, despite the massive unpopularity of the Weimar Republic and all the advantages which the NSDAP increasingly gained over existing parties, Nazism showed no signs of breaking out of its ghetto of marginalisation until the Great Depression hit home – the word 'home' here will turn out to be a deeply significant one.

Against this well-rehearsed history, however, it is possible to find an exception that both complements existing accounts, and makes the appeal of Nazism to the German electorate accessible to forensic investigation. This view draws upon insights from three disciplines in the humanities: social psychology, social philosophy, and cultural anthropology . Most conventional historians are understandably wary of consulting these disciplines because the historical theories they provide are highly speculative, and hence difficult to empirically prove with the sort of data and explanatory models and concepts traditional historians feel comfortable with. Since there are many competing theories and approaches in each of these three areas, it is particularly important to use ideas derived from them in a tentative, 'heuristic' spirit, seeking to complement and extend existing explanations rather than replace them.

The perspective of social psychology

The first set of insights derives from a form of social psychology which assumes that all human beings have certain, basic existential needs. Once human beings leave the paradise of the womb they become insecure, exiles in an alien and threatening world, so that a significant part of the way they collectively think and act may be interpreted as the result of a deep subliminal drive to overcome the sense of being exposed and vulnerable; to be 'inside' rather than 'outside'; to feel psychologically 'at home'. In *The Anatomy of Human Destruction* (1973), Erich Fromm, a pioneer of this type of social psychology, lists the preconditions for such a sense of belonging as a frame of reference (a system of beliefs or 'world-view'); a sense of rootedness; unity (a sense of harmony with the world); effectiveness (the feeling that your life makes a difference); and 'excitation' (regular periods of intensity or pleasure associated with participating in some event or process larger than oneself).

All traditional societies – whether a small African tribe like the Dogon, or an entire civilisation like the ancient Egyptians – were bound together by an elaborate set of traditions, rituals, and beliefs rooted in a cosmology which catered to all these needs. They had a cohesive or total 'culture'. In this sense, medieval Europe had more in common with ancient Egypt, since a blend of Christianity with traditions and practices whose origins are lost in the mists of the pre-Christian, 'pagan' past made the world meaningful for the vast majority of its inhabitants in an instinctive and unquestioning way. What characterises a 'modern' society is the loss of such a shared cosmology, and hence the breakdown of culture into a countless alternative world-views and values. Symptomatic of this is the rise of individualism, and the proliferation of 'isms' to believe in and live out.

Nevertheless, again on a subliminal level, a major source of psychological security is a broadly shared image of the state of society and history which all the members of a modern nation can take for granted, and which forms a slowly changing but stable backcloth to the personal dramas and experiences which make up each individual life. In a stable society (such as twentieth-century Switzerland), even two citizens who speak different languages, uphold conflicting values, and enjoy contrasting lifestyles can take for granted a broadly similar sense of Switzerland and 'Swissness' which provides a collective foundation upon which to construct their individual lives. Even if one is a communist and the other a capitalist, so that they both belong to different political cultures at a 'micro'-level, their political culture at a 'macro'-level, the unquestioned basis of their everyday normality is shared no matter how individualistic and diversified, the Swiss, in this example, may be said to share a 'collective identity'. There is relatively stable and uncontested ('common sense') perception of contemporary history and of 'the world' through Swiss eyes.

A 'sense-making' crisis

When a society enters a profound crisis, when an entire socio-political system suddenly fails and is replaced by another, as in the French or Russian revolutions, it is more than political, social, and economic institutions which are involved, even if these are the visible manifestations and primary focus for historical study. Political culture at a macro-level, the national 'collective identity', also disintegrates, and with it the very psychological foundations of normality and stability, of an existential 'home'. In those who do not have firm spiritual anchorage in a stable value system of faith, this can trigger an experience of acute turmoil, isolation, and distress at the deepest level of the psyche. According to the psychohistorian Gerald Platt (1980), when anxiety at the collapse of a socio-political system becomes pandemic (generalised), society as a whole enters a 'sense-making crisis'. It seems to be a tragic trait in human beings that, for the vast majority, the need to make sense of the world – the will to find a new existential home when the old one is devastated by a historical hurricane – goes much deeper than their need for coherent, rational values, or their capacity for compassion and humanitarian solidarity with fellow human beings.

A widespread sense-making crisis produced by the dramatic collapse of society can thus drive millions suddenly herd-like into an alternative world-view, or ideology, which diagnoses the crisis and offers a way out in terms of a 'new' sense of their surroundings, no matter how crudely irrational, mythic, or potentially destructive (and ultimately self-destructive) it is: indeed it is precisely because of these things that it seems to offer simple solutions to complex dilemmas. For those sufficiently desperate for order in the midst of chaos, the only thing that matters about the new cosmology is that it restores to the world a sense of solidity, firm foundations, collective purpose, belonging, community, home – whatever the cost in terms of 'truth' and whatever the human consequences. The key phrase here is 'sense of', since the experience of solidarity and unity which each convert enjoys in the new community is largely illusory, as each will have an individual understanding of the meaning behind this new cosmology and construction of a 'home'. The vision which the ideology promises to realise will eventually prove to be a mirage. The utopia can thus all too easily become a dystopia.

Post-modernism

The second element of interdisciplinary convergence is provided by a branch of social philosophy called 'post-structuralism', which has been concerned with exposing the constructed, subjective nature of all value systems which seem so self-evident and solid to those who live them out instinctively in daily life. It is particularly interested in demystifying the subtle psychological processes by which value and significance come to be attached to the world, and in the way (naked) power disguises its true nature by cloaking itself in a mixture of myths and images (or 'look'), causing the reality it installs to be systematically misread by those whom it rules and exploits. Felix Guattari, for example, has stressed the way any socio-political system achieves and maintains power (hegemony) by 'coding' reality with a subtle network of signs and symbols essential to instilling a particular 'normality' and behaviour at a subconscious level – the study of such signs and symbols is called 'semiotics'. Thus the erection of vast neon advertisements for Marlborough cigarettes and the opening of a McDonalds in Moscow only weeks after the collapse of Soviet Russia had a deep symbolic, semiotic resonance. It signalled the end of the communist era and the beginning of the capitalist one far more eloquently than any official pronouncement. Sponsors would not pay fortunes for their logos to be displayed on Grand Prix racing cars and sporting champions were they not wholly conscious of 'signs' in conditioning the values and behaviour of a captive audience.

In short, capitalism is not just a set of institutions. Through brand-names, adverts, and signs, capitalism as a socio-political system weaves its way 'stylistically' into the fabric of everyday life; dying the strands of each individual's experience of normality, conditioning the way people speak and feel. In history, the power of the semiotic is vividly illustrated by the French Revolution. Though 'officially' based on Enlightenment reason, it was accompanied by a host of symbolic acts – such as dedicating to the use of 'the nation' buildings and spaces previously for exclusive use of the nobility – by changes to the way people dressed and the vocabulary they used; by the adoption of a national anthem and a new flag; by the appearance of new rituals such as the Liberty Tree; by the creation of a new mythological heroine, Marianne; and by the introduction of a new calendar.

What follows from such considerations is that there can be no genuine revolution without a revolution in world-view, in collective identity, in semiotics, giving rise to a new political culture, a new normality. A tyranny imposes itself from above by taking over the institutions of political, economic, and cultural power through coercion. Just as when enemy troops occupy a foreign country, the population become subjected to it without their inner lives necessarily being touched (though of course, through history occupations have generally involved considerable brutality and coercion to maintain 'social control').

However, to exercise power effectively as a regime the state must as far as possible 'win hearts and minds', not just through improvements to the material conditions of existence (e.g. supplying water and electricity), but by colonising the largely non-verbal inner space of individuals where meaning and values are generated. This involves decoding and recoding everyday reality, rather like a company refitting all the shops of a chain that it has taken over with its own logo, lay-out, and colour scheme.

The final element of complementary analysis is provided by cultural anthropology, which investigates the central role which – even in modern societies – ritual and myth continue to play in creating a lived experience of wholeness and purpose. Of particular interest in the present context are studies which show the way these combine to provide a psychological refuge from the flood of meaninglessness to which human beings are constantly exposed once the protective shield of 'culture' breaks down (what one expert has called 'the Terror of History')[3]. A deep-seated crisis in national life can unleash a collective sense of existential panic at the realisation that the fabric of normality is being torn apart by events, that society itself is somehow running out of time. The panacea to this mass neurosis is the enactment of new rituals and myths signifying a new beginning, the opening of a new era in history. There is nothing peculiarly modern about such a 'syndrome'. As the Roman Empire entered its protracted period of decadence from the second century AD, Romans became increasingly obsessed with *rinovatio*, the need for the life-blood of Rome itself to be ritually renewed if it was to continue to be 'the eternal city'. Of course, this 'psycho-dynamic' factor is only one factor in the appeal of the promise of a new order. If I have dwelt on it here it is because it is one that is neglected in much conventional historiography of the Third Reich.

The psycho-historical dimension of the Nazi revolution

In the light of such considerations, we can now sketch the outlines of a psycho-cultural dimension of the NSDAP's rise to power thus far neglected by all standard histories. For the five years which followed the 1923 hyperinflation, the Weimar Republic, though deeply unpopular, nevertheless created sufficient political stability and economic growth to create, at a macro-level, a new political culture and collective identity to replace the one destroyed at the end of the Second Reich in 1918. German interwar democracy thus managed to generate a fragile sense of legitimacy, normality, and viable future in the mind of the general public. Like the crew on the doomed trawler before the final hurricane in the film *The Perfect Storm* (2000), most Germans were still able to treat the Weimar Republic, no matter how reluctantly, as the basis of their existential 'home', so that extremist alternatives of left and right were marginalised and contained. However, during this time the NSDAP invested enormous resources and resourcefulness into raising awareness of its alternative cosmology into the subconscious lives of most Germans, using theatrical and ritualistic forms of politics (marches, rallies, uniforms, inflammatory rhetoric) and a powerful logo, the Swastika (a symbol of the rising sun, of national rebirth, of the people's reawakening from the slumber of inertia, decadence, and decay). As long as the republic remained stable, however, Nazism's promises of a Third Reich, of a new order and a new beginning, fell on deaf ears. However uncomfortable, they still felt 'at home' in the Weimar Republic.

When the Great Depression hit the German economy in 1929, it struck at the lives of millions not firmly anchored to a traditional micro-political culture, rather like the monstrous wave that finally sank the boat in George Clooney's film. It unleashed a profound 'sense-making crisis', which made the alternative, comprehensive world-view (*Weltanschauung*) offered by the Nazis suddenly seem 'reasonable', 'obvious', and 'normal' to a significant percentage of them, precisely because it offered a deeply mythic, simplistic, and radical diagnosis of what was happening in Germany. The electorate's ears were now receptive to this diagnosis because it built upon the deeply ingrained sense of national humiliation and resentment which most Germans felt at the conclusion of the Great War, and because the Nazis had already carefully prepared the ground 'semiotically' for their message to take root in the public consciousness. The crucial factor tending to be neglected by conventional historians is precisely this psychological distress unleashed in millions of Germans by the sense that the world was disintegrating, that the future was evaporating, that anarchy was about to engulf them and sweep them away. It was ultimately the hard work that the NSDAP had put in during its years in the political wilderness that suddenly paid off. Rather than drown in a sea of despair, millions of Germans jumped onto the shiny new ship that was waiting for them alongside the sinking Weimar Republic, one seemingly able to whisk them to the safety of a new regime, a never-never land just over the horizon free from the crushing humiliation, poverty, and impotence many had known since 1918. This new cosmology was a land on which the sun would not set: A thousand-year Reich.

In such extreme conditions, so many Germans now succumbed to the spell of Nazism that it finally took off as a mass movement, creating a powerful momentum that seemed to legitimise Nazism's claim to represent the answer to all of Germany's problems, thus attracting even more voters. For genuine converts (and not all were), a transformative process of recoding took place to create a new normality: everything 'wrong with' Germany was given the stamp of the failed Weimar 'system' and the work of domestic enemies, primarily Communists and Jews. Everything healthy was invariably stamped with the Swastika. The precondition to the external socio-political and economic transformations subsequently introduced by the Third Reich was the rapid emergence of a new political culture, even before Hitler became Chancellor.

Indeed, the personification of the Nazi revolution was Hitler himself. By serving as the articulator of, and focal point for, the nation's hopes of an alternative future, for a reborn Germany, Hitler acquired his infamous 'charisma'. It was thus not only a power which emanated *from* him, but which was also projected *onto* him.[4] The well-documented state of ecstasy, of rapture, of trance which he induced in the crowds for most of the 1930s points to a deep psychological process at work, one through which Germans could find a haven from the traumas of chaos and isolation they had been suffering. At the heart of this experience of being 'saved' was the sense that Germany was at last arising Phoenix-like from the ashes of the decadent Weimar Republic in the shape of a new realm, the Third Reich. All committed Nazis – never a majority of the adult population, let alone 'all Germans' – 'knew' with their minds and bodies they were living through marvellous times: a time of rebirth and renewal. Destiny had chosen them to consecrate a new era in history.

Hermann Broch captured the essence of this aspect of Hitler's success in a novel dramatising the psychological and moral crisis which had characterised the last years of Weimar. In one passage, Bloch describes how the desperate situation could awaken those who became 'aware of [their] isolation':

> A doubly-strong yearning for a Leader to take [them] tenderly and lightly by the hand, to set things in order and show [them] the way [...] the Leader who will build the house anew that the dead may come to life again [...] the Healer who by his actions will give meaning to the incomprehensible events of the Age, so that Time can begin again.[5]

Wings over Germany

There are several important implications of this psycho-historical account regarding why people voted in droves for Hitler from 1929. In the main, they were ordinary, modern, educated human beings not obsessed with genocidal fixations about Jews, or with dreams of territorial expansion and heroic wars. Instead, they were driven by the urgent need to find what Erich Fromm called a new 'frame of reference', a sense of rootedness, unity, effectiveness, and 'excitation'. To all of these Nazism offered the answer to those willing to take its *Weltanschauung* to heart and play an active role in the regenerated *Volksgemeinschaft*. As such, Nazism is explicable in terms of normal psychological and historical processes. Explanations which assume that there is something 'different' about Germans which predisposed them to Nazism are essentially racist. Nor should too much be made of the German special path (*Sonderweg*) to becoming a nation-state, since there is no paradigmatic 'normal path' to statehood. More attention should therefore be devoted to analysing the psycho-historical factors which underpinned Nazism's electoral success between 1929 and 1933.

Crucial to such analysis is the recognition that even before the Depression, Nazism had been able to insinuate itself into the everyday life of German society 'transversally' (from the side), making effective use of semiotics in spreading awareness of the alternative political culture which it embodied. The omnipresent Swastika, the uniforms, and rallies were far more important to its gaining a foothold in society than the deployment of paramilitary violence by the SA or crudely racist slogans. The key to the Nazi revolution was this 'lateral' revolution in political culture that occurred before Hitler's movement was escorted into the citadel of power in January 1933. It meant that, for millions of Germans, Nazism had already become a new collective identity. After that, the Nazis were in a position to impose their 'new order' from above; yet until they started tangibly losing the war in 1943, Nazism could still count on a vast movement of spontaneous popular support and enthusiasm permeating society 'laterally' as well. The Third Reich increasingly became a tyranny, but it started out as a regime far more popular than most democratic governments of the time (or since, for that matter).

In the light of this analysis, the Nazis' extensive use of myth and ritual politics to convert Germans to their cause should not be dismissed as a masquerade, a façade concealing a lack of revolutionary substance. Certainly, in their own terms, the Third Reich was a revolutionary regime, and they constantly stressed the need for a revolution in people's minds and hearts, in their 'political culture', as the precondition for the transformations they would bring about in all other spheres of national life. They seemed to know instinctively how to devise and enact political spectacles, and use mythically charged language in a way calculated to whip up irrational emotions in the masses, making its followers fully identify with the regenerated *Volksgemeinschaft*. It is thus necessary, when examining the role of 'propaganda' in the success of Nazism, not to dismiss it simply as a tool of social engineering and brainwashing. The propaganda of the Third Reich was driven by genuine and fanatical belief in the imminence of Germany's rebirth, and its purpose was to instil this belief in all 'healthy' members of the population as a whole, much as the Vatican (which invented the term 'propaganda' in 1622) wants to spread Catholicism throughout the world. Similarly, the term 'totalitarian' needs to be handled with caution. It was a totalitarianism created by the drive not to simply crush liberal freedom, but to create the 'total' culture necessary to realise the utopia of a new order, a racially purified and regenerated state.

This approach to the electoral appeal of Nazism also reinforces the argument for treating Nazism not as an aberrant product of German history but as a form of fascism – now increasingly seen by scholars as a revolutionary movement bent on bringing about the rebirth of the nation. The Nazis' obsession with regenerating and cleansing every area of German society has structural parallels with the 'cleansing' programmes of some other fascist movements, notably the Ustasha regime in Croatia and *Garda de Fier* [Iron Guard] in Romania. Treating Nazism as the major expression of generic fascism, and hence the product of processes shaping modern European history as a whole, also complements the most recent Anglophone attempt to write a comprehensive history of Nazism, Michael Burleigh's *The Third Reich*.[6] He makes no reference to 'fascism', but describes Nazism instead as a 'political religion'. In doing so, he appeals to the overtly mythic and ritual aspects of Nazism which he demonstrates were intended to create a sense of a 'new era' and produce 'the new man' as an integral part of German national rebirth. Finally, it is important to note that, however speculative, the account of Nazism's appeal to voters outlined here is corroborated in painstaking scholarly detail by Ian Kershaw's two volumes on Hitler, *Hubris* and *Nemesis*. These document the way Hitler's rise to power, the sudden growth of popular appeal after 1929, and the explosion of spontaneous joy which greeted his appointment as Chancellor from all over Germany (but of course not from *all* Germans) are all inextricably linked to the deepening crisis of the Weimar Republic and the longings of ordinary people for Germany's totalising rebirth.

In short, the Third Reich should not be studied as something beyond history, but the tragic product of processes, events, and situations that fall within the scope of the human sciences and human understanding. Nor should it be viewed, as Peter Adam (1992) put it in his *Art of the Third Reich*, 'through the lens of Auschwitz'. What happened under Nazism was an unfolding catastrophe that had a completely different significance to ordinary people at the time than the one it assumes with hindsight. On 30 January 1933, millions of Germans from all walks of life were convinced that Hitler's appointment as Chancellor meant not destruction, but a momentous process of renewal which would sweep though every nook and cranny of the land. For example, it prompted the head of the Anti-alcoholism Association, Professor Gonser, to declare

> We Germans stand at an important turning point: new men are shaping the destiny of our fatherland, new laws are being created, new measures put into place, new forces awakened. The struggle touches on everything that has been and is unclean.[7]

In the same vein, a Lutheran pastor captured the mood of the times in these words: 'It is as if the wing of a great turn of fate is fluttering above us.'[8] Such individuals had been overwhelmed by powerful historical and psychological forces which made it difficult for them not to feel in their bones that they could make a new start by voting for Hitler, to find a new home in the (utopian) *Volksgemeinschaft* he promised. They did not realise that the sound they were hearing was not the wings of the Phoenix, but of the vulture.

5
Hooked Crosses and Forking Paths
The Fascist Dynamics of the Third Reich*

The 'virtual' nature of this chapter

In *The Garden of the Forking Paths*, Luis Borges evokes a continually unfolding world of virtual realities which are either actualised or not according to the route taken by the protagonist. Borges' Library of Babel, described in minute detail in another short story, contains books written with identical alphabets and vocabularies, but in which every sentence means something else. At one point, the narrator asks 'You who read me, are you sure of understanding my language?' The applicability of the concept 'fascism' to Nazism is so contested that investigations of its generic fascist dynamics invariably has a certain Borgesian quality.

The premises underlying the following account are as follows: first, that fascism is to be seen as a revolutionary form of nationalism driven by the myth of the nation's imminent[1] rebirth from decadence; second, that analysing Nazism as a variant of fascism in this sense not only complements much scholarship applying other approaches, but also provides a new dimension to historical understanding by revealing important aspects of the goals, policies, and acts of the Third Reich. Also highlighted here are causal factors at work in Nazism's genesis, seizure, and maintenance of power, whose significance might otherwise be not fully appreciated unless placed in a comparative perspective. In

*This chapter was commissioned for a Spanish political science book on twentieth-century fascism published as Mellón, Joan (ed.). *Orden, Jerarquía y Comunidad. Fascismos, Autoritarismos y Neofascismos en la Europa Contemporánea*. Madrid: Tecnos, 2002: pp. 103–157. It then appeared in an English form in the German periodical *Bulletin für Faschismus- und Weltkriegsforschung*, 23 (July 2004) published by Organon (Berlin) in special issue on 'the dynamics of fascism', edited by Werner Röhr. The Spanish editor asked for a comprehensive treatment of various aspects of Nazism that he specified, hence the considerable length of the final version reproduced here. It appears with the kind permission of Tecnos publishers (Madrid).

particular, this chapter (necessarily briefly) considers Nazism's characteristics as a 'political religion'; the role the 'national community' was intended to play as the vehicle of Germany's rebirth; typically fascist aspects Nazism displayed once it was transformed from anti-systemic movement to regime, from the generator of envisioned utopias to the formulator of concrete policies after 1933; the Third Reich's structural relationship to Fascism in Italy; and its function as the midwife of a socio-historical revolution. This chapter concludes with some brief comments on the features making Nazism the principal role model for post-war fascists and racists the world over, in addition to stressing the central role played by the contingent historical conditions of Europe which determined German fascism's success and failure as a twentieth-century revolutionary political force.

It should be stressed that the aim here is not to offer a potted history of Nazism or the Third Reich, but to give some idea of the fresh insights into the causes, nature, and rationale of Nazism which can be disclosed by considering it within the framework of comparative Fascist Studies, a framework which has no monopolistic or territorial aspirations with respect to existing scholarship or alternative historiographical perspectives. Before getting down to the analysis of Nazism as a form of fascism, however, it is necessary to concentrate on salient methodological issues, so as to maximise the possibility that whoever has embarked upon this Borgesian chapter might come to be reading the same text I am writing.

The controversy over Nazism's relationship to fascism

In the first instance, several eminent academics within Fascist Studies categorically reject Nazism's basis in generic fascism. For example, in his article 'Fascist Ideology' the Israeli scholar Ze'ev Sternhell – one of the foremost authorities on French fascism and the ideology of fascism – states 'Nazism cannot, as I see it, be treated as a mere variant of Fascism: its emphasis on biological determinism rules out all efforts to deal with it as such'.[2] The Italian biographer of Mussolini, Renzo de Felice, and the maverick US scholar of Fascism and totalitarianism, A. J. Gregor have also rejected the classification of Nazism as a form of fascism for their own idiosyncratic reasons. Yet it is principally German experts in the history of Nazism who have been most uncomfortable with the term 'fascist'. Thus Klaus Hildebrand and Andreas Hillgruber, both central to studies of the NSDAP since the late 1970s, stressed the factors unique to German history which accounted for the genesis of Nazism, and precluded it from being treated within the category of European fascism – an approach deeply bound up with the widely held thesis that Germany has followed a 'special path' (*Sonderweg*) to state formation that set it apart from the 'normal' patterns of Western modernisation.[3]

Underlying such a premise is the understandable assumption that no generic term (even 'totalitarianism') can do justice to the devastating specificity of Third Reich, and that its use could trivialise and relativise the Holocaust. Thus the Israeli scholar Saul Friedländer spoke for many when he rejected the concept on the grounds that 'it leads to an excessive normalising of the Holocaust on the basis of a preconceived conceptual framework'.[4] Karl Bracher, perhaps the best-known German historian of Nazism, makes a similar point in *The German Dictatorship* when he states that the definitional vagueness of the term 'fascism', and the uniqueness of German national history, make the term unhelpful.[5] In an encyclopaedia entry written for a German readership, he introduces another reason why it is 'unfruitful' for use by liberal historians of the Third Reich, namely that it smacks of Marxism.[6] Ever since the early 1930s, it had become part of Comintern orthodoxy to see both Fascism and Nazism as symptoms of the readiness of forces of reaction throughout the capitalist world to resort to authoritarianism and naked terror in order to crush the genuinely revolutionary forces of socialism. In the peculiar situation created by the Soviet occupation of Eastern Germany and the Cold War, the assumption that the Third Reich was the product of 'German fascism' (i.e. terroristic capitalist reaction) was incorporated into the DDR's [*Deutsche Demokratische Republik*, the German Democratic Republic] charter myth, providing a vital rationale for State Communism's only way of cleansing fascism from the Augean stables of German socialism. Bracher's claim that the tendentious use of 'fascism' by Marxists had rendered it unusable by apolitical historians was thus more than understandable in the highly politicised climate of West German academia prevailing in the early 1970s.

For non-Germans – in the fortunate position of being able to study the Third Reich without implicitly engaging in *Vergangenheitsbewältigung* ['mastering the past'] – it is not its Marxist connotations which make the term 'fascism' unusable, nor the fact that it dilutes the specificity of German history. Rather, it is the definitional vagueness which dogged the use of the term for decades, thereby depriving it of forensic value. The British academic and Marxist Tim Mason, made comments in the concluding session of the conference 'Re-evaluating the Third Reich' held at the University of Pennsylvania in the late 1980s, observations which he later developed into a short essay, published after his death as 'Whatever happened to fascism?' Despite his socialist convictions, he found the Marxist-Leninist orthodoxy on fascism unhelpful, and was concerned that 'the extreme peculiarities of German Nazism have come to dominate our moral, political, and professional concerns'.[7] He exhorted his colleagues to realise that 'if we can do without much of the original contents of the concept of fascism, we cannot do without comparison', and concluded by reasserting a fundamental conviction which had informed his life's work on the Third Reich; namely that 'fascism was a continental phenomenon and that Nazism was part of something much larger'.[8] But according to Ian Kershaw, Britain's most eminent historian of Nazism, by the end of the 1990s all that had happened since Mason artic-ulated the dilemma over establishing the relationship of Nazism to fascism is that the debate has lost its 'vibrancy', and that the latest books claiming to have discerned the nature of fascism are unremarkable.[9] As for his own ground-breaking works on Nazism, though the stress which the Nazis placed on their vision of 'national salvation' is central to his interpretation of Nazism's success and Hitler's charisma, Kershaw remains unconvinced by the capacity of the generic concept of fascism, and the comparative dimension of Nazism to do justice to the specificity of the Third Reich. As a result, his magnificent two-volume biography of Hitler, which runs to nearly two thousand pages, does not contain a single reference to generic fascism.[10]

The same is true of Michael Burleigh's prize-winning *The Third Reich: A New History*, which makes extensive use of the term 'political religion' yet studiously avoids the complementary term 'fascism'. This is hardly surprising, since in an earlier work, Burleigh claimed that the Third Reich's attempt to create a 'racial state' made it a 'singular regime without precedent or parallel', with the result that he dismisses terms like 'totalitarian' or 'fascism' as 'poor heuristic devices' for investigating Nazism.[11] In *Hitler's Germany* (1999), Roderick Stackelberg at least shows an awareness of the existence of new works on fascism appear-ing in the last decade which might throw some light on the issue of how Nazism can be located within generic fascism. Yet it is symptomatic of the sorry state of the relationship between historians of the Third Reich and comparative Fascist Studies at present that Stackelberg is still content to offer a disappoint-ingly negative, sub-Marxist, and heuristically useless definition: 'Fascism was a political movement (and later a system of rule) to generate mass support by radical and violent means for anti-democratic and counter-revolutionary ends'.[12]

In short, confusion continues to reign over the relationship of Nazism to fas-cism. Attempting to resolve (some of) this confusion here will commence with an explanation of why it is methodologically naïve to insist that the uniqueness or peculiarity of Nazism precludes it from being treated as a species of a political scientific genus. Even if Kershaw, Burleigh, and Wippermann seem oblivious to recent studies on comparative fascist movements in their latest studies of Nazism, a partial consensus or convergence of approaches has begun to emerge within Anglophone studies on the use of the term 'fascism' which makes it particularly illuminating when applied to Nazism.[13]

Fascism as an 'ideal type'

The key to resolving the first issue lies in Max Weber's theory of the 'ideal type'.[14] True to the spirit of philosophical nominalism, he stressed that, given the infinite variety of singular phenomena comprising human experience and human history, every generic concept used in the human sciences is a cognitive construct. A generic concept thus artificially tidies up a highly messy array of singular realities into a 'working definition' through an act of idealising abstraction similar (but only *similar*) to the sort that goes into producing a diagram of how 'the' diesel engine works or the reproductive system of 'any' mammal. Through this conjuring trick of human cognition, the discrete realities of historical reality become species of an imaginary, or at least 'imagined', genus. Unlike *genera* in the natural world, however, generic terms such as 'revolution', 'middle class', or 'capitalism' do not describe objectively existing classes of natural phenomena, let alone 'essences' which have been 'found'.[15] Nor should ideal typical definitions of such terms be treated like scientific hypotheses, which offer total explanations of a particular phenomenon and thus have somehow to be 'proved' through the use of data in line with 'Popperian' principles of falsification. Instead, they are *heuristic* devices used for exploring singularities in a comparative spirit – one seeking those regularities and patterns in human behaviour and social realities without which the conceptualisation of the world, verbal or otherwise, would be impossible. Every historical phenomenon – every 'actual' feudal system, parliamentary system, civil war, dictatorship, national identity, path to statehood, genocide – is made up of irreducibly unique features. The application of one or more ideal types to exploring these, or raising and resolving questions about them, serves simply to throw into relief aspects which become more intelligible in a comparative or explanatory framework.[16]

In consequence, the stress on the uniqueness of Nazism is totally compatible with the application of generic terms like 'fascism'. Kershaw is characteristically clear-headed about this:

> the uniqueness of specific features of Nazism would not itself prevent the location of Nazism in a wider genus of political systems. It might well be claimed that Nazism and Italian Fascism were separate species within the same genus, without any implicit assumption that the two species ought to be well-nigh identical.[17]

Occasionally, German historians have also recognised this, as when Heinrich Winkler saw Nazism as 'also but not only "German fascism"'.[18] Jürgen Kocka went further by arguing that there is no incompatibility between the uniqueness of Nazism and attempts to locate it within a wider framework which treated it as a variant of fascism. Indeed, he saw such attempts as vital for a proper investigation of Nazism's ideology.[19]

In this perspective, Juan Linz's description of Nazism as 'a distinctive branch grafted on the fascist tree'[20] is, methodologically, doubly muddled. All fascisms, like all specific examples or specimens of a generic phenomenon, are 'distinctive'. Nor was Nazism somehow 'grafted' onto the genus: all the 'branches' of a generic phenomena have been artificially brought together to form a conceptual 'tree' in a nominalist and not an idealist spirit, a process that has more to do with the creation of Frankenstein's monster than with natural organic processes such as 'grafting'. Like beauty, a political genus is constructed in the mind of the researcher. Moreover, its value is not descriptive but heuristic. The question to ask of an ideal type is not whether it is 'true', but whether it is *useful*. To treat Nazism as a manifestation of generic fascist is not to deny that there may be some value in seeing it is as a form of personal dictatorship,[21] reactionary modernism, nihilism,[22] totalitarianism,[23] political religion,[24] 'religion of nature',[25] millennarian movement,[26] or any other generic term. Nor does it imply that scholarship is somehow mistaken in treating the Third Reich as *sui generis*, as a unique product of Germany's *Sonderweg* to nationhood, or as the product of Hitler's pathological ambitions and fixations. Ideal type theory only stipulates that it should not be seen *exclusively* in those terms, and warns that important aspects of Nazism may be obscured by such exclusivity. In this sense, Ze'ev Sternhell was quite right when he claimed that Nazism is not to be treated as a 'mere variant of fascism'.[27] According to ideal type theory, it would be wrong to treat Nazism as a *mere* variant of fascism or of any other generic concept, but it may well be of heuristic value to treat it *also* as a variant of fascism. That value is, of course, entirely dependent on how fascism is defined.

The 'new consensus' on generic fascism

The analysis in this chapter is based on an emergent consensus or growing convergence of opinion within Fascist Studies, which sees its definitional core (the 'fascist minimum') in the vision of the imminent or eventual rebirth of the nation's political culture from its perceived current decadence.[28] For scholars working within this broad and somewhat unruly 'school' of thought pioneered by George Mosse in the 1960s, what sets fascist movements apart from authoritarian conservative regimes, no matter how modernised, technocratic, or 'fascistised' they appear, is their genuine aspiration to pioneer a 'third way' between communism and liberalism, to create 'new men', and to revolutionise political, social, and artistic culture. Such a collective 're-awakening' is seen as marking a definitive sea change in the nation's current state of decline, and can even be thought by some fascists to inaugurate a new era within the development of Western civilisation itself by putting an end to liberal and Enlightenment concepts of a linear, increasingly rationalised and globalised progress. It is this revolutionary dynamic distinguishing the fascism of Mussolini's regime, the Falange, and the Third Reich from the modernising, fascistised conservatism of Franco's Spain, Salazar's Portugal, Schuschnigg's Austria, Pilsudski's Poland, or Imperial Japan.[29] My own variant of the consensus is summed up in the definition of fascism as 'a genus of political ideology whose mythic core in its various permutations is a palingenetic[30] form of populist ultra-nationalism'.[31] The emphasis the 'new consensus' places ('ideal-typically') on the revolutionary and populist thrust towards national regeneration in a *new* order – a feature empirically demonstrable in some variants of twentieth-century ultra-nationalism – makes it particularly applicable to Nazism. Kershaw himself acknowledges this when he states in his evaluation of rival definitions of fascism that 'Griffin's emphasis on "palingenetic ultra-nationalism" – extreme populist nationalism focused upon national "rebirth" and the eradication of presumed national decadence – as the core of fascist ideology, self-evidently embraces Nazism.'[32] Arguably in heuristic terms, definitions based on the new consensus mark a decisive advance over earlier, 'negative' definitions approaching Nazism by identifying what it is against rather than what it is for. For example, Nolte's original (1963) claim that fascism is born of 'theoretical and practical resistance to transcendence',[33] and takes the form of an 'anti-Marxism' which it sets out to destroy through a 'radically opposed but related ideology', is simultaneously too vague and negative to have taxonomic value when applied to concrete examples of 'putative' fascist movements.

The 'new consensus' also marks an advance on even the most sophisticated 'checklist' definitions, such as those of Stanley Payne,[34] Emilio Gentile,[35] and Ian Kershaw [36]: Without being supplemented by a brief, synthetic formulation of the ideal type being applied their practical value is limited since not all the definitional features they include are present in all fascisms (Le Faisceau, e.g., did not have a charismatic leader); the domestic use of terror by the Fascist regime was worlds apart from its deployment by the Third Reich; Italian Fascism harboured no major plans for imperialist expansion when it came to power; the Spanish Falange's imperialism changed after its absorption into the Falange Española Tradicionalista y de las JONS from being 'territorial' to 'spiritual', while the Romanian Iron Guard was never imperialist at all, even if it was eager to support Franco's fight against Republican Spain). Nor is a celebration of war and militarism a trait of all fascisms, since the BUF declared a commitment to pacifism per se in 1938 (though this meant opposition to a war with Germany rather than a belief in the principles of peace). Moreover, if such 'shopping lists' even mention the revolutionary thrust of fascism towards a new order able to overcome national decadence, then it is relegated to being just another characteristic among many. Instead, the new consensus locates the palingenetic obsession with destroying decadence, 'cleansing' or 'purifying' the nation, and creating a total new order as the core component of the fascist cosmology ('fundamental ideology') shaping and providing the underlying rationale (matrix) for all its policies and actions ('operational ideology').[37] This approach also serves as a major factor of continuity between Nazism as a movement and Nazism as a regime by interpreting the 'totalitarianism' of the Third Reich as the practical outcome of its policies on a comprehensive range of social, economic, political, and cultural issues which were conceived as necessary in order to achieve the utopian goal of inaugurating a new epoch in the history of the Germany and the Europe.

The Third Reich as a palingenetic 'political religion'

Once the definitional feature of fascism's fundamental ideology is seen through the quest to transform the nation's political culture for *revolutionary* ends in order to overcome its perceived decadence and decay, then Nazism may be seen as a member of the same family as (though obviously not identical twins of) Fascism, the BUF, or the Falange. Moreover, a number of well-documented facts about Hitler's regime acquire a fresh significance. One is the obsessive recurrence of palingenetic imagery in Nazi texts. To take just three examples from amongst scores of other examples, the first, a speech which Hitler made in Munich in the spring of 1923, six months before the abortive putsch of 9 November, opens with the words 'If the first of May is to be transferred in accordance with its true meaning from the life of nature to the life of peoples, then it must symbolise the renewal of the body of a people which has fallen into senility.'[38] Second, in December 1940 Alfred Baeumler specified in one of his 'expert reports' (*Gutachten*) on ideological issues (not intended for public consumption as propaganda) that '[a]t stake is nothing less than to create anew in the light of consciousness a form of existence that hitherto resided in the unconscious [...] to nurture the irrational with rational means [...] proceeding from the purest impulses of the race'.[39] Five years later, one of the final reflections by Alfred Rosenberg on the regime he had served to the bitter end – formulated in the shadow of his execution by the Nuremberg War Crimes tribunal – was that its political ideal had been 'the rebirth [*Neugeburt*] of national-*völkisch* character in a system of government and life which overcomes the damage inflicted by democracy'.[40]

As long as Marxists dismissed all Nazi ideology as the mask for terroristic capitalist reaction, and even distinguished non-Marxist historians effectively viewed Nazism as 'bestial Nordic nonsense',[41] the three quotations above could be routinely treated as the cynical propaganda of a barbarous regime. As to a basic question widely neglected by conventional historiography, namely, *why* the Nazis went to so much trouble to seize and exercise power at the cost of so much human suffering, the answer provided by most Marxists has focused on the way it succeeded in defending monopoly capitalism through the destruction of socialism. Most non-Marxists, on the other hand, have implied that it was acting out essentially pathological impulses, such as power-lust, megalomania, the hatred of weakness and effeminacy,[42] dysfunctional nation-building, the bottomless *Angst* induced in the middle classes by modernity, or unbridled individualism. Typical of such superficiality concerning the motivation behind the Third Reich is the pronouncement in one English school textbook that:

> When 'a group of personal failures animated by a desire to destroy liberalism and pluralism in Germany and grouped round a fanatical, charismatic and unstable leader took over the reins of one of the most sophisticated governmental structures in Europe' the consequences were bound to be chaotic and to defy any rational analysis.[43]

Not surprisingly the same book assures students that the ideology of National Socialism 'implied that a Nazi social revolution would be primarily a *völkisch* counter-revolution aimed at unscrambling the contemporary pluralist and industrial state', thereby reducing it to a form of reactionary anti-modernism.[44] The average Agatha Christie novel devotes far more consideration to establishing the psychology and motivations for a single murder than many histories of Nazism spend on what lay behind one of the most destructive regimes in history directly or indirectly responsible for the deaths of as many as 25 million European lives.

In marked contrast, the new consensus treats such declarations as testimonies – no matter how carefully scripted for public consumption in the tradition of all institutional attempts to propagate a religious or secular faith[45] – of the genuine underlying revolutionary commitment of (convinced[46]) Nazis to realising the utopia of a regenerated nation, in which the decadence of the era of liberal pluralism and Marxist materialism would finally be transcended. Such believers expressed the vision of a movement whose revolutionary – and hence simultaneously destructive and creative – thrust was inextricably bound up with its aspiration to make the NSDAP not just a conventional political party, but the embodiment of the regenerative forces of the whole nation. Thus it became the principal organ for the dissemination of a new secular creed intended to make the Third Reich synonymous with the imminent rebirth of the *Volk*. It is precisely this aspect of Nazism which is thrown into stark relief by the emergent consensus in Fascist Studies, as well as by the most recent developments in the theory of totalitarianism,[47] and political religion.[48] Consistent with this interpretation, visions of the reborn nation are traceable in the directly highly variegated world-views of the Nazi leadership,[49] just as much as in the writings of minor party ideologues,[50] or in the main organ of party propaganda, *Völkischer Beobachter*.[51] Nor should one react solely with cynicism when finding Nazi ideologues, in their more visionary moments, presenting the 'new Reich' as uniquely capable of reversing the otherwise ineluctable decline not just of Germany but of Europe,[52] hence becoming the main protagonist in the shaping of a new type of civilisation destined to last for hundreds, if not thousands, of years.[53]

An important corollary, however, to seeing Nazi texts as something more than brainwashing – the verbal manifestation of the NSDAP's attempt to institute a mass 'political religion' as the basis of an entirely new type of socio-political culture – is that words are not treated as the principal locus of Nazi ideology.[54] From this perspective, even the delivery of a major speech by Hitler to a Party rally which, under the Third Reich, might be seen by millions in the cinema as part of the week's news-reel, or one of Goebbels' radio broadcasts heard throughout the nation on the '*Volksempfänger*' (the radio affordable by all but the poorest members of the new society), is treated as no more than one element in a constant stream of the 'performative acts' disseminating the Nazi world-view to which the German population was exposed. Altogether, these rituals constituted the spectacular, liturgical style of politics for which the regime is famous.

Indeed, in Marxist analyses, the theatrical nature of fascism has long been recognised as one of its most important aspects. Within years of the Nazi seizure of power, Bertolt Brecht and Ernst Bloch, who both lived through the dismemberment of the Weimar Republic, had stressed the crucial role of spectacle in winning mass support. Meanwhile, Walter Benjamin had not only identified this liturgical style as a definitional feature of fascism, but immortalised his theory in a concept that has made a permanent impact on left-wing Fascist Studies ever since, 'the aestheticisation of politics'. This implied the continuous *mise-en-scène* of spectacular displays of 'people power' that effectively left political control of society in the hands of (what Marxists saw) as a small reactionary elite operating on behalf of the bourgeoisie.

The result has been a number of works tending to reduce fascism to an insubstantial spectacle, a vacuous 'mythic discourse' focused on Hitler as a 'floating signifier'.[55] Yet this approach diverts attention from the substantive debates that emerged between fascists over the nature of their revolution, and encourages the treatment of fascism as a primarily 'cultural' phenomenon in a way which makes its devastating impact on twentieth-century history unintelligible. To be historiographically sound, any comprehensive account of a concrete manifestation of fascism must give due weight to the political, economic, institutional, and social dimensions of both its genesis and its bid to transform society.[56] As before, it is only in the context of attempts to produce an ideal-typical definition of the genus 'fascism' that the new consensus attributes primacy to fascism's ideological core and to Nazism's attempted cultural revolution. In the strictly historiographical context of reconstructing what 'actually happened' under the Third Reich, emphasis would naturally shift to the concrete aspects of Nazism's exercise of power. However, historians recognising the central significance which the vision of imminent national rebirth acquires will tend to give far more weight to the sphere of culture than was generally the case until recently (with the notable exception of G. L. Mosse). As long as scholars' main preoccupation continues to be the political analysis on how a 'civilised' and advanced nation as Germany could devote its social and economic resources to realising a programme of imperialist war and mass murder mind-numbing in the sheer scale of the atrocities it involved, the instinctive equation of Nazism with an 'anti-culture' – aesthetic, social, and political – will also continue.[57]

To summarise, then, comparative Fascist Studies entails a focus upon Nazism as a permutation of European fascism. Premises on the nature of fascism underpinning this view also entail a focus upon fascism's fundamental ideology and its wider implications for the understanding of the Third Reich. However, this should not be taken to imply the deeply unhistorical view that Nazism is merely an ideological or cultural phenomenon, or is to be treated exclusively as the variant of a generic 'ism', thus falling into the trap of 'essentialist' or 'idealist' fallacies. What this reading does suggest is that the empirical history and interpretation of Nazism necessarily involves conscious or unconscious assumptions about its fundamental nature as a historical phenomenon. Without a grasp of fascism's ideological dynamics, or its generic components on the basis of the approach adopted here, it is all too easy to lose sight of vital aspects in the genesis and nature of the Third Reich, as well as the profound nexus which connects Nazism to supranational processes at work in European and modern history.

The Third Reich as a substantive (though failed) revolution

The distinctive features of Nazism, when considered in the context of the new consensus on generic fascism, should now be clear. Central here is an understanding of the primacy which culture, rather than economics or even politics, occupied in the Nazis' concept of power and the transformation of society, not just politically but 'totally'. Moreover, in marked contrast to Marxist preconceptions (with the honourable exception of those who work in the Gramscian tradition),[58] culture is not regarded by the regime as the locus for enacting a grotesque counter-revolutionary spectacle designed to brainwash the masses, but instead as the laboratory for regenerating the 'national community' and creating the 'new men' needed to inaugurate the new age. Certainly, Nazi discourse is peppered with grotesque euphemisms to manipulate reality – such as 'special treatment' for execution; 'resettlement' for transport to an extermination camp; and the 'New Order' for a state whose power increasingly came to depend on violence and terror.[59] Yet the Orwellian nightmare the regime enacted was not conceived as an attempt to inflict as much suffering as possible or to gain total power, but to exploit the full potential of a modern state in order to translate the utopian longing for a reborn nation into reality. Nazism's view of the malleability of external reality was shaped by the nineteenth-century 'revolt against positivism', and the radical rejection of the Enlightenment project of 'progress', which had produced such writers and thinkers as Fyodor Dostoevsky, Henrik Ibsen, Richard Wagner, Henri Bergson, Sigmund Freud, Friedrich Nietzsche, Georges Sorel, and Gustave Le Bon. Moreover, many leading Nazis had experienced at first hand the awesome power of collective nationalist myths in the First World War (and at second hand, the power of socialist myths which unleashed the Russian Revolution) to mobilise the masses, sweeping aside any rationalist and humanitarian values standing in their path. The Nazi elites deliberately set about building a state that fomented and channelled these forces towards the comprehensive overhaul of society; an attempt to literally change the direction of history, to proactively 'make' history.

There is no shortage of testimonies to the lucidity with which some Nazi ideologues understood the radical implications of their project. In December 1925, at a time of deep crisis for the NSDAP (following the failure of the attempted putsch in Munich, the imprisonment of Hitler, and the outlawing of its activities), Franz Pfeffer von Salomon was one of those contributing to the intense debate within the NSDAP about his Party's core values and strategy, and had no illusions about how decisive the break with traditional Western morality had to be for the Nazi revolution to succeed. In a confidential memorandum, he warned of the danger of Nazi values being watered down and corrupted by Gregor Strasser's scheme for a Fascist-style corporate state, one based on egalitarian ideals which Von Salomon claimed smacked of 'the Jewish-liberal-democratic-Marxist-humanitarian mentality'. He went on: 'As long as there is even a single minute tendril which connects our programme with this root then it is doomed to be poisoned and hence to wither away to a miserable death.' Von Salomon then proceeded to outline a scheme to quantify the national worth of every German, and expressed in prophetic words his utter lack of compunction about the fate awaiting those deemed to have nothing to contribute to society: 'This bottom category means destruction and death. Weighed and found wanting. Trees which do not bear fruit should be cut down and thrown into the fire.'[60]

A decade later, the Expressionist writer Gottfried Benn, who, like other prominent Germanophone intellectuals such as Ernst Jünger, C. G. Jung, and Martin Heidegger, succumbed temporarily to the heady palingenetic climate engendered by the apparently irresistible rise of Nazism after 1930, equated the appearance of a new breed of man with a new type of state:

> No one can doubt any more [...] that behind the political events in Germany there lies a historical transformation of unfathomable consequences. The cultural sheen of an epoch starts to flake and break up. Along sutures in the organic the forces of heredity begin to ooze out; from defects in the centres of regeneration the human gene pushes towards the light. It is there that values which were once stable and authentic melt into the shadows. There

accomplishments are transformed and become unrecognisable: the centuries of propagation are at an end. The unfathomable historical transformation initially manifests itself politically in the central concept: the total state. The total state, in contrast to the pluralistic state of the last epoch, the state of thwarted plans and ambitions, announces itself by asserting the complete identity of power and spirit, individuality and the collective, freedom and necessity: it is monist, anti-dialectic, enduring and authoritarian.[61]

True to the radical ethos articulated by von Salomon and Benn, the Third Reich had, within a few months of its mythic thousand-year rule, effectively destroyed the pluralism and liberalism of the Weimar Republic, and laid the foundations of the 'racial state' – one prepared to eradicate anyone considered to be of no use. In its mercifully short life, the Third Reich attempted to bring about a revolution affecting every sphere of German society. Even if the class structure of Weimar Germany was not radically altered under the Third Reich, a profound trans-formation in sociological reality was involved in the partly voluntary, partly enforced collusion of all classes and social groupings with the persecution, enslavement, torture, and extermination of many millions of human beings in the name of this new order. It is thus disconcerting to find scholars suggest-ing that Nazism's 'social revolution' was in the last analysis more 'verbal' than substantial, as David Schoenbaum maintained in his influential *Hitler's Social Revolution* (1966), which by concentrating on the social sphere pays little atten-tion to its intended *anthropological* revolution and its genocidal consequences. As for Ian Kershaw's assertion that Nazism attempted a 'transformation in sub-jective consciousness rather than in objective realities',[62] such a verdict rightly implies that the Reich strove exclusively to bring about a change in world-view rather than in the distribution of power and wealth. Nevertheless, however little Germany's social structure and capitalist institutions were altered between 1933 and 1945, the attempt to create a 'New Order' had enormous consequences for concrete social realities and not just for ultimate reality; that is, the human flesh and blood taken from literally millions of the Reich's victims.

The *Volksgemeinschaft* as the vehicle of national rebirth

The key to the revolution that the Nazis had undertaken thus lay not in the sys-tematic destruction of capitalist institutions or of the existing class system, let alone a Pol-Pot-style eradication of city life, technology, or civilisation. Instead, it involved the simultaneous transformation in the ethos and function of all these elements, so that they served the regeneration of Germany instead of act-ing as agents of its dissolution. Modernity was not to be reversed, but rather purged of its decadent components and given a radically new orientation, one which would actually intensify its momentum and dynamism.[63] Nazi ideology accommodated many rival visions of how such a broad goal was to be achieved in detail, both within the leadership and within the ranks of the movement. However, all its ideological currents converged in the belief that the atomised, decadent, self-destructive 'society' into which Germany had allegedly degenerated under the impact of individualism, materialism, and pluralism, had to be replaced by the reborn *Volksgemeinschaft* for the nation to exist in any meaningful sense.[64]

Seen in Durkheimian terms, the Nazis conceived of this 'national community' as the basis for a recreated sociological existence, ordered according to a perceived racial health. Germany was to grow into a 'community of destiny' living out its unique historical fate on an epic scale in a way which emulated 'pre-modern' societies.[65] However, the sheer complexity of a European nation-state in the twentieth century meant that this new Germany could only be held together through a dense web, woven from the artificial strands of 'organic solidarity' – albeit in a far tighter mesh than was conceivable under liberalism. In the first instance, these strands had to be deliberately fostered through the destruction of liberal pluralism; the elimination or suppression of all institutions and ideologies construed as openly hostile to Nazism; the creation of mass organisations, and the inculcation of Nazi values and goals. This so called 'co-ordination' (*Gleichschaltung*), in turn, involved the regime in a vast project of social and cultural engineering discernable in education, the mass–media, propaganda, through state intervention in the economy, family life, demographic and health policy, welfare, social mores, art and culture, and through a liturgical, cultic style of politics.[66] Such attempts to achieve 'cultural hegemony' had to be reinforced by the exercise of what Gramsci calls 'domination', necessitating specialised state institutions dedicated to surveillance, repression, and terror. Though the commercial metaphor would have appalled them as the fruit of a decadent mind, the Nazis saw the Weimar Republic as something akin to what a ruthless entrepreneur might see in a vast industrial conglomerate that had gone bankrupt but which – given a new management team, radical restructuring, new buildings, the closure of uneconomic divisions, the firing of inefficient workers, and a brilliant publicity campaign – could be 'turned round' so as to produce a successful new range of products and markets. The Nazis' goal, however, was not increased financial profit or unprecedented dividends for investors, but enhanced racial strength and unparalleled national security for the German people.

The central point being made here is that an important practical consequence of treating Nazism as a major species of the genus fascism is that the creation of the Reich was not approached *a priori* as the nihilistic destruction of the Weimar Republic, the annihilation of the working class as a political force, the ruthless attempt to establish a totalitarian state, or the conquest of dictatorial power by a megalomaniac dictator. Instead German fascism should be seen as driven by the urgent need to eradicate every perceived symptom of decadence in order to induce its rebirth as quickly as possible. This was a dual process which involved co-opting, requisitioning, and overhauling everything in the existing state that could be perpetuated, salvaged, or recycled (leading to tactical alliances with such conservative forces as big business and the army, and an uneasy tense compromise with the most malleable elements within the Christian churches), while at the same time marginalising, neutralising, or destroying all that could not be used, or stood in the Third Reich's way. The Nazi revolution thus took the form of an elaborate process of transforming reality by spreading and normalising the National Socialist *Weltanschauung*, the 'grand narrative' of how history was unfolding, to a point where rival value-systems were silenced or drowned out by the sheer volume of official Newspeak[67] and the invasion of civic space by their symbology of the New Order.[68] To this extent, the Nazi revolution was indeed 'psychological' and cosmological. However, it should be remembered that all major revolutions in the age of the masses have a parallel psychological and cosmological dimension. The French Revolution, the Russian Revolution, China's Cultural Revolution, the *Khmer Rouge's* Revolution in Cambodia all involved the attempted transformation of the 'normality' and world-view of their polities through a combination of 'cultural hegemony' and domination. In each case, their ultimate aim was not to destroy and manipulate, nor even to create a new type of state, but to give birth to a new type of man (and woman) and so carry out totalitarianism's 'anthropological revolution'.

However, this recognition should not divert attention from the considerable amount of institutional and structural change which was brought about under the Nazis' proliferating ministries and organisations, not by systematically following some fundamentalist doctrinaire blueprint, but by improvising policies 'on the hoof'. This was something to which Nazism was already predisposed by its vitalistic stress on action, dynamism, and charismatic leadership (though here again the element of spontaneity in the French and Russian Revolutions should not be underestimated). What imparted ideological and mythic coherence to Nazism's improvisations was the palingenetic logic of destruction and creation which paralleled the vision of national rebirth. Whichever sphere of Nazi reality is considered – Hitler's tactical decisions for gaining power, the evolution of the NSDAP's political programme, foreign policy, agricultural policy, the institutionalisation of Nazi authority and power, the economy, class, the armed forces, anti-Semitism, aesthetics – the picture emerges not just of rampant opportunism, pragmatism, and tactical flexibility, but of conflicting policies, personality clashes, and sheer confusion. The seemingly superhuman dynamism of the Third Reich – the ability to mobilise national resources and accomplish massive tasks, such as the creation of the Autobahn system, or the rapid rebuilding of the armed forces – becomes intelligible once they are seen as the products of the mobilising power unleashed by the shared utopia of national rebirth, a vision nebulous enough to accommodate an infinity of variations at the level of the individual 'believer'. It was Nazism's promise to realise this utopia at whatever cost that formed the basis for so much of its appeal in the exceptional period 1930–1938. It was Hitler's ability to embody this promise in his person that lay at the heart of his legendary 'charisma'.[69]

This analysis also resolves much of the ongoing conflict between 'intentionalists' and 'functionalists'. Functionalists (sometimes known as 'structuralists') are right to stress the institutional chaos and lack of fixed plans and goals within the New Order, which meant that many policies and actions were more often than not the product of contingent situations and *ad hoc* decisions, rather than emanating from a cohesive leadership single-mindedly pursuing a master plan for the creation of 'New Order' with Machiavellian ruthlessness. However, their interpretations are deeply flawed as long as they deny that there was a basic *intent* which forms an integral part of Nazism's nature as both an ideology and regime: purging decadence so as to make possible the rebirth of Germany. The tensions between Darré's ruralist 'Blood and Soil' strand of Nazism and the technocratic vision of Todt or Speer, or between Goebbels' commitment to Expressionism as embodying Nordic vitalism and Rosenberg's rejection of it as epitomising a literally soul-destroying modernism, are merely internecine disputes over the precise diagnosis of the decadence which has to be destroyed. Yet, the many specific debates amongst the Nazi leadership took place within a shared utopian vision generating the energy, policies, and action which fuelled the 'movement'.

An example of the way this approach can illuminate important issues raised by historians was the so-called 'Jewish problem'. There was no blueprint about how this was to be resolved. Rather contradictory policies and deep uncertainties existed at the highest level, and there were notable lulls in the intensity of official anti-Semitism before 1939. It is thus a fundamental misreading of the nature of Nazism to assume that the physical liquidation of all European Jews was the ultimate goal of Nazism towards which Hitler and the leadership single-mindedly worked from the earliest days of the NSDAP.[70] Instead, in harmony with much *völkisch* and eugenic thinking of the time, the Jews had already been identified by the fledgling Nazi Party, the *Deutsche Arbeiterpartei*, as embodying decadence, and thus was seen as one of the factors preventing Germany's rebirth. Accordingly, Jews were axiomatically denied a place within the new *Volksgemeinschaft*. 'The Final Solution of the Jewish Question' in its genocidal form thus became a latent possibility contained within the rise of Nazism, one which was not an inevitability, but could only be actualised by a contingent configuration of circumstances; by a particular route taken through forking paths of virtual futures. The conscious decision to implement the final solution was probably only taken in the Autumn of 1941 after logistical difficulties following the launching of Operation Barbarossa, and it was only after the envisioned conquest of Russia collided with the reality of defeat at Stalingrad that the industrialised process of extermination pioneered in the euthanasia campaign – the application of 'Fordist' (and highly modern) principles of technical, logistical, and managerial efficiency – went into full production.[71] Here, as in every sphere of the Third Reich, we see the rampant polycentrism, duplications, and tensions in centres of policy-making and execution, as well as the arbitrariness and improvisation of sometimes crucial decisions by the leadership. In addition, considerable tensions over the regime's short-term objectives, and the conflicting visions of the New Germany and New European Order persisted at the heart of Nazism, though they were given a high degree of ideological cohesion and teleological impetus by the nebulous myth of the war against racial and spiritual decadence, of national rebirth, and its incarnation in Adolf Hitler. This made the existence of an actual *'Führer* Order', written or verbal, commencing the Final Solution, a legalistic rather than a historical issue. Had the Third Reich not been collectively 'imagined' as the rebirth of the national community, the Final Solution could never have been conceived or executed as one of its potential strategies of implementation. It was one of the many forking paths leading out of the Nazi 'Seizure of Power' in 1933.

The Third Reich as a fascist regime

This analysis is now in the position to highlight some of the basic inferences to be drawn from the consideration of the Third Reich as a permutation of fascism. First, the picture of Nazism changes radically once it is investigated on the basis of 'methodological empathy'; that is, how fascists themselves conceived their revolutionary task, a point which George Mosse, the main pioneer of this approach, saw as pivotal to the scholarly understanding of both fascism and Nazism in the early 1960s when he started applying a 'cultural' approach to modern ideologies.[72] It is thus diametrically opposed to those, consciously or not, applying the approach adopted by the historian Alexander de Grand who, in analysing the 'fascist' style of rule exhibited by the regimes of Mussolini and Hitler, explicitly dismisses the search for a definition of generic fascism as so much 'spilled ink'; opting instead for an 'outside in' approach based on surface comparison.[73]

Stressing the need to work from 'inside out' in the study of Nazism by taking its ideology and utopianism seriously is, of course, strictly a methodological device, and is hence emphatically not to be associated with 'revisionist' attempts to rationalise, relativise, or legitimise the Third Reich as at least one Marxist theorist has recently alleged. What it *does* mean is that the Nazis are not treated *a priori* as 'psychotic', or as the products of a pathological national culture. Nor are all Germans assumed to be latent anti-Semites, Nazis, or clinical mass murderers.[74] Rather, supporters of Nazism are approached as 'ordinary', modern human beings; about a third of whom, at a time when the fabric of social normality was being shredded in the aftermath of the Wall Street Crash, were attracted to a movement which held out the prospect of a new order. As a result, millions found themselves drawn into varying degrees of enthusiasm for, or active collaboration in, the creation of a system of authoritarian power that in the age of the modern state and mass society was able to develop a juggernaut-like momentum of its own in the realisation of its utopian schemes.

Second, the system created under the Third Reich was far from being the monolithic 'evil empire' so often portrayed in war films – a hermetic regime relying on perfect organisation and robotic obedience presided over by a deranged genius in his pursuit of total power, of the type familiar from the plots of science fiction epics and James Bond movies. Hitler is not to be imagined as controlling everything like a huge poisonous spider sitting in the middle of a vast, perfectly woven web. As functionalists delight in pointing out, the more closely his empire is explored, the more Hitler appears the 'weak dictator'[75] of a regime which not only has many centres of power (a 'polycracy'), but where an extraordinary amount of fundamental policy and decisions are made in an *ad hoc* manner,[76] as a response to situations rapidly unfolding in an unforeseen way.[77] It was also a regime in which reality was far more squalid and banal than the propaganda machine portrayed it. Leni Riefenstahl's *Triumph of the Will* shows documentary footage of scores of thousands of uniformed men and boys sculpted into geometrical shapes at the 1934 Nuremberg Rally. Yet, apart from its function as a tool of social engineering, her film was part of an elaborate cosmetic exercise to cover up the less aesthetic aspect of the Nazi style of rule, epitomised in the mafia-style massacre of opponents which had taken place only a few weeks before, in the so-called 'Night of the Long Knives'. Riefenstahl's clumsy insertion of the faces of god-like Aryan warriors into the scene in which Hitler inspects a line of very ordinary-looking soldiers (one wearing thick glasses!) symbolises the triumph of wishful thinking over the reality principle that was increasingly to be the nemesis of his new order.[78]

This raises the question why such an improvised, shambolic, delusional regime did not burst like a soap bubble on its contact with the hard facts of power, but achieved a strength that its enemies could only finally destroy through the mobilisation of social, material, and military resources unprecedented in history. The answer suggested by the new consensus is that in its formative period, the Third Reich was animated by a collective (even if far from universal) will not just to reverse the Versailles Treaty, but to bring about the nation's comprehensive rebirth or 'redemption'.[79] It was this longing for palingenesis animating every level of the Party hierarchy and every constituency of public support that turned the regime into what could be called 'palingenetic adhocracy'. The fanatical efforts of the new ruling elite to transform the state entered into a sinister synergy with a tide of populist energies from below, longing to inhabit a reborn nation in what Ian Kershaw has termed 'working toward the *Führer*'.[80] Aiding and abetting them were untold numbers of state employees bequeathed by the Weimar state apparatus, whose instincts were conservative rather than revolutionary, but whose animus against liberals, Communists, and Jews made them quite prepared to 'go with the flow' and serve the administrative and executive needs of the new regime. As a result, the ideals, energies, and activity of millions of Germans were channelled, no matter how chaotically, first towards creating the foundations of the 'new order', and then to preserving them from destruction by enemy forces once the tide of war turned against the Third Reich. Precisely because of its nebulousnesss, its openness to myriad specific interpretations at a personal level, the myth of the 'new Germany' incarnated in Adolf Hitler enabled millions to internalise the ethos of the Third Reich, to the point where they enthusiastically 'worked towards the *Führer*' often with no explicit orders from above or threats of violence, something which a purely coercive regime based on brainwashing and terror could never achieve.

In other words, Hitler's regime was an improvised system of social and political authority, infused by such a powerful convergence of highly dispersed ideological energies on the project of national regeneration, that in the 1930s when public support was at its height, Nazism could produce policies both explicit and unspoken which mobilised a significant minority of the masses and produced concrete changes in every sphere of society. Even some sceptics of the new consensus acknowledge this. For example, at the end of his comparative study, Alexander de Grand, so scathing about the existence of 'generic fascism', concludes that the 'intent' of fascism in Italy and Germany 'was exactly the same: to provide a quasi-religious alternative to Marxism. Central to this was the idea of national rebirth in a new social and political system' which would 'shape a new type of humanity'.[81] Similarly, Roderick Stackelberg, who defines fascism as a counter-revolution, realises that 'the mood of national revival that accompanied the Nazis' entry into the government greatly abetted Hitler's task', and concedes that 'many Germans were genuinely convinced that the hour of national rebirth had struck'.[82]

This leads to the third point to emerge from this account of Nazism: the central role played by populist palingenetic fervour in establishing and consolidating the power of the Nazi state. Leni Riefenstahl had no need to stage the ecstatic reaction of the crowd which greeted Hitler when he landed at the airfield in Nuremberg. The expressions of pure joy, reminiscent of post-war pop-star cults, point to a feverish sense of relief that the dark days of Weimar were over and that a new age had begun; a wave of frenzied expectancy that turned Hitler into a secular messiah, the Saviour of the Nation, to a point where between 1929 and 1936 Nazism had more in common with millenarian religions than with party politics. Goebbels' Propaganda Ministry was bombarded with unsolicited songs, poems, and plays from members of the public which celebrated the dawning new era, or effused about the *Führer*'s providential role in the nation's reawakening. Some German housewives even spontaneously tended a shrine to Hitler like those dedicated to a divinity common in Hindu households.

Goebbels clearly recognised the need for the Nazi revolution to be based on perceptions of popular consensus rather than military might. As he told the assembled faithful at the 1934 Nuremberg Rally 'immortalised' in Leni Riefenstahl's *Triumph of the Will*:

> May the bright flame of enthusiasm never be extinguished. It alone gives light and warmth to the creative art of political propaganda deployed by a modern state. This art rose from the depths of the people, and in order to search out its roots and locate its power, it must always return to these depths. It may be all right to possess power based upon guns; how much better and more gratifying it is to win and keep the hearts of the people.[83]

What sets the regimes of Hitler and Mussolini apart from those of Franco and Salazar is the fact that they not only came into being as revolutionary movements bent on overcoming the decadence of liberalism and impotence of conservatism; but in their ascendancy, both Nazism and Fascism unleashed mass populist energies directed towards the total renewal and regeneration of the nation. In essence, then, both regimes were as anti-conservative as they were anti-socialist. The basis of the power of Hitler and Mussolini, in complete con-trast to authoritarian Spain and Portugal, was their ability to articulate, channel, and literally embody – in a time of genuine structural crisis – the widespread longings for a new beginning. Dollfuss, a kindred spirit of Salazar, was killed in 1934 because he embodied a conservative rather than a revolutionary solution to the interwar crisis of the newly formed Austrian state and was seen by them as an obstacle to the rebirth of the pan-Germanic *Volk* rather than the vehicle of its longed-for regeneration.[84]

The myth of a reborn Germany not only supplied the revolutionary energy of Nazism, provided the ideological cohesion of the otherwise highly chaotic regime, and fuelled Hitler's charismatic powers. It also underlay the fearsome pattern of creation and destruction that ran through every sphere of the 'new order'. A deep structural nexus linked the eradication of liberal institutions and rights with the setting up of new ministries, administrative bodies and mass organisations, the burning of books and paintings, and the cultivation of particular forms of aesthetics which were associated with wholeness and the eternal truths of the national community. The cultivation of youthful, repro-ductive, heroic bodies was 'dialectically related' to the degradation, torture, and murder of 'asocials', the 'unfit', and racial enemies. Approaching Nazism as a variant of fascism can help understand the inner logic of this dialectic.

Nazism's relationship to Fascism

Important in furthering this exposition is a brief consideration of the relationship between Fascism and Nazism. In pre-consensus days, it would have seemed perfectly acceptable to adopt Alexander De Grand's approach in *Fascist Italy and Nazi Germany: The Fascist Style of Rule*; that is, to address this topic by comparing the two regimes under various headings – youth, the Churches, imperialism, economics, and so on– thus creating a list of common features (e.g. paramilitarism, spectacular politics, leader cult) and points of divergence (e.g. anti-Semitism, cultural policy, corporatism). Another approach leading to conclusions cognate with De Grand's could be derived from the theory of fascism propounded by the German scholar Wolfgang Wippermann, who sees Fascism in Italy as the 'real type' or paradigm of all fascisms, and who would thus proceed by presenting Nazism as one of its idiosyncratic variants.[85] The way of comparing the two regimes which follows from conceiving generic fascism as an ideal type differs from that proposed by de Grand and Wippermann in two vital respects. First, this approach recognises that the 'fascist minimum' cannot be found simply by drawing up a checklist of features the two regimes – and all other putative fascist movements – had in common, nor can it be found by seeing in Italian Fascism the essentialised paradigm of all fascisms. Instead the new consensus stresses that a leap of 'idealising abstraction' is necessary to select significant generic attributes from the welter of empirical 'facts' on the phenomena characterising Nazism and Fascism. Ze'ev Sternhell expressed this with great lucidity in his groundbreaking analysis of French fascism, *Ni droite, ni gauche ('neither Right nor Left')*:

> It falls to the researcher to extract the common denominator, the fascist 'minimum' which is shared not only by different movements and ideologies which claim to be fascist, but also those which reject the adjective but nevertheless belong to the same family.[86]

Thus whatever factors are objectively shared by Fascism and Nazism, they only become significant as definitional components as the result of a deliberate act of theorising, hopefully one as empirically substantiated as possible. In addition, such theorising should at least select definitional elements which feature prominently in Italian Fascism, since it was Mussolini's movement which provided the name of the generic term in the first place; not just for opponents, but for its emulators as well, such as the BUF.

The background to Fascism was the incomplete nature of the *Risorgimento* summed up in d'Azeglio's famous remark that unification had succeeded in making Italy, but that it was still necessary to 'make Italian'. Vast areas of the peninsula were, in social and economic terms, chronically 'underdeveloped' compared with Britain or France, and the nation lacked the industrial, military, and colonial might to be a 'Great Power'. The traditional corruption and weakness of the political system made it unable to deal with the pressing problems posed by the 'primitiveness' and ungovernability of 'the South', the persistent refusal of the Church to recognise the Italian state, and the militancy of revolutionary socialists. Pre-Fascist Italian governments also proved unresponsive to the longing for an improvement in living conditions which was rife among the millions of 'ordinary people' from all over Italy whose lives had been affected – and in many cases devastated – by the 'sacrifices' necessitated in order to participate in the war. The treatment of Italy by its Allies in the peace settlement of 1919, which was shabby (even if not the 'mutilated victory' D'Annunzio claimed it to be), only reinforced the widespread sense, for decades common among the intelligentsia and ruling elites, that Italy was in the vice-like grip of decadence. This was a process of perceived decline which could be felt to have manifested itself culturally since the Renaissance, constituting the underlying reason for the country's contemporary problems.

Fascism achieved power within conditions of protracted crisis, not the sudden collapse that occurred in Germany in 1929. The PNF did not 'conquer the state' through a surge of mass electoral and social support, or a tide of revolutionary energies, but exploited the ineffectiveness of Giolitti's liberal government in tackling the threat from the revolutionary left. However, when Mussolini set about replacing the parliamentary system with a totalitarian state in 1925, no mass protest movement arose to voice its opposition. Indeed, the majority of Italians welcomed the Fascist experiment, not just as a new basis for law and order, but as the only way that their nation would reverse the decline and become 'great' again. From then on Fascism's popularity grew, arguably reaching its highest point when, in May 1935, Mussolini was able to announce from his balcony to an ecstatic crowd in the square below, and to 20 million Italians listening via radio to his speech at home, that 'Ethiopia is Italian'.

By contrast, the Germany emerging from the war in 1918, even though a nation 'late' in unifying like Italy, had already 'nationalised' its citizens to a high degree. This was an undertaking considerably aided by the fact that, at the turn of the twentieth century, even if Britain remained the greatest colonial power on earth, Germans felt their country had become the most productive military, industrial, and cultural power in Europe. Yet the Germans' formerly secure sense of national identity was to suffer a series of blows following a requested armistice that took many by surprise, and bequeathed the myth of the nation being 'stabbed in the back' by (Jewish) Social Democrats. The collective misery which ensued was experienced within a society already saturated with the hypercharged chauvinist sentiments affecting all combatant nations in the cauldron of the Great War, but which had been given a particularly aggressive dynamic by a powerful tradition of belief in the cultural superiority and unique destiny to greatness of Germany. This tradition had been growing in strength ever since the German provinces had been crushingly defeated by Napoleon in the first decade of the nineteenth century, and by the last decade of that century was finding expression in a proliferation of *völkisch* literature evoking the myth of a 'true Germany' travestied by the existing nation-state, as well as through politicised forms of pan-Germanism and anti-Semitism emerging in the nineteenth century.[87]

What imparted a particular colouring and intensity to German nationalism was the fact that the rapid urbanisation and secularisation of society, accompanied by the growth of science and technology in what had until recently been a predominantly rural area of Europe, had by the late nineteenth century given rise both to powerful 'anti-modern' currents of nostalgia for connectedness with virgin nature, but also to pseudo-scientific, biological, and eugenic forms of a highly 'modernised', *scientistic* racism, and biopolitics. To make matters worse (from a liberal perspective), there was also a long and complex history of Christian anti-Semitism in Germany which created a backlash against the growing emancipation and integration of Jews in the nineteenth-century German provinces. Apart from influential nationalistic associations like the Pan-German League, Wilhelmine Germany also hosted numerous societies devoted to paganism and esotericism, some of which, in the early 1900s, were refining occultist varieties of racism and anti-Semitism practically unknown elsewhere in Europe. The result was that, when the collective national identity underwent the trauma of 1918, a sense of brooding *anomie* gripped many Germans who lacked deep spiritual anchors. This, in turn, added to swelling currents of hyper-nationalism which had started flowing well before the outbreak of war. Inevitably, a powerful ultra-right subculture came into existence almost immediately, articulated by authors who, in different ways, argued that Weimar was not a true state: what was needed was a German revolution allowing the nation to arise Phoenix-like from the ashes of defeat and humiliation to become once more the great cultural and political nation it essentially remained, despite defeat, betrayal, and humiliation.

It was against this background of a highly diffused, multifaceted, and racist ultra-nationalism (one which had no real equivalent in Italy), that the spark of national revolution represented by the minute *Deutsche Arbeiterpartei*, founded in 1919, could be fanned by Hitler into the later pyre of the NSDAP. On its reformation in 1925, the Party became a populist movement and parliamentary party – albeit one with a very small electoral base till 1930 – and within the ensuing three years, Hitler had managed to use it as the vehicle for bringing together into a single ecumenical force all the major currents of German ultra-nationalism which existed in 1919. These ranged from extreme anti-urbanisation and 'blood and soil' ruralism to an intense commitment to modernisation and technology; from pagan blood mysticism to genetics and eugenics, and from overtly religious to extremely secular varieties of thought – all of which could be manifested by all sectors of society, as long as they were committed to the vision of German rebirth. Nazism also could build on the existence of a highly developed civic society, and also on the widespread 'Prussian' cult of obedience, efficiency, and duty which had no counterpart in Italy.

Nevertheless, once Fascism and Nazism are seen 'nomothetically', that is, comparatively focusing upon on their similarities rather than their differences, what is striking is just how much they had in common: both cultivated an organic view of the nation and a cyclic vision of the fundamental processes of history; both rejected, in principle, materialism, conservatism, communism, socialism, and liberalism in the name of a new order, and both tended to promote a vitalistic, idealist concept of reality which celebrated action, the will, and the mythic. Yet the structural parallels go even deeper. From a sociological or anthropological perspective, both regimes offered a solution to the centripetal forces of modernity, abstractly described by such terms as *anomie*, alienation, and decadence. At an experiential level, these translate as an acute sensation of the breakdown of a 'genuine' community, a shared cosmology, and collective identity; of the atomisation of society; of the erosion of the 'spiritual', metaphysical dimension of life due to the spread of materialism and individualism; of the reduction of culture to self-expression, sensuality, or sensationalism, to the point where artists and intellectuals had ceased to be the interpreters and articulators of the healthy values of the 'people'; and of the decay of traditional values and hierarchies through the impact of egalitarianism, democracy, and secularisation.

To reverse this decay, to stop the rot, neither regime attempted to go 'back' to an idealised past of the nation (as conservatives desired). Instead, apart from the most futuristically inclined ideologues – notably Gottfried Benn in Germany and Filippo Marinetti in Italy – both set out to forge a mythic link between the present generation and a glorious stage in the past (the Roman Empire, the pristine age of the Aryans) to enable the 'eternal values' to live once more in the new order. Both regimes thus upheld a cyclic vision of historical time and intended their revolution to inaugurate a new era of national greatness. Their politics were informed by a totalising view which naturally expressed itself in a 'totalitarian' style of politics, not in the sense of intended oppression, but in the attempt to make each Italian and German belong mind, body, and soul to the new regime. Citizens in both countries were meant to internalise the cosmology and values of Fascism and Nazism as fully as medieval Christians were meant to live out the values of Christianity in every aspect of their lives. The natural expression of this concept of politics was, in both cases, a highly developed theatrical, liturgical style of politics which implicitly and explicitly sacralised the regime. Both Hitler and Mussolini intended belief in the new order they had created to eventually replace conventional religious faith, no matter how many concessions to Christianity were necessary in the short term.[88]

In this respect, both Fascism and Nazism were very much children of their times. The style adopted by both was perfectly adapted to an age in which a devastating European war had taken the nationalisation of the masses to new heights, putting millions in uniforms, habituating the general public to leader cults, the power of rhetoric and propaganda, the regimentation of society, the by-passing of democracy, the intrusion of the state's centrality into every sphere of life, the aesthetics of parades, and march-pasts, not to mention 'spectacular' politics. Needless to say, there was also something relentlessly chauvinist about the way both regimes celebrated the virtues of war and treated women as little more than the vehicles of demographic revitalisation and the backbone of domestic and moral stability, and as a reserve labour force (though there was also a subcurrent in both aspiring to create a 'new woman' as a counterpart of the 'new man').

To be sure, there are specific areas where major differences between the regimes become apparent, such as the relative absence of anti-Semitism in Fascist Italy before 1938, or the Fascist embrace of artistic modernism (notably Futurism) compared with Nazism's rejection of radical or innovative art after 1935. Yet when these topics are subjected to thorough investigation it becomes clear that, in those areas too, the regimes are more kindred spirits than has often been assumed. For example, some Fascist artists cultivated an anti-urban, 'back to nature' form of art known as *Strapaese*, which had a deep affinity with neo-classical Nazi art associated with the cult of 'blood and soil'; and while Nazism is reputedly 'anti-modernist', a genre of Nazi paintings existed that celebrated the construction of motor-ways and factories in a spirit similar to Futurism, even if stylistically remote. Indeed, a vociferous faction of Nazi art theorists (who had Goebbels' support) argued that Expressionism was pervaded with a deeply anti-decadent Aryan dynamism, and it was not until 1935 that they lost out to the vehemently anti-modernist lobby spearheaded by Rosenberg's *Kampfbund für deutsche Kultur* [Combat League for German Culture], a movement finally endorsed by Hitler, most notably in the 'Degenerate Art' exhibition touring Germany in 1937.[89] Similarly, currents of anti-Semitism and biological racism existed within Fascism from the outset, which makes the race laws promulgated in 1938 something more than a simple import from Germany (although this was its immediate impetus).[90]

The picture that emerges from such considerations is that the relationship between homogeneity and heterogeneity in comparative Fascist Studies is a subtle one. Stereotypes about Fascism and Nazism (which are sometimes influenced by racist stereotypes about Italians and Germans) make it tempting to assume that everything about Mussolini's regime was chaotic and improvised, in stark contrast to a Third Reich which was well co-ordinated, and punctiliously planned. In fact, both regimes contained conflicting currents of ideology, many centres of power, and a great deal of improvisation. Yet in both regimes, the shared vision of national rebirth enabled their most fervent activists and theorists to feel they were part of the 'same' revolution, that they were working towards the rebirth of the nation, and 'working toward' the leader.

Thus it is that, despite the contrast in 'image' between the two regimes, scholarly observations on the anarchic pluralism hosted by Fascism are also relevant to Nazism. For example, Marla Stone advanced the term 'hegemonic pluralism' to express the way the new Italian state achieved the illusion of being the instigator of revolutionary change, not by imposing uniformity on every aspect of social and artistic life, but by deliberately associating itself with all areas of activity, creativity, and reconstruction, irrespective of 'style'.[91] By contrast, the control exercised by Goebbel's *Reichskulturkammer* (Ministry of Culture) over every aspect of cultural production in the Third Reich drastically limited the range of styles within which artists could work. Nevertheless, the regime continued to accommodate a certain amount of diversity in subject matter and style, as long as artists were personally compatible with the racial revolution, or could be presented as contributing to it. Were this not the case, Karl Orff's *Carmina Burana* could never have been premiered in 1937 in the Frankfurt Opera House, and paintings of motorway bridges and bombing raids would not have been hung in the same exhibition space as German landscapes and classical nudes. To take another example, David Roberts has argued that everything in Fascist Italy was a 'mess', its cultural production made up of a welter of different projects for remodelling political and social reality. Yet he sees as the factor giving them cohesion as a whole 'the exciting sense of possibility [...] that Italians [...] could create a wholly new form of state buttressed by a whole new political culture.'[92] There was a parallel belief in Germany's potential to be regenerated through the creation of a racially and culturally homogeneous *Volksgemeinschaft* that supplied a powerful subjective sense of unity in the Third Reich, despite the conflicts and divisions that it undeniably hosted. In both regimes, a shared transclass myth of imminent rebirth generated not just from above but from within society through the forces of 'cultural hegemony' assured the social cohesion of both Fascist Italy and Nazi Germany in their years of consensus more effectively than attempts to impose ideological uniformity from above through techniques of domination.

Parenthetically, it is worth pointing out that any serious investigation of Nazism's fascist dimension should not stop at a comparison with Fascism. Since Mussolini's movement bequeathed the term 'fascism', and was the only other movement to seize state power, it is only natural that comparative studies tend to focus on parallels and contrasts between Europe's main Axis powers. Yet it would be a valuable exercise to compare Nazism as a movement and ideology with other forms of revolutionary nationalism – such as the Iron Guard, the

BUF, or the Falange – an exercise which would bring out another complex pattern of correspondences and divergences.[93] It would be equally valuable to compare the Third Reich with some 'para-fascist' regimes, particularly those of Salazar and Franco, to illuminate the radicalness in every area of social policy and political programme which stemmed from Nazism's revolutionary mission to reverse national decadence and decline in a new Germany, in contrast with the restoration of traditional forces of order and hierarchy in modernised forms behind a façade of dynamism and youth in the Iberian peninsula. Both Franco's decision to absorb the Falange into the conservative *Falanga Española y Tradicionalista y de las JONS* and Salazar's decision to crush Preto's National Syndicalists reveal the essentially reactionary instinct of the two dictators, no matter how scrupulously they were prepared to 'fascistise' their regimes as long as the Axis powers seemed ascendant.[94]

The evolution of Nazism and neo-Nazism: an endlessly bifurcating path?

In the event, Franco and Salazar astutely steered a course away from association with Hitler and Mussolini once the utopias of Fascism and Nazism started breaking on the rocks of military defeats. However, the deaths of Mussolini and Hitler in April 1945 did not spell the end of fascism, even though the horrendous events of the Second World War had, in the minds of the vast majority of Europeans, utterly discredited its rhetoric of national rebirth. Fascist ideology survived, but only by adapting to a post-war era which was an age not of the crisis of capitalism and democracy, but of its restoration and dominance. It is in this context that the 'new consensus' in comparative Fascist Studies has one further contribution to make to understanding Nazism, one which has a direct bearing on contemporary society. The analytical framework used here strips fascism down to the purely ideological core of 'palingenetic ultra-nationalism': this makes it possible to identify several important ways in which fascism has had to adapt to the post-war era.[95] First, one of the features that, in the interwar period, remained a marginalised aspect of orthodox fascism, the pan-European or 'Europeanist' vision of rebirth from decadence, has now developed into a major manifestation of ultra-nationalist longings for a new order, fostering supra-national alliances between extreme right-wing ideologues and activists.[96] Second, now that the preconditions for mass movements, and the charismatic politics which depend on the energy of the crowd are missing, fascism has learnt to operate with minute, highly scattered memberships made up of activists who may never even meet in person.[97] Third, one of the chief symptoms of 'decay' for most post-war fascists is no longer a single nation's specific characteristics (e.g., military weakness or lack of colonies), but its transformation into a multi-cultural, multi-faith society under the impact of mass immigration and cultural globalisation which profoundly threatens the sense of collective identity and cultural homogeneity.

Nazism was bound to provide a role model to post-war fascists committed to a racist vision of national 'cleansing' from degeneration. For one thing, it was one of only two of 'their' movements to have achieved state power (and no fascist ideologue has ever confused a reactionary conservative movement with the revolutionary brand of nationalism they so admire).[98] Additionally, in contrast to Fascism, Nazism managed to realise its goal of creating a new Germany within a new European order to a terrifying (to supporters, awe-inspiring) degree. Moreover, Nazism took its fight against Bolshevism seriously, to the point of launching the biggest invasion in history against the Soviet Union, while its eugenic concern with purging society of decadence and purifying the race involved a vast programme of cultural transformation, sterilisation, euthanasia, internment, enslavement, forced labour, mass murder, and genocide which was carried out with ruthless determination from above, but with the compliance of a vast number of ordinary subjects of the Third Reich. It also developed (largely for propaganda purposes) the concept of a New European Order, which by the end of the war was being defended by International Brigades of the Waffen-SS made up of racists and anti-communists drawn from all over Europe. This made it particularly attractive to European fascists who, in the Cold War era, saw in Nazism a serious attempt to save Europe from the twin menace of American and Marxist materialism – a vision of the 'true' purpose of fascism already anticipated long before the defeat of Nazism evident in the writings of a few fascist intellectuals, notably Pierre Drieu La Rochelle, Martin Heidegger, and Julius Evola.

It was the racist aspect of Nazism, however, that was the most significant for a new generation of white neo-fascists who were less alarmed by the political or military weakness of their 'home' nation than by the erosion of their pan-European ethnic identity through the impact of mass immigration and multi-culturalism. The Nazi Aryan myth was unique among interwar fascist varieties of ultra-nationalism in the degree to which it identified the reborn nation with racial purity. This deeply mythic construct has been taken up by white supremacists all over the world, and has become implicated in Holocaust Denial, revisionism, anti-Zionism, Third Positionism, eco-fascism, anti-Semitic conspiracy theories, and racist perversions of Christian fundamentalism. This may be just as easily adopted by a Caucasian living in California – concerned with the corruption of 'his' America by Hispanics, homosexuals, Jews, or liberals and the growing power of 'ZOG' (Zionist Occupation Government) – as one living in the East End of London, who sees a direct link between the poverty and urban decay which form the fabric of contemporary life and the presence of Asian and Afro-Caribbean Britons. It may prove equally attractive to an unemployed youth in Granada feeling threatened to the core of his existence by the mounting migratory pressure from across the Straits of Gibraltar and the erosion of 'Spanishness' by American fast-food chains. Obviously, each dialect of neo-Nazism will reflect the unique political culture, history, and immediate concerns of the 'host' national community where it thrives, but each variant will contain a core of common components, such as the celebration of Hitler's genius, an admiration for the SS, and the belief that 'wrong side' won in the Second World War. Such views will often be associated with the contention that the Holocaust 'never happened', a belief somehow reconciled with the call for Jews and other 'aliens' to be removed from society, or that each racially mixed relationships are destroying Aryans, allowing it to be outbred by inferior races.[99]

Nazism has universalised itself into the main dialect of revolutionary fascism to a point where even Italy, which until the 1980s had a strong Fascist legacy, now hosts groups of militant racists known as *'naziskin'*, who are the most likely to carry out physical attacks against economic refugees, 'gypsies', and asylum seekers. The single most important ideological influence on Italian neo-fascism and fascist terrorism since the 1970s, Julius Evola, also saw Nazism, not Fascism, as coming closest to realising his idiosyncratic vision of the rebirth of the 'Tradition' as the basis of a regenerated Europe.[100] It is perhaps worth stressing at this point that though 'neo-populist' parties such as the *Vlaamsblok* [Flemish Bloc], Jörg Haider's *Austrian Freedom Party*, and Jean-Marie Le Pen's *National Front* are frequently termed by the left-wing 'neo-fascist' or 'neo-Nazi', they lack the revolutionary dream nurtured by genuine fascists of a post-liberal 'New Order'. Even Gianfranco Fini's *Alleanza Nazionale* [AN] and Vladimir Zhirinovsky's perversely named Liberal Democratic Party of Russia, which contain genuine neo-fascist elements, have renounced the concept of a radical rebirth in a post-liberal regime, and instead operate as parliamentary parties in a spirit far removed from Mussolini's National Fascist Party or Hitler's NSDAP, which made no secret of their plan to destroy democracy as soon as they were in the position to do so. It is perhaps more appropriate, therefore, to see such parties as 'ethnocratic liberal parties' rejecting the pluralism and multi-culturalism of genuine liberal parties. However, this taxonomy is complicated by the fact that Umberto Bossi's regional separatist *Lega Nord* is more vociferous in its rejection of multi-culturalism and espousal of openly racist positions than the 'post-fascist' AN, even though the AN is directly descended from the formerly unashamedly Fascist *Movimento Sociale Italiano*.

Consistent with this picture of the vitality, influence, and longevity of Nazism as the main variant of fascism, the text which has probably had more influence on post-war 'black' terrorism than any other (outside Italy at least) has not been *Mein Kampf*, but *The Turner Diaries*. Both Timothy McVeigh's attack on the Federal State Building in Oklahoma in 1995 and David Copeland's three nail-bombings in London four years later drew some of their inspiration from this book. Written by William Pearce, leader of the America's neo-Nazi AN, this novel vividly portrays the Armageddon which will inevitably take place between healthy Aryans and *all* other races as the prelude to a new golden age of white civilisation. Pearce concludes with a thinly veiled dedication to Adolf Hitler as part of the evocation of a post-apocalyptic global 'new world order' in which the remaining human beings are Aryans:

> But it was in the year 1999, according to the chronology of the Old Era – just 110 years after the birth of the Great One – that the dream of a White world finally became a certainty. And it was the sacrifice of the lives of uncounted thousands of brave men and women of the Organisation during the preceding years which had kept that dream alive until its realisation could no longer be denied.[101]

This chapter has argued that the emergence of a partial consensus in Fascist Studies had made 'fascism' a heuristically useful term for investigating the ideological dynamics of Nazism, without reducing it to a capitalist counter-revolution or denying its uniqueness as a revolutionary form of racism. This is an interpretation which places Nazism in a different category of generic phenomenon from authoritarian conservatives such as *Franquismo* and *Salazarismo*, or the politics of neo-populists such as Le Pen and Haider. Such a perspective also forms the basis of an approach helping to locate the origins and 'success' of Nazism less in the 'special path' of Germany to nationhood than in the 'forked paths' of European modernity. It was a freak configuration of long-, medium-, and short-term factors that enabled German fascism to seize power and take major steps towards realising its vision of a new order once the fragile subjective consensus underpinning the Weimar Republic evaporated after the Wall Street Crash. In the following 12 years, political and social realities in Germany were increasingly bent and twisted to conform to the vision of a new order – one symbolised by the hooked cross of Nazism, emblem of the rising sun and racial rebirth. As a result, the entire resources of the state – from technocratic to social engineering – were dedicated to realising the utopia of a new era purged of decadence. The emergent new consensus on fascism also allows the ghostly trajectory of Nazism to be plotted after 1945, when it becomes a universal discourse of racist fascism, the rebirth of any one nation or community being conceived as inseparable from Hitler's war to ensure the final triumph of Aryan health over the forces of decadence.

As for the future of generic fascism outside the sphere of neo-Nazism, some of its energies have vaporised into the metapolitics of the New Right, some has been absorbed into right-wing populism, some has contributed to Third Positionist groupuscules, and has turned up even in such unlikely places as ecological politics and the anti-globalisation movement, despite the radically anti-fascist nature of the anti-globalisation movement as a whole.[102] There is even evidence of some collaboration between neo-fascist cells and al-Qaeda members in the planning of the attacks which suggests the possibility of curious hybrids resulting in the future.[103] Whichever of the Borgesian forking paths in contemporary history we find ourselves actually treading, it is time for historiography as a whole to help move Nazism in the way it is generally conceived out of the conceptual exile in which it has been trapped for decades so that the Third Reich is fully accepted as a terrible episode in 'our' history, the history of Western modernity, and not in a demonised 'theirs'. As a liberal humanist, I can only hope that the slogan heard under Hitler – *Ein Volk, Ein Reich, Ein Führer* – will one day have been finally drowned out by voices which, in their different languages declare, with Bob Marley, 'One Heart, One Love, One Song', a principle rooted not in racial but planetary belonging.

Part III
Fascism's Evolution Since 1945

6

'No racism, thanks, we're British'

How Right-Wing Populism Manifests Itself in Contemporary Britain*

The conspicuous absence of a 'right-wing populist' party in Britain

'This sceptred isle [...] this other Eden, demi-paradise, this fortress built for nature by herself, against infection and the hand of war.' Shakespeare's words from Act 2 Scene 1 of *Richard II*, written some four hundred years ago, express how many Britons still fondly imagine their homeland. As any visitor passing through British passport control soon becomes aware, one of the infections we are so determined to stop desecrating our holy soil with is rabies (though in the interest of fair play we try to keep foot-and-mouth disease to ourselves: British diseases for the British, foreign diseases out!). Another is an open, full-blooded indulgence in sensual pleasure, the national aversion to which is summed up in the title of a play engendered by the permissive 1960s, which became more famous than either its plot or its author: *No Sex, Please, We're British*. (A few weeks in an English summer generally suffice to convince most newcomers that our climate in any case acts as an effective prophylactic to unbridled lust). A third continental illness that is supposed to beat a retreat in the vicinity of the White Cliffs of Dover is politicised racism. However, this chapter will argue that racism is as persistent in entering British politics as any clandestine economic migrant intent on settling in this 'green and pleasant land'.

---

* This chapter is based on a conference paper presented in Graz, Austria, in 2000 and first appeared in German in Wolfgang Eismann (ed.) *Rechtspopulismus in Europa. Analysen und Handlungsperspektiven* (Czernin-Verlages: Graz, 2001), pp. 90–111. The book, on the rise of European neo-populism, was directed at the general public and not an academic audience. This explains the distinctly 'journalistic' aspects of tone and referencing, particularly the use of primarily website references. It would have to be significantly updated in the light of events in Britain since 9/11 and the partial success of Nick Griffin's 'new' BNP in achieving the image of a neo-populist party, but hopefully retains some value as a snapshot of the state of political racism in Britain when the twentieth-first century was still very young. It appears with the kind permission of Czernin-Verlag.

What helps confirm Britain's whiter than white self-image is the fact that, in contrast to Austria, Germany, France, Italy, Scandinavia, and a number of Slavic countries, Britain has no right-wing populist[1] party to speak of.[2] Clearly, there is no British equivalent of Jörg Haider's *Freiheitleiche Partei Österreichs* [Austrian Freedom Party, FPÖ], Germany's *Republikaner*, Jean-Marie Le Pen's Front National [FN], or Vladimir Zhirinovsky's Liberal Democratic Party of Russia. Twenty-five years ago in Britain the National Front [NF], an openly racist party blending home-grown British fascism with imported Nazi elements, perhaps had a window of opportunity to become such a party. At its peak, the NF could boast 17 500 members and won nearly a quarter of a million votes in the 1977 national elections – 119 000 votes in London alone. However, despite a considerable media panic at the prospect of fascists replacing Liberals as the 'third force' in some inner city areas, the NF quickly faded from the scene when the Thatcher era began. It now has a negligible following and was superseded in the 1990s by the British National Party [BNP], originally another thinly camouflaged neo-Nazi party, whose pathetic performance at the ballot box ensured it could never function as a vehicle for a dynamic 'movement'. By the turn of the millennium, the BNP could count on a mere 1500 members in the whole country, and even in the Midlands, where race relations are traditionally a major social issue, the party only managed to attract 9342 votes in the 1999 European elections, a percentage of 1.29 per cent. This result proved to be only slightly than that achieved by The Official Monster Raving Loony Party.[3]

Unlike the NF, after the BNP's disastrous performance in the 1997 General Election, the ageing and singularly uncharismatic neo-Nazi John Tyndall was replaced by the younger and more media-friendly Nick Griffin (no relation!), who immediately set about turning it into a 'modern' right-wing populist party on continental lines. Griffin's aim was to find a way of appealing to Britons who felt unrepresented by 'the system' and threatened in their sense of Britishness, a political constituency far wider than the minute flock of hard-core support attracted by the prospect of a revolutionary 'new order' or national rebirth ('palingenetic ultra-nationalism)[4] that I have elsewhere argued to be the core myth of fascism. At first, he looked to Le Pen's FN to help the BNP become a major factor in shaping the nation's political landscape by a careful 'makeover' of the latter's fascist agenda. However, his efforts to forge a working relationship with the FN came to naught in 1997, when they were cruelly exposed by British TV's *The Cook Report*, a programme specialising in uncovering frauds and confidence-tricks. Masquerading as Le Pen's envoys, the Cook team met with Griffin on several occasions, filmed his 'secret' negotiations, and then confronted him on camera about his grandiose plans in a hotel car-park.

Undeterred by this fiasco, Griffin has brought out two new party newspapers, *Identity* and *Freedom*, both devoted to covering the key topics of the 'modernised', *salonfähig* (socially respectable or 'clubbable'), and speciously democratised racism which lies at the heart of right-wing populism's success abroad. The leader in the first issue of *Identity* (which appeared on the symbolically significant date of January 2000) explicitly stated that the BNP was committed to a 'new, modernist [sic] nationalism', and to providing the British electorate with 'the chance to vote for a party like the FN'. The newspaper told its readers that, according to a poll carried out by the *Daily Express* in 1997, 9 per cent of the population wanted to be able to vote for such a party, and that a further 17 per cent would be 'prepared to consider' one as the truest representative of their interests. Griffin has also been actively seeking to involve his party in popular anti-government issues, such as the Country Alliance's fight to preserve some traditional aspects of rural Britain, the national campaign against the Euro, the protests against Britain's exorbitant petrol prices; and, most important of all, the concern over the rising number of asylum seekers. Yet more than ten years after the Cook Report exposé, the BNP remains as irrelevant to mainstream politics as it has ever been.

Nevertheless, if media researchers and academics want to find specimens of 'the Queen's English' being used to express the undisguised resentment of multiculturalism associated in Europe with the Belgian *Vlaamsblok* or the Norwegian Progress Party, then they need only consult the press and websites of the NF[5] and BNP[6]. *Freedom* reported (with relish) in September 2000 that, according to *The Observer* and *The Times*, 'the British are going to become a minority in our country within the next hundred years – possibly even within just sixty years'.[7] Apparently, London has already become 'a modern Tower of Babel', anti-white racial violence in some inner cities has reached a level where it can be described as a form of 'ethnic cleansing', and those who join the 'white flight from multiracism' are being pursued by enforced cultural mixing wherever they move. Thus, *Freedom* claims, the mainstream parties who have repeatedly made bland assurances that British culture and identity will not change under the impact of immigration have been simply '*lying* to us' all along. Other typically populist/ethnocratic front pages of *Freedom* have declared that Britain is 'full up' and can take no asylum seekers (February 2000), and asked a year later:

> as illegal asylum seekers pour into the EU, how many more can we take? The bottom line is this: They will just keep coming until Britain simply ceases to be British – or until the British people say 'Stop!' and turn to the only party which will take any notice of what ordinary voters want: The British National Party (January 2001).

Signs that the mangy leopard of British fascism is indeed attempting to change its spots is further found in a short article published in several numbers of *Freedom*, entitled 'The BNP and Race'. Whereas the 'old' BNP was closely associated with a British variant of Nazi Aryanism expounded in such publications as John

Tyndall's unashamedly neo-Nazi *Spearhead*, here we are treated to the sophisticated discourse of 'differentialist' racism and ethnic 'ecumenicalism' originally advanced by Alain de Benoist's *Nouvelle Droite* [New Right], later tactically employed with enthusiasm in the 1980s by Le Pen's FN. *Freedom* explains: 'The BNP is not a "race supremacist" party. The BNP does not claim that any one race is superior to any other, simply that they are different. The party merely wishes to preserve those differences which make up the rich tapestry of human kind.' Some clue as to how it would 'preserve' those differences once in power can be gleaned from an article in *Freedom* (January 2001) insisting on the material and cultural benefits which apartheid South Africa gave to Bantustan black citizens.

Yet it makes little sense to dwell on the racism of a party which is so marginalised that, in August 2000, only a few hundred could be bothered to attend its 'Red-White-and-Blue' rally modelled on the annual celebration of French culture held by the *Front National*. Nick Griffin proclaimed in the pages of *Freedom* that the event had taken the BNP 'to a new level': it was now 'much, much more' than a political party, namely a 'movement for the cultural and spiritual rebirth of our land and people'. The hollowness of such ultra-nationalist rhetoric is cruelly exposed by contrasting the pathetic turn-out in that rural English field with the many thousands who flock to mass open-air festivals of music and dance wherever local authorities allow them to be staged. The heart of today's youth beats faster not to the drums of military bands but the drum sets of rock bands, and more people usually attend the Notting Hill Carnival each year than vote for all the British fascist parties combined at general elections. When British youth makes a spontaneous show of force, it is not at a military parade but a love parade. He would do well to meditate on the fact that in 2001 'Homelands' was not the name of a fascist rally, but of one of the biggest dance festivals to be held in the United Kingdom that year. The stubborn fact which all would-be British *Führers* have to contend with is that all blatantly right-wing movements have ground to a halt: overtly racist populism is deeply unpopular. Nick Griffin's *Kampf* is not against communists and foreigners, but against indifference to extremist politics. Undoubtedly, his claim in the first issue of *Identity* on the *Daily Express* poll assessing the electoral prospects of a British version of the *Front National* – showing, in Griffin's mind that 'a staggering 26 per cent of British voters are prepared to admit to being willing to vote for a party which is committed to stopping immigration and to taking action to reverse the relentless darkening of our ancient homeland' – is pure self-delusion.

Why neo-populism makes no headway in Britain

The conventional reasons given for the absence of a British Le Pen or Haider concern the absence of proportional representation and a deeply rooted 'civic society' imbued with humanism and tolerance. Others might also argue that the more decisive factor in the famed resilience of the national ego to extremism is a collective self-image that leads most indigenous white Britons to see themselves as intrinsically tolerant, hospitable to foreigners, peace-loving, and anti-racist. As for the persistent 'troubles' in Northern Ireland (fuelled for decades, on both Loyalist and Republican sides, by political parties which could be seen as 'right-wing populist' yet curiously are never included in European surveys), most mainland UK citizens accommodated them within the myth of a land of moderation by the simple psychological ploy of subliminally editing out the whole of Ireland from their subjective map of the world. Indeed, the average mainland Briton probably feels closer to New York than to Belfast, let alone to Dublin, even if both of the latter are both a fraction of the flying time away of the former.

A cynic might go so far as to suggest that what makes British politics even more temperate than its climate is not the moderation and reasonableness celebrated in the national self-image, but a blend of complacency and indifference. Most Britons cannot be bothered to get worked up about major issues, even unemployment and immigration (let alone human suffering in the Third World and the breakdown of the ecosystem), and far prefer the sofa to the street when it comes to political engagement. When his hosts carried on eating politely during a Nazi air-raid on London, the exiled French leader Charles De Gaulle commented that what they displayed was not heroism but a lack of imagination: the idea of being blown up at any moment was inconceivable. If such a lack of imagination remains operative, British voters tend to be motivated by a drive towards non-participation, by a hatred of having their routine ways of life disturbed, by a phobia of people 'making a fuss', by an aversion for anyone who 'goes too far'. On one level this national 'trait' (if one can speak in such potentially racist terms) makes for good democracy. Any British party that overtly appeals to racist sentiments, tries to unleash 'charismatic' energies, or chooses a leader with demagogic reflexes is liable to be simply ridiculed or ignored as being 'over the top'.

However, these characteristics can make for bad democracy. Major issues tend not to be confronted openly, but in a round-about, hypocritical way. Topics which arouse visceral hatreds may unleash a series of innuendos and euphemisms, or may be passed over in awkward silence. Just as 'I think you're rather nice' can be the declaration of an Englishman's burning passion, so 'I am not very fond of' or 'I'd rather not' may register a nine on the Richter scale of emotions. There is an innate tendency in many indigenous Britons to enter a state of amnesia or denial when dealing with anything which might rouse sleeping dogs from their slumber, disinter buried skeletons, or necessitate radical change. Perhaps the symbol of Great Britain's national character should not be the lion, but the ostrich.

The fallacy of British 'exceptionalism' on race

It is, of course, a basic function of national mythology to repress memories of any shameful episodes of inhumanity lurking in the national past and to maintain a flattering self-image. Here Britain is certainly not alone in refusing to stare some of its negative traits in the face, past and present. However, precisely what constitutes this self-deception varies from country to country. Whereas some nations find it difficult to master the past, the British find it more difficult to master the present. A key area in which basic issues are continually neglected is race and racism. In both the 2001 and 2005 General Elections, the issue of asylum seekers – high up on the unofficial list of public concerns – was dealt with by a tacit agreement among the major parties not to raise it in alarmist language for fear of being accused of 'playing the race card'. In 2001, the Conservative leader of the opposition, William Hague, pledged to build new detention centres so that all new asylum seekers could be interned pending the decision on their case, while Tony Blair kept to Labour's policy of turning round applications more efficiently, yet both parties were careful not to let a hint of xenophobia be heard in Party statements.

Playing down the issue of asylum seekers sustains the optical illusion for most Britons, and many Britain-watchers abroad, that the country is a comparatively racism-free zone. Even British academia colludes in this white lie. Since the 1950s, experts on race relations have tended to assume that we are the pioneers of the truly multi-cultural society in Europe, and that it is more appropriate to compare our experience of racial integration and assimilation with the United States and Australia than with Germany or France (yet another symptom of the ambivalence which most Britain's feel about being part of Europe). Yet this ignores the valuable experiences of absorbing former colonial subjects accumulated by other former 'Great' Powers – notably Holland, Portugal and Spain – and diverts attention from the issue of non-colonial immigration, such as European Jews in the 1930s, and now asylum-seekers, where Britain has much to learn from the mistakes and achievements of its neighbours in Europe (not to mention Canada which has many examples of best practice to offer when it comes to viable forms of multi-culturalism).[8]

If the exceptionalness of Britain's multi-ethnic experience is questionable, then so is the image of relative racist harmony which is given spurious empirical corroboration by the absence of an overtly right-wing populist party along the lines of Haider's FPÖ. Given the structural forces at work, some form of populist racism of the type exploited by the radical right throughout Europe is unavoidable. In 2001, over 6.5 per cent of Britain's population comprised ethnic minorities, representing literally scores of countries of origin (a number of them white: the equation of 'immigrant' with 'non-white' is itself a racist reflex), languages, and religious communities; furthermore, relative birth rates mean that the percentage is rising rapidly, independent of fresh immigration. There are estimated to be over two million Muslims in Britain and in 2000, 105 000 refugees from a wide variety of East European, African, and Asian countries unconnected with our colonial past claimed asylum. Moreover, there are particular urban areas in London and the Midlands where the percentage of 'non-whites' rises to over 50 per cent, and many of these areas contain concentrations of poverty, social deprivation, poor standards of housing, education, and health care, high long-term unemployment, and crime which are statistically well above the national average. To compound the sense of threat that 'indigenous' whites are prone to experience when they live in such an environment of decay, several long-term processes are combining to turn the traditional British sense of identity into a siege mentality: Britain's dramatic decline since 1945, first from being the world's largest colonial power, and then from its status as an economic and military superpower; the perceived erosion of sovereignty due to membership in the EU; industrial and cultural globalisation, and, if the Briton is also English, devolution of power to Scottish, Northern Irish, and Welsh regional assemblies.

The realisation that Britain is suffering an image crisis, and that the national identity of 'the English' in particular is undergoing a radical transformation, is a theme regularly taken up by the 'quality press'. Thus an article in the *Sunday Times* of 19 March 2000 described the emergence of a 'post-British' generation who feel neither British or European but solely 'English', even if they display considerable confusion about what Englishness means to them. The most authoritative source for anyone undertaking a reappraisal of Britain's benign image as a non-racist country is the *Report of the Commission on the Future of Multi-Ethnic Britain*, published by the Runnymede Trust in July 2000, the result of two years of research and deliberation by 23 experts. What emerges is the picture of a country where much has been achieved with respect to establishing racial harmony, but which has a long way to go before it creates a genuinely multi-cultural society based on egalitarianism and human rights. The precondition for these values is a sense of collective national identity that does not engender stubborn habits of prejudice, resentment, and alienation. The report argues that only when more is done to remove the racial discrimination endemic to institutions and social structures is there a chance that most Britons will cease to look at 'their' nation through lenses – which distort either through crude stereotypes, ignorance, and complacency – and begin to form not only a 'community of citizens but also a community of communities', both 'cohesive and respectful of diversity'.[9]

The report reinforced the findings of the Stephen Lawrence Inquiry, which a few years earlier had exposed the degree of racial prejudice that had perverted the course of justice; in this case, when police in a racially diverse and socially deprived area of East End of London badly investigated the racist murder of a young black man. Such reports combine with those of specialised organisations – such as the Commission for Racial Equality, Searchlight (which produces an important magazine of the same name),[10] and the Institute for Jewish Policy Research (which publishes *Patterns of Prejudice*) – and of good investigative journalism to portray a Britain where racism is rife but widely unacknowledged, where a deeply divisive class system based on race and gender has grown up to replace the traditional three-tier one based on economic and social background. Though hard statistics are extremely difficult to obtain (especially since the category of 'racially motivated crime' has only recently been introduced),[11] serious attempts to quantify racist violence in Britain – ranging from verbal abuse, racially motivated problems in earning promotion or finding accommodation, threatening behaviour and harassment, to physical violence and actual murder – suggest that, sadly, Britain is not the exception to the rule it would like to think. Certainly some experts maintain that levels of violence are comparable with countries such as France and Germany, and higher than in countries like Austria and Italy, all of which do have 'right-wing populist parties'. If this is true, then mass circulation tabloids like *The Sun* – notorious for its 'Gotcha' headline on the occasion of the sinking of the Belgrano during the Falklands/Malvinas war – are a more reliable barometer of how most 'ordinary' Britons feel about race than broadsheets such as *The Times*.

Such was the deep malaise at the heart of our multi-cultural society that Tony Blair's declaration at the height of the foot-and-mouth epidemic (on 30 March 2001) that Britain's country-side was 'still open for business' inspired a scurrilous *Sun* article. It attacked the squandering of resources in the effort to make asylum seekers feel welcome under the headline: 'Visiting this country? How you can help yourself'. One passage read

> There have been fears that the general election fever sweeping the country [English irony!] would hit imports of illegal immigrants. But Mr Blair made it clear that he was giving the highest priority to supporting the lucrative bogus asylum industry. The Government invests billions of pounds a year in illegal immigration [...] Mr Blair said: 'We may no longer have a car industry, a steel industry, a coal industry, a fishing industry or a farming industry, but we still lead the world when it comes to bogus asylum.'

Given the deeply entrenched British habit of never saying quite what is meant (e.g., *The Sun* is here using sarcasm to make a point similar to the BNP's *Freedom* when it claimed the United Kingdom was 'full up'), there are good grounds to infer from most strident anti-EU or anti-asylum-seeker articles the populist xenophobia which Nick Griffin would like to further exploit. For example, on 25 November 1998 the front page of *The Sun*, entirely written in (schoolboy) German, asked whether the German Finance Minister Oskar Lafontaine was 'der gefährlichste Mann Europas' [The most dangerous man in Europe] (and promised a glimpse on 'page 3' of 'der große Busen von Helga' or her 'ample bosom'). In March 2000 a front-page article informed its readers that 'Gypsy spongers are building themselves palaces with the vast fortune they're making from soft-touch Britain', and that the British state's generosity to economic migrants was making it 'the stock of Europe'. Even the slightly more restrained *Daily Mail* asserted the same month that 'Romanian gypsies begging on the streets of Britain to pay for dream home', while its sister newspaper, *The Evening Standard*, revealed that 'a gipsy township in Romania is sending beggars to London on organised expeditions that support a community of 4000 people'.[12] Such articles are symptomatic of the degree to which, when push comes to shove and the spectre of mass immigration looms, a powerful stream of British chauvinism and xenophobia flows not at the extremist margins of society, but straight down the middle.

Britain's 'centrist populism'?

Our paradox thus explored in this chapter should be clear: British political culture contains a deeply ingrained element of racist populism which thrives independently of credible or significant right-wing populist party representation. It would be natural to assume, therefore, that millions of Britons must feel politically frustrated with the current situation. However, I would like to suggest that, just as populist ethnocentrism and xenophobia is an integral part of 'normal' political culture and finds an outlet in mass circulation newspapers, so too this mentality of exclusion finds representation in mainstream politics. The principal party-political outlet for populist racism is the Conservative Party itself. The reason why there is no public pressure for a British *Front National*, or for the introduction of the proportional representation necessary for it to win seats in parliament, is because it is tacitly understood that the instinct of most died-in-the-wool Tories once in government is to do everything in their power to stop immigration and impede the social advance of ethnic minorities, while conserving the mask of humanism and tolerance. True to the national spirit of compromise, Britain has resolved the tension between centrist liberalism and right-wing populism by pioneering a surreptitious form of racism that might be termed 'centrist populism'. It is a phenomenon which corresponds closely to the concept invented by the political sociologist Seymour Lipset in the 1960s to explain interwar fascism; namely an 'extremism of the centre', and which throws a new light on the appropriateness of the name adopted by Holland's 'right-wing populist party': *Centrumpartij* [Centre Party].

The key role which racism plays in the Conservative Party has not escaped liberal and left-wing commentators. Writing for *The Guardian*, Polly Toynbee argued 'Race is a subterranean river running through Tory party motivations',[13] while Mike Ingram of the World Socialist Web Site referred to the Conservative Party's 'racist underbelly'.[14] There are several notorious examples of this underground river pushing its way to the surface, of this obscene underbelly being briefly exposed to the light of day: Enoch Powell's infamous 'river of blood' speech in 1968, warning that Labour immigration policies meant that Britain' was 'busily engaged in heaping up its own funeral pyre' and that, like the Roman poet Virgil, Powell was destined 'to see the river Tiber foaming with much blood'; Norman Tebbit's extraordinary claim while he was Thatcher's Party Chairman that ethnic minorities who did not cheer for England when they played cricket matches should be denied the right to stay; the racist backlash provoked from within the party when a black barrister was selected as Conservative Candidate for Cheltenham in 1992; but also, the existence of a 'loony right' within the Conservative Party, which has informal contacts with fascist groups. In the 1980s the latter's forum was The Monday Club, but it is now catered to by a glossy quarterly magazine, *Right Now!*, run by Derek Turner, the former leader of an Irish neo-Nazi group, Social Action Initiative. *Right Now!* regularly attacks multi-culturalism and immigration, in addition to publishing interviews with a number of prominent Conservative MPs, including Ann Widdecombe, recently the Shadow Home Secretary.

Thus it should not shock Anglophile foreigners who admire British tolerance and moderation to learn that at a fringe meeting of the Conservative Party Conference in October 2000, David Heathcoat-Amory, then Shadow Trade and Industry Secretary, shared the platform with Don Martin, head of the Federation of Small Businesses; but also, the distributor through his own bookclub 'Bloomfield' of extreme right-wing literature promoting a deeply anti-Semitic conspiracy theory. Nor should it come as a great surprise if retiring MP John Townend embarrassed ex-Conservative Party Leader, William Hague, in March 2001 with a speech claiming that Britain's 'homogeneous Anglo-Saxon society has been seriously undermined by the massive immigration – particularly Commonwealth immigration [a code word for "non-white"] – that has taken place since the war'; Townend further claimed that Enoch Powell would have become Prime Minister if people had appreciated the accuracy of his forecasts. A month later, Tory MP Sir Richard Body published a new book called *England for the English*, voicing alarm at the erosion of his imagined homeland of cultural harmony, tradition, and purity (though how many ordinary Britons would have silently completed the title with 'Foreigners Out' can only be guessed at).

Hague hastened to put the lid on this untimely eruption of core Conservative racism by declaring on 21 April that 'the Tories have no room for racism', and that he was happy to sign a pledge drawn up by the Campaign for Racial Equality, even if he did not expect all Tories to sign it (in fact, Townend refused). Yet Hague himself had given a key speech at the party's spring conference in March in which he evoked the 'foreign land' that Britain would become under the Labour Party and declared 'Elect a Conservative government and we will give you back your country'. Though he insisted later that he was referring particularly to the erosion of British sovereignty by the EU (especially through the 'loss of the Pound'), the subtext was clearly anxiety about immigration and asylum-seekers. It was, after all, his Shadow Home Secretary Ann Widdecombe, who had earlier rung alarm-bells in a parliamentary speech about the way Britain was opening its doors to a 'flood of bogus asylum seekers'.

In such a speech she was not behaving as a maverick, but stepping in the shoes of the very incarnation of Britain's 'centrist populism', Margaret Thatcher. After all, it was Thatcher who, in the run-up to the 1979 general election, signalled toughness on immigration in suggesting that she understood the fears of those who felt the country was being 'swamped by immigrants'. As good as her word, the Nationality Act of 1981 was passed: legislation expressly designed to deprive black and Asian Britons of their citizenship rights, which also abolished the right to British citizenship by virtue of birth on British soil, the *ius soli*. Since then, British citizenship has been the gift of the government. (It is no coincidence that Le Pen has campaigned to replace *ius soli* by *ius sanguinis*, restricting citizenship to those of 'ethnic French origin': (again an incredibly complex concept from a scientific point of view). There is every reason to believe that the dramatic collapse of the NF in the 1979 elections – and its virtual self-liquidisation thereafter – was directly due to the way the Conservative Party was perceived by all racists and 'crypto-racists' as occupying the political space on immigration which the NF had carved out for itself in the previous ten years. In short, in Britain's two (and a half) party system, public perceptions that the government is tough on immigration deprives right-wing populism of a central plank for the construction of a mass base. Thus it is not only proportional representation that acts as a barrier to right-wing populism in Britain, it is also the Conservative Party. No foreign imports of populism thanks, we have our own.

A natural reaction to this argument would be to wonder why Tony Blair's landslide victory in 1997 did not automatically lead to a dramatic surge in support for the FN and the BNP. But this is to misunderstand a crucial aspect of New Labour. While much has been made of Blair's retention of Thatcherite economics, there has been less attention devoted to the way his 'New Labour' government retained Thatcherite immigration policies as well. Indeed, Blair has actually gone beyond traditional Conservative politics in making Britain inhospitable to asylum seekers. Its Asylum and Immigration Act of 1996 introduced 'fast-track' procedures to speed up deportations and replaced the cash benefits payable to those waiting for a verdict with vouchers; by February 2000, 7 per cent of applicants were granted asylum, compared with 13 per cent in the last quarter of 2000. Jack Straw, then Home Secretary (and now Foreign Secretary), had demanded changes to the 1951 United Nations Convention on Refugees intended to dramatically curtail the right of asylum. He also proposed the same year, that only those who apply for asylum *before* leaving their country of origin should be eligible for residence rights, and only if that country has been internationally condemned for human rights abuses.

In April 2000, *Searchlight* reported that Labour ministers had given in to the racist media over the need for draconian measures against asylum seekers in the wake of the panic over the arrival of entire families of Roma gypsies in Dover. Some might comment that they did not need too much persuasion. Clearly Blair's Third Way does not embrace the Third World, and 'Cool Britannia' has no intention of giving those desperate to escape economic and social misery a warm welcome. When Blair warned against 'playing the race card' in electioneering, he did so as Prime Minister of the country which, in the last 30 years, has kept its doors more tightly shut to 'non-white' immigration than any other in Europe.

Ein feste Burg ist unser Land[15]

In conclusion, there are several inferences worth drawing from this analysis. The first is that, as far as racism is concerned, 'tutto il mondo è paese' as the Italians say: 'the world is a village' and xenophobia and ethnocentrism are integral parts of village life. But just as the village idiot comes in different shapes, there are significant differences in the way racism is articulated, mediated, and politically implemented in each modern state. It would be useful if political scientists, journalists, and MEPs learned to distinguish between fascist forms of racism – of which Nazism is the most radical manifestation – and those generated by ethnocratic liberalism, which lack the revolutionary assault on the democratic state but seek principles of racial separation and exclusion. Thus the tide of international concern when the FPÖ entered government in 2000 was badly focused in raising spectres of the rebirth of fascism and of Nazism. However, there is every reason why the EU should condemn the access to power of parties such as the *Lega Nord*, which openly attack the viability of multi-culturalism as the basis for a modern European society, or for finding that ethnic heterogeneity saps the health and vitality of an allegedly homogeneous, indigenous people. In a more subtle way, both the Italian *Alleanza Nazionale* and the FPÖ represent ethnocratic preconceptions of democracy, even if the realities of power-sharing mean there is little they can do to put them into practice.

What emerges even more clearly from this analysis is that radical humanists should look much more carefully at the disguised xenophobia and non-party-political forms of racism often informing the politics of mainstream parties of a particular country; and of the EU itself, when assessing levels of organised racism in Europe. Otherwise inequalities may appear in the way countries are treated by the international community on the issue of racism which border on racism itself. Britain shows that a Jörg Haider, Umberto Bossi, or a Jean-Marie Le Pen are not necessary in order to have a thriving climate of populist racism both societal and political. I am convinced that if Jörg Haider had publicly supported Pinochet's attempts to escape extradition for crimes against humanity like Margaret Thatcher, or had proposed a 'Waltz test' on the lines of Norman Tebbit's 'cricket test' to establish the right to Austrian citizenship, or spoke of Austria becoming a 'foreign land' to its own citizens under the impact of the EU like William Hague, he would have once again been pilloried in the European press as a new Hitler.

While they are having new lenses made in order to examine contemporary racism in Europe, political scientists, journalists, and politicians would do well to study the pronouncements on multi-culturalism, not of political scientists, journalists or politicians, but of a number of artists who have experienced the human implications of narrow chauvinism 'on their skin'. One is Salman Rushdie, a writer of Anglo-Indian descent, secular English and religious Muslim culture, and British citizenship. Some of the essays in his *Imaginary Homelands* contain penetrating reflections on race relationships in Britain, and on the threats to creativity and humanism posed by fanatical belief anywhere in the world. A memorable passage on this theme occurs when he is explaining the cultural dynamics informing *The Satanic Verses,* whose alleged blasphemy in Muslim eyes caused a *fatwah* to be imposed on him by Islamic fundamentalists, one forcing him to write the following lines in hiding.

Standing at the centre of the novel is a group of characters, most of whom are British Muslims, or not particularly religious persons of Muslim background, struggling with just the sort of great problems of hybridisation and ghettoisation, of reconciling the old and the new. Those who oppose the novel most vociferously today are not of the opinion that intermingling with a different culture will inevitably weaken and ruin their own. I am of the opposite opinion.

The Satanic Verses celebrates hybridity, impurity, intermingling, the transformation that comes of new and unexpected combination of human beings, cultures, ideas, politics, movies, songs. It rejoices in mongrelisation and fears the absolutism of the Pure. Melange, hotchpotch a bit of this and a bit of that is how newness enters the world. It is the great possibility that mass migration gives the world I have tried to embrace it. *The Satanic Verses* is for change by fusion, change by conjoining. It is a love song to our mongrel selves.

Throughout human history, the apostles of purity, those who have claimed to possess a total explanation, have wrought havoc among mere mixed up human beings. Like many millions of people, I am a bastard child of history. Perhaps we all are, black and brown and white, leaking into one another, as a character of mine once set, *like flavours when you cook.*[16]

On the day I finished this chapter (27 May 2001) a traditional parade by the Loyalist (pro-British Protestant) Orange Order through a Catholic (Republican) area of Northern Ireland led to violence, and the worst riots in Britain for decades took place in Oldham, a run-down city in the former industrial heartland of England with a high population of British Muslims from Pakistan and Bangladesh. For several weeks the National Front had been mounting a campaign of intimidation in Oldham in order to incite racial conflict, including a highly provocative march (permitted by the authorities in the name of 'freedom of speech') through an ethnically mixed area of the city where there is high unemployment, poor inter-community relations, and a growing sense among Asian male youths of being let down by society. On 26 May a group of white youths from outside Oldham violently assaulted some Asians on the street. Several hundred Asian youths then gathered and started attacking the police who were there to defend them from racist attacks. They barricaded streets with burning cars and vans and assaulted the police with petrol bombs and stones. Only a massive police action and repeated calls by community leaders for calm prevented the situation from deteriorating further.

The explanation given by some of community leaders was that many Asians harboured resentment of the police since they had failed to protect them from the harassment and physical attacks from white racists in the past. A Liberal Democrat MP put some of the blame for the violence on the inflammatory racist language used by some Tories in recent months to address issues of sovereignty, immigration, and asylum which indirectly legitimised extremism by validating the claim of racists that Britain's way of life is under threat and its multi-cultural society is in a state of crisis. The epicentre of the troubles was a pub called the 'Live and Let Live'.

There are many Britons deeply committed to achieving a genuinely cohesive multi-cultural society. But as long as the majority of their fellow-citizens and their elected government, whether Labour or Tory, refuse to contemplate the radical measures needed to ensure steady progress towards multi-culturalism on the lines suggested by the Stephen Lawrence Inquiry and the Runnymede Trust, then Britain is destined to continue to oscillate between complacency and rude awakenings to the fact that we still have a lot more to learn from a number of countries, than to teach them about how to run a culturally pluralist democracy.

For some citizens of this not very 'United Kingdom' finding themselves on the 'wrong' side of the largely invisible ethnic divides and racial barriers which criss-cross British society, this country is no 'other Eden', whatever Shakespeare suggested so long ago. For the socially excluded, it is much more like a 'demi-hell' than a 'demi-paradise'. The British Isles may be a natural fortress militarily, but it has signally failed to prevent the infection of racism. Salman Rushdie suggests that, as Anglo-Saxon Britons have now lost their world empire, their colonial mentality has been redirected against ethnic minorities living in their own country. Whatever the structural reasons for Britain's white racism and the counter-racism it breeds in its victims, such intolerance will not be rooted out until most Britons (of whatever background) not only tolerate the steady mongrelisation of British society, but celebrate it as the laboratory of exciting new forms of culture and human coexistence.

7

Europe for the Europeans

Fascist Myths of the European New Order 1922–1992*

Introduction: The 'New Europe' as a mythic construct

'The century that began full of self-confidence in the ultimate triumph of Western liberal democracy seems at its close to be to be returning full circle to where it started.'[1] These words are taken from the second paragraph of the now-famous article published in the (at the time somewhat obscure) neo-conservative journal *The National Interest* in which Francis Fukuyama outlined his vision of the imminent victory of the West – or rather what he calls the 'Western *idea*' – over all rival ideologies, and coined a phrase which has since become a catchphrase of liberal capitalist triumphalism, 'the End of History'. Intimately bound up with this vision is that of a Europe and a North America leading the pack of other cultural systems 'in the vanguard of civilisation',[2] thus fulfilling (against all the odds, when the upheavals of the twentieth century are considered) what Hegelians consider history's hidden agenda; namely, the inexorable progress of liberal freedom. Little wonder, then, that a section of Fukuyama's article pays homage to the neo-Hegelian Alexandre Kojève, who managed to convince himself that the creation of the European Economic Community gave concrete form to the dream of forging Europe into an example of the universal, homogenous state – one alone capable of resolving 'all the contradictions of earlier stages of history' and of satisfying 'all human needs'. True to his beliefs, Kojève spent his later years working tirelessly as an EU bureaucrat.

---

* This chapter was written for a conference that was held by the Western European Area Studies Centre, Minneapolis University (7–9 November 1991). Obviously, many more events demonstrating the vitality of history have occurred since. The international context in which it was written was one of rising concern about the apparently explosion of dangerous forms of ultra-nationalism and the imminent 'return' of fascism, which helps explain the alarmist tone of the final paragraphs, common among academics at the time. It was subsequently reprinted in Marius Babius. (ed.) *European Influenza: Venice*, Romanian Pavilion, La Biennale de Venezia, 51st International Exhibition D-Arte, 2005, pp. 242–305 (a source book on aspects of European enlargement).

Since the summer of 1989, when Fukuyama's article appeared, 'world-historical' events directly impacting Europe have flowed thick and fast: the independence of the Baltic states; Czechoslovakia's Velvet Revolution; the bloody overthrow of Ceauçescu; the unification of the two Germanies; the Gulf Wars; the comprehensive collapse of European state communism in the wake of the dissolution of the Soviet Empire; the outbreak of a horrific civil war in, and then the US-led war on, Yugoslavia; the division of Czechoslovakia; and the rapid enlargement of the EU, to mention only the most spectacular. In a less spectacular way, another major process in the history of nation-building has been taking place, one profoundly influenced by the end of the Cold War: the movement towards the 'European Superstate'. The implications of this phrase obviously vary enormously according to how the EU project of alignment between member states and its eventual relationship with non-EU states is conceived, and there is an important distinction to be drawn between the European Union and Europe. Nevertheless, issues such as the economic and political integration of Western and Northern Europe with the former Eastern bloc countries, the inclusion within the EU of Turkey – a democratic Islamic state beyond the Bosporus – and the real possibility of Europe becoming one of three super-power blocs of economic and military power in the new world order alongside China and the United States, all point to changes which may not be as dramatic as those which followed in the wake of the Napoleonic or the two world wars, but in their own way are just as profound.

What is easy to lose sight of while so many 'real' events stream forth is that 'Europe' becomes a utopian and mythic concept whenever it is used by liberals or their enemies to connote anything more than a specific, geographically, or politically delimited area whose boundaries are agreed upon by cartographers. In evoking the vehicle of progress or the agent of destiny, let alone a homogeneous cultural entity or primordial racial community, then mythopoeia is at work no less strongly than it was for the Greeks, who identified Europe with Jupiter who, disguised as a bull, kidnapped Crete.

Such books are only the latest exercises in a pan-European project, which some might trace back to the attempts of the Holy Roman Empire to unite Europe into a single system in the late Middle Ages within the framework of feudal Christendom (or even the Roman Empire itself). Modern initiatives in this direction have their theoretical roots in the thought of Gottfried Herder and Immanuel Kant. As for practical experiments in Europeanisation, Napoleon Bonaparte might even be presented as a pioneer in a very qualified sense. An even stronger case can be made for beginning with the scheme for Young Europe, a republican brotherhood of nations emancipated from their oppressors, conceived in the 1830s by Giuseppe Mazzini in exile. The formation of Young Italy, and its kindred movements in several other countries, was part of what was conceived as a pan-European initiative for an alliance of free nation-states. Given the profoundly fragmented state of Europe in Mazzini's day, his passion for Europe is an outstanding example of mythopoiea at work, and it is significant that Georges Sorel cites his contribution to the *Risorgimento* as a case-study in the power of myth to change history.[3] The cataclysm of the First World War naturally engendered a wave of visionary idealism among some politicians and political scientists concerning the possibility that the defeat of Germany and her allies might be seized upon as an opportunity to recast the whole of Europe on liberal principles. This idealism is epitomised in Woodrow Wilson's 'Fourteen Points' and their supporters at the ensuing peace conference at Paris in 1919.

More well-known, but in the short term equally doomed to failure, was the liberal Paneuropa movement, founded in 1922 by the Viennese count, Richard Coudenhove-Kalergi, in the pursuit of pacifism and egalitarianism. By 1924, the movement was drawing up its own scheme for a United States of Europe, and two years later it held an international congress in Vienna. One of the delegates at that conference – and Paneuropa's honorary president in 1927 – was Artistide Briand, 11 times Prime Minister of France and the dominant voice in its foreign policy between 1925 and 1932. In 1929, he attempted to move Paneuropa's vision one step closer to reality by putting to the League of Nations what became known as the Briand Plan, which proposed the idea of a federal European Union based on close economic and political ties, an entity which, by 1930, he was referring to as a European Community or a Union of United States. The essential idea behind the plan was that Europe would not only move decisively out of the age of international conflict, but become a major power bloc to rank alongside the USSR and the United States. However, of the 26 countries responding to the proposal only five were positive, the position of a number of nations (especially Britain) being that the proper channel for integration should be the League of Nations. The onset of the Depression in 1929 and Briand's death in 1932, not to mention the Nazi seizure of power a year later, ensured that the plan remained a dead letter.

It was the horrific consequences of the next cataclysmic breakdown of European unity, the Second World War, which was to inspire a new wave of liberal palingenetic mythopoeia, one centring on the post-war order.

In an October 1942 letter to the British War Cabinet, Winston Churchill had already written, 'Hard as it is to say now, I trust that the European family may act unitedly as one under a Council of Europe. I look forward to a United States of Europe'. By the time he announced on 19 September 1946 in a speech given at the University of Zurich, 'We must build a kind of United States of Europe'[4] he was articulating ideas which, by the end of the war, had become the common sense of democrats of many complexions and nations on the continent, no matter how alien they were to the average Briton. It was to be other politicians who were infected by the visionary ideal of democratic Europeanism, men like Robert Schuman and Jean Monnet, who led to the launching of the European Movement and the formation of the Council of Europe. Out of this grew another initiative, the European Coal and Steel Community which became the nucleus of the European Economic Community.[5] Since the Treaty of Rome, the EU has been the main focus for pan-European visions, but not the only one. In the 1980s, one of the more original contributions to the theme came from a source which would have been unimaginable in the Stalinist era. It was as part of the scheme for Russia's palingenesis set forth in his 1984 *Perestroika: New Thinking for Our Country and the World* where Gorbachev first outlined his concept of the Common European Home. Though he was careful to stress in a speech two years later that it was a home with different apartments and entrances, he still set his sights on some sort of harmonious cohabitation of the communist and capitalist worlds. An analysis of his concept of a European home soon reveals its essentially utopian and a historical nature; but in any case, his bold policies for the restructuring of superpower politics were overtaken by a series of revolutionary events which *perestroika* and *glasnost* had done so much to unleash, while Mikhail Gorbachev himself was swept away by the tide of change like some latter-day sorcerer's apprentice.

It is not the purpose of this chapter, however, to discuss how far the New Europe envisaged by Eurovisionaries of reformist socialist, liberal, or reconstructed communist persuasion remains an 'imagined community'.[6] It sets out to examine another way Europe can be mythically created in the mind of the beholder – another example of what might be called 'Europoeia' at work – whose reality principle is even weaker than theirs: the fascist one. There is, of course, a major debate about what is to be understood by the term 'fascism'. The understanding of the term which informs the following analysis assumes it is characterised by a special genus of political myth, namely a palingenetic (rebirth) form of ultra-nationalism. In its many different permutations, the thrust of this myth is the attempt to inaugurate the Phoenix-like rebirth of the nation from the terminal cultural and political decay.

Though in the interwar period, the dominant forms of Fascism and Nazism – both permutations of rebirth nationalism – pursued national interests at the expense of international ones, nothing in fascist ideology ruled out, in principle, the possibility of alliances with other nations with kindred palingenetic aspirations. In fact, as this chapter seeks to show, certain strands of interwar fascism were actively concerned with resolving the decadence brought about by the *status quo* as a whole, not just in a particular nation, and thus thought of rebirth in pan-European or even Western terms. Indeed since 1945, this ecumenical fascism, or 'Eurofascism', far from remaining marginalised, has moved to the mainstream of far-right thought.

Part One: Eurofascism before 1945

Pan-European currents of thought within Italian fascism

An account of fascist quests to build a new Europe has at least one major figure in common with the liberal tradition, namely Giuseppe Mazzini. In contrast to the monarchical and bourgeois liberalism central to Count Camillo di Cavour's quest to bring about Italian unification through *Realpolitik*, Mazzini's anti-clerical and republican vision of the whole nation rising up heroically against its oppressors not only made more overt appeal to palingenetic myth, but was helpfully more ambiguous regarding the most appropriate constitutional framework for the new state. This made it possible for the Fascists to claim that they were completing the *Risorgimento* perverted by earlier generations of liberal politicians.[7] The other Mazzinian aspect of later Fascism is that the national reawakening in Italy was repeatedly seen by zealots of Benito Mussolini's 'Third Rome' as the local manifestation of a process of cultural and political regeneration affecting the whole of Europe. The colossal historical impact of the aggressive imperialist policies adopted by Fascism and Nazism, as expressions of exclusivist forms of chauvinism, has led to an understandable tendency for academics to lose sight of the *internationalist* form which fascist ideology assumed whenever its activists sensed a kindred spirit with the crusades of ultra-nationalists abroad. Once the various pre-1914 tributaries to Fascism are considered from this perspective, each reveals an in-built internationalist dimension which refutes simplistic notions that ultra-nationalism precludes a Europeanist dimension of historical speculation.

Thus Enrico Corradini, founder of *Il Regno* and the foremost theoretician of the Italian National Association (which would finally merge with the PNF in 1923), had as early as 1909 developed a theory of proletarian nations pitted against plutocratic ones like Britain and France, an ultra-nationalist counterpart to the Marxist analysis of class war within nations.[8] In this way, the renaissance of Italy was placed firmly within a pan-European context. Another major influence on integral nationalism in Italy was Giovanni Papini, whose periodical *La Voce* [The Voice] preached the need for a cultural and political revolution in Italy which would not only sweep away the decadence of the Giolittian system, but would form an integral part of the revitalisation of European civilisation. Papini conceived his role as being the theoretical midwife of a generation of '*homines novi*' or 'new men' who would supply the heroism and vision which, according to Nietzschean thinking, were vitally necessary if the whole of the Western world were not to fall into a terminal state of cultural decay.[9] Under Marinetti's influence, Political Futurism, an important component of nascent Fascism after 1918, considered itself as part of a crusade against a *passatismo* forming part of a European, and not merely Italian, cultural crisis. Meanwhile, some neo-syndicalists, such as Sergio Panunzio, were adapting the internationalist analysis of liberal democracy bequeathed by Marx and Sorel to the national context, placing such thinkers on a collision course, and thereafter convergence with the Fascist revolution.[10] All these strands of political culture became intertwined in the interventionist lobby of 1914–1915, when their spokesmen formed a common front. They did so in the conviction that participation in the First World War would launch Italy on the (quite differently conceived) revolutionary process they saw as the only remedy to its malaise. The *Fasci di azione rivoluzionaria*, with their nebulous call for national rebirth in an ultra-nationalist key, can be seen as the main proto-fascist force in Italian politics.[11]

With the formation of the *Fasci di combattimento* in March 1919, Mussolini's fascism took its first uncertain steps towards the road to power. Since it sought from the outset to capitalise on the revolutionary spirit of *combattentismo* – brought back from the front by war veterans (*combattenti*) – in the midst of an acute domestic crisis, it is hardly surprising if the nationalism of Sansepolcro Fascism and of the *squadrismo* which took off so spectacularly in the *biennio rosso* ('two red years'), the period of intense communist agitation between 1919 and 1920, lacked an internationalist dimension; its mythic focal point being the struggle of the 'new Italy' against the 'old'. It is thus particularly significant for discussion here that the variety of ultra-nationalist myth informing Gabriel D'Annunzio's attempt to create a role model for the Italian revolution at Fiume (1919–1920) contained an internationalist (though not a European) component. With the adoption of the Charter of Carnaro, he was giving the national syndicalist Alceste De Ambris the chance to carry out a full-scale experiment in the reorganisation of political and economic structures on corporatist lines, and so to establish a blueprint for the regeneration of all modern societies.[12] Moreover, under the influence of the Belgian poet Leon Kochnitzky, who headed the Regency's Foreign Office, in spring 1920 D'Annunzio set up in the League of Fiume, a sort of anti-League of Nations designed to form a common front of oppressed nations against hegemonic ones (echoes of Mazzini and Corradini are clearly audible here). Kochnitzky actively sought support from Egyptians, Indians, Irish, Croatians, Montenegrans, Albanians, Hungarians, Flemings, Turks, Arabs, and even Russians, who – in the heady constructivist phase of the Revolution – could still be seen as allies in the fight between young and old nations. He saw the League as shattering the old order and establishing a world based on 'Italy and Life', a new International based on the vitalistic and visionary energies incarnate in D'Annunzio himself. The 'Christmas of Blood' in which government forces finally ousted the '*Dannunziani*' (in December 1920) spared the advocates of the League the humiliation of their utopian expectations being exposed by the sombre realities of the power politics and nationalist conflict. But the very fact that the project was taken so seriously bears out the fact that the Fiume 'adventure' was not conceived merely as a domestic affair but, as Ledeen puts it, a revolt 'directed against the old order of Western Europe and carried out in the name of youthful creativity and heroism'.[13]

Yet it was Mussolini's variant of fascism which proved to be the most durable, not least because he possessed the tactical and ideological flexibility to weld together highly disparate forces (including after 1921 many Dannunzians), whose protagonists projected their own disparate schemes for Italy's ultra-nationalist regeneration onto his movement. Certainly in the period from 1922 to 1929, when the juridical, political, and socio-economic foundations of the Fascist State were being put into place, Fascism's domestic struggle for hegemony absorbed the bulk of Mussolini's interests and he appears to have formally renounced any international implications for his cause captured by the oft-quoted assertion (made in a speech in 1928) that 'Fascism was not for export'. However, the preconceived idea encountered in some studies on Fascism held that it was only in the 1930s (i.e. after the period of the regime's consolidation was over) that Mussolini came to be interested in the exportability of his movement is nevertheless erroneous. After all, he had started out political life as an idiosyncratic but assiduous supporter of internationalist socialism. Moreover, there is documentary evidence to show that the turning point towards a nationalist form of socialism came not on the eve of Italy's intervention, but as early as 1907 when, partly under the influence of *La Voce*, he became convinced he was a *homo novus* of Nietzschean ilk, called upon to induce the birth to a new nation as part of the transvaluation of values needed to regenerate the West as a whole.[14] Correspondingly, the profound influence of Oswald Spengler's analysis on the decay of the West has also been traced in Mussolini's thinking.[15] It is thus unsurprising if the spectre of decadence on an *international* scale haunts his letter to Henry Massi written (in French) in June 1927:

> The East is a danger, if you like an infection. But through which channels does this infection pass? I will list them: liberalism, democracy, socialism, freemasonry. The organism of the West has been weakened, debilitated by these ideologies. Well, there is in existence only one movement existing at the present time which has the courage – possessing the power of a great nation – to be fundamentally, openly, ferociously anti-liberal, anti-democratic, anti-Freemason: Fascism.[16]

Within a few months, Mussolini was writing in the preface to a book by the English philo-Fascist, Major John Barnes (significantly entitled *The Universal Aspects of Fascism*):

> Fascism is a purely Italian phenomenon in its historical expression, but its doctrines and postulates have a universal character. Fascism sets and solves

problems which are common to many peoples and precisely to those peoples who have experienced, and are tired of, Demo-liberal rule.[17]

In terms which might profitably be taken to heart by scholars wrestling with the concept of generic fascism ever since, Mussolini then proceeded to point out that the precise form which fascism took would necessarily, like liberalism, vary from country to country:

> the fact that Fascism possesses a specific and original Italian stamp does not prevent its principles having an application in other countries, in other forms, as indeed has already occurred. It is our proud prophecy that Fascism will come to fill the present century with itself, even as Liberalism filled the nineteenth century.[18]

Thus, while he realised that the specific state apparatus which Fascism had created in Italy was clearly not for wholesale export to other national contexts, Mussolini seems to have been convinced, early on in his dictatorship at least, that its spirit offered a shining example to other, modern nations grappling with local permutations of what he considered the true enemies of progress, 'demo-liberalism', and communism. No U-turn is to be read, therefore, into Mussolini's 1930 statement that 'today I affirm that Fascism is universal in spirit',[19] or the famous declarations in the *Enciclopedia Italiana* of 1932 that the twentieth century would be a 'Fascist century' and that 'Fascism has henceforth in the world the universality of all those doctrines which, in realising themselves, have represented a stage in the history of the human spirit.'[20] A similarly global perspective on decadence underlay a number of pronouncements on race, made well in advance of the 1938 decision to integrate Nazi-style racial laws within Fascist doctrine and celebrate the Aryan heritage of the Italians. An example is the 1931 article written for the *Popolo d'Italia* [The People of Italy], on 4 September, 'Is the White Race Dying Out?', which shows that official Fascism had both a supra-Italian and a racist dimension quite independent of the 1936 Pact of Steel with Nazi Germany.

Mussolini's most comprehensive biographer, Renzo de Felice, points out that it was after the 1935 Abyssinian War, and under the influence of the nationalist Alfredo Oriani, the demographer Richard Korherr, and Oswald Spengler that 'Mussolini underwent a decisive phase of ideological evolution and involution' which

> led him to believe that Europe and the world were undergoing a profound 'crisis of civilisation' from which would emerge a 'new civilisation' characterised by the rapid decline of countries like France and England and the rise of Germany, Japan, Russia and Italy. In this view, Fascist Italy had to fulfil its

own special 'mission' by exercising its 'moral primacy' over other nations, in addition to realising its Mediterranean hegemony.[21]

While this is doubtless true, it is clear that Mussolini was building on convictions about the state of the world arrived at well before the First World War and refined ever since the 'conquest of the state' in 1922. Whatever Mussolini's personality problems,[22] part of his emotional circuitry was – no less than Hitler's – fired by a boundless, visionary optimism about the regeneration of Italy; and, thereafter, of the entire 'West'. One telling symptom is evident in 1936, just as the edifice of Fascism gave the first ominous signs that it would eventually collapse around his ears like the House of Usher, the *Duce's* reaction was not to relapse into solipsistic brooding, but to embark instead on a heady piece of futurology to be called *Europe 2000*. This project was destined to remain as incomplete as all his would-be contributions to the New World of the *uomo fascista*.[23]

Mussolini's preoccupation with the repercussions of Fascism beyond the frontiers of Italy, far from being a private pipe-dream, was an integral part of mainstream Fascist thought. A generation ago, Pier-Giorgio Zunino has made an impressive attempt to carry out an analysis of the dominant themes in Fascism on the basis of a comprehensive study of official publications in the late 1920s. The results continually highlight the notion that European civilisation as a whole was going through the profound crisis prophesied by Nietzsche, analysed by Spengler, and exploded by the First World War and the chaos which ensued. The ubiquitous symptoms of a world out of joint were, for the Fascist mentality, no grounds for cultural pessimism, but the birth-pangs of a 'new civilisation whose essence no one could know'.[24] One seam within this regenerative philosophy of history which Zunino mines (and which is of immense significance for post-war fascism) is that Europe was caught in a pincer movement between two empires of decadent materialist ideology, the capitalist USA and communist Russia.[25] James Gregor also stresses the internationalist dimension of Mussolini's 'Third Rome' in *The Ideology of Fascism*,[26] claiming that by 1935 theoreticians were envisaging a 'pan-European federation of fascist nations' that would function through a 'polyarchic directorate'; and that by 1942, the conception of a European consortium of fascist nations united within a 'European regime of federal union' had become a commonplace of Fascist literature.

The Europeanism of several leading Fascist ideologues further bears out this analysis but, as in the case of Mussolini, is detectable well before the 1930s. For example, Curzio Suckert, better known as Malaparte, founder of *La Conquista dello Stato* [The Conquest of the State] and a major representative of the Fascist intelligentsia in the regime's early years, set forth the premises to his own conversion: his *L'Europa vivente*, as the title 'Living Europe' suggests, offered a comprehensive pan-European perspective for assessing the 1922 March on

Rome, as well as his own conversion in the next year. In the same year, albeit in a very different spirit, Giovanni Gentile rationalised his conversion to Fascism in terms of his right-wing neo-Hegelian philosophy of history. Gentile was soon tirelessly producing lectures and essays celebrating the March on Rome as a turning point, not just of Italy's history but of the entire West: Mussolini was a world-historical individual, 'an instrument used by providence to create a new civilisation'.[27] Yet another justification for Fascism was elaborated by Giuseppe Bottai, who, in his indefatigable propagandist activity for the regime – as Minister of Corporations, Minister of Education, and the editor of *Critica Fascista* – constantly sought to demonstrate the way in which Fascism found solutions to structural problems faced by European states still committed to the West's bankrupt, liberal economic system; a technocratic argument radically at loggerheads with Gentile's elaborate idealist rationale for Fascism.[28]

Another point within the broad spectrum of positions accommodated by Fascism is occupied by Carlo Costamagna, founder of the periodical *Lo Stato* [The State] and the most important legislator in the corporatist state after Alfredo Rocco. Costamagna went on to be adopted as an important ideologue by Italian neo-fascists after the war, for he was a major advocate of Fascism's pan-European significance. In an article of 1943, 'The Idea of Europe and the War', written even as the regime was crumbling, he was still arguing that a new Fascist International was becoming a reality due to the heroic efforts of the Axis powers. Presenting Fascism in now familiar terms as an international crusade against the European 'old order' of British imperialism and the League of Nations, Costamagna took issue with another of the regime's convinced Europeanists, Camillo Pellizzi, who saw cultural bonds as a sufficient basis for international co-operation, stressing instead the need for harmonising political and juridical institutions. Costamagna added that 'the new order, the bond (*fascio*) of the forces of several peoples', which he saw as the fruit of the Italian and German struggles for national unification in the nineteenth century, 'will deserve the name European only if its component nations have their own territory in a portion of Europe and have European traits of civilisation'.[29]

It is against this background that the scholarly investigation of the internationalist component of Fascism provided by Michael Ledeen's 1972 *Universal Fascism* becomes clear. Here, he documents the many initiatives launched by Fascists of the younger generation – the so-called Second Wave – to impart a pan-European thrust to the regime's foreign policy, and so to fulfil its mission to lead the way into a new phase of Western civilisation. Failure to do so would, they believed, condemn the regime to being no more than a national dictatorship imposed by a state hierarchy, one which the universalists saw rapidly degenerating into a blinkered and reactionary gerontocracy. Among the most ardent and articulate advocates for this universalist mode of Fascism's palingenetic myth was Benito Mussolini's brother, Arnaldo, editor of *Il Popolo d'Italia* from the March on Rome until his death in 1931. In October 1930, for example, he wrote an article which declared,

> The fascist spirit – as the essence of a new civilisation – is universal. It is based on the trilogy: 'authority, order, and justice.' An unstable, unquiet Europe, failing in its millenarian function, hemmed in by the vague formulae of liberalism and democracy, cannot find its health, or rather, its salvation any other way than in a new order [...] it is for that reason that in all countries we now see currents analogous to the fascist movement.[30]

Another family spokesman for this vision was Mussolini's son Vittorio who, between 1929 and 1935, was the leading light of *Novismo* [literally Newism]. As its distinctly palingenetic name implied, the movement sought to promote a process of renewal in every sphere of Italian society. One acting as a catalyst for the regeneration of Western civilisation as a whole. Another prophet of Fascism's mission as the agent of international renewal was Silvano Spinetti, whose journal *La Sapienza* [Wisdom], which appeared from 1933, campaigned for Fascism to recover the dynamism it had exhibited in the immediate post-war crisis. Spinetti spoke for all the universalist Fascists when, in *La Sapienzia* of April 1933, he declared,

> We are [...] the precursors of a new era, of a civilisation which we will not hesitate to call fascist, because our value must not consist in being the first to predict the universal reaction, but in having nourished and guided it, in having shaped our doctrine to it.

Three years later, Spinetti was still sufficiently confident in Fascism's potential for self-renewal that he predicted 'within a century the world will be fascist...given that universality is one of the characteristics of European civilisation which is essentially Roman'.[31] Spinetti offered elaborations of his pan-European fascist vision in two books, *Fascismo Universale* [Universal Fascism] (1934) and *L'Europa verso la Rivoluzione* [Europe towards the Revolution] (1936), the latter anticipating much post-war thinking by focusing on the twin threats to European civilisation: inner decadence brought about by 'demo-liberalism', and the external threat posed by Bolshevism. And his was no voice crying in the wilderness. Pan-Europeanism was a major theme in official Fascist texts from the 1930s. Two of the new publishers were called 'Europa' and 'La Nuova Europa', both of which brought out a steady stream of the universalist interpretations of Fascism. The year 1932 saw the appearance of the journal *L'Universalità Romana* [Roman Universality], one year after the respected intellectual Oddone Fantini launched *L'Universalità Fascista* [Fascist Universality], leading to a full-scale exposition of their message in a book entitled *Universalità del Fascismo* [The Universality of Fascism] (1933). *L'Universale* [The Universal], a periodical published by Ricci between 1935 and 1936, also portrayed Fascism as saviour of Western civilisation. Little wonder that the theme of fascism as a Rome-led yet universal revolution found its way into the official history of Fascism published in 1936 by Gioacchino Volpe, *La storia dle movimento fascista* [The History of the Fascist Movement].

The chief publicist of Fascist Europeanism, however, was Asvero Gravelli, a Fascist 'of the First Hour' and an indefatigable propagandist for Fascism's youthful revolution. Apart from a number of books (e.g. *La marche de Rome et l'Europe* [The March on Rome and Europe], 1932; *Europa con noi!* [Europe with us!], 1933), Gravelli was the editor of two important reviews. One, subtitled *Quotidiano del Fascismo Universale* [The Daily Paper of Universal Fascism], made its first appearance on the tenth anniversary of the March of Rome under the title *Ottobre* [October]. But three years earlier, just as Mussolini was endorsing Major Barnes's interpretation of Fascism's universality, Gravelli published an even more important journal entitled *Antieuropa* [Anti-Europe]. Gravelli himself explained the paradox in an article setting out the journal's aims in the first issue:[32]

1) Fascism is anti-European, because the present Europe, in the throes of a spiritual crisis and a material crisis is, in part, still under the influence of the immortal principles [of the French Revolution] while vast sections of society look to Moscow. Given *this* Europe, Fascism is anti-Europe.

2) The anti-Europeanism of Fascism is not an end in itself, but a provisional historical position, which will last till Fascism has enabled Europe to regain its ideal and spiritual equilibrium, the starting point of a new European role in the world. [...]

3) Fascism transcends democracy and liberalism; its regenerative action is based on granite foundations: the idea of hierarchy, of the participation of the whole population in the life of the State, social justice in the equitable distribution of rights and duties, the infusion of public life with moral principles, the affirmation of religious values, the prestige of the family, the ethical interpretation of the ideas of order, authority and liberty.

In the light of this transcendence, Europe will be able to find its way to enter a new phase of History.

From its first appearance in 1929, *Antieuropa* established itself as the main forum for advocates of fascist internationalism, publishing a steady flow of articles assessing the strength of Bolshevism and liberalism in shaping world events, and publishing reports on philo-Fascist initiatives in France, Poland, Switzerland, Croatia, Belgium, England, Austria, Egypt, China, Spain, the Ukraine, Hungary, and Finland. The constant theme is that a battle is being fought between the forces of decadence and resurrection: Fascism is showing Europe the way out of the cul-de-sac of history created by liberal democracy and the deep crisis provoked by Communism. Notable articles (some of which were written in French and German, as well as Italian) focus on the problem of ethnic minorities,[33] the radical incompatibility of Fascism with the 'anti-Roman' Aryan myth of the Nazis when the latter was still an opposition party,[34] and a series of articles specifically attacking the federal proposals of *Pan-Europa* and the Briand Plan.[35] For a sample of the periodical's tone, some of the principles laid down by a Belgian sympathiser as a basis for collaboration with Italian Fascism is expressed an article entitled 'Pour une internationale Fasciste'. This states that a fascist international must:

1) while fighting communism, defend the oppressed classes against the magnates of finance and capitalism and against the tyranny of the rich;

2) fight liberal parliamentarism, because it derives from a false ideology and, under the pretext of popular sovereignty, reduces the masses to slaves and hands over power to a minority of business men;

3) promote the corporatist organisation of society and proclaim the right of the state to solve economic conflicts as the only party able to act as intermediaries between different professional groups and control neo-capitalist enterprises, such as trusts, cartels, large banks etc.

4) propagate the idea of the European Union, not in the sense meant by Briand, but according to the Christian and fascist conception of international life [...] All the forces of European youth must be united as quickly as possible to fight effectively against the forces of dissolution: communism, socialism and liberalism.[36]

Just as significant as the textual expressions of Fascist internationalism were various attempts to organise a fascist equivalent of the Marxist Internationals. One of the forerunners of these was the *Centre International d'Études sur le Fascisme* (CINEF) [International Centre for the Study of Fascism] headed by Major Barnes, with a three-man executive that included Giovanni Gentile. These were supported by a governing body made up largely of professors representing Holland, Greece, Spain, Poland, Hungary, France, Norway, the United States, Romania, Germany, Belgium, and Ireland. Its first and only yearbook in 1928 contained articles by four eminent members of the Fascist hierarchy, Gioacchino Volpe, Luigi Villari, Edmondo Rossoni, and Filippo Turati; the dominant theme of which was that Fascism, while unique to Italy in the precise institutions it had created, showed how common European problems could be solved through a national reawakening at once anti-liberal and anti-communist.

Official sanction for the tireless proselytising of Gravelli and CINEF seemed to come in 1932, when Mussolini allowed a major international conference, the Volta Congress (named after the Italian scientist), to be held in Rome in order to debate the future evolution of Europe in the era of Fascism. Encouraged by the success of the meeting of so many foreign dignitaries favourable to Fascism, Gravelli then started planning an international youth congress to launch Young Europe, thus deliberately reviving the Mazzinian organisation in an international fascist key. Another organisation at the forefront of fascist pan-Europeanism in this period was the *Istituto Europa Giovane* [Institute of Young Europe] which, in its journal *Nazionale* [National] published articles with such suggestive palingenetic titles as 'The Rejuvenation of Europe'. By 1933 there were so many publications and initiatives dedicated to internationalising fascism that Mussolini was prompted to assert his authority over them. He did so by setting up the *Comitato d'Azione per l'Universalità di Roma* (CAUR) [Action Committee for the Universality of Rome] which found enthusiastic support from the new Foreign Minister Ciano. In 1934 CAUR held an international congress in Montreux attended by leading lights of kindred European movements, such as Frits Clausen (Denmark), Marcel Bucard (France), Eoin O'Duffy (Ireland), Vidkun Quisling (Norway), Ion Motza (Romania), and Giménez Caballero (Spain). Nazi representation was conspicuous by its absence: the exclusivity of Aryan racism precluded ecumenical fascist ventures of the sort.

At the level of political reality, all such initiatives were doomed to be stillborn. The adoption of the aggressive imperialist policy which led to the 1935 invasion of Ethiopia, the international repercussions of the Spanish Civil War a year later, the weakness of fascist movements outside the Berlin–Rome Axis – and the domination of this alliance by Hitler rather than Mussolini – the radical incompatibility of National Socialism's biologically oriented Aryan theory with Fascism's 'cultural' nationalism, and the expansionist ambitions of Nazism in Europe: all made nonsense of any schemes for real co-operation between fascist movements, let alone any sort of confederation of European fascist nations. So powerful was the utopianism built into fascism's palingenetic dynamic, however, that the purblindness to considerations of *Realpolitik* and to brute facts clouded the minds of most protagonists of Fascist Europeanism until defeat overtook them.

Yet even in the Nazi puppet-state, the Republic of Salò, where Fascism's *intransigenti* (i.e. the 'die-hard soldiers'), intellectuals, and 'hierarchs' (including Giovanni Gentile, Roberto Farinacci, and Giorgio Almirante, the future leader of the post-war *Movimento Sociale Italiano*) rallied round Mussolini, there were enough of universalist persuasion left to leave their stamp on the Manifesto of the Fascist Republican Party, issued in Verona in November 1943. This document states that the foreign policy of the Republic was to be directed to

> the realisation of a European community, with a federation of all nations which accept the following principles: (a) the elimination of age-old British intrigue from our continent; (b) the abolition of the capitalist system;

(c) the struggle against the world's plutocracies; (d) the development, for the benefit of European peoples and of the natives, of Africa's natural resources, with absolute respect for those peoples, especially Muslims, who, as in Egypt, have already achieved civil and national organisation.[37]

Pre-1945 Eurofascism outside Italy

Clearly then, many Fascists convinced themselves that their revolution was a national response to a generalised crisis of Western or European civilisation, as well as that Italy had a providential mission to inspire parallel national reawakenings abroad. The starting point for an appraisal of fascist internationalism outside Italy is the recognition that the sense of a crisis of civilisation was far from being confined to the land of Dante. This view also long predates the First World War, even if it was only this cataclysm which created the socio-political conditions which could generate mass followings for national revolutionary movements.[38] The 'decline' of the West had become a highly diffuse current of speculation among the European intelligentsia in the late nineteenth century, and formed a central component of *fin-de-siècle* culture, rightly identified by Ze'ev Sternhell as the incubation period of fascism.[39] Though this is a period of intellectual history widely associated with the terms 'cultural despair',[40] the striking feature in much of the aesthetic, moral, philosophical, physiological, racial, religious, and political theorising that dwelt on the sense of degeneration at the time is that it is far from pessimistic.[41] Rather, in a myriad ways, these perceptions testify to the desire to spin threads of Ariadne capable of leading 'modern man' out of the labyrinth of contemporary society, thereby *transcending* the present decadence. In other words, the prevalent thrust of the 'revolt against positivism'[42] was a palingenetic one of regenerating society, which is why figures such as Vilfredo Pareto, Georges Sorel, and, above all, Nietzsche – with their lurid depictions of Europe's malaise and the 'transvaluation of values' necessary to move into a new era – exercised such a fascination.[43] In many respects the 'revolt against positivism' could thus equally well be called the 'revolt against decadence'.

Given the pan-European diffusion of both cultural pessimism *and* regenerationist mythopoeia before 1914, it is not surprising to find a number of political theorists and movements which, while rejecting the 'scientific' path to humanity's palingenesis propounded by Marxism, were obsessed with the possibility that a new ideological synthesis of democracy, socialism, conservatism, and nationalism might be found, one able to renew European society and even 'the world'. Nationalist revisions of Marxism, integral nationalisms, spiritual and racist revivalism, anthropological, philological, and historical myths of renewal, visions of decadence and regeneration, and apocalyptic and millennaristic futurologies were all in the air. In this disorienting but heady cultural climate, those of an ideological bent not firmly ensconced within the liberal human-ist tradition were all too easily lured into formulating syncretic diagnoses of the perceived crisis, and concocting home-brewed remedies to it. Several Italian manifestations of this phenomenon have been discussed thus far, all of which eventually became suffused within Fascism. Pan-Slavism, pan-Germanism, Zionism, the national socialism of Maurice Barrès, Charles Maurras' *Action Française*, national syndicalism, Karl Lueger's Christian Social Party, the far-flung and heterogeneous *völkisch* movement in Germany (which, thanks to the pervasiveness of Romantic nationalism in the nineteenth century, had a counterpart in most European countries): all are examples of the new political syntheses of ultra-right thought emerging before 1914.

For those susceptible to palingenetic fantasies, the First World War and the 1917 Russian Revolution could all too easily appear as the objectification of the spiritual crisis they had identified, and hence the sign that history was expe-riencing the birth pangs of a vast transformation. This conviction formed an essential precondition for Mussolini's March in 1922 to encourage responses from abroad that located an international process of rebirth without any prompting from Fascist propagandists. Before long, parties were set up spon-taneously in several countries (e.g. Britain, Sweden, Romania) which, while asserting their own creed of national identity and destiny, incorporated the term 'fascist' into their name so as to betoken an underlying kinship with the Italian process of national rebirth. What needs to be stressed is that movements identifying with Fascism did not do so on the basis of direct mimesis, which their nationalism precluded *a priori*, but rather of a perceived 'elective affin-ity', that allowed culture-specific mythic elements to be combined with the universalist pretensions.

This blend of the derivative and the home-grown is clearly evident in the case of the BUF, formed in 1932. Its leader, Oswald Mosley, had devel-oped his own idiosyncratic theory of national palingenesis by blending (*inter alia*) the Superman concept of Nietzsche and George Bernard Shaw with elements of Spenglerian cultural analysis, Christian values, and Keynsian eco-nomics. Though the ritual style of his movement was heavily indebted to the *squadrismo* and *ducismo* of Fascism, it adopted an overt, cultural form of anti-Semitism in 1934 which made it superficially closer to Nazism than Fascism on racial questions. As for its foreign policy, by 1936, the BUF was resolutely committed to preserving Britain's foremost position as a trading and colo-nial superpower, while treating Italy, Germany, and Japan (but not Russia or America) as natural allies. They were all free to expand their own empire as expressions of national vitality as long, as they did not trespass on Britain's spheres of interest. This position led the BUF to officially adopt a neutralist stance towards Hitler's aggressive imperialism, though many of its members were active philo-Nazis by the outbreak of war in 1939.[44] What gives Mosley particular importance in the context of this analysis is that, even before the war, he was fusing British imperialism with a pan-European version of fascism that anticipates post-war developments. In 1937, he published *The World Alternative*, which claimed that 'the only force that can unite is a consistent faith in the essential one-ness of Europe', and argued that a form of European union which did not involve the 'suicide' of separate national governments would make a second world war avoidable.

Yet, once other abortive interwar fascist movements are taken into account, any neat pattern in their international linkage soon breaks down. Rolão Preto's National Syndicalism in Portugal and José Antonio Primo de Rivera's Falange, though strongly influenced by elements of the New Italy, did not officially associate themselves with Fascism, or with an international fascism. The leaders of the Iron Guard, however, though perhaps less ideologically indebted to foreign role models than any other European fascist movement, openly acknowledged the fact that Fascism and Nazism were kindred phenomena. Corneliu Zelea Codreanu sympathised with the goals of CAUR and the Montreux Conference, while Ion Motza lost his life in the Spanish Civil War fighting against the Republicans in what he believed was the defence of the same national-Christian values underlying the rebirth of Romania. In the countries of Northern Europe, especially Germanic ones, it was the NSDAP which naturally tended to provide a role model for palingenetic ultra-nationalist movements, especially after its spectacular ascendancy in the centre of the German political arena after 1929. While some merely tailored Nazism to the local situation by adopting the notion of a Nordic or Germanic reawakening, others, such as Quisling's *Nasjonal Samling* were far more ideologically independent at first, and only gradually became Nazified as the decade wore on.

Léon Degrelle's Belgian Rexism provides another illustration of the way highly original forms of ultra-nationalism could gradually align themselves with Nazism, to the point of becoming overtly fascist by 1939. Under Nazi occupation, *Rex* mutated into a collaborationist force with a fully developed pan-European vision of the New Order envisaging Belgium, or even a recreated Burgundy, becoming a junior partner of the Third Reich. So seriously did Degrelle take this scenario that he became a major protagonist of the Walloon SS Brigade and survived the war to become one of the main figureheads of ecumenical fascism.[45] Two other Belgians also persuaded themselves that the Nazis were in the process of uniting European states into a resurgent European Order. Pierre Daye, also a Rexist leader, wrote *L'Europe aux Européens* [Europe for the Europeans] (1942), a cry now familiar in Le Penist circles, which saw a Nazi Europe as finally immune to both Bolshevism and the divisive foreign policies of Great Britain. More surprising is the manifesto of Henri de Man, president of the Belgian Worker's Party and a tireless propagandist for a planned society based on social democratic principles. Published after he had become a collaborator with the Nazis in 1940, the manifesto talks of Nazism bringing about a 'European peace' and of a Europe 'unified by force of arms'. In his post-war memoirs he explains how, in 1940, it seemed as if the liberal world had collapsed, 'leaving the way free for popular aspirations towards European peace and justice', simultaneously admitting having underestimated the power of the old system to fight back and win the war.[46]

However slavishly imitative or doctrinally original they were, most genuine fascist movements in the interwar period shared the belief that the problems which they sought to resolve in national life were the local manifestation of a wider crisis, a crisis of civilisation itself. This is true just as much of fully fledged non-European fascisms, such as the Chilean National Socialist Movement, Plinio Salgado's sizeable Integralist Brazilian Action, and the 'Christan Socialist' *Ossewa Brandwag* in South Africa, as it is true of European groups like the Finnish *Lapua* movement (which became the People's Patriotic Movement) or Ferenc Szálasi's Arrow Cross, or Hungarist, movement. They all legitimated their revolutionary onslaught against the *status quo* through a philosophy of history that gave their movements a regenerationist mission whose significance went far beyond the narrow confines of national political life.[47] The difference is that the Eurocentrism so instinctive to most Europeans meant that fascists in the 'old world' tended to identify the wider crisis with a crisis of Europe rather than the West in general, and hence, if they had universalist inclinations at all, to see their movement specifically as part of the creation of a new Europe. This tendency has been encouraged both by the idea of Europe as an 'old' continent in need of rejuvenation, and by the image of it caught between the two superpowers of the United States and Soviet Russia.

Just how idiosyncratic European fascism can be is shown by the case of Szálasi, leader and main ideologue of the Hungarian Arrow Cross movement. Not even being installed as the impotent head of a puppet-state of the Third Reich in 1944 could shake his belief that Hungary was eventually destined to become the hegemonic nation in the Carpathian–Danube basin alongside Italy and Germany – each sovereign in their own geo-political spheres. They would eventually be joined by France and Russia: Britain was not included in this scheme since 'it had always behaved as if it was outside Europe!'. Under the leadership of these nations, Europe would eventually form a harmonious community based on national socialist principles, including the revitalisation of the peasantry and the removal of Jews to their own homeland, as a suitable candidate for which Szálasi suggested Madagascar. In a speech which he delivered as nominal head of state in February 1945, 'I see from the point of view of national socialist ideology the whole of Europe as a state of nationalities: the European Community is nothing other than the extension of Hungarian problems and their solution to Europe as a whole.'[48]

In a similar vein, Ze'ev Sternhell has pointed out that France 'offers particularly favourable conditions' for the study of fascism.[49] France also provides a
valuable case study in the study of fascist pan-Europeanism. French intellectuals had played a major role in the *fin-de-siècle* revolt against positivism and
cultural decadence, and the need to revitalise European civilisation was a recurrent theme well before 1914. It is hardly surprising, then, if one of the earliest
parties inspired by Fascism was a French one, the *Faisceau*, founded by Georges
Valois in 1925, a former member of the French *Action Française* and founder of
the national socialist *Cercle Proudhon* [The Proudhon Circle] before the war. He
envisaged France's regeneration as part of a Latin fascist bloc alongside Spain
and Italy, and even expressly invited Jews to contribute to the *'New Age'*, the
appropriately palingenetic name of the movement's newspaper.[50] By 1933, the
NSDAP could also provide a role model for a supra-national force of regeneration, as is shown by Marcel Bucard's attempt to create a French version of
Nazism with a movement called *Francisme*. Although Bucard was convinced
that Nazism was 'the only way to emerge from the universal mire',[51] his solidarity with other fascisms was strong enough for him to participate in CAUR's
Montreux Conference held in 1934, aiming to export the values of the New
Italy.

Inevitably, it was the 1940 victory of the *Wehrmacht* over the French and the
subsequent occupation of Northern France which precipitated mass conversions
of indigenous French fascists to pan-Europeanism. As Algazy puts it, 'those who
till yesterday had been nationalists became partisans of a "New European Order"
under the guidance of the German Reich'.[52] Marcel Déat, originator of a current of ultra-nationalism called 'neo-socialism', and Eugène Deloncle, former
head of the anti-communist terrorist group *Cagoule*, both formed new organisations – the *Rassemblement National Populaire* [The Popular National Rally] and the
Mouvement Social-Révolutionnaire [The Social Revolutionary Movement], respectively – which strove towards integrating France within the Nazi New European
Order. Even more significant was the alacrity with which the charismatic leader
of the *Parti Populaire Français* [French Popular Party], Jacques Doriot, emulated
Degrelle's headlong rush into the arms of Nazism – to the point of fighting on
the Eastern Front as part of the *Légion de Volontaires Français* [Legion of French
Volunteers]. In June 1943, Doriot was still claiming that his party had 'always
struggled for the defence of Europe, its life-principles, now more in danger
than ever before, in the East by Bolshevik barbarianism and in the West by
Anglo-American barbarianism'.[53]

It was this new rationale explaining the fact that, within months of the
German occupation, a highly prolific and variegated collaborationist press
(exemplified by *Les Nouveaux Temps* and *Le Rouge et le Bleu*) emerged in France,
the common denominator of its output being a vision of France gaining pride
of place in the New European Order, one which would follow the seemingly

inevitable Nazi victory over the forces of liberal decadence and the Jewish–Communist menace. Pierre Drieu la Rochelle, Robert Brasillach, and Lucien Rebatet were only the most famous figures to ally their pen with the Nazi sword. Typical was Brasillach's declaration, in a piece entitled 'For a French Fascism' (published in July 1944, even as the Allied liberation of France was taking place), that only French youth were in a position 'to understand what now exalts the hearts of so many young hearts, whether in Germany, in Italy, in Spain or elsewhere, wherever the great cry rings out of "Nation awake!"'.[54]

The single intellectual offering the greatest insight into the inner logic of pan-European fascism, however, is Pierre Drieu la Rochelle. Obsessed with the decadence of European civilisation throughout the interwar period,[55] Drieu came to the conclusion as early as 1922 that, as he wrote in *Mesure de la France*, 'we must create a United States of Europe, because it is the only way of defending Europe against itself and against other human groups'.[56] He was thus temperamentally predisposed to see in the ultra-nationalism embodied in Fascism and Nazism the timely antidote to the West's malaise. On this score, Drieu is unequivocal: 'I am fascist because I have taken stock of the advance of decadence in Europe. I have seen in fascism the only way to contain and reverse this decadence'.[57] Drieu subsequently elaborated this theme in such works as *Le jeune Européen* [The Young European] (1927) and *L'Europe contre les patries* [Europe against individual countries] (1931), and came to believe that Hitler's NSDAP and Doriot's PPF were vehicles for the realisation of his dream. The psychological and ideological process by which cultural despair could become alchemically transformed by fascism into manic optimism was meticulously reconstructed in fictional form in his novel *Gilles* (1939), which appeared on the eve of the Nazi conquest of Europe. No wonder, then, that Drieu became one of France's highest profile intellectual collaborators with Nazism, providing important expositions of the vision of a new confederation of nations under the Third Reich in *Notes pour comprendre le siècle* [Notes for understanding the age] (1941) and *Le Français d'Europe* [The European Frenchman] (1944). The latter anticipates an important post-war theme, seeing the white race (whose superiority over other races was self-evident for Drieu) as divided into three geo-political spheres: Russian, American, and European; each with its own distinctive destiny. Consequentially, the Second World War was a fight to preserve the hegemony of Europe, the only source of cultural health.

If the pervasive presence of native literary and publicist fascism in France played a major role in the normalisation and legitimation of collaboration, its effect was mightily reinforced (in glaring contrast to the stubbornly uncooperative stance maintained by Denmark) through collaborationist Vichy's adoption of a para-fascist, but parallel, policy of 'national revolution' to bring the country into line with the new Europe.[58] As late as June 1944 Fernand de Brion, Vichy's Secretary of State, was still affirming that 'We will help Germany on every front and in every way to preserve the West, its enlightenment, its culture, its traditions.'[59] Algazy comments that hard-core French fascists who, having tried in vain to fully fascistise Vichy, went into hiding with the Allies' advance, or were among the favoured few who withdrew to temporary safety in the castle at Sigmaringen when Paris 'fell'. To be sure, these French fascists saw Italy and Germany as 'brothers in arms whose aspirations they shared: to combat the communist danger and the decadence of liberal democracies and create a fascist Europe'.[60]

Such pan-European illusions were actively fostered by the Nazis themselves. Clearly the bulk of the Third Reich statements relating to pan-Europeanism disseminated by the Nazis in the occupied territories can be dismissed as cynical propaganda calculated to encourage, if not the active co-operation, then the passive acquiescence of the new vassals. Neither Hitler nor many of his leading hierarchs such as Goebbels had the slightest intention to compromise absolute German hegemony through the creation of a European confederation, 'subsidiary', or otherwise.[61] The numerous international bodies and events organised in occupied Europe for various trades and professions (e.g. the European Youth Organisation) are thus to be seen as little more than organs of *Gleichschaltung* and would-be totalitarian social control. The same is to be said of the pan-European journals circulated by the Nazis in conquered Europe (e.g. *European Review*, *Young Europe*), even though their feigned Europeanism complemented the local collaborationist press which was at least partly in the hands of genuine 'believers' in the federal fascist New Order. Everything we know about Hitler suggests that when, for example, he told Degrelle in person that the victory of the Third Reich would bring about the 'brotherhood of the European peoples', it was yet another manifestation of his Machiavellian manipulation.[62] What is more significant in the context of post-war fascism is that in the unpublished exposition of his foreign policy, his 'Second Book' of 1928, the future *Führer* stressed the need for Europe to become a bulwark against the encroachment of the United States, already seen by him both as a superpower and the citadel of Jewish decadence, and hence as an ultimate foe. In this sense Hitler was a Europeanist, but in an ultra-integralist sense who made Napoleon's imperialism, and even Ancient Rome's, look positively liberal and federal in comparison.

Nevertheless, if mainstream Nazism never aspired towards an equivalent of the federal vision of Europe which Gravelli propagated with *Antieuropa*, many leading Nazi ideologues were convinced that their movement held the key to a crisis which was not just German but Europe-wide. It is intriguing to note, for example, that the Draft of a Comprehensive Program of National Socialism drawn up by Gregor Strasser, Joseph Goebbels, and others in the winter 1925–1926 (overruled by Hitler at the Party's Bamberg conference in 1926), the proposals under Foreign Policy included 'United States of Europe as a European

league of nations with a uniform system of measure and currency'.[63] Another
example is contained in Alfred Rosenberg's *Der völkische Staatsgedanke* which
appeared in 1925 just before *Mein Kampf*. In it he argues that the purely legalistic (i.e. non-racial) 'concept of the state' disseminated by the French Revolution
was 'symbolic of an age of decline' and an act of 'betrayal that all the peoples
of Europe had committed against its essence'. However, thanks to the *völkisch*
world-view, Germany had rediscovered the organic and ethnic concept of state
which would allow it to fight off the liberal, Bolshevik, and Jewish threat.
'But because this battle at the same time encompasses problems which plague
the whole of Europe today, and which Europe is trying in vain to solve, so
in the last analysis, National Socialism is bringing about a solution to these
problems for all of Europe too.' However, just how little genuine concession
Rosenberg is prepared to make to the autonomy of other nations in his theory
of internationalism is hinted at darkly in the next paragraph:

> Two deadly enemies can use the same words and yet seek opposite goals.
> If today the international banks and international conferences discuss the
> League of nations and the United States of Europe, the exact opposite is
> meant when, for example, National Socialism speaks of a drawing together
> of the extreme nationalists among the European peoples. [...] There is, of
> course, no purpose in expounding possible or utopian ideas at this point;
> only the core of the battle must be pointed out and the already-characterised
> symbol of the swastika, *which will someday be victorious in all of the European
> states* (My emphasis).[64]

How seriously Rosenberg took the Nazi mission to save Europe from itself is
shown by the way he returned to the theme on the eve of the war in *Die Neugeburt Europas als werdende Geschichte* [The Rebirth of Europe in Contemporary
History] (1939).

Herzstein's *When Nazi Dreams Come True* (1982) provides abundant evidence
that a number of high-ranking Nazis genuinely saw the regeneration of Germany as indissociable from the regeneration of Europe as a whole, and did
not see this simply in terms of the spread of the swastika. Building on the
pan-European themes embedded in the cultural theories of several thinkers
who influenced Nazi ideology (e.g. Nietzsche, Moeller van den Bruck, Spengler,
Haushofer), a host of Nazi ideologues great (Carl Schmitt, Frank, and Ley) and
small (e.g. Srbik, Freisler, Gross, von Müller, Halfeld, Scharp, Landes, Bauer, Pas-
tenaci, Ganzer, Six, Steding) projected their distinctive palingenetic fantasies
onto Europe as a whole, seeing the Nazis as the agents of order and harmony
to a continent plunged into decadence and chaos, as the harbingers of a post-
liberal order. The very titles of some of their works evoke the tone of this vein of
speculation: *Legal Thinking of Young Europe*, *The Reich as the European Organising*

Power, Europe's Civil Wars and the Present War of Unification, Europe: Tradition and Future, The Reich and the Sickness of European Civilisation.

Nor did Nazi Europeanism remain confined to nebulous cultural, historical, and legal theorising. Even as the war began to turn against Germany, Himmler started to take seriously the idea that international SS formations (originally to be made up of men of Germanic stock, though the criteria for qualifying as an 'Aryan' became increasingly lax as time wore on) could provide the new elite necessary to underpin the Greater German Reich. By 1945 the efforts of Himmler and his recruiting officer and main propagandist Gottlob Berger had resulted in the ranks of the SS being swelled by hundreds of thousands of 'volunteers' (some of them genuine believers), recruited from non-German stock within the occupied territories. The SS Newspaper, *Das Schwarze Korps* [The Black Corps] constantly harped on about the imminent prospect of Europe's palingenesis, as in the autumn of 1941 when it justified the Russian campaign in the following terms:

> Without a basis for existence, driven to self-laceration by hunger and anxiety, those of this Continent, the cradle of the Nordic race and of all culture, are doomed to vegetate, able neither to live nor to die, so long as they are cut off from the maternal life-source in the great regions of the East. Now the doors into this immensity have been thrown wide open. Where isolation was designed to choke us, streams of life will flow. *Europe has been reborn* (My emphasis).[65]

Another area of Nazi policy where pan-Europeanism was taken seriously was in the sphere of forward economic planning. Walther Funk, Economic Minister from 1940, was charged with working out the reconstruction of the post-war economy specifically within the framework of a New European Order and a new world economy, subjects he was still warming to as lecture topics as late as January 1945. The European Working Group which he set up under Schlotterer formulated plans for a European economic union under German leadership (something which has an uncannily contemporary ring to it until it is realised what *sort* of Germany a victorious Third Reich would have been). Naturally, some major industrial concerns such as IG Farben took an active interest in such schemes. A parallel initiative was the Society for European Economic Planning and Macroeconomics (*Grossraumwirtschaft*), the brainchild of Werner Daitz. His book *What the New Order in Europe Brings to the European Peoples* is a sustained eulogy of the Nazi-dominated EC which he believed would result from a Nazi victory.

A symptom of how well established this 'universal' strand of thinking became within Nazi orthodoxy was the formation in late 1942 of the 'Committee on the Restructuring of Europe' by the foreign minister Joachim von Ribbentrop. The committee brought together a number of academics and politicians who gave free reign to their palingenetic fantasies in the formulation of several rival scenarios for the immediate development of European and world history. Rarely can what T. S. Eliot calls the 'the shadow between the idea and the reality' been wider and darker than in the minds of the countless hollow men who supplied the Nazi subjugation of Europe and the mass transportations, murder, and enslavement it involved with Eurovisionary rationales.

Part Two: Eurofascism after 1945

The Europeanisation of post-war fascism

One of the salient properties of the palingenetic mentality is that it tends to be sealed off from empirical refutation of the predictions it infers from its 'vision of the world' or *Weltanschauung* – key terms for the radical right with which its thinkers set their ideologies apart from those 'contaminated' by the liberal and socialist rationality they so despise. Thus the collapse of Fascism from within and the destruction of Nazism from without, far from dispelling the sense that a new culture was being born out of the chaos of modern society, could merely intensify the sense of the decadence of the present stage of world history and the need for it to be regenerated. Generally, though, the objective conditions in which the populist radical right could hope to form the nucleus of mass movements have evaporated since 1945,[66] and the state organs of propaganda and social control which mass-produced ideology under Fascism and Nazism have been destroyed. The manufacture of radical right culture has nevertheless continued to prosper uninterrupted as a much reduced but highly diversified and prolific cottage industry throughout the Westernised world.

For this minute but highly voluble political constituency the Allied victory clearly called for new rationales of fascism, especially for those who were not content to adopt wholesale the programmes and organisational style of pre-1945 movements, believing them to be at the root of fascism's failure. Despite the extraordinary fragmentation of post-war fascism into countless grouplets and different rationales for continuing the struggle, there is an overwhelming consensus between them on one point: the palingenetic ultra-nationalism of classical fascism, in particular mainstream Fascism and Nazism, was too narrowly chauvinistic and sectarian, and hence not sufficiently universal and ecumenical, to enable it to make headway against its internationalist enemies, liberalism, and communism. Fascists the world over could see that the principle of strength through unity symbolised in the bound rods of the *fasces* had to be applied to their own movement on a supra-national basis, though not at the price of watering down the essential differences between the groupings which at a national level were their *raison d'être*.

An outstanding example of the unbroken continuity between interwar and post-war Eurofascism is to be found in the work of Julius Evola, one of the most prolific and influential ideologues of the radical right in Italy and increasingly important abroad, even if he is still largely neglected by Anglo-Saxon Fascist Studies.[67] His dubious claim to fame within the history of Mussolini's regime is to have written a *Synthesis of Racial Doctrine* (1941) which for a time satisfied the *Duce*'s need for a version of racism which was distinct from Nazi genetic theories. It also argued that Italians were even more perfect Aryan specimens than the Germans because of their judicious blend of physical with intellectual and spiritual qualities. However, the theory which informs Evola's book is anything but orthodox even within Fascism, for it draws on his alternative philosophy of history which was given its most exhaustive exposition in the 1934 work *Revolt against the Modern World*. A tour de force of radical right eclecticism on a par with *The Decline of the West* (of which it is the Italian counterpart), the book blends Spenglerian, Guénonian, and Hindu themes into a vision of contemporary history as the nadir of a protracted process of decline from the hierarchical, metaphysically based imperial order of 'the Tradition', a decline embodied in the rise of the undifferentiated masses, or the 'fifth estate' in modern times. The last pale reflection of this golden age had been the Holy Roman Empire under the Ghibellines when the Continent was still ruled by an aristocratic caste of 'warrior-priests'. After this 'European spring cut off in its first bloom, the process of decadence took over once more'[68] leading to the *kali yuga*, the 'black age' of modern civilisation. However, the emergence of fascism in Italy and Germany heralds the long-awaited sea-change in history: the rebirth of the true organic, hierarchical state being pioneered by the Third Reich and the Third Rome is ushering in the dawn of a new golden age.

The power of this European fascist vision was not lost on the notorious literary Nazi, Gottfried Benn, who reviewing the German edition of *The Revolt against the Modern Age* in 1935 praised it for its keen insight into European decadence and its accurate depiction of modern man as

> cut off from tradition and the spirit, and left wandering around the earth investigating, sniffing, touching, holiday-making: the universality of Thomas Cook revelled in as if it was something Faustian or Promethean. Evola sees in Fascism and Nazism, based as they are on the axioms of a religiously racial world view, the possibility of a new connection being forged between nations and the world of the Tradition.[69]

Evola's contribution to fascist Europeanism was not confined to *The Revolt*, however, but took the form of a number of articles written between 1932 and 1943. One was prompted by the Volta Congress held in Rome in 1932, Mussolini's major concession to the universalist ideas referred to earlier. It offers a Traditionalist critique of the various papers delivered the likes of the Italian Nationalist Francesco Coppola, Charles Petrie from England, the Iron Guard legionary Michele Manoilescu, the Nazi Alfred Rosenberg, and the German writer Stefan Zweig.[70] More revealing of Evola's own views are the war-time essays 'Elements of the European Idea' (1940), 'Towards a True European Law' (1941), and 'Perspective on the Future Order of the Nations' (1941). In them Evola argues that the new Europe must be based on a symbiosis of Roman and Germanic (Aryan) cultural components on the lines pioneered by the Holy Roman Empire and calls for the creation of a European Empire based on the emergence of a new hierarchy which would govern an alliance of those nations which had recovered the organic principle of the state.

The destruction of fascism in 1945 naturally dispelled Evola's optimism about any imminent end to the *kali yuga*. Nevertheless, he continued to work on the elaboration of his Traditionalist vision of a united Europe, the clearest formulation being in the essay 'On the Spiritual and Structural Premises of European Unity' (1951). His first major book to take stock of the new situation, significantly called *Man and the Ruins* (1954), is informed by the same 'imperial' palingenetic scheme which underlay *The Revolt* and his subsequent essays on Europe, except that the emergence of America and Russia not only as victors over Nazism but also as superpowers makes the pan-Europeanism of his message even more emphatic. He sees Europe torn apart by these two alien empires and disparages the materialism and small-mindedness of the Common Market. Instead the need is for a 'nation Europe', or rather an *Empire* of European nations ('a European *nation* implies the levelling and cancelling of all "rival" nations').[71] This Traditionalist Europe would transcend obsessions with the fatherland (*Patria*) while avoiding at all costs the type of homogenisation which would blur national differences. However, the moral disease which afflicts modern Europeans means that a sustained course of spiritual disintoxication would be necessary before Traditional values could be relaunched, and only a handful of natural aristocrats are left who are even aware of this need.[72] It is in this context that Evola wrote the reflections on the 'true Europe' which became a major theme of his post-war writings.

Evola's subsequent books and articles are diatribes against modern decadence and appeals to the Tradition, even if until his death in 1974 he became increasingly devoid of hopes for of a way out of decadent, inorganic modernity in the foreseeable future, preaching instead a stoic philosophy of *apolitìa*.[73] Nevertheless, a new generation of Italian fascists has grown up which has embraced Evola's overarching philosophy of history with its built-in Europeanist perspective while at the same time discarding the pessimism of the post-war books. Instead, they fit it into the rationale of terrorism and subversion.[74] It is significant that all his key essays on Europe were republished as recently as 1989 in the volume *Saggi di dottrina politica* [Essays in Political Doctrine].

While Julius Evola remains a shadowy figure within Fascist Studies, the case of Oswald Mosley is notorious. The destruction of the Third Reich, far from bringing him back into the fold of liberal politics which he had abandoned so clamorously in October 1932, led him to attribute the failure of interwar fascisms to their narrowly chauvinistic vision of their historical mission, and to become one of the most ardent exponents of 'the Europe of Nations' principle, which as we saw earlier, he had first adopted in 1937 in *The World Alternative*. The first major post-war exposition of the new creed was *The Alternative* published in 1947, which showed that he had now 'modernised' his pre-war vision with elements taken from Jungian and post-reductionist science. This work placed high on the agenda the concept of a 'Nation Europe' economically supported by a fully colonised Africa ('Eurafrica'), a theme which has an intriguing parallel with the foreign policy of the Salò Republic already referred to.[75] As Mosley saw it, the war had dealt a severe blow to European hegemony, and only the voluntary co-operation of European peoples could free the Continent (which for him included Britain) from the pernicious influence of the USSR and the United States. To further this idea he founded the Union Movement with a section to foster European contacts, and he continued to campaign for the 'European idea' in numerous speeches and articles for the party newspaper *Union* as well as for *The European*, offering fuller expositions of his position in *Europe: Faith and Plan* (1958) and *Mosley – Right or Wrong?* (1961). Indeed, the whole first section of the latter is devoted to the theme 'Europe a Nation' and he made this the central plank of his campaign in the run up to the 1959 General Election.

Meanwhile several French representatives of 'classical' fascism were treading a parallel path. Marcel Déat, former head of the RNP, having taken refuge in Italy, was within a year of the end of the war talking menacingly of an invisible army preparing to fight without quarter for the cause of international fascism.[76] The less well-known ideologue, René Binet, was typical of the many former small-fry philo-Nazis in France who soon after the war was over sought to have a major fascistising impact on post-war Europe. His starting point was that the Continent, now under the thumb directly or indirectly of America and Russia, could only be saved through a co-ordinated uprising of all the 'national workers' of Europe. He went on to embrace a racial theory of the superiority of what was now significantly termed 'Indo-European' rather than 'Aryan' civilisation and became a major force behind the *Nouvel Ordre Européen* [NOE] which flourished in the 1950s and 1960s. Another fascist of the older generation, Charles Luca, worked tirelessly to create a 'national Europe' which 'took account of national sovereignties'. He was the *éminence noire* behind the paramilitary formations the *Commandos de Saint-Ex* and *Citadelle*, as well of the *Mouvement National Citadelle*. He also played an active part in the *Mouvement social européen*, also known as the *Phalange française*, and *Mouvement populaire français*, all Europeanist formations of the ultra-right. The periodical *Fidélité* associated with these organisations became a major source of propaganda for what Binet called 'the liberation of the peoples of Europe and the creation of a Europe both national and armed'.[77] He blamed the Allies for having forced Germany and Italy into a war which prevented them from 'realising pan-European unity' based on 'the mystique of youth', but believed 'the hour of awakening' would still come.[78]

Another influential French propagandist of fascism's new Europeanism, however, was Maurice Bardèche. His *Qu'est-ce que le fascisme?* (1961) is a major statement of the principle that the belief in the need for national rebirth (or what I have called 'palingenetic ultra-nationalism') forms the common ground between the most diverse fascist movements and should be channelled into an international crusade against Bolshevism and Americanisation. In the early 1950s he was already talking of the need for Euro-MPs to co-ordinate the creation of a European empire with its own colonies (cf. Mosley's 'Eurafrica') declaring that 'the aim of this European revolution will be the spiritual regeneration of Man, society and the state'.[79] It should be noted *en passant* that the intransigent and murderous stand taken by the French 'liberal' state against *Algérie Française* to resist forced decolonisation was vociferously supported in such Eurofascist periodicals as *Jeune Europe*, *Europe-Afrique*, and *Junges Europa*.

If post-war German fascism lacked an ideologue of the originality and output of Evola or Bardèche, it certainly has not been short of pan-European initiatives. In 1949 former SS Officer Arthur Erhardt founded the monthly *Nation Europa* which, as its subtitle makes clear, sets out to be a forum for all those who cherished the dream of a post-liberal and anti-communist 'European New Order'. This periodical has become one of the pillars of ecumenical fascist publicism and propaganda, regularly reporting on radical right activities in other countries under the rubric 'Europe on the right', publishing lists of 'recommended texts' across the whole spectrum of fascist ideologies, and giving monthly reports 'von der Überfremdungsfront' (roughly 'from the front-line of the battle against being swamped by foreigners' – the term *'Überfremdung'* has become as important for contemporary German racism as *'Verjudung'* or 'semitisation' was for the Nazis). It has thus been well placed to accommodate the many new permutations of palingenetic ultra-nationalism which have arisen since 1945 and to embrace as comrades in arms the organisations and parties which covertly or overtly seek to promote them (e.g. in recent years Le Pen's *Front National*, Frey's *Deutsche Volksunion*, Schönhuber's *Republikaner*, and Terreblanche's *Afrikaner Weerstandsbeweging*). It has also been at pains to capitalise on all conflicts between the European and non-European cultures (e.g. in Algeria and South Africa).

A parallel initiative of the immediate post-war period was the *Deutsches Kulturwerk Europäischen Geistes* [The German Cultural Project for the European Spirit], set up in 1950 to establish links to like-minded organisations in Europe, the United States, South Africa, and Argentina. It set the pattern for numerous neo-Nazi organisations great and small, ephemeral or well established, whose commitment to the 'Europe of nationalities' concept is reflected in their titles (e.g. *Aktionsfront Nationales Europa, Europäische Volksbewegung, European Freedom Movement, European National Union, Neues Nationales Europa, Kampfbund für Europa, Germania International,* and *Stahlhelmkampfbund für Europa*).[80]

The exponents of the Europeanisation of Nazism have not been confined to Germany, however. As early as 1946 *Combattant européen* and *Le Drapeau noir* were already circulating clandestinely in France, both portraying the international brigades of the Waffen SS as the heroic nucleus of the 'new Europe'. In August 1946 *Drapeau noir* organised a national conference of the Black Front which set about forging links with Nazi-oriented fascists abroad with a view to countering the 'pernicious' influence of the Soviet Union and the United States and to creating a fascist International.[81] The year 1951 saw the formation in Zurich under the aegis of Bardèche and the Swiss fascist Armadauz of the neo-Nazi New European Order of the neo-Nazi NOE which in all held some ten congresses in Paris, Hanover, Lausanne, Milan, Barcelona and Lyon. One of its branches was the *Mouvement Social Belge* which organised a Eurofascist congress in Brussels in 1954. Its organ, *L'Europe Réelle*, became NOE's major publication, and in 1962 actively campaigned for a New European Order. NOE became defunct in the early 1980s, but not before it had established links between numerous fascist groups in Europe and abroad, and formulated a racially based ecological vision.

In 1962 another internationalist neo-Nazi group was formed, the World Union of National Socialists (WUNS), led for a time by Colin Jordan and Françoise Dior. Though the group's aspirations were global, Europeanism was an important aspect of their strategy for changing history, as shown by the 1963 creation of the West European Federation [FOE] under its aegis. This led to the founding of the European Movement, which held congresses in 1985 and 1987. Central to the world-view of both WUNS and FOE is the belief (already promoted by Heinrich Himmler and the SS-journal *Das Schwarze Korps* [The Black Corps] before the end of the war) that the international Waffen SS constituted the nucleus a new European elite. One of the 13 points constituting FOE's charter affirms a principle dear to the bulk of post-war fascists: 'The Europe which we national socialists intend to create will be neither German nor French, any more than it will be English or Italian. It will be *one and diverse*, one in its political unity, diverse in its national cultures.'[82]

No less significant as a source of ecumenical neo-Nazi propaganda is CEDADE, *Circulo Español de Amigos de Europa* [The Spanish Circle of Friends of Europe]. This organisation for 'friends of Europe' was set up in 1965 by fugitives of the regimes of Mussolini, Hitler, and Franco, and has sister organisations in France, Ecuador, Argentina, and Portugal. More important is the network of affiliations it has built up with fascist groups all over the world, notably NOE (till the 1980s), the *Faisceaux Nationalistes Européens* [The Fasci of European Nationalists] based in France, and the Portuguese *Ordem Nova* [New Order]. The latter runs both a women's and youth organisation in Spain, and publishes numerous periodicals, one of them *Joven Europa* [Young Europe]. Neo-Nazi youth is also catered for by the German *Wiking Jugend* [Viking Youth] which has branches in Belgium, France, Norway, the Netherlands, Spain, Switzerland, as well as in Australia, New Zealand, and South Africa.

But in the aftermath of the Second World War neo-Nazism was far from enjoying a monopoly as the animating force behind international fascism. As early as 1946, the *Movimento Sociale Italiano* [Italian Social Movement], Italy's legally constituted neo-Fascist party – led by Giorgio Almirante, former head of propaganda in the Salò Republic – organised a European Study Committee and published a broadsheet *Europa Unita* [United Europe]. In this way, contacts came to be forged between MSI delegates and Nazis, Rexists, Falangists, followers of Anton Mussert and Vidkun Quisling, and members of the National Renaissance Party in the States. A few years hence, in May 1951, 60 delegates from every West-European country (including such prominent internationalists as Oswald Mosley, René Binet, Maurice Bardèche, and the Swede Pier Engdahl) met in Malmö to set up a European National Congress. Vitally, the result was a ten-point programme, entitled 'The Malmö Declaration', for collaboration between national fascisms and the formation of the European Social Movement. More-over, a neo-Nazi splinter group from this conference set up the New European Order a few months later. Then, in a congress held in Paris in 1953, an attempt was made to fuse the two factions of Fascist International in a new body, the European People's Movement, committed to saving 'Christian Civilisation' from the ravages of Judaism, Communism, and Freemasonry. With the backing of the Malmö committee, Engdahl formed his own 'European New Order' in 1954, which gave birth to an international youth movement, the Young European Legion. Given his long-standing Europeanist convictions, it is not surprising that Mosley was also keen to lead a Eurofascist party. At another international congress, this time held in Venice in 1962, he was co-founder of the National Party of Europe – whose logo was adopted from the Union Movement, a flash of lightning in a circle. Mosley also helped draft a European Protocol leading to 'the Venice Declaration', whose by now familiar theme was that Europe should become a third power to combat the encroachment of Russia and America. Not for the first time, the English *Duce* thought his time had come.

Perhaps because of its size, Belgium's fascists have been prominent instigators of pan-Europeanism after 1945, in tandem with the country's central role in the EU. The Congo crisis was as important a catalyst to the Belgian New Europe myth as the Algerian War was to the French one, and gave birth to the group *Jeune Europe*, which folded in 1968 after leaving a number of heirs, notably *Les Groupes Révolution Europe* [Groups for European Revolution], *Jeune Garde d'Occident* [The Young Guardians of the West], and the *Parti Européen* [The European Party]. The Flemish counterpart to such groupings, the Flemish Militants Order (VMO or Odal Group, now subsumed within the *Vlaamsblok* or Flemish Bloc) has been playing a major role in co-ordinating links with racist fascist groups in Europe. As for its media output, in addition to *Europe Réelle*, and especially influential magazine to spread the ecumenical gospel is *Nouvel Europe Magazine* [Magazine of the New Europe] launched in 1944, even before the Nazi defeat. A Flemish equivalent to *Jeune Europe* is *Were Di* [Protect Yourself], which in magazines such as *Dietsland-Europa* and *Rebel*, seeks to promote the creation of a greater Flanders, or 'Dietsland', within a reborn Europe. What confirms Belgium's pivotal role in the diffusion of Eurofascism is the yearly international rally, held at Dijksmuide, hosted by the VMO. Less well publicised are the activities of former government minister Baron Benoit de Bonvoisin, who for a time not only financed the NEM groups and the closely associated *Front de la jeunesse* [Youth Front], but held a meeting of European fascists in his castle in 1976 and set up a European Union of Entrepreneurs in the early 1980s.[83]

Given the marked pan-Europeanism of its most prominent fascists both before and after the war, it is also not surprising to find a profusion of universal radical right organisations in France. Those associated with Bardèche, Binet, and Luca were discussed above, and in 1951 the sons of the Vichy collaborator Joseph Darnand founded *Jeune Nation* [Young Nation] which, like its successor *Europe-Action*, had strong ecumenical leanings. The most important of these to date is *Faisceaux Nationalistes Européens* [FNE], which, as we saw, has been associated with the Europeanist CEDADE and NOE. FNE is a reformation of the *Fédération d'Action Nationaliste Européenne* [Federation of Nationalist European Action] banned in 1980. It is a small but potent neo-Nazi group responsible for anti-Semitic outrages and active collaboration with a wide range of neo-Nazi groupings abroad. Its organ is *Notre Europe* [Our Europe]. Smaller, likeminded groups or publishing houses with titles indicating a commitment to right-wing Europeanism have included *Devenir Européen, Occident, Mouvement de Libération de l'Europe, Europe Jeunesse, Parti Ouvrier Européen, Europe 2000, Europe Unie, Revue Internationale des Problèmes de Nationalisme*, and *Europe, Notre Patrie*. The ethos of all these publications is perhaps best summed up by a poem (or piece of doggerel) written by Jean Buzas of the French chapel of WUNS:[84]

Frères Nationaux- Socialistes, unissons- nous, Afin de bâtir l'Europe, Patrie de notre Devenir. Il faut nous grouper partout En vue de luttes à venir.	[National Socialist Brothers, let us unite To build Europe, Fatherland of our destiny. We must group everywhere To prepare for struggles to come.
Nous voulons construire un 'Ordre Nouveau' Où règnera la Justice Sociale. Mais, avant, déblayons les ruines Qu'a entassés la 'démocratie' bestiale.	We want to construct a 'New Order' Where Social Justice will reign But, before we do, let us sweep away the ruins Which bestial 'democracy' has piled up.
Alors triomphera notre Révolution Nationale et Sociale, pour un avenir merveilleux! En vue de ce But, avec résolution Pourchassons les trâitres et les politiciens véreux. Il faut comprendre, ô Camerade! Que pour unifier l'Europe-Nation Il ne suffit pas de monter sur les barricades Mais il convient avant tout avoir FOI en notre Mission.	Then our Revolution will triumph, A National and Social one leading to a marvellous future! With this goal in mind, and with resolution, Let us chase out traitors and corrupt politicians. O comrade, you must understand That to unite the Nation Europe It is not enough to mount the barricades, But above all we must have FAITH in our mission.]

In his famous work, *Three Faces of Fascism*, Ernst Nolte maintained that the age of fascism ended in 1945,[85] but, clearly, reports of its death have been greatly exaggerated. Though highly debilitated as a party-political force and extinct as a credible revolutionary challenge to state power, European fascism had, by the early 1980s, continued to maintain its vitality in a myriad of movements and periodicals, some of them ephemeral and minute, others tenacious and sizable. Internecine power-struggles and ideological divides – many of these microcosms of the pre-war split between Nazi biological and Fascist cultural nationalism – have hampered any initiatives for international collaboration, while structural conditions have condemned fascism, as a whole, to marginality. Yet particularly notable are the innovations setting post-war fascism apart from 'classical fascism', the most important of which is the projection of the myth of rebirth onto Europe as a whole rather than just the nation. As a result, the universalist vision of fascism's historical mission has now moved very much into the mainstream.

Another symptom of fascism's vitality is the diffusion of a new rationale for fascism since the late 1960s, which provides radical right visions of the new Europe with a highly sophisticated ideological foundation to retain structural distinction: the *Nouvelle Droite*.

The Europeanism of the New Right

The *Nouvelle Droite* (for which we will use the term 'European New Right' or ENR, shorn of the neo-liberal connotations it has acquired in Britain and America) is inseparable from the figure of Alain de Benoist, very much a child of post-war Europe (he was born in 1943). In 1968, year of the left-inspired Paris 'Events', De Benoist helped found a major think-tank for the radical right, the *Groupement de Recherche et d'Études pour la Civilisation Européenne* (which by no coincidence forms the acronym GRECE). Displaying an eclectic mind and the yearning for an overarching 'vision of the world' so typical of right-wing auto-didacts (cf. Spengler, Rosenberg and Evola), De Benoist has produced a number of key books over the years, as well as numerous articles for the reviews *Nouvelle École*, *Valeurs Actuelles*, *Le Spectacle du Monde*, and *Élements*. His heroes range from Friedrich Nietzsche and Arthur Moeller van den Bruck, the foremost thinker of the proto-Nazi 'Conservative Revolution' in Germany (whose main historian, Armin Mohler, is an important contributor to the ENR), to those without fascist pedigree, like Pierre Teilhard de Chardin, Jean Piaget, and Karl Popper.

De Benoist's voluminous writings converge on a constellation of interrelated propositions:

(i) for scientifically demonstrable reasons, humanity can only remain healthy as long as the dynamic principle of cultural diversity is safeguarded and the distinctive roots of each human group are retained;

(ii) for concrete historical reasons, Europe is made up of distinctive national cultures (*ethnies*) whose bedrock of community is their roots in a common Indo-European tradition;

(iii) this communal heritage is under threat from a number of ideologies tending to promote egalitarianism, homogenisation, materialism, cosmopolitanism, and the ideal of an undifferentiated 'One World';

(iv) the two main sources of the diffusion of such pernicious, culture-cidal forces are the liberal capitalism and democracy emanating from American economic power, lifestyles, and entertainment, and the evangelistic brand of communist materialism once embodied in Soviet Russia;

 (v) the presence of immigrants (and by implication Jews) in Europe is inimical to cultural health, and assert their cultural identity within their own nations;

(vi) by establishing the cultural hegemony of heroic (and intrinsically anti-democratic and anti-Marxist) ideas native to Indo-Europeans it is still possible to create the preconditions for a socio-political reversal of decadence, and for European history to be 'regenerated'.

These are the organising principles behind the vast compilation of articles which de Benoist published in his *Vu de Droite* [Seen from the Right] (1977), earning him the coveted Academy Française prize for literature a year later. With the specious facticity so typical of New Right 'science', this text finds that the '450 million human beings in Europe [...] are heirs of the same culture, they have a common origin. Their ancestors are called Indo-Europeans'.[86] This forms the preamble to De Benoist's affirmation that

> I define myself first and foremost as a European, as one who is at home in Europe. Maybe you could even say that the will to see Europe come into her own again, to be an example to the world, to retrieve a communal identity and existence, is the fixed point of my entire life.[87]

For an exposition of his special brand of Europeanism, however, the articles collected in *Les Idées à l'endroit* [Ideas in the right place] (1980) are even more illuminating. In one of the articles written in the wake of the Vietnam War, de Benoist asserts that 'between American Vietnam and Communist Vietnam there isn't much to choose. My votes are for a Vietnamese Vietnam, as for an Algerian Algeria, a French France and a European Europe'.[88] In another article, entitled 'Against the Superpowers', he expands this point:

> Between the materialism of the West and the materialism of the East, between an America of vulgarity, egalitarianism and the mercantile spirit and a Russia of the Gulag, of oppression, of prisons and concentration camps, there is now a void. This void is Europe. A Europe under occupation: in the East by barbarianism, in the West by decadence. The worst thing that can be done is to end up thinking that one occupation is, in the last resort, *preferable* to the

other. As far as I'm concerned I am inclined neither to dress up as a Cossack nor in Levis. Caught between Moscow which kills bodies and Washington which kills souls I am waiting for Europe *to return to its being*.[89]

In the following piece, called 'The Rise of Europe', the thesis is similar: the only way out of the spiritual crisis which has overtaken Europe is for a higher new consciousness to be born. Citing Carl Gustav Jung and Friedrich Nietzsche he rejects a rectilinear for a spherical image of time, suggesting that history could take an entirely new direction at any moment. A Europe-wide 'gnostic revolution' could lead to the 'regeneration of history' and the salvation of the West. The time is ripe for such a transformation, for the time has come where 'those who have stayed awake during the long night encounter those who appear in the new dawn'.[90]

The mythopoeia of the ENR has been a major factor in the overhaul of intellectual fascism since the 1970s. By concentrating on the primacy of 'cultural' over 'political hegemony' (perversely enough, the New Right draws upon the theories of the Italian Marxist Antonio Gramsci), and by stressing a pan-European philosophy of contemporary history, this current of palingenetic ultra-nationalism enables modern fascists to dissociate themselves from the narrower nationalisms of the interwar movements. Their common denominator is that they are all in one way or another linked to anti-reductionism, anti-materialism, and anti-egalitarianism, but free of links with Fascism or Nazism in the public mind. Examples are Carl Jung, Arthur Koestler, Konrad Lorenz, Hans Eysenck, Mircea Eliade, the last three of whom are directly linked to GRECE publications (Eliade was in fact an apologist for the Rumanian Iron Guard before the war, and before becoming Professor of Comparative Religion in the United States). Nevertheless, the fascist tendency of this New Right is shown not only in the overt rehabilitation of Aryan racial fantasies through the diffusion of 'Indo-Europeanism', but in the respectability given to arguments concentrating on the threat posed by 'alien' world views, and hence their human carriers, to European culture. Fascist Newspeak allows new ideological concerns such as ecology, Aids, and the Third World to be easily accommodated, as well as the more up-market versions of historical revisionism (i.e. the international pseudo-academic industry bent on denying the Holocaust and euphemising Nazism).

Illuminating in this respect is the report on a meeting of the Thule Seminar, held in West Germany in the late 1980s under the auspices of Pyramid Media. The predominantly yuppie participants heard a lecture on the civil war being fought out by the combined forces of excellence and diversity against an alliance of egalitarianism, materialism, cosmopolitanism, and mediocrity. The speaker, Pierre Krebs, French-born but a major contributor to the German New Right, reassured his audience (which included some neo-Nazis notables) that

We intend to take over the laboratories of thinking. Our aim is to combat egalitarian ethics and socio-economics with a world-view which stresses differentiation. In other words a culture, an ethical and socio-economic vision which respects the right to be different. We are new. We are committed to the homeland of the Indo-Europeans, to Athens and not to Jerusalem.[91]

Krebs' earliest contribution to the Europeanism of the New Right was a small volume, entitled *Die europäische Wiedergeburt* (1982) [The European Rebirth]. There he quotes freely from Nietzsche, Spengler, Hölderlin, and particularly from Heidegger who, before the war, had developed his 'ontological' interpretation of Europe as the custodians of genuine Being, caught between the two materialistic superpowers of the United States and Russia. It was this theory which predisposed him to lend his weight to the NSDAP for over a year as Rector of Freiburg University during the co-ordination of the German State with the Third Reich. Heidegger's argument has naturally exercised a profound fascination on the New Right. Krebs portrays Europe as a unique cultural entity growing out of a heroic Indo-European tradition, one now threatened by the forces of egalitarianism and multi-culturalism that are destroying its organic roots. Europe is faced by decadence and decay, but if it can reconnect with its roots, there is still time for it to recapture its identity and regenerate itself. In a typically palingenetic conclusion he summons his readers to enlist themselves in the cultural war for the rebirth of Europe:

> Ortega y Gasset announced that the moment has arrived for Europe to focus on its national idea. For today it is less utopian to think and believe in this way than in the 11th century when the unity of Spain and France were prophesied. We call upon Europe to achieve self-determination and for a comprehensive awareness of our selves and of the freedom which we must conquer. The 21st century will be European. For now our will is our only home, for Europe is about to be reborn.[92]

In 1988, Krebs was also the editor of *Mut zur Identität. Alternativen zum Prinzip der Gleichheit* [The Courage to Have an Identity: Alternatives to the Principle of Equality], one of the most influential works of New Right cultural criticism written in German to date. Apart from contributions by Krebs, it contains essays by Alain de Benoist, Guillaume Faye, and Jean Haudry of the French New Right, alongside essays by a 'cultural philosopher', a banker, an anthropologist (all German), and a former general of the Austrian army and prisoner of war. It also contains a vast bibliography of texts which either contribute to the analysis of contemporary decadence or foster 'healthy' forms of knowledge necessary for it to be overcome. Preaching a secular heroism which travesties the existentialist (and anti-nationalist) nominalism of Nietzsche as much as it perpetuates that of

Heidegger, the essays explore various aspects of Europe's present decline brought about by the principles of Judeo-Christianity, equality and multi-culturalism. In different ways, all of the texts in Krebs' volume stress a collective return to the organic roots of Europe, in order the continent to save itself from 'genocide'. This perverse use of language is not fortuitous: we are assured in the section of *The Courage to Have an Identity* entitled 'the challenge of the multi-racial society' that Anne Frank's diary was a forgery and that evidence for the Holocaust is dubious and, moreover, it is the proponents of the multi-cultural society who are racists and responsible for counter-attacks by those who value the distinctive racial identity of *all*.[93]

First, an overtly palingenetic philosophy of history informs the whole work, as when Guillaume Faye invokes 'the Faustian spirit of the old European civilisation, which bears the youthful stamp of the Phoenix', and calls for 'moribund religions' to be replaced by a 'second paganism'. The 'true war of values' is between:

> the protagonists of the *decline* of mankind (apostles of the humanitarian, egalitarian, Soviet-American global state, which will be ruled by the bourgeois materialism of the cult of economics and the dissolution of any sense of belonging) and the defenders of identity, rootedness, and the diversity of species which is ultimately the only guarantee for the species Homo. By bearing witness to this European identity and defending the people [*Volk*] we belong to, we will contribute to the preservation of *homo sapiens sapiens* [sic] and to the only higher values which he can assert and impose on the indifferent, blind flow of life.[94]

It is passages such as this which bring out the key role that myth plays in New Right thought: they see it as the deliberate imposition of human will and spirit upon an intrinsically meaningless world.

Yet GRECE's influence is not confined to Germany. Sister publications to *Élements* are published in Italy, Luxemburg, Belgium, and Switzerland, while the English contribution to 'Grecian' fascism is the periodical *The Scorpion*. This magazine, the brain-child of former National Front activist Michael Walker, regularly publishes articles by *Nouvelle Droite* thinkers. An example is Issue 10, 1986, which contains two articles dedicated to an exposition of De Benoist's ideas, addressed to 'a post-war generation unresigned to Europe's exit from history'. For good measure, the magazine preaches Evolian Traditionalism, even though Alain de Benoist had explicitly rejected Evola's Traditionalist ideas on 'Nietzschean' grounds in *Les Idées à l'endroit*.[95] Predictably then, Europeanism is one of the periodical's recurrent themes, forming the sub-text of its highly diverse pieces on cultural history, nationalism, and political theory. On occasion it becomes explicit, however, as in an article which appeared in Issue 2 (1982), dedicated to the theme 'For a European Renaissance'. Even more significantly, in October 1985, the *Scorpion* hosted an international conference in London on the topic 'A Third Way for Europe', reported on at length in Issue 9, 1986 entitled 'When Europe Awakes'. The conference followed on from one held earlier in the year by the *Cercle Proudhon* on 'Europe: The Right to an Identity' (naturally, Krebs was one of the delegates), and another in Paris at which Guillaume Faye, one of Krebs' collaborators, gave an impassioned account from his recently published work *Nouveau discours à la Nation Européenne* [New Address to the European Nation]. The London congress was attended by 50 participants, representing France, Ireland, Luxemburg, Belgium, Italy, and Switzerland.

A phrase from Michael Walker's introduction sums up neatly the New Right vision of a Europe, based not on the abolition of nationalism, but its simultaneous *intensification* and *subsumption* within a continental federation: 'We do not need a Europe under one flag – we need a Europe of a thousand flags of free communities from the Atlantic to the Urals'. The centrality of palingenetic myth to the fascist 'philosophy of history' is again highlighted in the choice of these lines from J. R. R. Tolkien to set the tone of the conference:

> From the ashes a fire shall be woken
> A light from the shadows shall spring
> Renewed shall be blade that was broken
> The crownless again shall be king.

In Italy, fascists have, in Julius Evola, a central figure in this pan-European fantasy. This has not deterred some young radical right intellectuals in Italy from espousing De Benoist's ideas to form a parallel New Right, the *Nuova Destra*, with its own publications, notably *Elementi*. Others have spawned a highly original strand of palingenetic myth by blending Evolian and New Right themes into a celebration of fantasy literature, especially that of Tolkien, and of ancient legends (e.g. the quest for the Holy Grail) as the source of a new 'vision of the world' pointing beyond contemporary materialism and decadence. For both currents of thinking, this 'decadence' is usually seen as a threat to European civilisation as a whole, not just Italy.[96] It is important to reassert at this point that there are some neo-fascists who in no uncertain terms still reject any sort Europeanist vision. Here is a particularly vitriolic passage from the pen of the Evolian Franco Freda, one which echoes many of the themes of Asvero Gravelli's *Antieuropa*:

> At first we thought that Europe really was a valid myth, and represented an *idée-force*. Even neo-fascists hardly out of school harp on about 'Europe-Fascism-Revolution' without checking to see if a homogeneous European civilisation really exists. We will have nothing to do with Europe of the

Enlightenment tradition [...] We have no truck with a democratic, Jacobin Europe. We have nothing in common with the Europe of the market-place, the Europe of plutocratic colonialism. With Jewish or Judaised Europe we have only scores to settle [...] Europe is an old whore who has plied her trade in every conceivable brothel and contracted every kind of ideological infection – from those of the medieval city-states to those of nationalist monarchies against the Holy Roman Empire; from Enlightenment humanism to Jacobinism, to free-masonry, to Judaism, to socialism, to liberalism, to Marxism. A whore whose belly conceived and gave birth to the bourgeois revolution and the proletarian revolt, whose soul is enslaved by the violence of merchants and the rebellion of the slaves. And, given all this, we are supposed to redeem her![97]

Yet it is significant that even when Freda rejects Eurofascism it is not for a narrow Italian chauvinism, but for an *international* revolt against 'The Modern World' in the spirit of Evolian Traditionalism. Nevertheless, the Europeanist version of palingenetic ultra-nationalism is more typical of contemporary Italian fascism: after all, it was Freda's guru himself, Julius Evola, who preached the vision of a European Empire. An outstanding example of the centrality of the 'Europe of Nations' concept in contemporary Italian fascist thought is the 1981 volume *Drieu la Rochelle: Il Mito dell'Europa* [Drieu la Rochelle: The Myth of Europe], containing essays by three intellectuals, Adriano Romualdi, Guido Giannettini, and Mario Prisco. In his preface, Romualdi dwells on the decadence of liberal-democratic Europe, and evokes Drieu's prophetic vision of the alternative. In the following passage, he touches on many of the favourite themes of contemporary Eurofascism (note the glowing account of the international SS):

European fascists for too long lingered on sterile nationalistic positions before being forced in the direction of a continental revolution by the inexorable initiative of Adolf Hitler. It was this total revolutionary initiative which fused into a single front the dispersed forces of the various fascisms. The Europe of Drieu stretches from Brest to Elbruz, from Narvik to Crete, resolved to defend its revolution against Yankee capitalism and Asiatic Bolshevism. It is this Europe that the French and Scandinavian volunteers rushed to defend. It is the Europe of the Danish, Dutch and Belgian SS who preferred annihilation to surrender in the tragic trap of Korsun [...] From a higher historical point of view, the sacrifice of a few hundred thousand of international SS fighters is more significant than the millions who fell in the name of the old national conceptions. The former bore witness for the old fatherlands, while the latter sacrificed themselves for the new Aryan fatherland of European fascism. Their witness is irrefutable. If there is to be a new fascism it will not be of the old school but that of a Drieu or an Evola, the precursors'.[98]

Romualdi goes on to baldly assert that there can be no true Europe without fascism: 'Europe will rise again as a fascist power or else it will slowly be extinguished in comfort and democracy till, in the inexorable hour of history's final judgement, it will be swept away by the global revolt of coloured races led by a fanatical, implacable China'. He quotes with relish Drieu's apocalyptic pronouncement *'D'abord les films américains et après la fin du monde'* [If we start getting American films, then its the end].[99]

It should be noted that in its quest for cultural hegemony, Eurofascism has been keen to take advantage of the opportunities offered by both liberal party politics and the EU itself, even though the vision of democracy and Europe they represent is anathema. Though generally failing to emulate Italy's MSI in being able to count on a stable political constituency, fascist parties have surfaced in every liberal democracy in Europe. Moreover, Le Pen's extreme right-wing *Front National* – which stops just short of calling for the overthrow of France's liberal institutions, but whose ideology and leading activists are demonstrably indebted to fascism – has played a major role in shifting the centre of gravity in French politics to the right, making xenophobia and the call for *apartheid* respectable in the bid to stem the 'Islamicisation' of France.

When representatives from such parties have been elected to Strasbourg they clearly recognised the common ground between them. In 1984 the Group of the European Right was formed of 17 MPs (ten from the *Front National*, five from the MSI, one from the Greek EPEN, and one from the Official Ulster Union). Le Pen spoke for all of them in an interview given to *Nation Europa* in the run-up to the European elections,[100] published under the title 'For a Europe of Europeans'. Asked what dangers he saw posed by the enlarged market of 1992 for France and other Europeans, he answered that 'The danger lies in international utopianism, in the One World Utopia, or Oneworlders who want to destroy peoples. The need for national boundaries is not removed by the European Union. Individual peoples must retain them so as to preserve their identity, freedom and independence'. Significantly, he identified as the twin dangers to Europe the United States and *Japan*. Even before the dramatic events of the autumn of 1989 and the summer of 1991, Le Pen apparently considered the Soviet Union too debilitated by internal problems to be worth mentioning.

The call for a 'return to history' in Eastern Europe

Though Western Europe may be seen as the historical heartland of fascist thought, since the collapse of the USSR ultra-nationalist milieux have lost no time in propagating illiberal visions of how their 'liberated' nations can be integrated into the non-communist world. It has become a cliché to observe that unresolved the ethnic hatreds and nationalist aspirations which pullulated in Eastern Europe before the war were deep-frozen by state communism after 1945, only to be microwaved back into new movements in the 1980s. What has attracted less comment is the way acute politico-economic, and hence socio-psychological uncertainties, that accompanied the collapse of the old order have proved a powerful seed-bed for elaborate ultra-right ideologies as well. This has led not only to the fragmentary revival of fascism, but a more pervasive diffusion of a peculiar vision of contemporary European history rooted in myths of national regeneration giving privileged place to the new democracies within Western civilisation. In particular, the Soviet suppression of both Christian and liberal-capitalist values, combined with the enforced isolation of the Eastern bloc from the 'decadent' West, has meant that emancipation from communism has tended to become identified – within broad swathes of chauvinists of an intellectual caste of mind – with the rebirth of Christianity. This, in turn, is to form the precondition for a cultural and national renaissance after nearly half a century of subjugation by a communist empire condemned both for its atheism and its hostility to the national identity of non-Russians.

At the heart of this ultra-right vision is, once again, the palingenetic myth of combating decadence. In terms all too familiar, ever since the days of Maurras' *Action Française* and the variegated *völkisch* movement before 1914, this decadence is alleged to be embodied in the pluralism, secularism, and individualism of liberalism itself. As a result, in the words of Tomasz Wolek, member of Poland's (moderate) Forum for Democratic Right, democracy itself comes to be seen by extremists 'as a great evil, a kind of moral putrefaction which made its way to us from the West'.[101] It is natural for ultra-nationalists with this mindset to identify the nation with an allegedly pure ethnic community, and hence to see the presence of racial minorities, Jews, Travellers, and 'guest-workers' from Vietnam, Turkey, and Cuba as the bacilli of cultural contamination. One symptom of the prevalence of this attitude has been the resurgence of anti-Semitic, anti-Polish feelings and out-and-out neo-Nazism in the former DDR, feelings which have also become more vociferous in western Germany. Racist sentiments were also openly expressed by Czechoslovakia's Republican Party, the Association for the Republic, founded in December 1989. Another group springing up in the former Czechoslovakia, The New Right Wing, pressed for the de-Bolshevisation of the country in an ultra-nationalist key, while the separatist claims of the Slovak extremists helping force the division of the country in January 1993 resuscitated memories of the Slovak puppet-state installed by the Nazis under the Hlinka Guard.

Meanwhile, Ferenc Szálasi's Arrow Cross has been revived in Hungary, again pursuing irredentist claims on Transylvania; and the Iron Guard has been brought back from the dead in Rumania and joined by a new ultra-right group, *Rumania Mare* [Greater Rumania], again. Even in the Baltic states there are

Latvians, Lithuanians, and Estonians whose fervour for their people and culture flows down illiberal channels. It is thus as part of a much wider historical process that, in the former Yugoslavia, Ustasha paramilitarism was revived in Croatia while Serbian ultra-nationalists also resuscitated old separatist passions. This forced Muslims to retrench into their own religious identity with the result that combatants on all sides of the Yugoslav Wars were impervious to appeals to tolerance or reason.

What gives such developments a bearing on 'Europoiea' is the claim by ideologues of movements asserting a resurgent national identity that authoritarian Soviet rule paradoxically made cultural resistance a vital necessity. This, they claim, succeeded in keeping the heritage of European culture more intact than was ever possible under the regime of post-war materialism and consumerism in the West. As a result it is they, not Western democrats, who are the 'real Europeans'. The phrase which sums up such aspirations is 'the return to Europe', by which is meant not merely re-entering the mainstream of liberal history à la Fukuyama, but forming the vanguard of Europe's spiritual salvation. It is when the ultra-right idea of what they mean by 'Europe' is scrutinised that close affinities emerge with the Eurofascist themes examined here. One scholar who has monitored the rapidly evolving situation in the former East bloc countries is the polyglot Israeli scholar Raphael Vago. His conclusion is that, in the minds of their ideologues, Europe becomes an 'almost mystic formula' serving as the rationale for a total repudiation of the Western humanist liberal tradition. In Romania, for example, the periodical *Europa* is published by a *Europa Nova* publishing trust, headed by Iosif Constantin Dragan – former member of the Iron Guard and advocate of the ultra-chauvinist aspects of the Ceaçescu regime. He preaches the need for the rebirth of the Rumanian people, not as citizens of a democracy but as members of an organic national community. A paper for expatriate Rumanians, *Cuvantul Romanesc* [the Romanian Voice], published in Canada, echoes *Europa*'s curiously European brand of anti-Semitism and anti-Hungarianism in the claim that 'the more authentic a Romanian is, the more he is European'. The same Europa issue also approvingly quoted the maxim of the nineteenth-century nationalist poet, Mihai Eminescu, that Romanians 'can only be free in our political thought and actions, only on condition that we do not confuse our culture and history with that of others'.[102]

Such sentiments are characteristic of the whole Eastern European New Right. Central to its logic is the notion that the end of Soviet rule has initiated a process of reattachment to Europe after years of being 'almost swallowed by Eurasia'. The journey 'from Asia to Europe' is thus conceived in terms keying into the same myths of cultural regeneration, and even ethnic purification, which were the driving force of interwar fascism. In the process, liberal ideas of pluralism, tolerance, and the multi-racial nation-state based on the principle of shared citizenship, all simply disappear from the agenda. To cite one example from Vago's paper:

> The Slovak extreme right, riding high on a wave of anti-Czech, anti-Hungarian and anti-Semitic feeling (although there are almost no Jews left in Slovakia), seeks its return to Europe by countering potential or actual threats against the integrity of Slovakia. Of course, the Slovak right argues, Slovakia is an integral and loyal part of the West, and its Catholic heritage is a living proof of this, but the existence of the Hungarian minority on Slovak soil is a perpetual threat to the territorial integrity of Slovakia.[103]

Meanwhile, the Greater Romania movement led by Corneliu Vadim Tudor, another chauvinist survivor of the Ceauçescu regime, was from the early 1990s mounting an irredentist campaign for the return of Moldavia couched in similarly extremist terms; with Jews, Hungarians, and Russians treated as scapegoats for the alleged dissection and desecration of the holy Romanian nation.

Not to be outdone, the propagandists of the rejuvenated Iron Guard have, since 1989, taken to celebrating the movement's most famous pre-war leaders, Ion Motza and Corneliu Codreanu, as interwar martyrs defending Christian Europe against the onslaught of communist materialism and atheism. Romanian extremists thus conceive of themselves as a vanguard in the struggle to re-Christianise Europe, and so redeem it from the materialism and cultural mixing which has brought it so low both in the East and the West. Thus Horia Sima, with Degrelle the most illustrious survivor of the interwar fascism, spoke for the whole of the East European ultra-right when, in the run-up to the EU parliamentary elections in the Spring of 1989 (and several months before the overthrow of Ceaçescu), he exhorted fellow Europeans in the 'free' West to choose their future role carefully. The wrong choice, Sima claimed, would mean that Europe would enter the third millennium as a multi-racial, multi-national society, and ultimately might go under altogether, 'drowned in the Afro-Asiatic deluge'. Certainly Eurovisionaries of Sima's ilk talk enthusiastically of integration, but they have in mind neither the harmonising of sausage specifications nor of frontier regulations. Instead, they look forward to the building of a 'Fortress Europe' (significantly, a phrase first used to describe the Nazis' military occupation of the continent under the Third Reich), one which will stand firm against the triple threat of Judeo-Bolshevism, contamination by alien cultures, and an invasion by hoards of economic and political refugees from Asia and Africa.

Given that waves of acute social crisis both institutional and collective are set to continue sweeping across the new democracies for the foreseeable future, the ethnic hatreds and neo-fascist myths to which they are host look set to become increasingly diffused and entrenched. While democrats may pin their hopes on a suitably idealistic, resourced, and mobilised EU and UN to address tensions and violence which are bound to erupt, ultra-right ideologues in the West are not slow to see in such tensions eloquent vindication of their stand against decadence. Here, for example, is a comment on the dissolution of Yugoslavia taken from Michael Walker's *The Scorpion* in late 1989, before the outbreak of the civil war.

> Day after day we witness that multiculturalism and multiracialism, as sentimental as they may sound in theory, in practice invariably lead to racism, xenophobia and evil war. The main reason for such a course of events lies in the egalitarian dogma which sets out from the premise that culture and nation are flimsy superstructures, and hence assimilable by all. It is very likely that the current West European strategy of multi-culturalism and multi-ethnicism will result in consequences already occurring in the Balkans. Unfortunately, when ethnic turmoil begins causes are usually mistaken for consequences and vice versa.[104]

It is symptomatic of the deep gulf which separates a genuinely humanist vision of Europe from the one cultivated by neo-fascists that the latter blame the growing tide of hatred and violence which they themselves foment on the egalitarianism and multi-culturalism of those who oppose it.

Conclusions: Eurofascism and the 'End of History'

Despite its chronic weaknesses at the level of parliamentary and extra-parliamentary movements, the vitality of fascism as an ideological force and the fomenter of racial hatred shows no sign of ebbing. Clearly, the notion that fascism could ever seize power by emulating the NSDAP, let alone achieve sufficient 'cultural hegemony' to overthrow liberal democracy in its own version of a Velvet Revolution, continues to be a chimera. Yet the insistence of fascists on the decadence of modern society, and their nebulous promises of an ultra-nationalist New Order have nonetheless established themselves as thriving components, and presumably *permanent* ones, of Western political sub-culture. Nowhere is the potential impact of contemporary fascism more dramatic than on the issue of 'Europe'. This is partly because the call for a 'Europe of nationalities' is one of the most persistent *topoi* of post-war fascist thought, as well as being the main basis for co-operation and ecumenicalism between the myriad groups and grouplets pursuing national rebirth. Eurofascism not only represents a major element of continuity between the countless dialects of pre-war and post-war fascisms, but provides common ground between party-political organisers and paramilitary activists, between skinhead racists and 'educated' ideologues, between thugs and (pseudo-)intellectuals, between neo-Nazis and neo-fascists, between fascists and conservatives on the cusp between liberalism and the radical right. To a non-believer, the ultra-nationalist myth of a new Europe has the glaring weakness of failing to offer any realistic blueprints to explain what the new order would be like, let alone any practical strategy for how it would be achieved. But it is precisely in this nebulousness that much of fascism's mythic strength lies.

The reason for this paradox is to be sought in the weak mythic forces emanating from the dominant, *liberal* myth of Europe. Despite the visionary humanistic fervour which may have inspired the initial impulses to create the EU, for the vast majority of Europe's citizens, the notion of its future unity is associated with bureaucracy and butter-mountains. The greatest passions it can arouse are negative, arising from the fear of losing sovereignty or seeing national traditions and cultural identity eroded. To this extent, Europe *qua* the EU is generally a source of apathy or resentment, the diametric opposite of a real 'community'. Who would rally to the star-spangled banner of the EU and be prepared to lay down his or her life for it in a fit of heroic self-sacrifice? As for a United Europe embracing all the nations which politically comprise it, for most this is an even greater abstraction, a mere 'geographical expression' more than nineteenth-century Italy ever was. In this respect, the collapse of communism and the 'liberation' of the Eastern bloc has simply made a vague, disquieting concept even more so.

By contrast, the fascist myth of Europe plugs directly into such half-expressed fears. It simultaneously celebrates nationalism at its most local level of regional culture and dialect – appealing to and fomenting separatist sentiments – while replacing the lukewarm liberal Europeanism of political, legal, and economic union with one based on the myth of common historical roots and unique cultural heritage: *e pluribus unum*. Thus there is no contradiction in the fact that, in the 1980s, some activists associated with the British National Front were forging links with Welsh nationalists while still other British neo-fascists were cultivating contacts with groups all over Europe. What enhances Euro-fascism's mythic pull is that it not only capitalises on the illiberal nationalism which has become a permanent feature of all societies affected by 'modernisation', but also keys into several areas of latent phobia already rife in Europe without its ministrations: anti-socialism, particularly anti-Marxism and anti-communism; anti-Americanism; xenophobia and 'cultural' (sometimes even biological) racism, especially in the form of anti-immigration and anti-Semitism. Perhaps an equally important source of sentiments conducive to illiberal visions of Europe is a vague sense of Europe's marginalisation as the centre of world power; and more generally, of the decay and chaos in the 'modern world'. These elements are welded together into the fascist myth of Europe's hegemony and cultural integrity under threat from America, the Far East (especially Japan), communism, immigration, the demographic explosion of the Third World, and all putative sources of cultural levelling and homogenisation. Having established the vision of Europe's decadence, the need for its rebirth through a co-ordinated movement of national 'reawakenings' then acquires a terrible self-evidence and inner logic. Despair is transformed into hope, narrow nationalist sentiments into visionary supranational ones, reactionary pessimism into revolutionary optimism.

Since 1989, this threat has deepened. The prevailing conditions of economic deprivation, social chaos, and ideological disorientation in former communist societies are hardly conducive to the spread of humanism, tolerance, and global compassion. Rather, the wave of integral nationalism and racism flooding through several of these countries is a predictable response to the feeling of cultural crisis and *anomie* which have followed in the wake of their dramatic liberation from the Soviet system. The intensification of separatist nationalism, ethnic hatreds, and anti-Semitism in the ex-Soviet republics is a manifestation of the same phenomenon. So is the formation of a new fascist group in Moscow and St Petersburg, *Pamyat* [Memory], which has already forged links with ecologist groups and sister organisations in the West. The rapid spread of international skinhead racism and fascism to Eastern Europe recently, the growth of support for anti-immigration parties in several solidly liberal countries (such as Norway and Denmark), the emergence of the Lombard League in Italy playing on resentments of the State, the South, and *terzomondiali* ('third worlders'), the unabated strength of Le Pen's *Front National* in France, the rise of support for the neo-fascist Republican Party in Germany, the parades of racists in full neo-Nazi and neo-fascist regalia celebrating the anniversary of Germany's unification, the burning down of hostels for asylum seekers and Turks in previously peaceful German towns: all are disturbing signs of the times.

Contemporaneously, with the resurgence of the extra-parliamentary radical right, Eurofascism at Strasbourg also extended its influence in the early 1990s. As a result of 1989 elections, the Technical Group of the European Right (as it has called itself since that year) lost its Ulster Unionist and also its MSI members (over the South Tyrol issue), but was joined by six members of Franz Schönhuber's Republican Party, and for a time, by a member of the *Vlaamsblok* who had successfully manipulated the issue of Flemish separatism. The group established links with various anti-immigrant parties and the Spanish far right, as well as with Jörg Haider, leader of the extreme right *Freiheitliche Partei Österreichs* [FPÖ]. The Eurofascist penetration of the Strasbourg Parliament enjoyed its fleeting moment of triumph when a procedural anomaly allowed 88-year-old Claude Autant-Lara, former film director and member of the National Front, to preside over the newly elected parliament in July 1989. More than half the members walked out on principle as he set about using the occasion to deliver a blistering attack on the Europe which the EU intends to create (but which, as he gleefully pointed out nearly half the electorate could not even be bothered to vote for). Autant-Lara warned his listeners that 'the threat to our culture, our cultures, dear fellow Europeans, is coming not from the Soviet

Union but from the United States, alas! And it is a terrifying threat'. Having cited various examples of the erosion of cultural uniqueness, he declared:

> All the dangers I have listed would not be fatal if they fell upon solid national tissue that was still able to generate antibodies and gain victory over death. This language shows just how much fear and disgust I feel at the mondialist, internationalist and egalitarian theories.

Autant-Lara then drew on his own life experience of the cinema industry to illustrate what he called the 'American invasion of Europe and the world'. Nor did he miss the opportunity to allude to the dangers of Europe's 'Islamicisation' preached by his hero Le Pen. Autant-Lara's final message to the 'young people of Europe' was that 'national cultural identity' is being lost. 'Lose that and there is nothing left to lose'.[105]

In short, the Fukuyamian school of triumphalism is not the only political force able to take heart from recent world events. The palingenetic mythopoeia of Eurofascists also has received an enormous fillip from the collapse of Russian communism and its chaotic aftermath. As far as they are concerned, only one of the twin citadels of evil has fallen. Moreover, Japan may well be already constructing another to replace it, thus compounding the residual fear of a 'red' yellow peril (China) with the prospect of being engulfed by a 'blue' one. Indeed, the original euphoria about a 'new era' that swept through both the 'freed world' and the 'Free World' (another mythic construct) over 1989/1990 may well turn out to have a negative backlash. As a sense of chaos and disillusionment replaces the utopian expectations which greeted the revolutions at home and abroad; as the relatively prosperous liberal democracies of the North face the prospect of an increasing tide of migration from the 'other' Europe and the 'South'; as environmental and demographical scares turn into sombre realities, so more mythic energy is likely to be generated on the margins of official society to feed fascist and radical right movements.

It is said that the 'devil always has the best tunes' and ideologically speaking, this has certainly been borne out by the recent history of Western civilisation. But fascism has a whole repertoire of its own melodies to play, arrangements of Golden Oldies beloved of ultra-nationalist and historical subculture, one now attuned to the age of drum-machines and rap. In its own Eurovision contest with representative democracy, fascism may well be dismissed by classical humanists as a meaningless cacophony, but its refrains and 'hooks' (what the Germans delightfully call 'ear-worms') continue to bore their way into the ideals of multi-culturalism and the One World ethic with a destructive force which the liberal intelligentsia would be advised not to underestimate in assessing Europe's immediate future.

Whatever the immediate future holds, Fukuyama's concluding assertion in his notorious article that only 'the prospect of centuries of boredom [...] will serve to get history started once again' smacks of a complacency which is as culpable as it is arrogant. Contemptuous of evangelism stemming from the 'evil empire', fascism's writers and activists will continue to preach their own vision of a New World Order. Theirs is an order based not on a restored American hegemony but a restored European one, a 'Fortress Europe' standing firm in the midst of mounting social chaos and cultural decay.

Moreover, fascists are arguably better placed than most liberal intellectuals to offer the bewildered and the myth-hungry public plausible diagnoses and tempting panaceas for the welter of social, ethnic, and nationalist tensions. In the very same month that *The National Interest* published Fukuyama's article, *Nation Europa*'s leader[106] was telling its subscribers with equal self-assurance that the abstract, individual human rights announced in 1789 are moribund and incomplete. The declaration of the 'immortal principles' of the French Revolution contained a glaring omission: the right to a homeland and to a distinctive (national, racial, cultural) identity. The piece closed with words which may better approximate the historical realities of the new Europe than the prognosis of terminal boredom: 'Whoever violates the right to identity is playing with fire'.

What can upholders of the Western humanist tradition, whether left or right, do to combat visions of Europe which deny plurality and tolerance, and hence the basis of a sustainable liberal democracy integrated not just internally, but with the rest of human society? As Bertolt Brecht made clear in his *Life of Galileo*, it is indefensible only to labour away at modern *discorsi* within the cocoon of our own disciplines, when the citadels of knowledge and power are being attacked from various quarters by the advocates of a Europe based on a vision of humanity akin to the very apartheid recently dismantled in South Africa. Nor can the liberal intelligentsia afford to pin its hopes on the possibility that the age of satellite TV and virtual reality graphics might eventually so anaesthetise and depoliticise 'the masses' that the energy will drain away from ethnic tensions and nationalist hatreds. Krebs' collaborators in *The Right to Have an Identity* have a point: there is an ongoing ideological war, a war for the survival and propagation of genuinely humane societies, and for the preservation of the ecosystem on which they are all ultimately based. On the issue of Europe, illiberal mythopoeia must be actively fought with a genuinely liberal mythopoeia. Significantly, it is a poet statesman, not a political scientist, who has arguably done most to blaze a trail towards such a future both in word and in deed: Vàclav Havel, former President of Czechoslovakia.

Havel's use of poetry and drama to appeal for basic freedoms had already made him the country's most famous dissident under Soviet rule, and after the Velvet Revolution of 1989, he set about becoming the ambassador of national self-determination in a spirit of universal humanism. Havel formulated the axioms of his vision when, in 1991, he received an honorary degree at Lehigh University in Bethlehem, Pennsylvania. At its core lies the powerfully charged mythic concept of 'home', formulated in a way that tears down curtains of dulled imagination and crippled capacity for love, to reveal a breathtaking vista. It is the prospect of a genuinely global and ecologically aware humanism which does not suppress national identity or ethnic passions, but rather subsumes them within a concept which is anathema to all ultra-nationalists. The timely principle reaffirmed at Lehigh is that civic rights and citizenship provide a framework within which all can celebrate our uniqueness without obscuring common humanity.

It is thus appropriate to conclude with Havel's words, quoted less as a primary source of contemporary Europoeia than as a passionate plea that a sane version of it might eventually prevail. If it does not, Europe, exposed to mounting demographic and ecological pressures from outside, might well degenerate into a Fortress without any help from those who would consciously turn it into one.

What a person perceives as his home can be compared to a set of concentric circles, with his 'I' at the centre. My home is the room I live in, the room I've grown accustomed to, and which, in a manner of speaking, I have covered with my own invisible lining. I recall, for instance, that even my prison cell was, in a sense, my home, and I felt very put out whenever I was suddenly required to move to another [...] My home is the house I live in, the village or town where I spend most of my time. My home is my family, the world of my friends, the social and intellectual milieu in which I live, my profession, my company, my work place. My home, obviously, is also the country I live in, the language I speak, and the intellectual and spiritual climate of my country expressed in the language spoken there. The Czech language, the Czech way of perceiving the world, Czech historical experience, the Czech modes of courage and cowardice, Czech humour – all these are inseparable from that circle of my home. My home is therefore my Czechness, my nationality, and I see no reason at all why I shouldn't embrace it since it is as an essential part of me as, for instance, my masculinity, another aspect of my home. My home, of course, is not only my Czechness, it is also my Czechoslovakness, which means my citizenship. Ultimately my home is Europe and my Europeanness – finally – it is this planet and its present civilisation, and, understandably, the whole world. [...] I certainly do not want, therefore, to suppress the national dimension of a person's identity, or to deny it, or to refuse to acknowledge its legitimacy and its right to full self-realisation. I merely reject the kind of political notions that attempt, in the name of nationality, to suppress other aspects of the human home, other aspects of humanity and human rights.[107]

8
Fascism's New Faces (and New Facelessness) in the 'post-fascist' Epoch*

Fascism in the eye of the beholder

The European New Right, so alarmed at the prospect of the comprehensive homogenisation of culture in the wake of the inexorable process of globalisation, should take comfort that there is no equivalent of McDonaldisation in the human sciences. On the contrary, the latter continues to host a steady proliferation of contested definitions, methodological assumptions, conceptual frameworks, and ethical positions in every sphere of academic specialism. The work by Ernst Nolte that helped (and only helped) pioneer comparative Fascist Studies thirty years ago was *Der Faschismus in seiner Epoche* [translated into English as *Three Faces of Fascism*]. One of its many pronouncements was that 'the era of the world wars is identical with the era of fascism'.[1] Since then, most works devoted to the comparative analysis of fascism (indeed, almost all produced outside Germany except for Marxist ones) have explicitly or implicitly corroborated this view, despite few of these texts applying the 'philosophy of history' that underpinned Nolte's interpretative scheme. In monographs, conference

* This chapter is a slightly shortened version of an article commissioned by Werner Loh, editor of the German periodical *Erwägen, Wissen, Ethik* to serve as the 'main article' subsequently discussed in two rounds of comment and criticism by academics invited to respond. The article was debated in two rounds of 'criticism' and included two 'replies' by Griffin to the criticism, all of which was then published in single issue 15.3, (Autumn 2004). The aim of the periodical is to encourage debate between academics over major issues of contention in their discipline. The whole issue was been reprinted in 2006 in the series *Ideas and Politics of the Radical Right* (edited by Andreas Umland of the University of Kiev) published by Ibidem Press, Stuttgart, as a contribution to informed debate between academics and politicians over the relevance of fascism to post-Soviet societies in Eastern Europe. The chapter appears with the kind permission of Werner Loh.

proceedings, and collections of essays devoted to reconstructing fascism's history, the post-war period has been treated perfunctorily, if at all, as little more than an anti-climactic coda for fascism's catastrophic spring-time.[2]

It is as if, with the advent of democracy's Indian summer in 1945, a once-raging mountain torrent had turned into a pathetic brook, or that a mighty river of ideological energies swelled by numerous tributaries had shrivelled into a delta of stagnant swamps and sluggish streams devoid of revolutionary momentum. The same publications have more often than not implied that fascism was almost exclusively a European affair. Italy's most industrious archival historian of Mussolini's regime, Renzo de Felice, thus spoke for the orthodoxy of the day when he declared:

> If we are to consider fascism one of the major historical events of our time, use of the word cannot be extended to countries outside Europe, nor to any period other than that between the wars. Its roots are typically European; they are inalienably linked to the changes in European society brought about by World War I and the moral and material crisis occasioned by conversion to a mass society with new political and social institutions.[3]

It is consistent with this assumption that, for the majority of political scientists, the anti-democratic forces of the right most worthy of study today are no longer openly revolutionary parties and groupings. After all, extremist movements are utterly marginalised within the party-political process and, in terms of the number of hard-core activists involved, they can count on a few thousand 'skin-head' racists and a few hundred disaffected middle-class intellectuals in the whole of Europe, which, when compared with the half-million who belonged to the Nazi SA on the eve of Hitler's seizure of power, is hardly a major threat to the stability of liberalism. No wonder the bulk of research resources that might once have been channelled into monitoring fascism are now devoted to the study of a new form of party-political illiberalism, variously called neo-populism or radical right populism, which operates within the party political system of a number of European countries and can claim a total electoral constituency of several million.[4] Gianfranco Fini articulated a widespread feeling when he described the formal transformation of the neo-Fascist *Movimento Sociale Italiano* [MSI] into the neo-populist *Alleanza Nazionale* [AN] in 1995 as the expression of the fact that in practical terms we all now live in a 'post-fascist' age.

Yet the sense of living in a post-fascist world is not shared by Marxists who, ever since the first appearance of Mussolini's virulently anti-communist *squadrismo*, have instinctively assumed fascism to be one of the 'faces' of capitalism worn just below its liberal mask. No matter how much it may appear to be an autonomous force it is, for them, inextricably bound up with the defensive reaction of bourgeois elites or big business to the attempts by revolutionary socialists to implement fundamental changes needed to create a classless society. According to which school or current of Marxism carries out the analysis, the precise sector or agency within capitalism acting as the protagonist or 'backer' of fascism's elaborate pseudo-revolutionary, pre-emptive strike, its degree of independence from the bourgeois elements who benefit from it, and the amount of genuine support it can win within the working class varies appreciably. But for all concerned, fascism is a copious taxonomic pot into which Nazi Germany, Francisco Franco's Spain, *apartheid* South Africa, Augusto Pinochet's Chile, Jean-Marie Le Pen's plans for the renewal of France, and Jörg Haider's ideal Austria can be thrown without too much intellectual agonising over definitional or taxonomic niceties.[5]

The fact that such conflicting perspectives can exist on the 'same' subject is to be explained as a consequence of the particular nature of all generic concepts within the human sciences. To go further into this phenomenon means entering a field of studies where the philosophy of the social sciences has again proliferated conflicting positions – this time concerning the complex and largely subliminal processes involved in conceptualisation and modelling within the social sciences.[6] An instinct of self-preservation has meant that in this article social scientific methodological issues, especially those of the post-structuralist and post-modern variety, have been avoided as a vast area of intellectual quicksands, probably because of a disturbing intuition that the solid foundations of all empirical work in the field of Fascist Studies may ultimately reveal themselves to be a comforting illusion.

For the practical purposes of discussing fascism as a generic phenomenon, it is far from self-evident that a century of intensive modern and post-modern speculation about such epistemological issues has significantly improved on the approach arrived at piecemeal by Max Weber over a century ago, one unfortunately never elaborated into a coherent or 'total' system of hermeneutics. According to him terms such as 'capitalism' and 'socialism' are ideal types, heuristic devices created by an act of 'idealising abstraction'. This cognitive process, which in good social scientific practice is carried out as consciously and scrupulously as possible, extracts a small group of salient features perceived as common to a particular generic phenomenon, assembling them into a definitional minimum which is at bottom a 'utopia'.[7]

The result of idealising abstraction is a conceptually pure, artificially tidy model which does not correspond exactly to any concrete manifestation of the generic phenomenon being investigated, since 'in reality' these are always inextricably mixed up with features, attributes, and surface details that are inherently unique, and which are not considered definitional to that example of it. The dominant 'paradigm' of the social sciences at any one time, the hegemonic political values and academic tradition prevailing in a particular country, the political and moral values of the individual researcher – all contribute to determining what common features are regarded as 'salient' or 'definitional'. Thus there is no objective reality or objective definition of any aspect of it, and no simple correspondence between a word and what it means (what later theory would call the 'signifier' and the 'signified'), for it is axiomatic to Weber's world-view that the human mind attaches significance to an essentially absurd universe and thus literally creates value and meaning, even when attempting to understand the world objectively. The basic question to be asked about any definition of 'fascism', therefore, is not whether it is true, but whether it is heuristically useful. Vitally, for the study of generic fascism, this entails heuristically gathering common features from a large body of independent phenomenon in interwar Europe and beyond.

In his theory of 'ideological morphology' the British political scientist Michael Freeden has elaborated a 'nominalist' – and hence anti-essentialist – approach to the definition of generic ideological terms, one highly compatible with Weberian heuristics. He distinguishes between definitional or 'ineliminable' attributes, that is properties without which an ideology would be unrecognisable, and those 'adjacent' and 'peripheral' to this ineliminable core, which vary according to specific national, cultural, or historical contexts. To cite the example he gives, 'liberalism' can be argued to contain axiomatically, and hence at its definitional core, the idea of individual, rationally defensible liberty. However, the precise relationship of 'liberty' to laissez-faire capitalism, nationalism, monarchy, the church, or the right of the state to override individual human rights in the defence of a collective polity or the welfare of the majority (universal human rights) is adjacent, and thus infinitely negotiable and contestable. The same goes for the ideal political institutions and policies that a state should adopt in order to guarantee liberty, which explains why democratic politics could never be fully consensual across a range of issues without there being something seriously 'wrong'. Given that each ideology is a cluster of concepts comprising ineliminable (uncontested, definitional) and eliminable (contested, variable) aspects profitably accounts for the way ideologies are able to evolve over time while still remaining recognisably 'the same', and why so many variants of the 'same' ideology can arise in different societies and historical contexts. It also explains why every concrete permutation of an ideology is simultaneously unique *and*, potentially, the manifestation of the generic 'ism', one which may assume radical morphological transformations in its outward appearance without losing its definitional ideological core.[8]

The fascist minimum as an ideological core

When applied to generic fascism, the combined concepts of the 'ideal type' and of 'ideological morphology' have profound implications for both the traditional liberal and Marxist definitions of fascism. For one thing, it means that fascism is not to be defined primarily in terms of style (e.g. spectacular politics, uniformed paramilitary forces, the pervasive use of symbols such as the Fasces and Swastika), or organisational structure (e.g. charismatic leader, single party, the corporatisation of economic or cultural production, mass youth, and leisure movements), but in terms of ideology. Moreover, this ideology is not seen either as essentially nihilistic or negative (anti-liberalism, anti-Marxism, resistance to transcendence, etc.), or as the mystification and aestheticisation of capitalist power. Instead, fascist ideology is reconstructed in the 'positive' (but not apologetic or revisionist) terms of its proponents' own professed diagnosis of society's structural crisis and the remedies proposed to solve it, paying particular attention to the need to separate out those 'ineliminable', definitional components from time- or place-specific, peripheral ones.

However, for decades the state of Fascist Studies would have made Freeden's analysis well-nigh impossible to apply to generic fascism, because precisely what was lacking was any conventional wisdom about what constituted the 'ineliminable' cluster of concepts at its (heuristic) core. Despite a handful of attempts to establish fascism's definitional constituents, combining deep comparative historiographical knowledge of the subject with a high degree of conceptual sophistication, there was a conspicuous lack of scholarly consensus over what constituted 'the fascist minimum' (a phrase popularised by Ernst Nolte).[9] Some scholars expressed serious doubts whether there was such an entity as 'generic fascism' to define in the first place.[10] Others, particularly within German-speaking academia, argued that Nazism's eugenic racism and the euthanasia campaign it led to, combined with a policy of physically eliminating racial enemies leading to the systematic persecution and mass murder of millions of 'undesirables', was simply too unique to be located within a generic category.

Both of these positions suggest a naivety about the epistemological and ontological status of generic concepts most regrettable among professional intellectuals, since (a) every generic entity is a utopian heuristic construct, not a real 'thing', and (b) every historical singularity is, by definition, unique no matter how many generic terms can be applied to it. Other common positions that implied considerable naivety in this regard were those dismissing fascism's ideology as too irrational or nihilistic to constitute any 'fascist minimum',[11] or generalised about its generic traits by simply blending characteristics of Fascist and Nazi movements.[12]

The emergence of a 'new consensus'

Throughout the post-war era, the sorry state of Fascist Studies rendered the term 'fascism' almost unusable to serious 'idiographic' historians of extreme right-wing phenomena for practical heuristic and forensic purposes. In particular, with very few exceptions both Italian and German non-Marxist historians of Fascism and Nazism, respectively, have avoided the generic term altogether. In doing so, they deprive themselves of the valuable comparative perspectives on the Mussolini and Hitler regimes, let alone their relationship to other mani-festations of ultra-nationalism in the West. Such a comparative perspective is needed more than ever now, to throw into relief the way divers phenomena – normally treated as symptoms of dysfunctions in the process of nation-building peculiar to Italy and Germany – were actually part of patterns woven into the fabric of European history.

Yet over the last decade, a growing explicit (theoretically formulated) or tacit (pragmatic) acceptance by Anglophone academics working in the field has emerged, holding that fascism's ineliminable core is composed of the vision of a regenerated political culture and national community established in a post-liberal age.[13] Inevitably such a consensus can never be total, and there are academics working in Fascist Studies who continue to apply a different ideal type to fascism, and some expressing deep scepticism about any convergence on the centrality to fascism of an ultra-nationalist myth of rebirth.[14] The most cited version of the consensus on fascist ideology applied by academics sympathetic to it is the highly synthetic formula used to encapsulate my own ideal type: '*Fascism is a political ideology whose mythic core in its various permutations is a palingenetic form of populist ultra-nationalism.*'[15]

The utopian nature of definitions formed through a process of idealising abstraction may imply to those still sceptical about the whole enterprise of searching for a 'fascist minimum' such theories have a fragile anchorage in empirical reality. It is important to stress, therefore, that the myth of Italy's imminent 'palingenesis' (rebirth) can be *objectively* documented by a close study of primary sources. These unmistakably recur across the copious texts expressing fascist ideology, as well as the main point of convergence between the many currents of thought and species of political project that formed a loose alliance initially – first within the Fascist movement, and then within the Fascist regime. The myth of national rebirth is also documentable as the main common denominator not only between the Fascist regime and a hand-ful of movements that in history have called themselves fascist – notably the *Faisceau*, the BUF, and the post-war *Faisceaux Nationaux Européens* – but a far greater number of revolutionary nationalist groups such as the Falange, the Romanian Iron Guard, and the NSDAP that rarely if ever applied the term to themselves.

As a definitional ideal type, the discriminatory value of this approach holds that *revolutionary* aspirations involving the attempted palingenesis of the nation's entire political culture are demonstrably missing in the core ideology of a number of regimes and movements commonly associated with fascism, such as Franco's Spain, Pinochet's Chile, or Le Pen's *Front National*. Moreover, some corroboration of the heuristic value of this 'minimum' is given by the fact that on the rare occasion when ideologues of the extreme right have offered a definition of fascism it has corresponded to this ideal type,[16] even when it is used by them to demarcate 'true' revolutionary nationalism from perverted forms which, for example, retain capitalism.[17] This burgeoning consensus is also consistent with the latest scholarship on totalitarianism and stress on political culture rather than organisation and style.[18]

To clear up another widespread misunderstanding about the nature of the 'fascist minimum' as it is increasingly widely perceived, it is worth citing reservations voiced by the British historian, Martin Blinkhorn. In the 'author's reply' to an electronic review praising his scepticism about the new consensus in his *Fascism and the Right in Europe 1919–1945*, Blinkhorn admits to being 'increasingly impatient with the whole "generic fascism" grail quest'. He goes onto state his relationship to the new consensus somewhat pointedly: 'I claim the right to say: "I am not part of it; therefore it does not exist." '[19]

Yet precisely what follows from a Weberian approach is that the fascist minimum of 'ineliminable' properties is not some sort of elusive, objectively existing essence to be found at the end of a search, something which would indeed smack more of romantic legend than humanistic science. As an ideal type, fascist ideology rather resembles an industrial diamond in being an entirely 'man-made' product, a deliberate cognitive act of construction which takes place *at the beginning* of an empirical investigation in the human sciences. If the more methodologically self-aware scholars working in this field are concerned with refining the way they conceptualise and 'problematise', it is not because of some perverse neo-Platonic belief in the primacy of ideas and essences over facts and empirical reality, but for mundane, strictly heuristic purposes of advancing conceptual understanding. For unless key concepts central to any research project are clarified at the outset, the cogency of the resulting analysis will be impaired to the detriment of any value it might have for other scholars.

Blinkhorn's decision to 'opt out' of the new consensus and hence demonstrate its non-existence also points to further confusion, since it has never been suggested that the agreement between academics on the fascist minimum has ever been more than emergent or partial. After all, this is true of consensus between experts over any highly contested area of academic investigation in the human (and natural) sciences. In any case, the function of such a consensus is not to put an end to debate, but to allow other aspects of the 'problematic' to be contested. Without this continuous process of generating shifting areas of convergence and divergence, academic knowledge and scientific understanding could never progress; the controversies generated could never 'move on'.

A final irony with the above is that the definition of fascism Blinkhorn actually applies in his survey of interwar and wartime Europe specifies that, at the core of its 'ideas and myths', lies the 'belief in a national and/or racial revolution' embodying rebirth from an existing condition of subjection, decadence or 'degeneracy' leading to the 'creation of [...] a "new fascist man"'.[20] This is fully consistent with, and actually deeply indebted to, the major expressions of the new consensus about which he has earlier expressed such deep scepticism.

However, though Blinkhorn tacitly adopts the new consensus, a later section of his book, in referring to fascism after 1945, indicates that he has not appreciated the radical change of perspective that it brings about when applied to the post-war era. As a result, he duplicates the standard historical view of postwar fascism in depicting the gamut of the post-war extreme right as stretching from highly conspicuous, significant parties – such as the MSI which at times makes significant inroads into the legitimate space of democratic politics – to a zone which 'seethes' with a 'profusion of *groupuscules* far too numerous to mention – organisations mostly too tiny to be worth mentioning', some of them 'psychotically violent'.[21]

Once the full implications of seeing fascism's definitional core as a belief in 'national and/or racial revolution' are grasped, the question of fascism's evolution after 1945 changes radically. In particular, the issue of how fascism 'naturally' manifests itself as a political and historical entity takes on a dimension not readily perceived on the basis of ideal types constructed exclusively through a study of the extreme right in inter-war Europe, such as Ernst Nolte's 'metapolitical' definition,[22] James Gregor's 'developmental dictatorship' model,[23] Ze'ev Sternhell's concept of a fusion of anti-Marxist socialism and tribal nationalism which made it 'neither right, nor left',[24] or Wolfgang Wippermann's 'real type' based on Italian Fascism.[25] The key to this reassessment of twentieth-century fascist ideology lies in the realisation of just how historically contingent the Fascist and Nazi forms of fascism were, even if these continue to exert such a powerful influence on historical memory and imagination.

Fascism's inherently protean quality

From the two variants of the 'new consensus' already cited (Griffin and Blinkhorn), it is clear that the core cluster of definitional concepts with which fascism is increasingly being identified by scholars contains room for an extremely wide range of specific ideological contents and policies. Both 'national' and 'racial' are intrinsically multivalent terms that can vary considerably in meaning, according to which particular nation or nation-state is examined, or which theory of race is applied. Even 'rebirth' may be interpreted in an ultra-conservative and hence restorationist sense as well as in a far more futuristic sense signalling a definitive break with the past. There should be no surprise, then, if each permutation of fascism, be it Spanish Falangism, the Hungarian Arrow Cross, or Italian Fascism itself, contains highly idiosyncratic features, exemplified by the central role of the Romanian Orthodox Church in the ideology and ethos of the Iron Guard. However, the applicability of this definition of generic fascism should also be clear for those studying German National Socialism. Nazism was a form of ultra-nationalism deeply imbued with notions of imperialism, anti-Semitism, Aryan supremacy, racial hygiene, and eugenics, making it highly idiosyncratic in terms of ideologies and policies. It systematically strove for the renewal and regeneration of the national community in every sphere: political, military, social, cultural, aesthetic, even the economic one (though achieved by adapting capitalism rather than abolishing it).

Yet also on account of the conceptual fuzziness at the ideological core of fascism, once any permutation of fascism becomes a mass movement, it naturally brings together many different – and sometimes deeply conflicting – concepts of nation, race, and rebirth. Fascism hosted a welter of schemes for a new Italy containing inherent tensions and contradictions that Mussolini never attempted to resolve. Nazism, though more centralised and intolerant of 'heterodoxies', was far from ideologically homogeneous, as any comparison of the visions for national rebirth promoted by leading Nazis such as Gregor Strasser, Alfred Rosenberg, Heinrich Himmler, Albert Speer, and Walter Darré demonstrates.

Moreover, it should be stressed that this ineliminable core does not itself prescribe any particular organisational or institutional form of politics, both of which will be largely determined by the precise historical situation in which the attempt to induce national palingenesis is carried out. In short, fascism has a protean quality, generating myriad permutations of the vision of national rebirth, and is thus intrinsically factious and fractious. It also can assume a number of different external organisational forms. Once seen in this way, the focus of historical explanations on the strength or weakness of specific variants of interwar European fascism naturally shift away from deep-seated pathological cultural traditions, or solely paths to nationhood undertaken by individual nations. Instead, investigations shift to the medium-term systemic factors and short-term socio-political factors determining whether fascism forms a larger, more cohesive movement or remains fragmented.

Similarly, attempts to trace fascism's overall development as a historical force that are informed by this approach cease to concentrate on attempts to simply emulate the Fascist and Nazi parties: attention moves to considering how its external form (styles and organisation) and central policies mutate in order to adapt to changing historical circumstances. Recast in terms of 'ideological morphology', this means that reconstructing the history of fascism involves clearly

distinguishing the definitional features of fascism from its adjacent or peripheral ones, and then tracing how, in different circumstances, fascist ideology
sheds some non-definitional features and loses others as it adapts to different
external forces. Thus the leader cult, spectacular politics, corporatism, the ethos
of militarism, and the youth movement can be treated as 'phenomenal' rather
than 'noumenal', as long as the 'noumen' here is understood to be an ideal
typical construct rather than fascism's essentialised 'thing-in-itself'.

It is all too easy for adjacent concepts to be smuggled into the definitional core of fascism, even by methodologically self-conscious theorists. Thus
Stanley Payne introduces the *Führerprinzip* and militarism into his one-sentence
definition,[26] both of which were peripheral products of the historical conditions of inter-war Europe rather than 'essentially' fascist. My original definition
in *The Nature of Fascism* included 'populism', which needs considerable qualifi-
cation for the post-war era, once fascism ceased to behave as a mass movement.
The more discursive version of the definition in the same chapter also refers to
the fascist belief in *imminent* national rebirth, which now appears inapplicable
to those believing that the Axis' defeat means they now find themselves in an
indefinite 'interregnum', waiting for the Godot of a sudden reversal (*Umschlag*)
of the meta-historical situation – of which there is no sign on the horizon.[27] In
each case, an 'adjacent' property of fascism has been centrally identified with
its ineliminable core, unwittingly corrupting the purity of the abstracted ideal
type with ephemeral, contingent properties.

It follows that the key to understanding the evolution of fascist movements
in the post-war era is to be alive to the way the myth of national rebirth can produce new adjacent properties spinning off from the ideological core of fascism.
Equally, it can assume organisational forms radically different from its interwar
manifestations, even if they may be unrecognisable as attributes of fascism –
especially for those convinced that its revival means the reappearance of a
movement-party setting out to emulate the NSDAP or PNF. As Pierre-André
Taguieff insightfully reminds us

> Neither 'fascism' or 'racism' will do us the favour of returning in such a way
> that we can recognise them easily. If vigilance was only a game of recognising
> something already well-known, then it would only be a question of remem-
> bering. Vigilance would be reduced to a social game using reminiscence and
> identification by recognition, a consoling illusion of an immobile history
> peopled with events which accord to our expectations or our fears.[28]

A consequence of this kind of academic vigilance means that it becomes easier
to recognise fascism's new guises once it has been understood why, in the
inter-war period, it took the form it did. The profound structural crisis which
each European countries underwent was the specific blend of a number of

factors: the *fin-de-siècle* loss of faith in rationalism and progress; impacts both material and social from the First World War; the Russian Revolution of 1917 and the subsequent rise of revolutionary communism; the consequences of the crisis of capitalism and the Great Depression; and the rise of the masses and the progressive tensions within both conservative authoritarianism and elitist liberalism. In both Italy and Germany, the structural crisis of liberalism, though configured extremely differently, were profound enough to allow the forces of the revolutionary, anti-conservative right to coalesce into a new type of formation, the 'armed party'.

The totalitarian aspirations of the PNF and the NSDAP, and the totalitarian regimes that they underpinned, thereafter became the role model for all revolutionary nationalists in the inter-war period and became synonymous with totalising, mass-based revolutionary nationalism itself. This became known as 'fascism' after the first such movement to achieve power, namely Mussolini's *fascismo*. However, it was only in Italy and Germany that the structural crisis of liberal society was profound enough to generate a genuinely charismatic form of populist politics, one which was not confined to the hard core of movement activists, but involved the particular type of consensus generated by a 'palingenetic political community', thereby creating the basis for a fascist regime.[29] Yet others seeking to emulate the PNF/NSDAP (e.g. the BUF, Spanish *Falange*, and the *Nasional Samling*) never approached the point where they created a genuinely revolutionary critical mass as a populist force, even if some achieved a small electoral following. The Romanian Iron Guard and Hungarian Arrow Cross eventually gained a substantial popular following, but only succeeded in enjoying a short-lived and largely nominal share of power because of exceptional circumstances (in the first case a tactical alliance sought first by King Carol and then by General Ion Antonescu, in the second the Nazis' need to install a puppet-state having effectively forced Admiral Horthy to abdicate).

Thus, on account of the fact that they were children of their age, both the PNF and the NSDAP combined a paramilitary, uniformed elite with a mass electoral base into a party headed by a charismatic leader combining the qualities of political statesman and military leader. Both parties envisioned themselves as the vehicle for the creation of a mass movement of national renewal that would enable the parliamentary system to be overthrown on the basis of a charismatic dictatorship. The critical mass of populist energies generated by, and contained within, both parties meant that they were able to embrace a vast range of activities and functions: from ideological elaboration and propaganda carried out by a small elite, to mass participation in party-related events and projects in every sphere of society; from the violent actions of paramilitary cadre formations, to mass leisure and youth organisations. In turn, these adjacent features were also incorporated by other European fascist movements.

Both parties therefore became the protagonists and animators of a vast programme of cultural production, the most conspicuous of which took the form
of 'spectacular' or 'aesthetic' displays of revolutionary energies unleashed and
co-ordinated by the movements. It was thus political parties which became
the basis for the transformation of both Fascism and Nazism into elaborate,
all-pervasive 'political religions'.

Furthermore, the image of fascism as the most dynamic and most successful
anti-communist force of the age also had a major impact on authoritarian conservatism. The highly visible modernising achievements of Mussolini's Italy in
the social, technological, and cultural spheres; Franco's eventual success in overcoming the combined forces of the Left thanks to Fascist and Nazi intervention
in the Spanish Civil War; the seemingly irresistible rise of Hitler's Germany in
quickly becoming a leading world political and military power – all combined to
shape popular conceptions of 'fascism' in the 1930s. To its converts, fascism certainly seemed to represent a new ideology born of the modern age, one which
was the only hope for the salvation of civilisation given that the age of political
liberalism and of secular humanism appeared to be drawing to such a dramatic
and sudden close. As a result, conservative regimes wanting to hold out against
the challenges of liberalism, socialism, and communism readily adopted some
of the trappings of fascism in order to seem modern, legitimate, and in harmony
with the new populist forces of the age.[30]

The death of the slime mould

What emerges from the above analysis is that the external form adopted by
fascism in the inter-war period was determined by a profound multi-factorial,
generalised sense-making crisis. This allowed revolutionary populist energies
to be generated that associated the term 'fascist' in the popular and academic
mind with charismatic and paramilitary mass-movements pursuing nationalist
goals. On closer inspection, however, the only indigenously 'successful' fascist movement-regimes (Fascism and Nazism) were coalitions and alliances –
sometimes loose to the point of factional conflict – between a large number of
diversified ultra-nationalist projects and visions, and different aspects of state,
cadre, and mass socio-political institutions, all forged into a superficial cohesion due to the populist energies released by the seismic structural upheavals
suffusing the Westernised at the time.[31]

It is clear that biological metaphors are rightly suspect within the social
sciences. They are all too easily perverted to political ends, especially in the
hands of right-wing ideologues and rhetoricians, because when social processes
and organisational structures are modelled on the dynamic processes found
within nature it lends spurious ('scientistic') corroborations to racist myths of

elitism, breeding, and cleansing which can have horrifically real human consequences as the basis of state policies. Thus, it should be understood that the two biological metaphors to be employed here are intended to help conceptualise the contrasting organisational structure of interwar and post-war fascism. Again, these terms are strictly heuristic devices. Both are used in the same spirit of demystification and exploration that led the post-modernists Gilles Deleuze and Felix Guattari, hardly open to charges of right-wing affiliations, to use the dyadic images of 'tree' and 'rhizome' in their interpretations of modern social processes. Pioneered in the spirit of post-structuralist radicalism, Deleuze and Guattari helped conceptualise social phenomena to which, metaphorically at least, the attributes of supra-personal organic life-forms can be ascribed, but which are not structured in a coherently hierarchical or systematically interconnected way that would make tree-based or 'dendroid' metaphors appropriate.[32]

With this caveat in mind, it is also worth pointing out that that even the most successful fascist mass movements in the interwar period were far from achieving the genuinely organic, tree-like (arboreal) unity that all political demagogues dream would lead into the socio-political clouds. As far as analogies with the natural world are concerned, their internal structure is instead illuminated by the remarkable phenomenon called the 'slime mould' (myxomycota).[33] This slug-like entity is formed from countless single cells in conditions of extreme damp found; for example, in abandoned English country cottages. Without a central nervous system, it has the mysterious property of forming into a brainless, eyeless super-organism that nevertheless moves purposefully, like a mollusc animated by a single consciousness (it can even negotiate mazes in search of food!). Once the conditions 'dry out' and its habitat disappears, the slime-mould disintegrates back into the countless cells that composed it and endowed it with the capacity to generate such a powerful replicant of centrally co-ordinated, organic life.

The metaphorical relevance of the slime mould to changes occurring in fascism's external manifestation after 1945 should be self-evident. It was only the extreme conditions of interwar Europe's political culture that allowed the disparate aspects of the extreme right to coalesce in the party-political equivalent of the slime mould – and even then only in certain countries. The most gigantic political myxomycota of all, the NSDAP, achieved such a high degree of internal cohesion that, for most victims and helpless observers at the time, it seemed to behave just like the fully integrated product of unified will and perfect *Gleichschaltung* (co-ordination) exemplified by the slogan 'Ein Volk, Ein Reich, Ein Führer' (One People, One Empire, One Leader), no matter how chaotic and polycentric Nazism proved to have been with hindsight.

In the post-war period, the habitat in which fascism has had to survive has been radically altered. For one thing the systemic crisis of liberal democracy and the capitalist West – which probably reached its nadir in the autumn of 1942, on the eve of Stalingrad – gave way to a triumphalist sense of the economic, technological, military, and moral superiority of the 'Free World' over both fascism and communism after 1945, a sense further vindicated for many by the eventual collapse of the Soviet Union (The Second World) in the late 1980s. In particular, the acute economic instability of capitalism was replaced by unprecedented growth and prosperity for average inhabitants with the First World. Equally important, fascism became indissociable for the majority of Western citizens from war, destruction, genocide, and moral evil, its rhetoric of national renewal glory thoroughly discredited. Furthermore, the draining away of fascism's mythic power and mass mobilising potential was further reinforced by a general rejection of imperialism, militarism, and ultra-nationalism, the dwindling of the power of the nation-state, and a considerable growth of cosmopolitanism and informal contacts between different Western cultures in the burgeoning transport and information revolutions of the late twentieth-century.

One political effect of this radical transformation in which fascism must now operate is that the ethnocentrism and xenophobia of the interwar period subsequently have found an outlet in overtly anti-liberal forms of conservatism and revolutionary nationalism, often dubbed 'right-wing populism', as an integral part of the party-political system. In structural terms, political racism has thus had to drop the revolutionary agenda within which it was subsumed during the interwar 'crisis of civilisation'. Even though fuelled by such threats to mythically constructed views of identity like multi-culturalism, mass-immigration, the European Union, American cultural imperialism and globalisation, the evaporation of this 'sense-making' crisis means that fascist movements have generally renounced anti-systemic forms of politics in favour of an illiberal form of democratic politics, one that may also be called 'exclusionary populism'[34] or 'ethnocratic liberalism'.[35] In party-political terms, the whole post-war era has indeed become 'post-fascist'.

New faces of fascism

The interwar period provided the ideal habitat for fascism to manifest itself as a charismatic mass movement, for its revolutionary power to seem sufficiently impressive and 'exportable' in Italy and Germany, and for its external trappings to be copied by anti-revolutionary authoritarian regimes. This meant that the international fascist right operated within discrete national party-political organisations in which all its various components coalesced, thus making it relatively easy for conventional historians trained in the reconstruction of macro-political events to trace its development, whether or not these scholars used generic terms such as 'totalitarian' or 'fascist'. Certainly, they had no cause to delve into post-structuralist theories of reality. However, the loss of that habitat and the transformation of the historical situation as a result of the Allied victory in World War Two meant that the realisation of fascist ideals has forced an adaptation in ideological content and the adoption of a number of new survival strategies. These have not only radically changed fascism's ideological content, but brought about a major mutation in the way it is outwardly manifested as a revolutionary political force.

One of the more conspicuous of these changes is that, though some forms of revolutionary nationalism still promote a narrowly chauvinistic form of ultra-nationalism, the dominant forms of fascism now see the struggle for national or ethnic rebirth in an international and supra-national context, an aspect of fascism that was comparatively underdeveloped during the interwar years.[36] Thus Nazism has been adopted throughout the Westernised world as a role model in the fight for Aryan or White supremacy, producing what can been called 'Universal Nazism'. Within Europe, most national fascisms see their local struggle as part of a campaign for a new Europe, one far removed from the vision of the EU. Third Positionism, meanwhile, especially in its more outspokenly anti-capitalist, National Bolshevik forms, campaigns for a radical new world order in which the dominance of the United State's economic, cultural, and military imperialism has been overturned. This ideological Third Way looks forward to an entirely new economic system and international community, and its struggle against the present system fosters a sense of solidarity with non-aligned countries such as Libya, Palestine, and even Iraq and Yugoslavia when they are seen as victims of US imperialist aggression in the need for maintaining the New World Order or *Pax Americana*.

The second, decisive change is a pervasive metapoliticisation of fascism. Many formations have vacated party-political space altogether, and many have even abandoned the arena of activist struggle, choosing to focus on the battle of ideas. The clearest expression of this development can be seen in the New Right, born of the growing recognition in French neo-fascist circles of the 1960s that the need for a radical change of 'discourse' in order to regain the credibility for revolutionary forms of anti-liberal nationalism destroyed by the Second World War and its aftermath. Taking the concept of 'cultural hegemony' to heart resulted in a 'right-wing Gramscism' that aimed to undermine the intellectual legitimacy of liberalism by attacking aspects of actual existing liberal democracy: materialism, individualism, the universality of human rights, egalitarianism, multi-culturalism, and so on. 'Metapolitical fascism' did so not on the basis of an aggressive ultra-nationalism and axiomatic racial superiority, but in the name of a Europe restored to the (essentially mythic) homogeneity of its component primordial cultures, and by the application of a 'differentialist' ideal which seeks to put an end to rampant 'vulgarisation' and ethnic miscegenation that they see endemic to modern societies.

The result has been a powerful anti-systemic ideology – self-consciously distinct from Fascism and Nazism – deeply indebted to Weimar's equally anti-systemic 'Conservative Revolution', which it considers the original and pure version of the transvaluation of Western values so grotesquely travestied by the Third Reich. Later versions of the extraordinarily prolific, logorrheic New Right have placed increasing stress on the need to transcend the division between Left and Right in a broad anti-global front.[37] In short, the metapolitical perpetuation of inter-war fascism's crusade against liberal decadence advocates in its varied factions the inauguration of a new global order which would preserve or restore (through policies and measures never specified) unique ethnic and cultural identities (first and foremost European/Indo-European ones) allegedly threatened by globalisation.[38]

The battle 'to take over the laboratories of thinking', as one German New Right ideologue put it,[39] takes place on other fronts as well. Historical Revisionism and Holocaust denial are widely dispersed but highly deliberate assaults on the collective memories of events surrounding the Second World War calculated to exploit scholarly historical and scientific enquiry in order to rewrite history in such a way as to minimise, relativise, or cancel out altogether crimes against humanity committed by fascist regimes.[40] The 1960s counter-culture also bred New Age, neo-pagan, and occultist variants of the Hitler myth,[41] in addition to forms of nationalism embracing various visions of the threat to humanity posed by materialism and globalisation (one strand of which led to Tolkien's *Lord of the Rings* becoming a prescribed text for the intellectuals of the Italian New Right).[42] Other currents of fascism have taken up ecological concerns, often as an integral part of the New Right critique of Western concepts of progress.[43]

Contemporary fascism's independence from a mass party-movement, or a regime with a centralised hierarchy of command and propaganda directorate, endows it with considerable ideological flexibility. In the United States, this has enabled it to enter into a sufficiently close relationship with certain forms of fundamentalist Christianity, producing new forms of collaboration and fusions between religious and secular racism and anti-Semitism (the Christian Identity network being the outstanding example).[44] At the other end of the spectrum, fascism has used the popularity of punk rock and heavy metal among (mostly) proletarian racists to create a rich and complex 'White Noise' music scene, geared to the legitimation of racial hatred and violent xenophobia.[45] At least the lyrics of fascist punk music make no attempt to disguise its racism under layers of metapolitical or differentialist discourse. Nor do they euphemise the palingenetic dream of 'purging' the nation from decadence though racial war, a major ideological artery leading back to interwar fascism and especially Nazism. Thus one of the songs of the seminal White Noise band, Ian Stuart's *Skrewdriver*, roars out to its audience:

Hail and thunder, the lightning fills the sky
Not too far it comes before the storm
Hail and thunder, we're not afraid to die
Our mighty fearless warriors marching on.
With high ideals we make our stand
To cleanse the poison from our land. [. . .]
They spread a flame, a wicked spell
To keep our people locked in Hell. [. . .]
But now the devil's cover's blown
The strength of light is going to break the evil seal[46]

The fact that White Noise CDs and concerts set out to whip up racial hatred and inspire 'racially motivated' crimes underlines how misleading it would be to imply that fascism's metapoliticisation and ideological diversification has uniformly led to an abandonment of the sphere of activism and violence by fascist movements. The difference is that, instead of being absorbed into massive paramilitary formations like the Nazi's SA, fascist activism is now often concentrated within specially formed cadre units such as the Combat 18 group in the United Kingdom, or the numerous 'black terrorist' cells which carried out bomb attacks in Italy during the 1970s.[47] Even more significantly, racist violence is increasingly carried out not by members of fascist parties, but by groups of extremists acting on their own initiative. Similarly, a number of terrorist outrages have been committed by 'lone-wolves' not under any organised command at all, but who had instead formed a deep sense of personal mission to further the cause communicated to them by a variety of fascist sources.

The ultra-nationalism of the 'Oklahoma bomber', Timothy McVeigh, had first been politicised by his exposure to the particular revolutionary subculture created by the patriotic militias, rifle clubs, and Freemen. His sense of personal mission to do something to break ZOG's (Zionist Occupation Government) stranglehold on America had then been crystallised by reading *The Turner Diaries* by William Pierce, the now-deceased leader of the National Alliance in the United States.[48] Similarly, London nail-bomber, David Copeland, though the police initially stated he had no connections with any right-wing organisations, proved to have been heavily influenced by Christian Identity and the UK-based National Socialist Movement, alongside *The Turner Diaries*.[49] In his case, the Internet played a crucial role in his recruitment into the private militia of lone terrorists personally dedicated to bringing about a radical change in the existing system.[50] It also provided Copeland with the information needed to make nail-bombs. Another example of this phenomenon recently hitting the headlines was the attempt by Maxime Brunerie to assassinate Jacques Chirac on Bastille Day, 14 July 2002. Among the groups influencing him were the Third Positionist student *Groupe Union Défense* (GUD),[51] the 'universal Nazi' *Parti Nationaliste Français et Européen*, and Christian Bouchet's 'National Bolshevik' *Unité Radicale* [UR].

The rhizomic structure of the groupuscular right

The way McVeigh, Copeland, and Brunerie internalised one adjacent strand of the extreme right world-view, carrying their self-appointed mission in a spirit of 'leaderless resistance', is symptomatic of the biggest change of all to affect fascism in the 'post-fascist age': groupuscularisation. There is a natural tendency to dismiss the thousands of minute and often ephemeral formations constituting the post-war extreme right as pathetically unsuccessful attempts to emulate the classical interwar mass movement-party; so numerous they are, as Martin Blinkhorn put it, 'too tiny to mention'. This has obscured the fact that the vast majority represent a new sort of formation, one making no attempt to gain an electoral following. 'Groupuscules' thus seek out a niche, not in conventional political space, but rather in 'uncivic space' – that area of civic society hosting radical rejections of the *status quo*.[52]

In the context of extreme right-wing politics in the contemporary age, 'groupuscules' can be defined as numerically negligible political (frequently metapolitical, but never party-political) entities formed to pursue palingenetic ideological, organisational, or activist ends with an ultimate goal of overcoming the decadence of the existing liberal-democratic system. Though fully formed and autonomous, they have small active memberships and minimal if any public visibility or support. Yet they acquire enhanced influence and significance through the ease with which they can be associated, even if only through linkages in cyberspace, with other grouplets which complement their verbal onslaught against the present phase of the West and attempt to lay the theoretical foundations of a new type of society.

As a result, the groupuscule has a Janus-headed characteristic of combining organisational autonomy with an ability to create informal linkages with, or to reinforce the influence of, other similarly minded formations. This enables groupuscules, when considered in terms of their aggregate impact on politics and society, to be understood as non-hierarchical, leaderless, and centreless (or rather polycentric) movements with fluid boundaries and constantly changing components. These 'slimemould' fascist movements have the characteristics of a political and ideological subculture rather than a conventional political party movement, and is perfectly adapted to the task of perpetuating revolutionary extremism in an age of relative political stability.

The outstanding contrast between the groupuscular and party-political organisation of the extreme right is that, instead of being formed into tree-like

hierarchical organisms, it is now 'rhizomic'. When applied to the groupuscular right, the concept of the 'rhizome' throws into relief its dynamic nature
as a polycratic, leaderless movement by stressing that it does not operate like
a single organism like a tree with a tap-root, branch, and canopy, with a well-
defined beginning and end. Instead it behaves like the root-system of some
species of grass or tuber, displaying 'multiple starts and beginnings which inter-
twine and connect which each other', constantly producing new shoots as
others die off in an unpredictable, asymmetrical pattern of growth and decay.[53]
If a political network has a rhizomic political structure it means that it forms
a cellular, centreless, and leaderless network with ill-defined boundaries and
no formal hierarchy or internal organisational structure to give it a unified
direction.

Thanks to its rhizomic structure, the groupuscular right no longer emulates
a singular living organism, as the slime-mould is so mysteriously capable of
doing. Nor is it to be seen as only comprising countless tiny, disconnected
micro-organisms. Instead, following an internal dynamic which only the most
advanced life sciences can model with any clarity, the minute bursts of spontaneous creativity producing and maintaining individual groupuscules constitute
nodal points in a web of radical political energy fuelling the vitality and viability of the organism as a whole. These qualities duplicate the very features of the
Internet, which first attracted US military strategists to its potential for making
it impossible to shut down or wipe out the information it contains simply by
knocking out any one part of it, precisely because there is no 'mission control' to destroy. The groupuscularity of the contemporary extreme right makes
it eminently able to survive and grow, even if some of the individual organisations which constructing them are banned and their websites are closed
down.[54]

One symptom of the extreme right's rhizomic structure is an ecumenicalism
unthinkable in the 'fascist era', expressed both in the way web-linkages exist
and in cross-currents of influence detectable between diffuse currents of fascism
such as Universal Nazism, Christian Identity, Third Positionism, the New Right.
The 'Eurasianism' of Arctogaia, for example, draws upon the influences of home-
grown, pre-Soviet tradition of Russian ultra-nationalism; Russian dialectics of
post-Soviet national Bolshevism; the French New Right; the Traditionalist Italian
New Right; Third Positionism; New Age and occultist fascism; and even the
punk-rock strand of 'White Noise', so that in August 1998 its website paraded
the name of Jonny Rotten (of the notorious anarchic punk band Sex Pistols)
next to those of Alain de Benoist and Julius Evola as prophets of the new age.[55]
Significantly, by the mid-1990s the leader of Arctogaia, Alexander Dugin, had
become official advisor to Gennady Seleznev, then President of the Russian
parliament.[56]

The contemporary threats of fascism

Applying the 'new consensus' on fascism by tracing its development after 1945 leads to an evaluation of its contemporary resonance, one radically different than that arrived at using definitions solely based on salient characteristics of inter-war fascist movements. Far from fading away to insignificance, fascism has displayed a vigorously Darwinian capacity for creative mutation. Post-war fascism has diversified, specialised, and groupuscularised in order to fill as many civic and uncivic spaces as possible now, given that mainstream political spaces is unavailable. Fascism may have withered on the vine as a would-be party-political mass movement, but it has also assumed a new capillary and rhizomic form that has become a new sort of weather-resistant organism. It is one difficult for traditional social sciences to conceive, and one extraordinarily well-adapted to the wintry climate prevailing since April 1945.

This remarkable metamorphosis makes the exercise of evaluating the threat fascism now poses to liberal democracy a challenge quite different from assessing the potential of the Fascist or Nazi type movements to re-conquer power. Clearly, present conditions mean that fascism cannot mount an attack on state power comparable to that of Mussolini or Hitler, either through a paramilitary putsch or a sweeping electoral victory. Nevertheless, it is worth noting the continued threats to democracy that it embodies (always remembering that this 'it' now embraces, even more than in inter-war Europe, a vast range of variants, many of them mutually hostile):

(a) It keeps an extremist agenda of revolutionary nationalism alive in a form that is practically uncensurable, since the groupuscular right shares with the Internet that it uses so readily the information and organisational intelligence diffusion guaranteeing that the system is not lost through the suppression of any one of its nodes. This reservoir of extremism ensures a plentiful supply of ideological fuel for small activist groupings and party political formations wherever they arise.

(b) The existence of countless autonomous but interconnected nodes of ideological, organisational, and 'lonewolf' activity ensures that fascist ideology is constantly evolving and incorporating new elements into its diagnosis of the contemporary decadence (e.g. the European Union, ecological concerns, globalisation). Whether this is conceived as one of imminent collapse or of a protracted 'interregnum', in activist or in metapolitical terms, the core vision centres on the longing for a radically new order based on organic principles and authentic spiritual/racial roots.

(c) In the years of Italy's 'Strategy of Tension', post-war fascism demonstrated its ability to maintain a network of groupuscules directly associated with elements within the state, inspired mainly by a highly abstruse metaphysical interpretation of the evils of contemporary society based on the 'Traditionalist' vision of Julius Evola. The most spectacular expression of this crusade against the modern world was the Bologna Bombing of August 1980. It now tends to spawn lone wolves who take it upon themselves to carry out sporadic acts of terrorist violence.

(d) In its groupuscular form, contemporary fascism right helps maintain a subculture of ideologically rationalised and organised hatred of multiculturalism and liberalism which, in local conditions of exacerbated socio-economic and ethnic tensions, can provoke racially motivated crimes.

(e) It also ensures the ideological education within a sometimes remarkably sophisticated revolutionary ethos of new activists who may go on to join mainstream reformist parties, thus ensuring that both mainstream conservative parties and neo-populist parties contain a fringe of hardcore extremists.

(f) It can subvert democratic, pacifist opposition to globalisation and to the perpetuation of global injustices by attempting to inject these with a revolutionary, violent dynamic exploited by governments to discredit the 'no logo' or 'Seattle movement' (sometimes).

(g) It can corrupt the cogency of left-wing critiques of the *status quo* by hi-jacking and editing them in the interests of 'cultural hegemony' for an extreme right-wing analysis and agenda, couched in metapolitical anti-Western terms.

(h) In its New Right incarnation, which in some countries has achieved a high degree of respectability within mainstream culture, it can help rationalise and legitimate neo-populist attacks on multi-culturalism, feeding fears about the erosion of national or ethnic identity (albeit in a 'differentialist', pseudo-xenophile, spirit rather than an openly xenophobic one). This, in turn, can reinforce a climate breeding traditional xenophobic racism and help ensure that the 'centre' position of particular liberal democracies shifts to the 'right', rather than the 'left' on such issues as international trade, citizenship, and immigration. To that extent, New Rightists would be justified in claiming some measure of success in their attempts to undermine the hegemony of actually existing liberal democratic values.

(i) As a groupuscular force, fascism has also become supra-national and has internationalised. Furthermore, post-Kennedy America and post-Gorbachev Russia have become two of the major incubators for new varieties of extreme right-wing palingenetic ideologies. Fascism is thus well-placed to provide the basis for collaboration and organisational linkages between the Western far right and other terrorist organisations from the non-Christian world with their own mission in order to fight a 'holy war' against the West.[57]

Beyond the Maginot lines of the historical imagination (and the need for a bit of magic)

Just as fascism has diversified and mutated as a movement, so has the risk it poses to liberalism. Clearly, fascist movements no longer threaten to topple regimes and install dictators bent on pursuing imperialist dreams, or realising fantasies of racial superiority and national rebirth at whatever the cost. However, occasional terrorist outrages are only the more spectacular expression of the threat posed by what has become a largely subcultural or counter-cultural extreme-right constituency of fanatics and utopians determined to prepare the way for the inauguration of a new order. Moreover, much of this constituency now operates in a polycentric, leaderless, and hierarchy-less 'movement', more ideological than practical, and largely invulnerable to conventional state counter-measures or military tactics.

Attempts by the state to combat fascism in its new forms have certainly not been helped by the general failure of academic scholarship to recognise its transformation from a party-political (and hence high-profile, conspicuous, and hierarchical anti-systemic) force to a predominantly rhizomic (and hence largely faceless) one. The evolution of military technology and tactics meant that the Maginot line, France's imposing line of fortifications built on her eastern border that would have been invaluable in the First World War, was irrelevant to its defence against modern forms of warfare by 1940. In the same way, mainstream academic thinking on fascism is still dominated by the way it manifested itself over 50 years ago. A 'Maginot mentality' still prevails within the social and historical sciences on the nature of fascism – as embodied in the verdicts on its post-war development by Ernst Nolte, Renzo de Felice, and Martin Blinkhorn cited earlier. It is this collective blind spot that renders the new ideological and organisational forms of fascism largely invisible and undocumented.

The Fascination of Fascism

A Concluding Interview with Roger Griffin

The following is an edited and revised version of a recorded interview of Roger Griffin [RG] by Matthew Feldman [MF], which took place in May 2005. The original dis-cussion was chaired by Dr Robert Pyrah as part of the University of Oxford's ongoing Central and South-Eastern Europe Seminar Series. As a result, this concluding text is both the most recent and most informal in this collection, and rounds out the previous essays by offering Griffin's synoptic reflections on his pursuit of the 'fascist minimum'. Note the tripartite structure of the interview, focusing first on the 'back story' to Grif-fin's involvement with Fascist Studies; then on his evolving approach and contribution to this interdisciplinary field of study; and finally, a summary and overview of the pre-ceding chapters in this volume. These discursive and synoptic aspects are also intended to provide a more accessible 'way in' to the debates surrounding fascist historiography – indeed, virtually none of the polysyllabic words in this sentence are either found in the ensuing questions or in Griffin's response to them. [MF]

*****

MF: *To start off on a biographical note, how did you first get involved in Fascist Studies, at a time when it wasn't yet a recognised academic discipline?*

RG: Two pivotal experiences, reinforced by pragmatic considerations, helped crystallise my abiding fascination with the nature of fascism as a multifaceted, protean political force that has had a major impact on modern history. First, in 1967, while I was an undergraduate studying French and German literature at University, I spent a day in the city of Weimar as part of a cultural tour of students from 'the West' to what was still the German Democratic Republic, and hence a Soviet satellite state. In the morning I saw the wooden desk – on which the world-famous German humanist and artist, Wolfgang Goethe, had written some of his greatest poetry. In the afternoon I also saw on the way to the permanent exhibition of the horrors of Buchenwald concentration camp – the site of the famous 'Goethe Oak', left intact as a cultural monument within the electrified fences by the camp's SS architects. Aware of its significance to German culture, its stump had been preserved and commemorated by the SS administration after the tree itself was destroyed in an Allied air-raid in 1944. This dramatic juxtaposition of experiences seems to have triggered obsessive – though largely subliminal – thoughts about the relationship between humanity and inhumanity, modern literature and modern history, 'good' and 'evil'. They were embryonic questions about the nature, not just of Nazism and fascism, but of the modern age, human nature, human culture, and modernity itself, which I was only able to revisit properly more than two decades later.

MF: *But you mentioned two pivotal moments in the 'pre-history' of your engagement with the study of fascist ideology.*

RG: Indeed. The second rather weird 'incident' occurred in 1981, when I was half-heartedly searching for a suitable research topic for a PhD. – my first attempt to write one in my twenties, code-named 'The Dark Realm', having been a disaster, though the fundamental issues I engaged with then as a postgraduate in German studies were eventually to be subsumed within my research into modernism 40 years later. I had a curiously 'auspicious' encounter with a total stranger who came to sit next to me in a *taverna* in Genoa as I read an English history book. He struck up a conversation and, intrigued by the fact that I was teaching in a history department in England, showed me the book *he* was carrying, assuring me with considerable earnestness that it contained the key to understanding the *real* forces determining the course of human civilisation. With a growing sense of mission, and what Hippies termed after Jung the 'synchronicity' of that meeting, I noted the title of the book, and tried to track it down. But the Bodleian Library in Oxford – which I fondly imagined contained all the important books in the world – had no trace of it. The book was called *La rivolta contro il mondo moderno* [published in English as *The Revolt against the Modern World*].

MF: *Given the revolutionary nature and Dadaist past of the author, however, this was not a book about a conservative revolt against the modern world, but was instead a radical call for a utopian modernity, a 'new' modernity, as it were.*

RG: Precisely. The book radically rejected linear schemes of progress or decline, instead expounding a cyclic scheme that saw periods of dissolution giving way to a new phase of regeneration and health. It turned out to be the brainchild of the highly prolific Baron Julius Evola who, following in the footsteps of Oswald Spengler and René Guénon, in the 1930s became an autodidactic cultural prophet, theorist of occultism, and evangelist of the so-called 'Tradition', whose alleged existence he rightly claims is ignored by mainstream historians – though not for the reasons he maintained. Evola also came to be a visceral pro-Fascist and pro-Nazi who, after 1945, went on to become one of the most important gurus of Italian neo-fascism, providing a spurious philosophical and 'metapolitical' rationale for highly political bomb outrages during the years of the European far right's 'Strategia della Tensione' [the 'Strategy of Tension' of the 1970s–early 1980s, according to which bomb outrages would destablise society to the point of inducing the state to adopt extreme anti-communist and anti-liberal measures].

My efforts to come to grips with his alternative reading of European history would eventually become the starting point for my investigation of the recurrent motifs, structures, and fluid dynamics found in fascist ideology. It was an investigation leading to what I believed was an 'improved' theory about an ideal type of the 'fascist minimum', based on its revolt against the 'degenerate' modern world in the name of a new, higher modernity based on the reborn nation. It also offered a clue to resolving the paradox I had encountered so graphically and memorably in Weimar: the readiness of human beings to ruthlessly 'sacrifice' their fellow human beings in order to purge the present phase of civilisation of its decadence so as to inaugurate a new one.

MF: *Surely there were also less epiphanic and more mundane, pragmatic reasons for your involvement in Fascist Studies? Meaning that, in practice, how did you start out your research on fascism?*

RG: At the time of my close encounter with someone who in retrospect was clearly a convinced neo-fascist and might even have been a fanatical activist – I now regret that I did not have the knowledge or Italian needed to interview him in depth about his worldview – I was teaching on a course on the debate about fascism at Oxford Polytechnic [now Oxford Brookes University]. It was run by my inspirational Head of Department, the late Robert Murray. I soon realised that, though I was 'delivering' this course, none of the history books on the bibliographies we were handing out to students seemed to make sense of fascism either by offering a satisfactory definition of it, or an explanation of its genesis or its goals. There was no shortage of texts on 'what happened' but very little on '*why* it happened'. Certainly nothing available accounted, to my satisfaction at least, for the extreme violence, destructiveness, and systemic inhumanity of which fascism was capable, beyond making ill-conceived allusions to barbarism, reaction, nihilism, or pathology. In fact, I had yet to study key works by Stanley Payne, Ze'ev Sternhell, and Emilio Gentile, who would have put me on the right track. In the event, I undertook to resolve the issues myself within the framework of a doctorate. This eventually enabled me to write the type of book I wish had been available to me [*The Nature of Fascism*, Pinter: 1991] when I was designing the course and setting those questions on interwar Europe that I could not answer myself: a case of the blind leading the blind.

Nonetheless, what was missing from *The Nature of Fascism* was a serious consideration of the role played by the ritual, political dimension of what I was looking at. It wasn't enough to talk about the ideas or ideology of rebirth, and how they cast light on the trajectories of individual fascisms. I needed to look much more seriously at the praxis, at the way it was implemented, the way it was lived out and experienced. I can see now that, in this respect, it was a defective thesis. But then you only have 100 000 words to play with in a PhD., and it was the thesis that basically became the book. The resulting interpretation inevitably shared many of the blind spots in understanding fascism that were so prevalent in the secondary literature of the time. And even if I had actually been aware of all the gaps in it, I probably wouldn't have been able to write it at all, because I would have been totally paralysed by the overwhelming sense of how inadequate everything I was writing was in order to do justice to the complexity of the topic. So I owe it to the fact that I had this 'crush' on the basic idea of interpreting fascism that grew out of my reading of Evola's *Revolt against the Modern World* that I had the one-sidedness to complete it in the first place. Nevertheless, I now recognise that it's a defective book. A few years ago I was asked to re-edit it for students, but I have come to the conclusion that it would be a really bad idea, because I would have to annotate it so heavily to make it more complete and correct the distortions that it would no longer be *The Nature of Fascism*.

MF: *Let's turn now to your subsequent work over the 1990s, and in particular, what seems to be the development of your thinking on a number of themes related to fascism, like 'totalitarianism', 'modernity', and the concept of 'political religions'. Could you comment on your increasing engagement with the latter concept; for instance, how you incorporated this into your research?*

RG: The issue of fascism's ritual dimension in the interwar period takes us to the heart of the problem of deciding which historical lens is most appropriate for interpreting fascism when we write its history. When we see those grainy black and white newsreels of what the Fascists called an 'Oceanic Assembly' with hundreds of thousands of people crowded in a square to hear the *Duce,* every different theory of fascism adopted makes us *see* what was happening differently. We can see workers being manipulated by the 'aestheticised politics' of capitalism to stop socialism in its tracks. We can see crowds of Italian enjoying a sort of political opera with Mussolini as a *prima donna.* Or we can simply see a megalomaniac hypnotising an entire population.

The new dimension added to what I argued in *The Nature of Fascism* – particularly through the use of Emilio Gentile's brilliant *The Sacralization of Politics in Fascist Italy* – is that what we are actually seeing is the manifestation of a serious attempt by an ultra-modern, totalitarian regime to create a new type of society and a new type of Italian. This is not to say the crowd formed some supra-individual organism of fanatical faith. Of course, there were a lot of fellow travellers or people simply going through the motions in that square. You only have to see a wonderful film by Federico Fellini called *Amacord* about the gap between the regime's image and reality to grasp just how superficially many Italians were 'Fascistised' by the regime. Nevertheless, what we are witnessing is a serious attempt by a state to socially engineer a new socio-political reality, a new modernity, and a new future made possible by the structural crisis of the West in the interwar period.

MF: *You say 'in the interwar period', which raises a major point of contention between you and others in the field. For you see 1945 as a watershed in the development of fascism, but not the end of the fascist epoch as such.*

RG: Yes, in contrast to the majority of historians, I see fascism as having an important after-life once the Second World War is over, entering a second period of sustained, if strongly diminished, vitality as an ideological project after 1945. Certainly the vision of a reborn national community had been so utterly discredited in the mind of the general public by the catastrophe of the Second World War and Nazi genocide that – particularly in the conditions of growing stability and wealth in the capitalist West and of totalitarian repression in the Soviet Empire – fascism was comprehensively denied the political space to develop into a mass movement during the Cold War. This explains why, as a party-political force of any consequence, it effectively died in Hitler's bunker, unable to operate as a 'cultic' or 'ritual' form of politics with a charismatic leader.

Still, currents of 'palingenetic ultranationalism' certainly survived the defeat of the two fascist regimes. Wherever levels of socio-political instability have become critical or, for example, when mass-immigration is experienced as profound threat to identity, 'old-style' fascists – modelling themselves on the fanaticism if not the paramilitary discipline of Nazi street fighters – have sprung up on a small scale to commit acts of ethnic violence. Meanwhile, other zealots of the new order have vacated the streets to focus on a different battle, the battle for 'cultural hegemony'. Others may become lone-warriors cultivating fantasies of triggering race wars through a gratuitous act of terror like David Copeland, or take refuge in neo-populist parties such as Le Pen's *Front National*. In doing so these moles, working for a more revolutionary species of politics, carefully modify and moderate their discourse by campaigning not for violence against foreigners and Jews, but for the 'indigenous population' to be protected from the ills of multi-culturalism and Americanisation. They are at pains to avoid talking – at least in public – the language of racial superiority or the need for ethnic cleansing, choosing instead to tactically foreground issues of identity and cultural difference. Some of those who, in the 1930s, would have been swept along by a fascist party must now be content to join minute groupuscules or simply run websites with delusions of grandeur about their ability to spread the 'religion' of race or the need for European rebirth.

MF: *Here again, the development of your scholarship on fascist ideology is of relevance. Generally speaking, are there some respects in which you have modified your theory of fascist ideology since it was published?*

RG: Critics of my whole approach – and there are many – would probably assume that I am still am basically recycling my one good idea of about 20 years ago, when I started out on my doctorate: concentrating on the myth of rebirth as a defining characteristic of fascist ideology, and to see how fascism 'looks' when you take it seriously as an ideological force – which includes tracking its evolution after 1945. But from my perspective it is obvious that I have changed quite a lot. It's as if I'm still living in the same house, but I've completely redecorated it and added a new storey to the building. And that 'story' is to integrate fascism more and more fully within non-fascist aspects of modern history, culminating in my latest work [*Modernism and Fascism. The Sense of a Beginning under Mussolini and Hitler*, Palgrave Macmillan: 2007], an attempt to look at fascism's relationship with a whole number of inter-related phenomena relating to modernity and modernism. This is part of a larger attempt to contextualise and historicise fascism, so that it ceases to be treated like some Kraken-like monster surfacing in the sea of early twentieth-century modernity, and instead can be recognised as something which is part of our age and belongs to *our* modern age, even if it pursued a wholly alternative form of modern 'progress'.

I should stress that this does not mean – as some people have alleged – that I am engaged in creating a complex *apologia* for what went on under fascist regimes. In this case *tout comprendre, N'EST PAS tout pardonner* [to understand all is NOT to forgive all]. There is a danger of normalising fascism, of saying 'fascism is *just* another modern phenomenon'. No, fascism is not *just* another modern phenomenon, it's a phenomenon that, in some of its forms – and I do believe that Nazism can be usefully seen as a form of fascism – created the most horrendous crimes against humanity ever witnessed in history. What I am trying to do is to suggest that one way of getting a handle on the horrific, unimaginable, unrepresentable things that went on in the concentration camps, killing fields, and labour camps, for example – *one way*, not *the* way into it – is to see these events through the lens of the study into comparative fascist phenomena. It is a one way of increasing our historiographical understand-ing, a way that complements the attempt of more empirically based scholarship and the testimony provided by memoirs and art and so on to capture 'what actually happened'.

MF: *One of the things you stressed in* The Nature of Fascism *is the need to approach fascism as another political ideology on a comparative par with, say, liberalism or anarchism. Certainly it is true that other political ideologies have also caused great suffering – one thinks here espe-cially of Stalinism's place in the history and ideology of Soviet Marxism-Leninism. Perhaps the most contentious aspect of your stress on the ideology of fascism, though, is the claim that its distinctive feature as an ideology is what you call its 'palingenetic' vision of a new era. Critics have objected that all revolutionary movements try, in one way or another, to renew society, and hence are no less 'palingenetic'. How is it you see revolutionary 'palingenesis' in fascism as distinct from these other movements?*

RG: Well, there you raise two distinct points that are prone to be misconstrued. When I came into this field it was standard practice for fascist ideology to be neglected as a causal factor in explaining what fascism actually did. When I took it seriously it was, at least, in part a deliberate attempt – following in the footsteps of George Mosse – to challenge widespread assumptions that fascist movements are to be approached as pathological or atavistic phenomena. No: the engines of fascism burn on the fuel of ordinary human nature. They are products of modernity, not throwbacks to prim-itive ages of barbarity. However, what I never attempted to do was *reduce* fascism to an ideology; or to argue it was *only* an ideology; nor did I imply that fascism could be understood without extensive reference to a whole range of material factors which made that ideology attractive to millions; or instead claim that its 'nature' could be fully understood without considering what it did in the pursuit of its vision for society, its praxis, as well as what it said it was going to do.

Point two: I completely agree that all revolutions are 'palingenetic' by definition. Yet what makes fascism distinctive is not the fact that it has got a palingenetic thrust, but that it projects palingenetic longings onto the *nation*, conceived as an organic or racial entity. That means fascism comes about only when you get the myth of immi-nent or eventual 'palingenesis' combined with what I have called 'ultra-nationalism'.

This convergence creates an ideological compound which, in a crisis situation, can unleash extraordinary affective power. It is this unique combination making the fascist myth of the reborn nation something distinct from all other types of revolution. For example, the Russian Revolution was in practice highly nationalist, but it was not carried out in the name or idea of the reborn nation, but of a reborn humanity, an age of universal socialism. In theory it was not ultranationalist but antinationalist.

MF: *Coming back to the theme of fascism as a 'political religion', you alluded to earlier, in* The Nature of Fascism *you argue against this approach. You refer to 'the need to distinguish between political and religious ideology', arguing that those who treat fascism as a political religion are comparing it directly 'to the vision of a new heaven, and a new earth which St. John described in the book of Revelations'. However, as we have seen, more recently you have taken up the term 'political religion' as an invaluable heuristic aid for understanding not just fascism, but totalitarianism, in general. Can you explain why and how this change came about?*

RG: The simple answer is that I was wrong! Basically, I hadn't done enough homework on the concept of political religion, which I simply identified with the theories of Eric Voegelin, whose theory of neo-Gnosticism I still find deeply flawed. For example, I was not aware of the degree to which Rousseau was actually postulating the idea of a 'civic religion' in order to replace the Catholic Church after the overthrow of the *ancien regime*. 'The Cult of the Supreme Being' introduced by the French revolutionaries was a conscious attempt to sacralise a secular phenomenon in a way that has a tremendous bearing on what went on under Fascism and Nazism. Without actually being a modern form of apocalyptic religion, there was a deliberate attempt by the Nazis, and the Fascists – and it certainly would have happened if any other fascist movement had got into power under it's own steam – to use ritual and belief for the 'sacralisation of politics'. Like all effective politicians, fascists understood intuitively that reason alone is not the basis of mass adhesion to a political order, and that for the new regime to work, it had to encourage a powerful irrational, symbolic, ritual dimension alongside 'normal' politics.

One eloquent expression of this was on the first of May, 1936 in Berlin. The Nazis hijacked the traditional May Day Celebration and erected a massive Maypole with a swastika on top in a famous Berlin square. The ensuing pageantry celebrated not just the birth of spring, but the Nazification of the labour movement and the rebirth of the German people – all in one go. Partly cynically, but partly genuinely, the regime was symbolically enacting the birth of a new age. They were instituting a secular, state religion to encourage the mass experience of national rebirth from decadence and collapse. Understood in this way, 'political religion' becomes an indispensable concept for understanding interwar fascism.

MF: *Let me press you on one more, specific aspect of 'political religion'. At a conference held in 2006 at Oxford Brookes University, entitled ' "Clerical Fascism" in Interwar Europe',*[1] *you called certain movements fascist which you initially [in* The Nature of Fascism] *had defined as 'quasi-fascist', or not even fascist at all, because of their explicit invocation of Christianity as a source of legitimation: I'm thinking particularly of the Romanian Iron Guard, the Belgian Rex, and the Croatian Ustasha. You even suggested that some genuine believers in Christianity could create a genuine hybrid between religion and fascism, one whereby fascism tended to prevail over Christianity and not vice versa. Can you clarify these shifts in position?*

RG: Well, in some sense at least, we're back to the problem of language. 'Religion' is such a horrendous term, because its so polysemic – it means so many things to so many people – and there is a real academic problem talking about it without creating all sorts of unnecessary confusions. But let's get to the heart of what you've asked me. My premise, if we go back to Max Weber – though others could go back to other theorists to argue this – is that ultimately there's a mismatch between the complexity of the world, the uniqueness of everything, and our attempts to model it and fit individual phenomena into patterns and 'generic concepts'. In practice, this means there's always going to be borderline cases where things don't quite fit. At the time, I put some things just the other side of the limit, and now I would put some of the 'secular' side of the line dividing politics from religion.

The bottom line is that there are many ways of being a fascist, several different styles that fascism can adopt as a movement, and several relationships it can adopt towards established religion – not to mention positions that everyday believers can adopt towards fascist ideology in turn. In addressing these issues it is useful, I believe, to distinguish three distinct uses of the term 'political religion': the ritual, charismatic form of politics that all revolutionary or anti-systemic movements tend to adopt when their popular support reaches a critical mass; the spectacular events staged by regimes attempting to impose their values on civic society, which are intended to 'sacralise' secular politics; and the *politicisation* of an established religion such as Christianity or Islam.

MF: *This, in turn, raises the frightening consideration of 'faith based' extremism as the characteristic product of the modern world, one where there is no longer a single, dominant narrative, but conflicting, competing narratives. This is something you address in your new book,* Modernism and Fascism. *Can you talk bit about 'modernisation' and 'modernity' with respect to fascism?*

RG: One of the things I have attempted to illuminate in that book – and it relates to what I was saying earlier – is the underlying dynamics of the obsession with the renewal of the nation perceived as 'decadent' leading to the projects to 'save' or 'redeem' the nation that have come to be known as 'fascism'. In other words, it focuses on the general cultural situation known as 'modernity' in which specific constellations of historical forces can nurture movements based on 'palingenetic ultra-nationalism', allowing it to become a powerful socio-political force. In the first instance, I try to explode the category of modernism as a purely aesthetic or cultural concept, and argue that aesthetic attempts at radical innovation and cosmological renewal are to be seen in relation to a wide range of phenomena that are conventionally not associated with modernism at all.

A trivial example: the spread of nudism. Naturism arose in the pre-1914 climate of preoccupation with health and 'life reform', one manifestation of which was a vogue for hiking and trekking. Another instance was groups of otherwise 'normal' people believing that if they could regularly get rid of all this superficial stuff known as 'clothing' they would be stripping off the veneer of a repressive, unhealthy 'civilisation' and thus contribute to regenerating a sick culture.

The cult of naked, athletic bodies under Nazism is inseparable from this pre-1914, pan-European social movement which was bound up with widespread impulses to renew contact with nature or break through to more ancient forms of wisdom in the late nineteenth century, all of which I see as part of a response to a perceived crisis of civilisation; just as much as artistic and architectural modernism. The rising concern with social and racial hygiene, biopolitics, and eugenics is also part of this anxiety about degeneration found throughout the West, not just Germany. It was a crisis concretised and externalised *objectively* by the First World War, but which was, as it were, experienced and anticipated *subjectively* by the *avant-garde* in the pre-1914 *fin-de-siècle* – a very significant phrase, meaning 'The End of an Age'; and therefore, understood palingenetically, the expected beginning of a new one.

In *Modernism and Fascism* I try to show that what drives this pandemic concern with regeneration and renewal is something incredibly ancient, something inextricably bound up with the reflexivity and awareness of death that helps to define human nature and drives the creation of human culture. In other words, there is an *archetypal* aspect to the modernist rebellion against existing modernity, the bid to create a new, more satisfying culture that has frequently surfaced in the midst of social crisis throughout history, but one which takes on new properties and aspects under modernity. By following this line of enquiry through, it becomes more intelligible that, after the 1929 Wall Street Crash had torpedoed Weimar Germany, millions of 'ordinary Germans' suddenly – and not because they were German, but because they were human beings – became susceptible to an ideology of national rebirth, belonging, and community, which promised them a new sense of collective redemption and communal transcendence. In that sense the new book provides the panoramic conceptual framework for several of the essays published here, all written before I had formulated a 'bigger picture' that locates fascism within the larger canopy modernity and modernism.

MF: *Moving on now from your general background and approach to the specific essays in* A Fascist Century, *I want to ask you about this particular selection of articles. What significance do you attach to them – apart, of course, from the fact that all but three have never previously appeared in English, and two of those were written in an essentially non-academic register?*

RG: The first two pieces in Part I are practical applications of the importance I attach to the rebirth myth as a definitional component of fascist ideology. They draw attention to the totalising vision of history as renewable, which I see as the precondition to all attempted fascist revolutions. 'I am no longer human. I am a Titan. A god!' is a somewhat speculative survey of the temporal implications of fascism's palingenetic myth, which originated as a seminar paper for the seminar 'Modern Italian History: 19th and 20th Centuries', organised by Carl Levy at the Institute of Historical Research in London. 'Modernity under the New Order' was my first attempt to address the crucial issue of fascism's relationship to modernity. Its genesis was a paper I gave for a seminar on Nazism at Sheffield University, held by Ian Kershaw – the external examiner of my doctorate – in the mid-1990s.

'Exploding the continuum of history', my attempt as a non-Marxist to offer a Marxist interpretation of fascism closer to mainstream liberal thinking on the topic, grew out of more anomalous circumstances. I had been invited to review recent attempts to define fascism at a major Marxist conference on 'British fascism and the Left' held in 2003, despite being known for my vociferous rejection of the Marxist insistence on its reactionary, anti-modern nature. The article grew out of my experience of general incomprehension with the position I took at that conference. It also builds on an earlier article I published on the possibility of convergence between Marxist and non-Marxist accounts of fascist aesthetics.[2] The resulting chapter is a concrete example of my efforts to promote collaboration – or at least fruitful dialogue – in Fascist Studies even between the seemingly implacably opposed approaches. I thus welcome the fact that, after being politely rejected by several 'liberal' Anglophone journals, it was finally published in translation in *Mondoperaio*, Italy's foremost socialist historical journal, and edited by Luciano Pellicani, one of the rare Marxists convinced of fascism's revolutionary credentials.

MF: *Again returning to your own, evolving approach to fascist ideology, what importance do you attribute to this group of essays within the context of your work on fascism?*

RG: All three result from the attempt to apply what George Mosse called 'methodological empathy' to understanding fascism not just empirically, but *phenomenologically*, by taking seriously the worldview and psychology of its actors – in a strictly non-apologetic, non-revisionist sense, of course. In particular, it underlines how important it is to take seriously their distinctive diagnosis of the state of civilisation and the shape they ascribe to historical time; what used to be called the 'philosophy of history'. Yet these essays also illustrate, in different ways, how this approach reveals the presence of subterranean links between fascism and all bids in modernity to 'make history' by derailing it from its present form and putting it onto new tracks that led to an alternative future, an enterprise familiar to historians as 'revolution'.

MF: *The two essays assembled in Part II assume that Nazism is to be regarded as a permutation of the fascist revolution against 'existing modernity'. In doing so, you take a position directly opposed to many scholars – such as Ze'ev Sternhell and Renzo de Felice, to name just two – who regard it as misconceived to even entertain the idea of a 'German fascism'. Indeed, there is a longstanding, empirical historiographical tradition amongst may prominent German and Anglo-American historians, whose extensive research into the Third Reich largely emphasises the destructive uniqueness of Nazism rather than any comparative kinship with more moderate fascist movements (like the BUF) and regimes (like the PNF).*

RG: Yes, as I indicated earlier, a corollary of my theory of fascism is that Nazism is – like any historical phenomenon – unique, but that important aspects of that uniqueness can be illuminated by approaching it comparatively; in this case, as a variant of fascism, hence locating important aspects of its genesis, dynamics, and goals outside the peculiarities of German history. The first essay in this section, 'Fatal Attraction', was written for *New Perspective*, a journal largely aimed at A-level and High School students aspiring to study history at university. Both apply to Nazism the understanding of fascism's attempted temporal revolution encountered in Part I, and present its bid to inaugurate an alternative modernity as essential both to its mass appeal and to the powerful sense of mission it had in the critical phase of progressively conquering state power in the early 1930s.

The second piece, 'Hooked Crosses and Forking Paths', is much more substantial (and demanding). It was commissioned by a Spanish historian, Joan Mellón, to appear in a collection of essays on twentieth-century fascism [entitled *Orden, Jerarquía y Comunidad. Fascismos: Autoritarismos y Neofascismos en la Europa Contemporánea*, Tecnos: 2002]. He wanted a 'survey' chapter illustrating the heuristic value of applying the concept of generic fascism to Nazism as a whole. This accounts for the way it deals superficially with issues of immense complexity. But like the essays preceding this one, I see its main value as lying in its sustained attempt not only to break out of a Hitler-centric view of Nazism, but out of a Nazi-centric and German-centric one.

MF: *Part III illustrates one of the major points of cleavage between you and other historians of fascism, namely the energy you have devoted to considering the post-war development of fascism and its relationship to other forms of extremism that have prospered in contemporary society. Historians, and perhaps even most academics concerned with comparative Fascist Studies, tend to specialise in interwar phenomena, leaving political scientists to grapple with post-war extremist movements of the right, and with the taxonomic challenges they pose. Can you comment on the three samples of your work in this area?*

RG: The premise of the chapters in Part III is that Mussolini was right to claim in his 1932 *The Doctrine of Fascism* that the twentieth century would come to be seen as 'a century of fascism', but certainly not in a way that either he or Hitler could have imagined. In fact, they would have been appalled to see the triumph of historical forces they equated with decadence – in the form of what is now termed 'globalisation' – and to discover in what reduced circumstances fascism has been forced to survive; often resorting to desperate strategies to ensure that the flame of belief in national palingenesis is not snuffed out altogether.

'No racism thanks, we're British' argues that powerful currents of right-wing populism manifest themselves in contemporary Britain, despite the absence of a major neo-populist party on a par with Le Pen's *Front National*. It was delivered at a conference on neo-populism organised as a thinly veiled academic protest against the way Jörg Haider's Austrian Freedom Party was making waves in Austria during the late 1990s. This chapter highlights the fact that, after its electoral debacle as a neo-Nazi party, the British National Party was attempting to masquerade as a neo-populist one with no overtly violent or revolutionary racist aspirations: a clear symptom of fascism's extreme political marginalisation since 1945 and lack of a mass electoral base. Yet it also shows its age as piece of analysis, underestimating the prospects for Nick Griffin's success in winning a measure of electoral credibility for the BNP with this tactic. Nevertheless, the modicum of success he has won since 2001 has been at the expense of renouncing openly fascist solutions to what Nick Griffin and his hard-line supporters see as the growing 'crisis' and 'decadence' of a Britain 'flooded' by foreigners.

MF: *'Europe for the Europeans' deals with a dimension of fascism rarely covered in surveys fascism, which almost always adopt a country-by-country focus – not least on account of fascism's oft-cited 'ultra-nationalism'. Could you say a bit about the idea of a pan-nation, 'European' fascism?*

RG: This chapter is another example of 'work in progress', having been written for a conference on post-war developments in fascism held in Minneapolis shortly after the collapse of the Soviet Empire. It underlines the strong element of continuity between interwar and post-war schemes of national regeneration, which sometimes nurtured a pan-European vision of rebirth. It also highlights the way an extreme right-wing form of 'Europeanisation' has become far more prominent since 1945 as a response to the Cold War, globalisation, and to the rise of a liberal-capitalist European Union fostering multi-culturalism.

Contemporary Eurofascism offers a motley group of ultra-nationalists, neo-Nazis, Third Positionists, New Rightists, and white-supremacists a way of dissociating themselves from the narrowly chauvinistic nationalisms of interwar Europe that were largely based on the nation-state – and hence from Nazi crimes against humanity – while smuggling nationalism into their policies in other guises, such as 'ethno-regionalism', or the war on 'Americanisation'.

MF: *This brings us on to the last piece in this collection, representative of the many pieces you have written over the years on the theory of generic fascism. It was first commissioned by the German 'discussion forum' journal,* Erwägen, Wissen, Ethik *[Deliberation, Knowledge, Ethics or EWE], which invited a wide range of academics to reply to a controversial 'leading article'. First of all, what points did you set out to 'air' in your leading article, which seems to have set out to deliberately provoke debate in an already highly contentious area.*

RG: Yes, 'Fascism's new faces (and new facelessness) in the "post-fascist" epoch' was supposed to encourage, or rather challenge, German academics in both history and the social sciences to open up the national debate about the historicisation of Nazism to the increasingly sophisticated perspectives that have evolved within the Anglophone historiography increasingly treating it as a form of fascism. Second, it aimed to expose the fallacy of assuming that the fascism simply ended in 1945. Though the article was meant to foster greater collaboration on such issues between academic cultures, the unintended, practical effect – in the short term, at least – was to divide both German and non-German contributors; between those who broadly accepted my approach to fascism and those who did not, some of whom were vitriolic about aspects of my argument.

MF: *How do you respond to critics who find your approach, in the words of one of the most strident, 'singularly unhelpful'? These words are actually taken from the EWE debate. One of the major criticisms in this issue was that you are illegitimately extending the term fascism once you divest major, characteristic features from the interwar period, such as paramilitarism, spectacular politics, charismatic leadership, and violence as definitional components.*

RG: I would argue that critics are perfectly at liberty to apply any definition of fascism they want, but with the proviso that its heuristic value must stand up to empirical testing. For example, an insistence on the backward-looking, nostalgic nature of Nazism has to make sense not just of the breathtakingly advanced technology and technocracy of the Third Reich but of countless statements by Nazis themselves that they did not want to go 'back' but resolutely forward, towards a future rooted in what they perceived were eternal values. Similarly, those who argue Nazism is not a form of fascism have to explain why the organisers of the BUF adopted elements of both Fascism and Nazism in creating their variant of what they saw as an international force for renewal. Moreover, it can be documented that Mussolini and Hitler recognised an affinity between their movements that they did not see, for example, in Salazar's Portugal. As for the argument that of a non-paramilitary, non-spectacular, leaderless form of right-wing extremism cannot be fascist, those who uphold this position are flatly contradicted by the following statement, made in 1961 by post-war France's most articulate fascist ideologue, Maurice Bardèche:

> The single party, the secret police, the public displays of Caesarism, even the presence of a Führer are not necessarily attributes of fascism [. . . .] The famous fascist methods are constantly revised and will continue to be revised. More important than the mechanism is the idea which fascism has created for itself of man and freedom [. . . .] With another name, another face, and with nothing which betrays the projection from the past, with the form of a child we do not recognise and the head of a young Medusa, the Order of Sparta will be reborn.[3]

Besides, on a methodological level it seems to me profoundly *unhistorical* to treat fascism as a static entity, incapable of profound outward transformations when historical circumstances change dramatically. This is like defining liberalism, socialism, or Christianity in terms of features which are dependent not on the core ideal of society each pursues – the *idea* – but the form it adapted in contingent historical circumstances. An Oxford scholar, Michael Freeden, has adopted a sophisticated theory of 'ideological morphology' to account for how ideologies change over time, which centres on the way a 'core' of ideas can remain the same while adjacent and peripheral components can come and go. In this sense, my work argues that, though the core ideas of fascism were retained after 1945, the adjacent and peripheral elements have undergone considerable development. This still does not mean that fascism has some mysterious 'essence', only that, like liberalism or Christianity, it has mutated in response to radical changes in the historical conditions in which it operates.

MF: *Given the misgivings and even criticisms expressed by a number of German and Anglophone academics responding the* EWE *article, surely the very fact this was subsequently published as a book* [Fascism Past and Present, West and East: An International Debate on Concepts and Cases in the Comparative Study of the Extreme Right, Ibidem-Verlag: 2006] *suggests that Fascist Studies is, in fact, moving towards some sort of theoretical agreement?*

RG: I still maintain that there is a healthy and conspicuous tendency towards synergy and convergence – but not, of course, unanimity – both within Fascist Studies and between Fascist Studies and wider European historiography. It is significant, for example, that all the major publications of the last ten years on generic fascism, with the solitary exception of the book by an unreformed Trotskyite, stress the centrality of its bid to purge, cleanse, renew, redeem, or regenerate the nation. Probably more significant is the appearance of a series of books by a younger generation of historians who find it a matter of 'common sense' to engage with fascism not as a reactionary, backwards-looking force, but as a revolutionary, futural one deeply bound up with the early twentieth-century revolt against existing modernity that took on myriad aesthetic, social, and political forms. Examples are Angelo Ventrone's works on Fascism, Heather Pringle's biography of Heinrich Himmler, and Michael Allen's study of 'the business of genocide'. In his prize-winning analysis of the Nazi economy Adam Tooze states, for example, that the destruction of European Jewry is only intelligible 'in terms of a violent theology of redemptive purification', adding that '[t]he cultural and ideological turn in the study of fascism has permanently remodelled our understanding of Hitler and his regime'.[4]

As more and more studies are published on particular permutations of both interwar and post-war fascism which cumulatively clarify the specific genesis, social dynamics, and politico-cultural project of each individual example of national fascism, it should become clearer how fascism is born not just of the catastrophe of the First Word War, but of a more generalised sense of the crisis of Western modernity that gathered strength well before the First World War and produced many other variants of programmatic socio-political modernism. The prospect of learning more in English about fascist phenomena in poorly charted areas – such as former parts of the Soviet Empire and Latin America – is particularly exciting, since the dissemination of in-depth knowledge within Fascist Studies at present is very patchy. In short, I see Fascist Studies gradually embracing the paradigm I helped articulate in the 1990s, partly as a continuation of the Mossean legacy – a development that would throw into relief the linkages and affinities between concrete phenomena and theories of fascism which, to many academics, still seem unrelated at present.

I am also hopeful that, as Fascist Studies matures into a more collaborative and trans-national venture, it will become more and more 'self-evident' that fascism is an ideologically driven, futural project, one that, in the interwar period, assumed the transition to a new era was imminent, but which since 1945 has largely resigned itself to the notion that humanity is trapped in an 'interregnum' of indefinite duration. It would also be important to see it more widely accepted that, in the conditions of extreme crisis following the First World War, fascism was predominantly narrowly nationalistic, charismatic, and aggressively militaristic, attempting through mass-mobilisation and mass-militarisation to pursue the mission of the imminent regeneration of society. Perhaps one day political scientists, many of whom routinely dismiss post-war fascism as a non-subject or have refused to recognise its kinship with its interwar forbears, will increasingly recognise that, in the relatively stable post-1945 conditions, the same ideological force that once assumed a charismatic style of politics is now forced to adopt a variety of new tactics and organisational forms, some with no apparent connection with interwar models, and many almost exclusively 'virtual', thanks to the power of the web.

MF: *What form do you envisage to be your own contribution to such future developments in research on fascist ideology?*

RG: *Modernism and Fascism* will, I hope, encourage ever more experts to look afresh at the utopianism and praxis of particular fascisms, even in their most apparently reactionary materialisation, and see that they are not the expressions of an ultimately reactionary political force. Instead, these movements externalise a revolutionary, politico-cultural vision of the ideal society, one inextricably related to both a generational rebellion against Western modernity and to the countervailing modernism that sought to institute a new society. This broad conceptual framework offers the prospect of synergies and collaborations in understanding not just fascism, but all modern forms of political extremism, that were unimaginable two decades ago. Despite the debates and arguments that the discipline will inevitably continue to host and provoke, Fascist Studies promises to be a far more exciting and welcoming field of studies than when I entered it in the mid-1980s. It is now a fully fledged branch of the Humanities, which, at its best, combines theoretical sophistication with sustained empirical research, in turn informed by the insights of several disciplines operating collegially across national and ideological divides. The prejudice and tunnel vision that stunted the development of Fascist Studies in a generation that had witnessed the horrors of Nazism unfold are now dissipating, while the growth of extremist forms of religious politics originating outside the Judeo-Christian West stimulates ever more intelligent engagement, especially from younger scholars, in order to undertake the task of locating fascism within a globalising modernity. As a result, it is a discipline becoming *more*, not less, enthralling as time goes on; one I am increasingly reluctant to abandon for pastures new. For the moment, I want my own research to focus on the *modernist* aspect of fascism, although its biopolitical dimension is also one that I hope to explore in more depth if time allows.

MF: *Finally, do you have any words for those remaining sceptical of your whole approach; for example, those who mistrust any arguments that suggest fascist ideology may be analysed comparatively or dispassionately?*

RG: I think it is healthy for readers to retain a dose of scepticism when reading any historian, however empirical or theoretical, and to focus on whether what is written helps or hinders understanding. I would stress for the umpteenth time that my whole approach, being based on the concept of the 'ideal type', axiomatically rejects essentialism and renounces definitiveness. It seeks, tentatively, to integrate various approaches and cluster a number of different key explanatory concepts in the attempt to make sense of fascist ideology, fascist praxis, as well as the events they unleashed and continue to generate – all from within a conceptual framework which is no more than a construct, a heuristic device. The theories and definitions it subsumes are to be ignored or applied as the researcher sees fit, along with any other approaches she or he has acquired or 'borrowed' in the global market-place of ideas. As I argued in respect of the debate about 'political religion',[5] considerable progress is possible in the human sciences when academics see themselves as part of a collaborative enterprise in which no one concept or theory can, or should, enjoy a monopoly of 'truth'.

It is when groups of terms and theories are seen as illuminating related aspects of a multifaceted reality, and when academics devote their energy to seeking areas of convergence with other approaches in a spirit of open-mindedness and mutual tolerance, that more and greater historical reality can be understood. Entrenched positions, territorial imperatives, dogmatic rejections of rival arguments or definition should have no place in serious academic engagement with the past and its legacies in the present. Fascist Studies is not about individual historians, but about history itself. A Zen proverb warns that when the finger points at the moon, only the imbecile remains staring at the finger. Ultimately, it is the phenomena I am pointing to in my work that matters, not the words and theories generated by the typing fingers – alas, still only two! – that I am using to formulate them. So my advice to students and researchers alike is to keep reading, keep debating, keep learning, and keep trying to arrive at your own way of seeing the moon.

Notes

Editorial introduction by Matthew Feldman

1. See *The Daily Telegraph* online, at: http://www.telegraph.co.uk/travel/main.jhtml? xml=/travel/2006/03/11/etloch11.xml&sSheet=/travel/2006/03/11/ixtrvhome.html (last accessed 13/04/06).
2. Griffin, Roger. *The Nature of Fascism*. London: Pinter, 1991: p. 26.
3. Griffin, Roger, with Matthew Feldman (eds). *Fascism: Critical Concepts*, 5 vols. London: Routledge, 2004, Vol. 1: p. 6.
4. Griffin, Roger (ed.). *International Fascism: Theories, Causes and the new consensus*. London: Arnold, 1998: p. 15.
5. Bracher, Karl Dietrich. 'National Socialism, Fascism and Authoritarian Regimes', in Hans Maier (ed.). *Totalitarianism and Political Religions: Concepts for the Comparison of Dictatorships, Vol. 1*. Abingdon: Routledge, 2004: pp. 312–313. This view also echoes the question raised in a 1990 essay by the same name, written by the late Marxist historian of Nazism, Tim Mason, frequently cited in Griffin's work: 'Whatever Happened to Fascism?' in Jane Caplan and Tim Mason (eds). *Nazism, Fascism and the Working Class: Essays by Tim Mason*. Cambridge: Cambridge University Press, 1995.
6. Two previously existed only as written-up conference papers, three were first published in translation (Italian, Spanish, and German), one has a virtual existence on an electronic research seminar website, one was published in a journal for high-school students, and the last appeared in a German forum discussion journal alongside articles written in German.
7. See, for example, Emilio Gentile's *Politics as Religion*, Trans. George Staunton. Oxford: Princeton University Press, 2006; Stanley Payne's *A History of Fascism: 1914–1945*. London: UCL Press, 1995; Turner, Victor. *The Ritual Process: Structure and Anti-Structure*. London: Routledge & Kegan Paul, 1969; and Bauman, Zygmunt. *Modernity and Ambivalence*. Oxford: Polity Press, 1991.
8. See Burger, Thomas. *Max Weber's Theory of Concept Formation: History, Laws and Ideal Types*. Durham, NC: Duke University Press, p. 37.
9. The terms 'core' and 'adjacency' are also taken from Michael Freeden's 'Political Concepts and Ideological Morphology.' *Journal of Political Philosophy* Vol. 2, No. 2 (June 1994): pp. 140–164.
10. Geertz, Clifford. *The Interpretation of Cultures: Selected Essays*. New York: Basic Books, 1973: p. 29.
11. Griffin, Roger. *Modernism and Fascism: The Sense of a Beginning under Mussolini and Hitler*.
12. For example, '*Accelerators*, or precipitating events, inaugurate revolutionary violence. These are the most contingent events of all, but they are not difficult to recognize or conceptualize'; and again, 'The transfer culture of a revolutionary ideology – that element which tells the revolutionaries what to do and how to do it in order to usher in the new order – in some cases dictates what will be the sufficient cause, or *accelerator*, of a revolution'; finally and most relevantly to the case of the First World War: 'Of all the *accelerators* directly affecting the armed forces, by far the most important is defeat

in war. This is the one occurrence that dissolves even well-trained military formations, and from a restricted perspective, revolution in modern times can almost be considered an invariable complication of international conflict', Johnson, Chalmers. *Revolutionary Change*. Harlow: Longman, 1983: pp. 190, 138, 106; emphasis added.

13. Manning, Frederic. *The Middle Parts of Fortune*. London: Penguin Books, 1990: pp. 108–109, xxi.

14. Platt, Gerald. 'Thoughts on a Theory of Collective Action: Language, Affect, and Ideology in Revolution', in Mel Albin (ed.). *New Directions in Psychohistory*. Lexington: Lexington Books, 1980: pp. 69–94.

15. For example, see Hong, Fan. 'Blue Shirts, Nationalists and Nationalism: Fascism in 1930's China', in Griffin with Feldman. *Fascism: Critical Concepts*, Vol. 4, pp. 204–226; Larsen, Stein (ed.). *Fascism Outside Europe*. New York: Social Science Monographs, 2001.

16. See Griffin. *Patterns of Prejudice* Special Issue, 'The Groupuscular Right: A Neglected Political Genus' Vol. 36, No. 3 (July 2002): pp. 31–50.

17. See Coogan, Kevin. *Dreamer of the Day: Francis Parker Yockey and the Postwar Fascist International*. New York: Autonomedia, 1999; Mosley, Oswald. *The European Situation: The Third Force*. Ramsbury: Mosley Publications, 1950.

18. Mathyl, Markus. 'The National-Bolshevik Party and Arctogaia: Two Neo-Fascist Groupuscules in the Post-Soviet Political Space'. *Patterns of Prejudice*, Vol. 36, No. 3 (July 2002): pp. 62–76; Durham, Martin. 'The Upward Path: Palingenesis, Political Religion and the National Alliance' in Griffin, Roger (ed.). *Fascism, Totalitarianism, and Political Religion*. Abingdon: Routledge, 2005: pp. 160–174.

19. Antonio Carioti. 'From the Ghetto to Palazzo Chigi: The Ascent of the National Alliance', Griffin with Feldman. *Fascism* (note 3), Vol. V: pp. 57–78; Taguieff, Pierre-André. 'Discussion or Inquisition? The Case of Alain de Benoist.' *Telos* Vol. 98/99 (Winter 1993–Spring 1994): pp. 34–54.

20. Lowles, Nick and Silver, Steve (eds). *White Noise: Inside the International Nazi Skinhead Scene*. London: Searchlight, 1998; Mathyl. 'The National-Bolshevik Party and Arctogaia: Two Neo-Fascist Groupuscules in the Post-Soviet Political Space'; Macklin, pp. 62–76; Macklin, Graham, 'Co-Opting the Counter Culture: Troy Southgate and the National Revolutionary Faction.' *Patterns of Prejudice* Vol. 39, No. 3 (September 2005): pp. 301–326.

21. For an example of Combat-18's unrepentant valorisation of National Socialism, see http://www.drypool.net/cgi-bin/system.pl?id=isdgb, http://www.combat18.org (both last accessed 28/3/2006); McLagen, Graeme and Lowles, Nick. *MR EVIL: The Secret Life of Racist Pub Bomber and Killer David Copeland*. London: John Blake, 2000.

22. For some accessible and effective examples here, see the British periodical *Spotlight* (also available at http://www.searchlightmagazine.com), or online publications like *The Hate Directory*, available at: http://www.bcpl.net/~rfrankli/hatedir.htm, and *Extremism and Democracy*, available at: http://webhost.ua.ac.be/extremismanddemocracy/newsletter/News8_1.htm (all last accessed on 31/10/2007).

23. 'German Army orders on the "Conduct of the Troops in the Eastern Territories", 10 October 1941', in Steve Hochstadt (ed.). *Sources on the Holocaust*. London: Palgrave Macmillan, 2004: p. 112.

24. Griffin. *The Nature of Fascism*, p. 237; and Turda, Marius, and Weindling, Paul J. *'Blood and Homeland': Eugenics and Racial Nationalism in Central and Southeast Europe*. Budapest: Central European Press, 2006.

25. Mann, Michael. *Fascists*. Cambridge: Cambridge University Press, 2004: p. 12. Yet while attempting to distance himself from Griffin, the apple appears not to have fallen far the theoretical tree: Mann's useful study is, consciously or otherwise, quite in keeping with the 'new consensus'. For example, the first subsection in Chapter 1 is entitled 'Taking Fascists Seriously', while the second subsection, 'Toward a Definition of Fascism', attempts a single-sentence definition of fascism – 'fascism is the pursuit of a transcendent and cleansing nation-statism through paramilitarism' – which all seem little different to Griffin's own characterisations, excepting both synonyms and the inclusion of paramilitarism.
26. Griffin. *The Nature of Fascism*, p. 237.
27. Taguieff, Pierre-André. 'Discussion or Inquisition? The Case of Alain de Benoist', p. 54.
28. Griffin, Roger (ed.). *Fascism*. Oxford: Oxford University Press, 1995: pp. 391–392.
29. Levi, Primo, 'Afterward' in *If This is a Man: The Truce*. London: Abacus, 1987: pp. 396–397, cited in Griffin (ed.). *Fascism*, pp. 392.

1 'I am no longer human. I am a Titan. A God!': The fascist quest to regenerate time

1. Ozouf, Mona. *Festivals and the French Revolution*. Cambridge, MA: Harvard, 1988.
2. Notably the essays published in the catalogue of the Council of Europe exhibition *Art and Power*. London: Hayward Gallery, 1995: pp. 120–182; Ben-Ghiat, Ruth. 'Italian Fascism and the Aesthetics of the "Third Way"'. *Journal of Contemporary History*, Vol. 31, No. 2 (1996): pp. 293–316; Affron, Matthew, and Antliff, Mark (eds). *Fascist Visions: Art and Ideology in France and Italy*. Princeton: Princeton UP, 1997.
3. Taylor, Brandon, and Wilfried van der Wil (eds). *The Nazification of Art: Art and Power*. Winchester: The Winchester Press, 1990.
4. Hitler, Adolf. *Mein Kampf*. London: Pimlico, 1992, Vol. 2, Ch. 6: p. 430. Maximilien Robespierre and Saint Juste (Jean Pierre Léaud) anticipated the deliberate creation of state religions in the twentieth century when they tried to institute a 'cult of the Supreme Being', but their understanding of 'crowd psychology' and the tools of social engineering, propaganda, and state terror at their disposal palled into insignificance when compared to those deployed by the Third Reich.
5. For example, William Blake, one of whose *Proverbs of Heaven and Hell* reads, 'The hours of folly are measured by the clock; the hours of wisdom no clock can measure.' Baudelaire's poem 'L'horloge' in *Les Fleurs du mal* [The Flowers of Evil] is also relevant here, its dissection of chronic 'ennui' contrasting so strongly with the ecstatic mood celebrated in a poem such as 'Élévation'. The whole cycle of poems can be seen as an attempt to transform 'anomic time' into visionary time through the alchemy of poetry (or as Baudelaire himself put it, 'Je prends de la boue, et j'en fais de l'or' ['I take mud and turn it into gold']).
6. Pickering, W. S. F. *Durkheim's Sociology of Religion*. London: Routledge & Kegan Paul, 1984: p. 120. It is revealing that on the eve of the First World War, Durkheim hoped that the *anomie* he felt in the air would be overcome in the near future through a period of 'creative effervescence, in the course of which new ideals will be born and new formulae emerge which will for a time serve as a guide to humanity' (quoted p. 392).
7. Max Weber wrote little specifically about the qualitative experience of time, though his wide-ranging research into the contrasts between societies based on religion and secular societies implies a deep interest in the topic, especially given his conviction

that the world is essentially meaningless and is given meaning through human values. His observations on the way prophetic revelation presents the world 'as a meaningful totality' has a profound bearing on our theme. It was this 'totalising' illusion that enabled the Nazis to use rhetoric and ritual to create a sense of transformation from an incomplete, fragmented 'decadent' existence to a complete, whole one, an experience which could assume the force of a secular epiphany for someone who found in Nazism an escape from the distress of *anomie*.

8. For example, Campbell, Joseph. *The Hero's Journey*. New York: Harper and Row, 1990.
9. See particularly Eliade, Mircea. *The Myth of Eternal Return*. Princeton: Princeton UP, 1971. Eliade was a supporter of the Romanian Iron Guard's quest to regenerate history in the 1930s before becoming a professor of comparative religion in the United States; see Jesi, Furio. *Cultura di destra*. Milan: Garzanti, 1979: pp. 38–50.
10. A phrase popularised by Hughes, Stuart. *Consciousness and Society: The Reorientation of European Social Thought, 1890–1930*. London: McGibbon and Kee, 1958.
11. Cf. Swart, Koenraad. *The Sense of Decadence in Nineteenth-century France*. The Hague: International Archives of the History of Ideas, 1964; Serra, Maurizio. *Al di là della decadenza*. Bologna: Il Mulino, 1994.
12. Some valuable insights into this aspect of modern culture are offered in Kern, Stephen. *The Culture of Time and Space 1880–1918*. Cambridge, MA: U of Harvard P, 1983. See also Hughes, Robert. *The Shock of the New*. London: BBC, 1980.
13. Quoted in Pynsent, Robert. *Decadence and Innovation*. London: Weidenfeld & Nicolson, 1989: p. 156.
14. This point emerges clearly from Hunt, Lynn. *Politics, Culture and Class in the French Revolution*. Berkeley and Los Angeles: U of California P, 1981; Stites, Richard. *Revolutionary Dreams: Utopian Dreams and Experimental Life in the Russian Revolution*. Oxford: Oxford UP, 1992; and Lasky, Melvin. *Utopia and Revolution*. London: Macmillan, 1976.
15. This is a prevalent assumption about the nature of Italian Fascism, best exemplified in Mack Smith, Denis. *Mussolini*. London: Weidenfeld & Nicolson, 1981.
16. Bloch, Jean-Richard. 'La democrazia e la festa'. *La Voce* 28 July 1914. See also Walter Adamson's summary of the article in Adamson, Walter. *Avant-Garde Florence: From Modernism to Fascism*. London and Cambridge, MA: Harvard UP, 1993: p. 190.
17. Documentation of this vital stage in Mussolini's development as an ideologue is provided by Gregor, A. James. *The Young Mussolini and the Intellectual Origins of Fascism*. Berkeley: U of Chicago P, 1979: pp. 87–100; De Felice, Renzo. *Mussolini il rivoluzionario*. Turin: Einaudi, 1965; Gentile, Emilio. *Il mito dello Stato Nuovo dall'antigiolittismo al fascismo*. Bari: Laterza, 1982, Ch. 3; and Adamson, *Avant-Garde Florence*, pp. 141–143.
18. Cited in Gentile, *Il mito*, p. 105.
19. See Roberts, David. *The Syndicalist Tradition in Italian Fascism*. Manchester: Manchester UP, 1979.
20. See particularly the analysis of the nationalist dimension of Futurism offered in Schnapp, Jeffrey. 'Forwarding Address'. *Stanford Italian Review*, Vol. 8, Nos 1–2 (1990): pp. 53–80.
21. Marinetti, Filippo. 'The Founding Manifesto of Futurism', in Umbro Apollonio (ed.). *Futurist Manifestos*. London: Thames and Hudson, 1973: pp. 21–22.
22. See particularly Gentile, Emilio. 'The Myth of National Regeneration in Italy: From Modernist Avant-Garde to Fascism', in Affron, Matthew and Mark Antliff (eds). *Fascist Visions*. Princeton: Princeton UP, 1997.
23. For a sample of the palingenetic expectancy of the *Squadristi*, see the extract from the memoirs of Mario Piazzesi in Griffin, Roger. *Fascism*. Oxford: Oxford UP, 1995: pp. 39–40.

24. See Ledeen, Michael. *The First Duce: D'Annunzio at Fiume*. Baltimore: John Hopkins UP, 1977. For a sense of D'Annunzio's palingenetic temperament before he developed his own form of fascism, see Bonadeo, Alfredo. *D'Annunzio and the Great War*. Madison and Teaneck: Associated UP, 1995.

25. See Gentile. *Il mito dello Stato Nuovo*, p. 108.

26. See Griffin. *Fascism*, pp. 28–29.

27. See Mussolini, Benito. 'Fascism: Doctrine and Institutions', in Griffin, Roger (ed.). *International Fascism: Theories, Causes, and the new consensus*. London: Arnold, 1998: pp. 249–250.

28. This position conflicts both with the assumption that Fascism had no ideology, held by the Denis Mack Smith and others, in addition to those treating Fascism as a coherent, extensively rationalised doctrine, such as A. James Gregor and (to a lesser extent) Ze'ev Sternhell. It is fully consistent, however, with the studies of the Italian scholars as Gentile, Emilio. *Le origini dell'ideologia fascista*. Bari: Laterza, 1975; and Zunino, Pier-Giorgio. *l'Ideologia del fascismo*. Bologna: Il Mulino, 1985.

29. See Mussolini's speech on the birth of a new civilisation in Griffin. *Fascism*, pp. 72–73.

30. Mussolini, Benito. 'Political and Social Doctrine of Fascism', originally published in Mussolini, Benito. *Fascism: Doctrine and Institutions*. Rome: Arditi, 1935, reproduced in Griffin, *International Fascism*, p. 250.

31. Giuliano, Balbino. 'Il fascismo e l'avvenire della coltura', in Giuseppe Pomba (ed.). *La civiltà fascista*. Turin: Torinese Unione Tipografica Editoriale, 1928: p. 96.

32. Gentile, Giovanni. *Fascismo e cultura*. Milan: Fratelli Treves, 1928: pp. 57–58.

33. Gentile, Giovanni. 'The Doctrine of Fascism', in Gentile, Giovanni (ed.). *Enciclopedia Italiana*. Rome: Istituto della enciclopedia italiana, 1932. Also quoted in Lyttleton, Adrian. *Italian Fascism from Pareto to Gentile*. London: Jonathan Cape, 1973: pp. 39–40.

34. Schneider, Herbert. *Making the Fascist State*. New York: Howard Fertig, 1968: pp. 222–223.

35. Ibid., pp. 223–230.

36. Gentile, Emilio. *The Sacralisation of Politics in Fascist Italy*. Cambridge, MA: Harvard UP, 1996: p. 90.

37. Ibid., p. 158.

38. Cited ibid., p. 55.

39. Falasca-Zamponi, Simonetta. *Fascist Spectacle: The Aesthetics of Power in Mussolini's Italy*. Berkeley: U of California P, 1997: p. 186.

40. Ibid., p. 31.

41. Schnapp, Jeffrey. 'Epic Demonstrations: Fascist Modernity and the 1932 Exhibition of the Fascist Revolution', in Richard Golsan (ed.). *Fascism, Aesthetics, and Culture*. Hanover and London: UP of New England, 1992: p. 30.

42. Ibid., p. 31.

43. See Cheles, Luciano. ' "Nostalgia dell'avvenire": The Propaganda of the Italian Far Right between Tradition and Innovation', in Luciano Cheles *et al.* (eds). *The Far Right in Western and Eastern Europe*. London: Longman, 1995: pp. 41–90.

44. Berezin, Mabel. *Making the Fascist Self: The Political Culture of Interwar Italy*. Ithaca: Cornell UP, 1997: p. 38.

45. Cited ibid., p. 182.

46. A 'fact' which is, of course, dependent on the assumption of the ideal type of Fascism which defines it in terms of such a core. See Griffin, Roger. *The Nature of Fascism*. London: Routledge, 1993.

47. Fest, Joachim. *Hitler*. London: Weidenfeld & Nicolson, 1974: p. 215.

48. Hitler, Adolf. *Liberty, Art, Nationhood. Three Addresses delivered at the Seventh National Socialist Congress, Nuremberg, 1935*. Berlin: Müller and Sons, 1936: pp. 38–39.

49. Vondung, Klaus. *Magie und Manipulation: Ideologischer Kult und politische Religion des Nationalsozialismus*. Göttingen: Vandenhoeck & Ruprecht, 1971. Klaus Vondung provided an English summary of his central thesis in his article 'Spiritual Revolution and Magic: Speculation and Political Action in National Socialism'. *The Modern Age*, Vol. 23, No. 4 (1979): pp. 391–402.

50. Vondung is citing Robert Lifton: Vondung. *Magie und Manipulation*, p. 165.

51. Ibid., p. 164.

52. For the most authoritative investigation into the impact of occult ideas of race on the genesis of Nazism, see Goodrick-Clarke, Nicholas. *The Occult Roots of Nazism*. Wellington: The Aquarian Press, 1985. The only major occultist dimension of Fascism in the 1930s is found in the circle which formed round Julius Evola's 'Traditionalism', which was profoundly influenced by esoteric theories of reality. See Ferraresi, Franco. 'Julius Evola: Tradition, Reaction, and the Radical Right'. *European Journal of Sociology*, Vol. 28 (1987): pp. 105–151.

53. Rauschning, Hermann. *Hitler Speaks*. London: Thornton Butterworth, 1939: pp. 237–242.

54. For example, Bergier, Jacques and Pauwels, Louis. *Le Matin des Magiciens*. Paris: Gallimard, 1960.

55. For example, in a speech to the 1938 Nuremberg Rally, Hitler declared that 'National Socialism is not a cult-movement, a movement for worship: it is exclusively a *völkisch* political doctrine based upon racial principles [...] We will not allow mystically-minded occult folk with a passion for exploring the secrets of the world beyond to steal into our Movement' (Hitler, Adolf. *My New Order*. Sydney and London: Angus and Robertson, 1942: pp. 397–398).

56. Theweleit, Klaus. *Male Fantasies: Vols. 1 and 2*. Cambridge: Polity Press, 1989.

57. Goebbels, Joseph. *Michael: Ein deutsches Schicksal in Tagebuchblättern*. Munich: Eher, 1929.

58. Theweleit. *Male Fantasies: Vol. 2*, pp. 242–243.

59. Whyte, Iain Boyd. 'Berlin, 1 May 1936', in Council of Europe (ed.). *Art and Power*, pp. 41–48.

60. Weigert, Hans. *Die Kunst von heute als Spiegel der Zeit* [The Art of Today as a Mirror of the Age]. Leipzig: Seemann, 1934.

61. Schulte-Sass, Linda. *Entertaining the Third Reich: Illusions of Wholeness in Nazi Cinema*. Durham and London: Duke UP, 1996.

62. Ibid., pp. 267–268.

63. Ibid., pp. 294–301.

64. For the association between the swastika, the vortex, and the idea of 'autokinesis' or self-generating life, see Quinn, Malcolm. *The Swastika*. London: Routledge, 1994: pp. 74–80.

65. See Jellamo, Anna. 'Julius Evola: il pensatore della tradizione', in Franco Ferraresi (ed.). *La destra radicale*. Milan: Feltrinelli, 1984: pp. 215–252.

66. Griffin, Roger. 'Revolts against the Modern World: The Blend of Literary and Historical Fantasy in the Italian New Right'. *Literature and History*, Vol. 11, No. 1 (1985): pp. 101–124. A crucial work for understanding this neglected aspect of contemporary Fascism in its more 'metapolitical' manifestations is Bologna, Piermario and Mana,

Emma (eds). *Fascismo oggi: Nuova destra e cultura reazionaria negli anni Ottanta*. Cuneo: Isr, 1983.

67. Cardini, Franco. 'Alle radici di una concezione del mondo dell'avvenire: La comunità che si ritrova: il mito, il rito, la liturgia, il gioco, la festa', in Cison di Valmarino (ed.). *Al di là della destra e la sinistra*. Rome: Libreria editrice Europa, 1983.

68. Tarchi, Marco. 'Tra festa e rivoluzione'. *Intervento*, Vol. 31 (1978): pp. 113–132. The essay is also reproduced in Griffin. *International Fascism*, pp. 264–275.

69. Ibid., p. 274.

70. Armin Mohler expatiates on the qualitative transformation of time to be brought about through a metapolitical cultural revolution in Mohler, Armin. *Die Konservative Revolution in Deutschland 1918–1932: Ein Handbuch*. Darmstadt: Wissenschaftliche Buchgesellschaft, 1972: pp. 78–108. His ideas have been extensively influenced by the concept of cultural rebirth elaborated by Friedrich Nietzsche and Ernst Jünger. For a sample in English of the palingenetic mood typical of the protagonists of the Conservative Revolution, see Mohler's text 'German Nihilism' in Griffin. *Fascism*, pp. 351–354.

71. In his *Cultura di destra*, Furio Jesi distinguishes 'sacred', and 'esoteric' from 'profane' and 'exoteric' neo-Fascism, a distinction of relevance here. Thus, while Himmler and Evola probed into the notion of a reality 'behind' History, and hence cultivated an 'esoteric' palingenetic myth, the 'indeterminate secular otherworld, "immortal" yet of this world' which according to Jeffrey Schnapp was supposed to be evoked by the Exhibition of the Fascist Revolution clearly belongs to what Jesi means by a 'profane' concept of time.

    It should be stressed, however, that even 'profane' neo-Fascism postulates a transcendent, meaningful, collective reality beyond that of anomic, individual time. Clearly, some work is necessary to refine a discourse, terminology, and taxonomy with which to address the topic of 'Fascist time'. Refining distinctions between religious, pseudo-religious, and non-religious phenomena would be an integral part of such an exercise. For the moment I prefer to treat Fascist time as a (travestied) version of 'sacred' as opposed to 'profane' time, one which usually takes the 'exoteric' form of a hypostatised, profoundly mythic 'History'. On occasions, this 'standard' Fascist time can be mixed with elements of an 'esoteric' supra-Historical metaphysics, as glimpsed in Himmler's *Ahenerbe*, the death cult of the Legionaries of the Romanian Iron Guard, or some of the more outlandishly pagan forms of contemporary neo-Nazism, such as the Odinism and Ásatrú cults in contemporary America. On the latter, see Kaplan, Jeffrey. *Radical Religion in America Millenarian Movements from the Far Right to the Children of Noah (Religion and Politics)*. New York: Syracuse UP, 1997.

72. Benjamin, Walter. 'Theses on the Philosophy of History' (1940). *Illuminations*. London: Fontana Press, 1992: pp. 252–253.

73. Some Nazi buildings bore as their date of construction the number of years that had passed since 1933, or what the film *The Triumph of the Will* calls in the opening title sequence 'The Year of German Rebirth'.

74. Which is impossible in the structural conditions currently prevailing in Westernised democracies. See Griffin. *The Nature of Fascism*, Ch. 8: pp. 208–236.

75. Galli, Giorgio. 'La componente magica della cultura di destra', in Bologna, P. and E. Mana, (eds) *Fascismo Oggi. Nuova destra e cultura reazionaria negli anni ottanta* (Notiziario dell'Istituto storico della resistenza in Cuneo, no. 23, 1983): p. 286.

2 Modernity under the new order: The fascist project for managing the future

1. Mosley, Oswald. *The Greater Britain*. London: BUF Publications, 1932: p. 100.
2. Strachey, John. *The Menace of Fascism*. London: Victor Gollanz, 1933: p. 146.
3. Moore, Barrington. *Social Origins of Dictatorship and Democracy*. Harmondsworth: Penguin, 1966.
4. Organski, Kenneth. 'Fascism and Modernization', in Woolf, Stuart (ed.). *The Nature of Fascism*. London: Weidenfeld & Nicolson, 1968.
5. Turner, Henry Jnr. 'Fascism and Modernization'. *World Politics*, Vol. 24 (1972): pp. 547–564.
6. Gregor, A. James. 'Fascism and Modernization, Some Addenda'. *World Politics*, Vol. 26 (1972).
7. Hughes, Arnold and Kolinsky, Martin. '"Paradigmatic Fascism" and Modernization: A Critique'. *Political Studies*, Vol. 24, No. 4 (1976).
8. For an overview of the state of the debate in 1980, see Hagtvet, Bernt and Larsen, Stein. 'Contemporary Approaches to Fascism: A Survey of Paradigms', in Hagtvet Bernt and Stein Larsen (eds). *Who Were the Fascists*. Bergen, Oslo: Universitetforlaget, 1980: pp. 38–41.
9. Nolte, Ernst. *Three Faces of Fascism*. London: Weidenfeld & Nicolson, 1980.
10. Klingemann, Carsten. 'Sociology and Social Research in the Third Reich', in Turner, Stephen and Dirk Käsler (ed.). *Sociology Responds to Fascism*. London: Routledge, 1992: p. 127.
11. For example, Herf, Jeffrey. 'The Engineer as Ideologue: Reactionary Modernists in Weimar and the Third Reich'. *Journal of Contemporary History*, Vol. 19 (1984): pp. 631–648; Herf, Jeffrey. *Reactionary Modernism: Technology, Culture and Politics in Weimar and the Third Reich*. Cambridge: Cambridge University Press, 1984.
12. For example, Zitelmann, Rainer. 'Die totalitäre Seite der Moderne', in Prinz, Rainer and Michael Zitelmann (eds). *Nationalsozialismus und Modernisierung*. Darmstadt: Wissenschaftliche Buchgesellschaft, 1991; Aly, Götz and Roth, Karl. *Die restlose Erfassung: Volkszählung, Identifizieren, Aussondern im Nationalsozialismus*. Frankfurt am Main: Fischer Taschenbuchverlag, 2000.
13. Kershaw. Hitler. 'Ideologe und Propagandist'. *Vierteljahrshefte für Zeitgeschichte*, Vol. 40, No. 2 (1992); Kershaw. *The Nazi Dictatorship* (34th edition). London: Edward Arnold, 2000. See particularly Chapter 7, which offers a valuable overview of the current debate. Another sceptic is Norbert Frei, as emerges from his article 'Wie modern war der Nationalsozialismus?' *Geschichte und Gesellschaft*, Vol. 19, No. 3 (1993).
14. Sternhell, Ze'ev *et al*. *The Birth of Fascist Ideology*. New Jersey: Princeton University Press, 1993.
15. Apthorpe, Raymond. 'Modernization', in Kuper, Adam and Jessica Kuper (eds). *The Social Science Encyclopedia*. London: Routledge & Kegan Paul, 1985: pp. 532–533.
16. Benjamin, Walter. 'Theses on the Philosophy of History', no. IX, in Benjamin, Walter *Illuminations*. London: Fontana, 1992: p. 149.
17. Hobsawm, Eric and Ranger, Terence. *The Invention of Tradition*. Oxford: Oxford UP, Oxford, 1983.
18. Eisenstadt, Shmuel. *Patterns of Modernity, Vol. 2: Beyond the West*. New York: New York University Press, 1987: p. 10.
19. Yasusuke, Murakami. 'Modernization in Terms of Integration: The Case of Japan', in Eisenstadt, Shmuel (ed.). *Patterns of Modernity, Vol. 2: Beyond the West*. New York: New York University Press, 1987.

20. Gentile, Emilio. 'Il fascismo', in Gentile Emilio *et al.* (ed.). *L'Europa del XX secolo fra totalitarismo e democrazia*. Faenza: Itaca, 1991: pp. 109–110.
21. Marx, Karl. 'The Eighteenth Brumaire of Louis Napoleon', in Feuer, Lewis (ed.). *Marx and Engels: Basic Writings on Politics and Philosophy*. London: Fontana, 1969: pp. 360–361.
22. Mussolini, Benito. 'Il discorso di Napoli', reproduced in Griffin, Roger (ed.). *Fascism*. Oxford: Oxford University Press, 1995: p. 44.
23. Sznajder, Mario. 'The "Carta del Carnaro" and Modernization'. *Tel Aviv Jahrbuch für deutsche Geschichte*, Vol. 18 (1989): pp. 447–448.
24. Ibid., p. 459.
25. Mosse, George. 'The Political Culture of Political Futurism: A General Perspective'. *Journal of Contemporary History*, Vol. 21, Nos 2–3 (1990): pp. 253–268.
26. Roberts. *The Syndicalist Tradition in Italian Fascism*.
27. De Grand, Alexander. *The Italian Nationalist Association and the Rise of Fascism in Italy*. Lincoln: University of Nebraska Press, 1978.
28. For example, Currey, Muriel and Goad, Harold. *The Workings of the Corporate State*. London: Nicholson and Watson, 1933.
29. See Stone, Marla. *The Patron State: Culture and Politics in Fascist Italy*. Princeton: Princeton University Press, 1998.
30. Adamson, Walter. 'Modernism and Fascism: The Politics of Culture in Italy, 1903–1922'. *The American Historical Review*, Vol. 95, No. 2 (1990): p. 365; cf. Adamson, Walter. 'The Language of Opposition in Early Twentieth-Century Italy: Rhetorical Continuities Between Prewar Florentine Avant-Gardism and Mussolini's Fascism'. *Journal of Modern History*, Vol. 64 (1992): pp. 22–51; Adamson, Walter. *Avant-Garde Florence*.
31. Gentile, Emilio. 'Impending Modernity: Fascism and the Ambivalent Image of the United States'. *Journal of Contemporary History*, Vol. 28, No. 1 (1993): pp. 7–29. Emilio Gentile's English essays on the modernity of fascism are collected in *The Struggle for Modernity: Nationalism, Futurism, and Fascism*. New York: Praeger Books, 2003.
32. For example Sarti, Roland. 'Fascist Modernization in Italy: Traditional or Revolutionary'. *American Historical Review*, Vol. 75 (1970): pp. 1029–1045; Tannenbaum, Edward. 'The Goals of Italian Fascism'. *American Historical Review*, Vol. 74 (1969): pp. 1183–1204; Zunino, Pier-Giorgio. *L'Ideologia del fascismo*. Bologna: Il Mulino, 1985.
33. Gentile, Emilio. *Il culto del littorio*. Rome-Bari: Laterza, 1993: p. 181.
34. Thomson, Alexander Raven. *Motorways for Britain*. London: Abbey Supplies Ltd., 1938: p. 8.
35. Mosley. *The Greater Britain*: p. 125.
36. Brender, Reinhold. *Kollaboration im Zweiten Weltkrieg*. Munich: Oldenbourg, 1993: especially pp. 264–267.
37. See Müller, Klaus-Jürgen. 'French Fascism and Modernization'. *Journal of Contemporary History*, Vol. 11 (1976): pp. 269–283.
38. Benoist, Alain de. *Vu de droite*. Paris: Copernic, 1979: p. 316.
39. Krebs, Pierre. *Die europäische Wiedergeburt*. Tübingen: Grabert-Verlag, 1982: pp. 68–70.
40. Dupeux, Louis. ' "Rivoluzione conservatrice" e modernità'. *Diorama letterario*, Vol. 79 (February 1985): p. 6.
41. Ibid., p. 7.
42. Ibid., p. 15.
43. Barnes, James Strachey. *Fascism*. London: Thornton Butterworth, 1931: pp. 49–50.

44. Shand, James. 'The Reichsautobahn: Symbol for the Third Reich'. *Journal of Contemporary History*, Vol. 19 (1984): pp. 99–134.
45. Bracher, Karl. *The Nazi Dictatorship*. Harmondsworth: Penguin, 1978: p. 415.
46. Rabinbach, Anson. 'The Aesthetics of Production in the Third Reich'. *Journal of Contemporary History*, Vol. 11 (1976): pp. 43–74.
47. Speer, Albert. *Inside the Third Reich*. London: Sphere Books, 1971.
48. Walker, Mark. *Nazi Science: Myth, Truth, and the German Atomic Bomb*. New York: Plenum Press, 1995.
49. Herf. *Reactionary Modernism*.
50. For example, Pois, Robert. *National Socialism and the Religion of Nature*. London: Croom Helm, 1986.
51. Rhodes, James. *The Hitler Movement*. Stanford: Hoover International Press, 1986.
52. Cf. Möller, Horst. 'Die nationalsozialistische Machtergreifung: Konterrevolution oder Revolution?' *Vierteljahresschrift für Zeitgeschichte*, Vol. 31, No. 1 (1983): pp. 25–51.
53. For example, Zitelmann. Die totalitäre Seite der Moderne.
54. See Kershaw. 'Hitler: Ideologe und Propagandist'.
55. Rauschning. *Hitler Speaks*, p. 242.
56. Giddens, Anthony. *Modernity and Self-identity*. Cambridge: Polity Press, 1991.

3   Exploding the continuum of history: A non-Marxist's Marxist model of Fascism's revolutionary dynamics

1. 'To articulate the past historically does not mean to recognise it "the way it really was" (Ranke). It means to seize hold of a memory as it flashes up at a moment of danger. 'Theses on the Philosophy of History' No. VI, Benjamin, Walter. *Illuminations*, p. 247.
2. Schleifer, Ronald. *Modernism and Time: The Logic of Abundance in Literature, Science, and Culture 1880–1920*. Cambridge: Cambridge University Press, 2000: pp. 13–31.
3. Kafka, Franz. 'Auf der Galerie' (1917), published as 'In the Gallery', in Malcolm Pasley (ed.). *The Transformation and Other Stories*. Harmondsworth: Penguin, 1995.
4. Bloch, Ernst. *The Principle of Hope*. Cambridge, Mass.: MIT Press, 1986: p. 130. Of relevance is the following passage in Bloch's 1935 essay, 'Inventory of Revolutionary Appearance', reprinted in Ernst Bloch (ed.). *The Heritage of our Time*. Cambridge: Polity, 1991: p. 64: 'Nazism first stole the colour red, then the streets, then the rhetoric of radical change and hatred of the bourgeoisie, satisfying anti-capitalist longings by kissing the Aryan arse of Old Nick. [. . .] Thus the enemy is not content with torturing and killing workers. He not only wants to smash the red front but also strips the jewellery off the supposed corpse. The deceiver and murderer cannot show his face other than with would-be revolutionary speeches and forms of combat'.
5. Debord, Guy. *The Society of the Spectacle*. Detroit: Black & Red, 1983, 1st edition 1967: paragraph 109.
6. Hewitt, Andrew. *Fascist Modernism*. Stanford: Stanford University Press, 1993: pp. 17, 100, 177.
7. Beetham, David. *Marxists in Face of Fascism*. Manchester: Manchester University Press, 1983: p. 82.
8. Woolf, Stuart (ed.). *European Fascism*. London: Weidenfeld & Nicolson, 1968, revised edition 1981: p. 55.
9. For an exposition of my theory of the 'new consensus' see Griffin, Roger. 'The Primacy of Culture. The Current Growth (or Manufacture) of Consensus within Fascist

Studies'. *The Journal of Contemporary History*, Vol. 37, No. 1 (2002): pp. 21–43. Though the existence of an emergent consensus is widely challenged, even works by those who repudiate it vociferously broadly corroborate the following tenets, notably Gregor, James. *Phoenix: Fascism in Our Time*. New Brunswick, NJ: Transaction, 1999; Paxton, Robert. *The Anatomy of Fascism*. New York: Alfred A. Knopf, 2004; and Mann, Michael. *Fascists*. New York: Cambridge University Press, 2004.

10. I am using the term here in the sense given to it by Emilio Gentile in his essay 'The Sacralisation of Politics: Definitions, Interpretations and Reflections on the Question of Secular Religion and Totalitarianism', Trans. Robert Mallet, *Totalitarian Movements and Political Religions*, Vol. 1, No. 1 (2000): pp. 18–55.

11. A pseudo-ancient form of mass theatre promoted by the Nazis for the ritual celebration of the nation.

12. Fest, Joachim. *Der zerstörte Traum: Vom Ende des utopistischen Zeitalters*. Berlin: Siedler, 1991: pp. 50–52.

13. I plead guilty to this myself in the past. See Griffin. *The Nature of Fascism*, pp. 2–4.

14. For example, Werner Röhr draws attention to the damage inflicted by imposition of the Dimitrov orthodoxy in the GDR in the article 'Faschismusforschung in der DDR: Ein Problemskizze.' *Bulletin für Faschismus- und Weltkriegforschung*, Vol. 16 (2001): p. 18. Shortcomings in the various permutations of 'Bonapartist' explanation that have flourished beyond the hegemony of Comintern have been explicitly indicted by Ernesto Laclau in his essay 'Fascism and Ideology', in *Politics and Ideology in Marxist Theory: Capitalism, Fascism, Populism*. London: Verso, 1982; implicitly by Tim Mason in 'Whatever Happened to Fascism?' *Radical History Review*, Vol. 49 (winter 1991): pp. 89–98, reprinted in Jane Caplan (ed.). *Nazism, Fascism and the Working Class: Essays by Tim Mason*. Cambridge: Cambridge University Press, 1995; and more recently by Renton, David in *Fascism: Theory and Practice*. London: Pluto Press, 1999, especially the chapter 'Towards a Marxist Theory of Fascism'.

15. I have explored the possibility of such collaboration in the study of fascist aesthetics in the essay, 'Notes Towards the Definition of Fascist Culture: The Prospects for Synergy Between Marxist and Liberal Heuristics'. *Renaissance and Modern Studies*, Vol. 42 (Autumn 2001): pp. 95–115.

16. Benjamin, Walter. 'Theses on the Philosophy of History', No. IX, in Benjamin, Walter *Illuminations*. London: Fontana, 1992: p. 149.

17. Koestler, Arthur. *The Sleepwalkers: A History of Man's Changing Vision of the Universe*. London: Arkana, 1989: p. 524.

18. After the war, Louis Althusser constructed a theory of ideology that offers an alternative way of conceptualising the relative autonomy of ideology from economics and the crucial role of culture in providing a sense of identity, normality, and autonomy to those living under even what on closer inspection reveals itself to be an oppressive regime. See Althusser, Louis. *Essays on Ideology*. London, New York: Verso, 1971.

19. One Italian theorist Gramsci could build upon in this context was Antonio Labriola. Other Marxist currents within Marxist thought acknowledging the 'relatively autonomous' role that ideology plays in the revolutionary phase of political struggle is the voluntarist tradition that bore fruit in Leninism and Sorelian forms of Syndicalism. While not abandoning a class analysis of society, what these variants of Marxism share is the recognition that myth, vision, will, and flights of the historical imagination all play a greater role in shaping events than the objective conjuncture of material conditions, thereby rejecting the crudely determinist and reductionist variants of Marxism associated with 'economism'. See, for example, Krasin, Yurii. 'Determinism or Voluntarism', in *Lenin and Revolution: A Reply to Critics*. Moscow:

Novosti Press Agency Publishing House, 1969; Mazgaj, Paul. *The Action Française and Revolutionary Syndicalism*.Chapel Hill, NC: University of North Carolina Press, 1979.

20. Antonio Gramsci cited in Hoare, Quintin, and Nowell-Smith, Geoffrey (eds). *Antonio Gramsci: Selections from the Prison Note Books*. New York: International Publishers, 1971: pp. 139–140.
21. Ibid., pp. 231–233.
22. Ibid., p. 115.
23. See Gramsci's reflections on Caesarism in Hoare and Nowell-Smith, *Antonio Gramsci*, pp. 219–223. For more on Gramsci's interpretation of Fascism, see Adamson, Walter. 'Gramsci's Interpretation of Fascism'. *Journal of the History of Ideas*, Vol. 41, No. 4 (1980).
24. Cited in Hoare and Nowell-Smith, pp. 118–120.
25. Ibid., pp. 119–120.
26. Althusser. *Essays on Ideology*, pp. 54–55.
27. Laclau, Ernesto. 'Fascism and Ideology'. In Ernesto Laclau (ed.). *Politics and Ideology in Marxist Theory: Capitalism, Fascism, Populism*. London: Verso, 1982: p. 100.
28. Ibid., p. 103. For a non-Marxist analysis of the appeal exerted by an anti-systemic ideology at the height of a 'sense-making crisis', see Platt, Gerald. 'Thoughts on a Theory of Collective Action: Language, Affect, and Ideology in Revolution', in Mel Albin (ed.). *New Directions in Psychohistory*. Lexington, MA: Lexington Books, 1980: pp. 69–94.
29. Laclau. 'Fascism and Ideology', p. 119.
30. Ibid., 124.
31. Ibid., 136.
32. Ibid.
33. Dimitrov, Georgi. 'The Fascist Offensive and the Tasks of the Communist International', in Georgi Dimitrov (ed.). *Selected Speeches and Articles*. London: Lawrence & Wishart, 1951: pp. 99–102; cited in Laclau, 'Fascism and Ideology', pp. 139–140.
34. Laclau. 'Fascism and Ideology', p. 142. A remarkable anticipation of the main thrust of Laclau's argument is to be found in Klara Zetkin's speech made to a Comintern session in June 1932, which is cited in Beetham, David. *Marxists in Face of Fascism*, Manchester: Manchester University Press, 1983: pp. 102–112. In it she warned that fascism 'offered a refuge for the politically homeless, for the socially uprooted, the destitute and the disillusioned. And the hopes which none of them expected to be met by the revolutionary class of the proletariat and by socialism, they now look to a combination of the cleverest, toughest, most determined and audacious elements from all classes'.
35. Benjamin. *Illuminations*, p. 255.
36. Shakespeare, William. *Macbeth*, Act V. Scene 5: line 20.
37. Benjamin. *Illuminations*, pp. 252–255.
38. See Bloch. *Heritage of our Times*, p. 68: 'Thus the enemy is not content with torturing and killing workers. He not only wants to smash the red front but also strips the jewellery off the supposed corpse'.
39. A term made famous by Jeffrey Herf in his book *Reactionary Modernism*.
40. A term commonly applied to such figures as Martin Heidegger, Ernst Jünger, and Carl Schmitt, who are collectively seen as the intellectual fellow-travellers of Nazism. This view underwent considerable conceptual and ideological elaboration, imbuing it with a profoundly palingenetic dimension, in Armin Mohler's *Die Konservative Revolution*

in Deutschland 1918–1932. Stuttgart: Friedrich Schiller Verlag, 1950. This work has acquired iconic status for the post-war New Right in its analysis of the contemporary phase of history as an 'interregnum', the prelude to a new era conceived by the revolutionary right in terms that contrast starkly with Gramsci's own analysis of the 'interregnum'.

41. Osborne, Peter. *The Politics of Time*. London: Verso, 1995: p. 163. For an illuminating article that complements Osborne's analysis, see Feldman, Matthew. 'Between *Geist* and *Zeitgeist*: Martin Heidegger as Ideologue of a "Metapolitical Fascism"'. *Totalitarian Movements and Political Religions*, Vol. 6, No. 2 (September 2005): pp. 175–198.

42. Jünger, Ernst. 'Nationalismus und modernes Leben' [Nationalism and Modern Life], *Arminius*, Vol. 8, No. 8 (20 February 1927): pp. 3–6, quoted in Herf. *Reactionary Modernism*, p. 82.

43. Osborne. *The Politics of Time*, p. 164. Independent corroboration of the existence of a genuine element of 'futurity' in the Conservative Revolution, and hence within Nazism, can be found in the work of another Marxist, Alex Callinicos in his *Social Theory: A Historical Introduction*. Cambridge: Polity, 1999: pp. 214–226. Similarly, Mark Neocleous, another Marxist, makes a major deviation from orthodoxy, when he acknowledges that fascism uses the past in order to generate utopian images of a new order in *Fascism*. Maidenhead: Open University Press, 1997. For example, he concedes that 'the cult of the romanità [...] while appearing to be a reactionary turn to the past, in fact constitutes an orientation to the future. The spirit of eternal Rome was invoked not to regress to a previous civilisation, but to encourage Italians to become a new race, a reborn great people', p. 72.

44. Osborne. *The Politics of Time*, p. 164.

45. Ibid., p. 166.

46. Hoare and Nowell-Smith. *Antonio Gramsci*, p. 276.

47. The heuristic value of the concept 'counter-revolution' conceived in very similar terms has been used to great effect by another Marxist, Arno J. Mayer, in his analysis of the two formative revolutions of modern history: see Mayer, Arno. *The Furies: Violence and Terror in the French and Russian Revolutions*. Princeton, NJ: Princeton University Press, 2000.

48. It might be pointed out that 'objectively' all revolutions by definition 'react' against the *status quo* and hence perceive those who stand in their way as 'reactionary'.

49. Popper, Karl. *The Poverty of Historicism*. London: Routledge & Kegan Paul, 1957: p. 3: 'I mean by "historicism" an approach to the social sciences which assumes that *historical prediction* is their principal aim, and which assumes that this aim is attainable by discovering the "rhythms" or the "patterns", the "laws" or the "trends" that underlie the evolution of history'.

50. On the scientism of fascism and Communism, see Todorov, Tzvetan. *Hope and Memory: Lessons from the Twentieth Century*. Princeton: Princeton UP, 2003. On Nazi scientism see also chapter 1 of Bauman. *Modernity and the Holocaust*. Cambridge: Polity Press, 1989; and Bauman. *Modernity and Ambivalence*. The utopianism of 'utopian socialists' such as Charles Fourier and Pierre-Joseph Proudhon, Benjamin's stress on 'messianic time', Bloch's emphasis on the 'principle of hope', Lenin's espousal of voluntarism, the embrace of Sigmund Freud by Wilhelm Reich, Erich Fromm, and Herbert Marcuse, Louis Althusser's and Ernest Laclau's debt to Jacques Lacan – all are arguably symptomatic of the need to blend 'historical materialism' with overtly irrational elements to make socialism a mobilising myth or give it existential

relevance, and point to the key role scientism plays at the level of ideological mythopoeia.

51. The formative role of the remembrance of the past is also central to other unorthodox Marxists, notably Georges Sorel: see Vernon, Richard. *Commitment and Change: Georges Sorel and the Idea of Revolution*. Toronto: University of Toronto Press, 1978. In Jacques Derrida's *Specters of Marx, the State of the Debt, the Work of Mourning, & the New International*. London: Routledge, 1994, the remembrance of Marx himself provides the ideological pixie dust needed to conjure up a radical 'now-time' in the aftermath of the collapse of the Soviet Empire and the 'end of history'.

52. Benjamin. *Illuminations*, pp. 14, 253.

53. Marx, Karl. 'The Eighteenth Brumaire of Louis Napoleon', in Feuer, Lewis (ed.), *Marx and Engels: Basic Writings on Politics and Philosophy*. London: Fontana, 1969: pp. 360–361.

54. Ibid., p. 362.

55. In the 1890s, this element in Marx's thought prompted the Polish Marxist, Kazimierz Kelles-Krauz to postulate his 'law of retrospective revolution' according to which 'the ideals with which each reform movement tries to replace existing social norms are always similar to the norms of a more or less distant past'. Kelles-Krauz draws attention to the importance to Marxism of the latent myth of 'primitive communism', even if it is only referred to explicitly in Marx's own writings. See Snyder, Timothy. *Nationalism, Marxism, and Modern Central Europe: A Biography of Kazimierz Kelles-Krauz (1872–1905)*. Cambridge, MA: Harvard University Press, 1997.

56. Courtois, Stéphane, Nicolas, Werth, Nicolas, Panné, Jean-Louis, Paczkowski, Andrzej, Bartosek, Karel and Margolin, Jean-Louis. *The Black Book of Communism: Crimes, Terror, Repression*. Harvard: Harvard University Press, 1999.

57. Dimitrov. 'The Fascist Offensive', 101.

58. See Wordsworth, William. 'Discourse of the Wanderer, And an Evening Visit to the Lake', *The Excursion*, Book Ninth (1795–1814): 'The food of hope/is meditated action; robbed of this/Her sole support, she languishes and dies./We perish also; for we live by hope/And by desire; we see by the glad light/And breathe the sweet air of futurity/And so we live, or else we have no life'.

59. A former terrorist declared to an investigator when interviewed about 9/11 that 'non-violence is a bourgeois luxury': see http://www.ainonline.com/issues/11_01/11_01_securitytrainingpg24.html (accessed 09/06/05).

60. This is not to call into question the value for activists of believing at a mythic level that they are objectively championing a 'true revolution'. Consider the following passage from Martin Luther King in his *The Trumpet of Conscience*. London: Hodder & Stoughton, 1968: pp. 41–42: 'In 1957 a sensitive American official overseas said that it seemed to him that our nation was on the wrong side of a world revolution. I am convinced that if we are to get on the right side of the world revolution we as a nation must undergo a radical revolution of values. A true revolution of values will soon cause us to question the fairness and justice of many of our past and present policies. A true revolution of values will soon look uneasily on the glaring contrast between poverty and wealth. [...] A true revolution of values will lay hands on the world order and say of war, "This way of settling differences is not just". This kind of positive revolution of values is our best defence against Communism'.

61. I have in mind several socialists who attempted to supplement Marx's work with neo-Kantian moral theory (another mythic additive to scientific analysis?), notably

the Austrians Max Adler and Otto Bauer, and Marxists associated with the German Marburg School, especially Karl Kautsky in his *Ethics and the Materialist Conception of History*. Chicago: Charles H. Kerr & Sons, 1906. For a contemporary exercise in this project, see Wilde, Lawrence. *Ethical Marxism and its Radical Critics*. London: MacMillan Press, 1998.
62. Williams, Howard. 'Metamorphosis or Palingenesis? – Political Change in Kant'. *Review of Politics*, Vol. 63, No. 4 (Fall 2001): pp. 693–722.
63. See note 58.

4 Fatal attraction: why Nazism appealed to voters

1. *If This is a Man. The Truce.*
2. Kershaw, Ian. *Hitler 1936–45: Nemesis*. London: The Penguin Press, 2000: p. xvii.
3. Eliade, Mircea. *The Myth of Eternal Return (or Cosmos and History)*. Princeton: Princeton University Press, 1946. The final chapter of this book is an extensive treatment of the 'terror of history' and its profound impact on the beliefs and behaviour of 'modern man'.
4. This assertion is corroborated in meticulous scholarly detail by the first volume of Ian Kershaw biography of Hitler: *Hitler. 1889–1936. Hubris*. New York: W. W. Norton, 1999.
5. Broch, Hermann. *The Sleepwalkers*. New York: Grosset and Dunlap, 1964: p. 647.
6. Burleigh, Michael. *The Third Reich – A New History*. London: Macmillan, 2000.
7. Cited in Proctor, Robert. *The Nazi War on Cancer*. Princeton: Princeton University Press, 1999: p. 35.
8. *Hitler. 1889–1936. Hubris*, p. 433.

5 Hooked crosses and forking paths: The Fascist dynamics of the Third Reich

1. Only in the interwar period – when there was a widespread sense of the crisis of civilisation – was the change generally experienced by fascists as 'imminent'. In the post-war period, many of the more intellectually disposed fascists believe Europe remains in an indefinite 'interregnum': Griffin, Roger. 'Interregnum or Endgame? Radical Right Thought in the "Post-Fascist" Era'. *The Journal of Political Ideologies*, Vol. 5, No. 2 (2000): pp. 163–178. Reprinted in Michael Freeden (ed.). *Reassessing Political Ideologies*. London: Routledge, 2001: pp. 116–131.
2. Sternhell, Ze'ev. 'Fascist Ideology', in Laqueur, Walter (ed.). *Fascism: A Reader's Guide: Analyses Interpretations, Bibliography*. Harmondsworth: Penguin, 1979: p. 328. See also: Sternhell, Ze'ev. *The Birth of Fascist Ideology*. Princeton: Princeton UP, 1994. In the latter, Sternhell asserts that 'Fascism can in no way be identified with Nazism' (p. 4), and his statement in private correspondence to me in March 2001: 'I believe that Nazism was something different (from Fascism), just as a prison, a labour camp or exile were different from Auschwitz. Even after its racial laws Italy was not Germany and this was due, not only but very much also to ideology. Fascism in my view was at war with the Enlightenment, Nazism with mankind.'
3. Alan John Percival Taylor and Fritz Fischer also stressed the uniqueness of German history as the main causal factor in the genesis of Nazism. On the *Sonderweg* thesis, see Kühnl, Reinhard. 'The German *Sonderweg* Reconsidered: Continuities and Discontinuities in Modern German History', in Alter, Reinhard and Peter Monteath

(eds). *Rewriting the German Past: History and Identity in the New Germany.* Atlantic Highlands: NJ Humanities Press, 1997: pp. 115–128. The most influential discussion of German exceptionalism remains Blackbourn, David and Eley, Geoff. *The Peculiarities of German History.* New York: Oxford UP, 1984.

4. Friedländer, Saul. *Kitsch und Tod: Der Widerschein des Nazismus.* Munich: Hanser, 1984: p. 112.

5. Bracher, Karl Dietrich. *The German Dictatorship.* London: Penguin, 1988: p. 605.

6. Bracher, Karl in Geiss, Imanuel (ed.). *Meyers Enzyklopädisches Lexikon: Vol. 8.* München: Bibliographisches Institut, 1973: pp. 547–551. See also Wippermann, Wolfgang. *Wessen Schuld?* Berlin: Elefanten Press, 1997: p. 16.

7. Mason, Tim. 'Whatever Happened to "Fascism"?' in Jane Caplan (ed.). *Nazism, Fascism and the Working Class: Essays by Tim Mason.* Cambridge: Cambridge UP, 1995: p. 324.

8. Ibid., p. 331.

9. Kershaw. *The Nazi Dictatorship,* p. 262.

10. Kershaw. *Hitler: Vol. 1 (Hubris) and Vol. 2 (Nemesis).* New York and London: Norton, 1998–1999. Since publishing this chapter, Ian Kershaw has acknowledged that Nazism's '"charismatic" politics of national redemption' makes it part of the extended family of generic fascism, an extreme variant of 'the quest for national rebirth' that lay, of course, at the heart of all fascist movements', corroborating this assertion with a reference to my book *The Nature of Fascism.* See Kershaw. 'Hitler and the Uniqueness of Nazism'. *The Journal of Contemporary History,* Vol. 39, No. 2 (2004): p. 247.

11. Burleigh, Michael and Wippermann, Wolfgang. *The Racial State.* Cambridge: Cambridge UP, 1991: p. 306. That Wolfgang Wippermann also subscribes to this statement is curious given his unstinting advocacy of the use of the term by German historians of Nazism. See Loh, Werner and Wippermann, Wolfgang (eds). *'Faschismus' kontrovers.* Paderborn: Lucius und Lucius, 2003.

12. Stackelberg, Roderick. *Hitler's Germany.* London: Routledge, 1999: p. 23.

13. I argue for the emergence of this partial consensus in Griffin, Roger. 'The Primacy of Culture: The Current Growth (or Manufacture) of Consensus within Fascist Studies'. *The Journal of Contemporary History,* Vol. 37, No. 1 (2002): pp. 21–43. Since then a major contribution to comparative Fascist Studies and the history of Nazism informed by the new consensus has appeared in German, namely, Reichardt, Sven. *Faschistische Kampfbünde.* Cologne: Böhlau, 2002.

14. I should really say 'one key', since ideal type theory is itself only one ideal typical reconstruction of the cognitive process involved in constructing heuristic concepts in the social sciences. There are various other theories of concept formation to be found, for example, in hermeneutics, the Wittgensteinian concept of 'family resemblances', and semiotics, opening up yet another Borgesian world in which methodological paths for the investigation of reality intersect, converge, and bifurcate.

15. It thus betrays a profound misunderstanding of basic methodological issues when, in a reply to a review of his book, *Fascism and the Right in Europe 1919–1945,* the British historian Martin Blinkhorn talks about becoming 'increasingly impatient with the whole "generic fascism" grail quest' (Blinkhorn, Martin. *Fascism and the Right in Europe 1919–1945.* London: Longman, 2000). The review was published electronically as an e-mail in the series *Reviews in History* on 24 September 2001. The definitional essence of fascism is not some priceless treasure to be found only

through a daring leap of the romantic or mystical imagination. Rather, it resembles an industrial diamond in being an entirely 'man-made' product, and is made at the outset of research, not unearthed at the end of it.

16. On Weber's ideal type theory, see Burger, Thomas. *Max Weber's Theory of Concept Formation*. Durham, NC: Duke UP, 1976.
17. Kershaw. *The Nazi Dictatorship*, pp. 41–42.
18. Winkler, Heinrich August. *Revolution, Staat, Faschismus*. Göttingen: Vandenhoeck & Ruprecht, 1978: p. 66.
19. Kocka, Jürgen. 'Ursachen des Nationalsozialismus'. *Aus Politik und Zeitgeschichte (APZ)*, 21 June 1980: pp. 3–15, cited in Kershaw. *The Nazi Dictatorship*, p. 21.
20. Linz, Juan. 'Some Notes towards a Comparative Study of Fascism in Sociological and Historical Perspectives', in Laqueur, Walter (ed.). *Fascism: A Reader's Guide*. Harmondsworth: Penguin, 1979: p. 24.
21. Kershaw. *Hitler; Vol. 1: 1889–1936. Hubris; Vol. 2: 1937–1945. Nemesis*.
22. Rauschning, Hermann. *Die Revolution des Nihilismus: Kulisse und Wiriklichkeit im Dritten Reich*. Zürich and New York: Europa Verlag, 1938.
23. Arendt, Hannah. *The Origins of Totalitarianism*. New York: Harcourt Brace, 1951.
24. Burleigh. *The Third Reich*. London: Macmillan, 2000.
25. Pois, Robert. *National Socialism and the Religion of Nature*. London: Croom Helm, 1986.
26. Rhodes, James. *The Hitler Movement: A Modern Millenarian Revolution*. Stanford: Hoover International Press, 1980.
27. Sternhell. *Fascist Ideology*, p. 328.
28. On the growth of the new consensus, see Payne, Stanley. 'Historical Fascism and the Radical Right'. *Journal of Contemporary History*, Vol. 35 (2000): p. 110; Griffin. *The Primacy of Culture, passim*.
29. I use the term 'para-fascist' to describe interwar European regimes which created an elaborate fascist façade while remaining at heart conservative. See Griffin. *The Nature of Fascism*, pp. 116–145.
30. The use of the term 'palingenesis' (literally 'rebirth'), for the transformation of a political and social nature, was pioneered by Immanuel Kant, who gave it the connotations of violent and hence unsustainable, abortive attempts to realise a secular utopia (in contrast to 'metamorphosis'), a distinction which applies very much to the Nazi project of the New Germany. See Williams, Howard. 'Metamorphosis or Palingenesis? Political Change in Kant'. *The Review of Politics*, Vol. 63, No. 4 (2001): pp. 693–722.
31. See Griffin. *The Nature of Fascism*, p. 26.
32. Kershaw. *The Nazi Dictatorship*, p. 42.
33. Nolte, Ernst. *Der Faschismus in seiner Epoche*. München: Piper, 1963: p. 51. For the English edition, Nolte, Ernst. *Three Faces of Fascism: Action Française Italian Fascism and German Nazism*. London: Weidenfeld & Nicolson, 1965.
34. Payne's original 'typological description' is a checklist but of an unusually perceptive sort, which he later supplemented with a single-sentence definition of his own, which places rebirth at the core of fascist ideology; see Payne, Stanley. *A History of Fascism 1914–1945*. London: University College London Press, 1995: p. 14.
35. For Emilio Gentile's checklist, originally published in *Enciclopedia Italiana* (1992) see Payne. *A History of Fascism*, pp. 5–6.
36. Kershaw. *The Nazi Dictatorship*, p. 42.

37. For this distinction, see Seliger, Martin. 'Fundamental and Operative Ideology: The Two Principal Dimensions of Political Argumentation'. *Policy Sciences*, Vol. 1 (1970): pp. 325–327. In his even more sophisticated model of political ideology, Michael Freeden refers to the 'ineliminable core' of an ideology as opposed to elements which are 'adjacent' and 'peripheral'; see Freeden, Michael. 'Political Concepts and Ideological Morphology'. *The Journal of Political Philosophy*, Vol. 2, No. 2 (1994): pp. 140–164. In this article Freeden introduces the theory explored in greater detail in his *Ideologies and Political Theory: A Conceptual Approach*. Oxford: Clarendon Press, 1998.

38. See 'Hitler's Speech in Munich' at http://www4.stormfront.org/posterity/ns/5-1-23.html (last accessed 31/05/08).

39. Institut für Zeitgeschichte, Hauptamt Wissenschaft, MA/610, pp. 57711–23. Cited in Tal, Uriel. *Religion, Politics and Ideology in the Third Reich: Selected Essays*. London and New York: Routledge, 2004: p. 90. This book of essays, written between 1971 and 1985, extensively uses primary sources to document the centrality of imagery of redemption and rebirth in the blend of the mythic, irrational with the scientific and rational, which Tal calls Nazism's 'political theology'.

40. Rosenberg, Alfred. *Letzte Aufzeichnungen: Ideale und Idole der nationalsozialistischen Revolution*. Göttingen: Plesse, 1955: p. 316.

41. Trevor-Roper, Hugh. 'The Phenomenon of Fascism', in Woolf, Stuart (ed.). *European Fascism*. London: Weidenfeld & Nicolson, 1968: p. 55.

42. Klaus Theweleit at least elaborates such assumptions in an impressively documented and considered psychodynamic theory in Theweleit, Klaus. *Male Fantasies: Vols. 1 and 2*. Cambridge: Polity Press, 1989.

43. Williamson, David Graham. *The Third Reich*. London and New York: Longman, 1995: p. 37. The quotation is from Orlow, Dietrich. *The History of the Nazi Party: Vol. 2, 1933–1945*. London: David and Charles, 1973: p. 17.

44. Williamson. *The Third Reich*, p. 37.

45. Significantly, the term 'propaganda' derives from the expression used by the Vatican: 'de propaganda fide' (concerning the propagation of Faith).

46. It is worth pointing out here that only a relatively small, but unquantifiable and fluctuating, percentage of Nazis belonged at any one time to the special category of those who believed whole-heartedly in the palingenetic vision of the movement, the real driving force behind Nazism as a revolutionary force. Most subjects of a totalitarian regime are to a greater or lesser extent 'fellow travellers' rather than core believers/fanatics, hence the speed with which a nation can make the transition to a pluralistic society based on different values once the totalitarian regime has collapsed.

47. For example, Tormey, Simon. *Making Sense of Tyranny*. Manchester: Manchester UP, 1995. The most important contribution to a radical rethinking of the concept 'totalitarianism', however, is to be found in a seminal article by Emilio Gentile that explores the nexus between totalitarianism, palingenesis, political religion, and the creation of a 'new man' via social engineering (Gentile, Emilio. 'The Sacralisation of Politics: Definitions, Interpretations and Reflections on the Question of Secular Religion and Totalitarianism'. *Totalitarian Movements and Political Religions*, Vol. 1, No. 1 (2000): pp. 18–55).

48. Recent Anglophone scholarship wisely avoids engaging with Eric Voeglin's questionable metahistorical speculation about the 'gnostic' nature of all modern political ideologies. One of the more important examples of the revitalised use of the concept is an article by Michael Burleigh, which uses the term 'political religion' with

the connotations given to it by Emilio Gentile, of the type of secular politics in religious guise produced by a totalitarian movement or regime attempting to realise the 'palingenetic' vision of a 'new man' (Burleigh, Michael. 'National Socialism as a Political Religion'. *Totalitarian Movements and Political Religions*, Vol. 1, No. 2 (2002): pp. 1–26). It hence unwittingly corroborates the heuristic value of applying the generic term 'fascism' to Nazism (even though, as we have pointed out, Burleigh himself studiously avoids the term himself in *The Third Reich*), as long as it denotes a 'palingenetic' form of 'ultra-nationalism', as the new consensus now suggests. Anglophone historians, such as Ian Kershaw and Richard Evans, nevertheless remain sceptical about the heuristic value of the term 'political religion' when applied to Nazism. Such observations should in no way be taken to endorse the thesis expounded in Richard Steigmann-Gall, namely, that Nazism's claim to embody a 'positive Christianity' should be taken at face value as a theologically coherent form of politics (Steigmann-Gall, Richard. *Holy Reich: Nazi Conceptions of Christianity, 1919–1945*. Cambridge: Cambridge UP, 2003).

49. Kroll, Frank-Lothar. *Utopie als Ideologie: Geschichtsdenken im Dritten Reich*. Paderborn: Schöningh, 1998.
50. See Griffin. *Fascism*, Part Two, pp. 129–165.
51. See, for example, Mühlberger, Detlef. *Hitler's Voice: The Völkischer Beobachter, Vol. 1 (The Organization of the Party); Vol. 2 (Propaganda)*. Bern: Peter Lang Verlag, 2004.
52. For example, Steding, Christoph. *Das Reich und die Krankheit Europas*. Hamburg: Hanseatische Verlagsanstalt, 1938.
53. Such a vision informs Ernst Jünger's 1932 essay *Der Arbeiter. Herrschaft und Gestalt*. Hambuug: Hanseatische Verlagsanstalt, 1932, and the debate within the Nazi hierarchy over Albert Speer's Theory of Ruin Value (see Speer, Albert. *Inside the Third Reich: Memoirs*. New York: Macmillan, 1970: pp. 55–56).
54. From this perspective, works illuminating the spectacular aspect of modern state politics thus assume a crucial importance in the context of Nazism, and the prescience of G. L. Mosse's pioneering study of the role played by the 'aestheticization' of German nationalism in preparing the ground for Nazism assumes even greater significance (e.g. in Mosse, George L. *The Nationalization of the Masses*. New York: Howard Fertig, 1975).
55. There is a tendency for this to happen even in such scholarly texts as: Spackmann, Barbara. *Fascist Virilities: Rhetoric, Ideology, and Social Fantasy in Italy*. Minneapolis: University of Minnesota Press, 1996; Falasca-Zamponi. *Fascist Spectacle*.
56. See Roberts, David. 'How Not to Think About Fascism and Ideology, Intellectual Antecedents and Historical Meaning'. *Journal of Contemporary History*, Vol. 35, No. 2 (2000): p. 208.
57. Mason, Tim. 'Primacy of Politics: Politics and Economics in National Socialist Germany', in Jane Caplan (ed.). *Nazism, Fascism and the Working Class*. Cambridge: Cambridge UP, 1995: pp. 53–72. This essay recognises that the Holocaust was driven by political rather than economic imperatives, but still betrays considerable confusion about the existence of any coherent ideology underlying the policies it pursued. In this respect, it is encouraging that the last chapter of Richard Evans' *The Coming of the Third Reich*, the first volume of his forthcoming trilogy, explores 'Hitler's Cultural Revolution' (Evans, Richard. *The Coming of the Third Reich*. Harmondsworth: Penguin, 2004).
58. Antonio Gramsci's concept of 'cultural hegemony' is a perceptive recognition by a Marxist theorist on the central importance of ideology, civic society, and political

culture in determining the success of any movement (and by implication Italian Fascism) in achieving and maintaining state power by supplementing the role of coercion ('domination'). See Adamson, Walter. *Hegemony and Revolution: A Study of Antonio Gramsci's Political and Cultural Theory*. Berkeley: University of California Press, 1980.

59. On Nazi 'Newspeak', see Klemperer, Victor. *The Language of the Third Reich: LTI, Lingua Tertii Imperii, A Philologist's Notebook*. London: Athlone, 2000. ('Newspeak' is the term used for the official language used by the totalitarian society described in George Orwell's *1984*, which was deliberately engineered by the state to make all genuine thought – and hence rebellion – inconceivable.)

60. Pfeffer von Salomon, Franz. *Zucht: Eine Forderung zum Programm*. (Internal Party memorandum, Christmas 1925, NSDAP-Hauptarchiv, Hoover Institution, Microfilm Collection, Reel, 44, Folder 896, 1–11). I am grateful to Detlef Mühlberger for bringing my attention to this source and making it available to me.

61. Benn, Gottfried. 'Züchtung I', in Gottfried Benn *Der neue Staat und die Intellektuellen*. Stuttgart and Berlin: Deutsche Verlags-Anstalt, 1933. Also reprinted in Benn, Gottfried. *Essays, Reden, Vorträge*. Wiesbaden: Limes Verlag, 1959: pp. 214–222.

62. Kershaw. *The Nazi Dictatorship*, p. 173.

63. Fritzsche, Peter. 'Fascism, desire and social mechanics'. *Ethik und Sozialwissenschaften*, Vol. 11, No. 2 (2000): pp. 298–300.

64. Such was the prevalence of the sense that liberal capitalist society was excessively atomised by individualism and materialism that the Social Democrats and Centre Party also talked of the need for Germany to become a 'national community'.

65. See Brooker, Paul. *The Faces of Fraternalism: Nazi Germany, Fascist Italy, and Imperial Japan*. Oxford: Oxford UP, 1991.

66. See particularly Vondung, Klaus. *Magie und Manipulation: Ideologischer Kult und politische Religion des Nationalsozialismus*. Göttingen: Vandenhoeck & Ruprecht, 1971.

67. See Griffin, Roger. 'Notes towards the Definition of Fascist Culture: The Prospects for Synergy Between Marxist and Liberal Heuristics'. *Renaissance and Modern Studies*, Vol. 42 (2001): pp. 95–115.

68. The concept of 'charisma' as a function of socio-political forces rather than personal qualities is one of the central concepts to Ian Kershaw's two-volume biography of History. *Hitler: Vol. 1 (Hubris) and Vol. 2 (Nemesis)*.

69. The position argued, for example, by the extreme intentionalist Lucy Dawidowicz, who claims 'Hitler openly espoused his plans of annihilation' as early as 1925 (Dawidowicz, Lucy. *The War against the Jews*. Harmondsworth: Penguin, 1977: pp. 193–208).

70. This argument can be seen as a 'moderate functionalist' position, the most scholarly exposition of which is found in Browning, Christopher. *Nazi Policy, Jewish Workers, German Killers*. Cambridge: Cambridge UP, 2000. For the timing of the crucial decisions regarding the planning of the Holocaust, see Chapter 1. For an excellent summary of the complex academic debate surrounding the authority for, and timing of, the series of decisions which led to the 'Final Solution', see the chapter 'Hitler and the Holocaust' in Kershaw's *The Nazi Dictatorship*.

71. This approach is already clear from his article: Mosse, George L. 'The Genesis of Fascism'. *Journal of Contemporary History*, Vol. 1, No. 1 (1966): pp. 19–20. See also: Mosse, George L (ed.). *The Fascist Revolution*. New York: Howard Fertig, 1998: p. x.

72. Grand, Alexander de. *Fascist Italy and Nazi Germany: The Fascist Style of Rule*. New York and London: Routledge, 1995.

73. This approach thus conflicts with the thesis expounded in Daniel Goldhagen's *Hitler's Willing Executioners*, which held that the Germans became the 'willing executioners' of the Jews because of peculiarities in their cultural and political history which predisposed them *en masse* to 'eliminationist anti-Semitism' (Goldhagen, Daniel. *Hitler's Willing Executioners*. London: Abacus, 1997). See Kershaw. *The Nazi Dictatorship*, pp. 253–262.

74. See the chapters 'Hitler: Master of the Third Reich' or 'Weak Dictator' in Kershaw's *The Nazi Dictatorship*.

75. An example is the fact that the plight of a single handicapped child, which became known as the 'Knauer case', precipitated the euthanasia campaign after Hitler's personal involvement in it in the winter of 1938–1939 resulting in the formation of an *ad hoc* committee called the Reich Committee for the Scientific Registration of Serious Hereditarily and Congenitally-based Illnesses. See Burleigh and Wippermann. *The Racial State*, pp. 142–145.

76. For an overview of this debate, see Kershaw. *The Nazi Dictatorship*, Ch. 4, pp. 69–92.

77. On the 'nemesis' dimension of the fate of the Third Reich, see Kershaw. *Hitler: 1937–1945. Nemesis*.

78. On the redemptive aspect of Nazism, see Kershaw. 'Hitler and the Uniqueness of Nazism'.

79. See Kershaw. *Hitler: Hubris*, especially Ch. 13. 'Working towards the Führer': pp. 527–591.

80. de Grand. *Fascist Italy and Nazi Germany*, pp. 2–3, 77–78.

81. Stackelberg. *Hitler's Germany*, pp. 100, 118, 143.

82. For the text of the film, see the Calvin College Website providing English translations of Nazi propaganda: http://www.calvin.edu/academic/cas/gpa/ww2era.html.

83. It should be pointed out, however, that the Nazis usually preferred non-fascist conservative governments to fascist ones to govern a puppet-state (e.g. in Croatia, Hungary, and Romania) because they were more likely to remain compliant.

84. Wippermann, Wolfgang. 'Hat es Faschismus überhaupt gegeben? Der generische Begriff zwischen Kritik und Autokritik'. *Ethik und Sozialwissenschaft*, Vol. 11, No. 2 (2000): pp. 289–334 (edited by Werner Loh); reproduced in Loh and Wippermann. *'Faschismus' kontrovers*, pp. 51–70.

85. Sternhell. *Ni Droite, ni Gauche*. Paris: Éditions du Seuil, 1973: p. 110.

86. See Pulzer, Peter. *The Rise of Political Anti-Semitism in Germany and Austria*. London: Peter Halban, 1988.

87. For an important article which explores the dynamics of Fascism as a political religion and a substitute for the Christian faith, see Gentile. *The Sacralisation of Politics*.

88. See Taylor, Brandon and Wilfried van der Will (eds). *The Nazification of Art*. Winchester: The Winchester Press, 1990.

89. See Ben-Ghiat, Ruth. *Fascist Modernities: Italy 1922–1945*. Berkeley and Los Angeles: U of California P, 2001.

90. Stone, Marla. 'The State as Patron: Making Official Culture in Fascist Italy', in Affron, Matthew and Mark Antliff (eds). *Fascist Visions: Art and Ideology in France and Italy*. Princeton: Princeton University Press, 1997: pp. 205–238.

91. Roberts, David. 'How Not to Think About Fascism and Ideology, Intellectual Antecedents and Historical Meaning'. *Journal of Contemporary History*, Vol. 35, No. 2 (2000): p. 208.

92. José Antonio Primo de Rivera's voluminous speeches and writings serve as an excellent basis for such a comparison.

93. See Payne, Stanley. *Falange: A History of Spanish Fascism*. Oxford: Oxford UP, 1962; Costa-Pinto, Antonio. *Salazar's Dictatorship and European Fascism: Problems of Interpretation*. New York: Columbia UP, 1995.

94. Though I should stress once again that this does not mean that the necessarily 'static' or 'abstract' quality of an ideal type somehow implies the primacy of the conceptual or ideological over the concrete and unique empirical realities forming a central concern for historians, it is intended as a heuristic tool for investigating them.

95. See Griffin. 'Interregnum or Endgame?', pp. 116–131. The article argues that the three main tactics that fascism has adopted to survive in a post-war environment that precludes that formation of mass-based paramilitary parties with charismatic leaders are internationalisation, metapoliticisation, and groupuscularisation.

96. See Griffin, Roger. 'GUD Reactions: The Patterns of Prejudice in a Neo-Fascist Groupuscule'. *Patterns of Prejudice*, Vol. 33, No. 2 (1999): pp. 31–50; Griffin, Roger. 'From Slime Mould to Rhizome: An Introduction to the Groupuscular Right'. *Patterns of Prejudice*, Vol. 37, No. 1 (2003): pp. 27–50.

97. It is interesting to note that, in the neo-fascist press, for example, in publications of the British Third Positionist group of the 1990s National Revolutionary Faction, Franquism and Salazarism are never invoked as sources of inspiration, but Cornelius Codreanu (leader of the Romanian Iron Guard) and José Antonio Primo de Rivera are frequently treated as martyrs to the cause, and an inspiration for today's 'political soldier'.

98. For some insight into the world of cybernazism, see the *Stormfront* Website at http://www.stormfront.org/.

99. See sections on Universal Nazism, Eurofascism, and Evola in Griffin, *Fascism*.

100. Pearce, William, cited in ibid., pp. 372–374.

101. In the early 2000s, some 'Third Positionists' were involved in turning peaceful protests against globalisation into episodes of street violence in various cities.

102. See especially Michael, George. *The Enemy of My Enemy: The Alarming Convergence of Militant Islam and the Extreme Right*. Lawrence, KS: University Press, 2006.

6   'No racism, thanks, we're British': How right-wing populism manifests itself in contemporary Britain

1. 'Right-wing populism' or 'neo-populism' are terms used by political scientists to refer to electoral parties which appeal to popular xenophobic and anti-government sentiments but without the fascist agenda to create a new order in a post-liberal society.

2. Elsewhere I have termed 'ethnocratic liberalism' what is generally known as 'right-wing' or 'neo-populism'; that is, perversions of democratic principles that axiomatically reject the multi-racial or multi-faith society, and equate cultural nationalism with civic nationalism. See Griffin, Roger 'Interregnum or Endgame? Radical Right Thought in the "Post-fascist Era"'. *The Journal of Political Ideologies*, Vol. 5, No. 2 (2000): pp. 163–178; Griffin, Roger 'Last Rights?' Afterword to Ramet, Sabrina (ed.). *The Radical Right in Central and Eastern Europe*. PA: Penn State Press, 1999: pp. 297–321.

3. See the OMRLP [Official Monster Raving Loony Party] Website at http://www.omrlp.com/ (02/04/06).

4. Notably in Griffin, Roger. *The Nature of Fascism*. London: Pinter, 1991.

5. http://www.natfront.com/ (02/04/06).

6. http://www.bnp.org.uk/ (02/04/06).

7. See the current BNP website at www.bnp.net. (02/04/06) to see whether back issues of BNP papers are still available.

8. See Favell, Adrian. 'Multi-Ethnic Britain: An Exception in Europe?' *Patterns of Prejudice*, Vol. 35, No. 1 (2000): pp. 35–58, part of a special issue on multi-culturalism and citizenship.

9. Available via the Runnymede Trust website: http://www.runnymedetrust.org/ (02/04/06).

10. See *Searchlight* website at www.searchlightmagazine.com.

11. See Website of Commission for Racial Equality for links with relevant literature http://www.cre.gov.uk/ (02/04/06).

12. See Craske, Oliver. 'Women and Children First'. *Central Europe Review*, Vol. 2, No. 12 (27 March 2000). Available at http://www.ce-review.org/00/12/craske12.html (02/04/06).

13. Toynbee, Polly. 'Old-Fashioned Racism and a Britain that Never was'. *The Guardian* (20 April 2001). Available at http://www.guardian.co.uk/racism/Story/0,2763,475548,00. html (02/04/06).

14. Ingram, Mike. 'Britain's Conservative Party Exposes its Racist Underbelly'. *World Socialist Web Site* (2 April 2001). http://www.wsws.org/articles/2001/apr2001/hag-a03.shtml/ (02/04/06).

15. First line of a famous Lutheran hymn: 'A strong fortress is our God'.

16. Rushdie, Salman. *Imaginary Homelands*. London: Penguin, 1992: p. 394.

7   Europe for the Europeans: Fascist myths of the European new order 1922–1992

1. Fukuyama, Francis. 'The End of History?' *The National Interest*, Vol. 16 (Summer 1989): p. 1.

2. Ibid., p. 5.

3. Sorel, Georges. *Reflections on Violence*. London: Collier-Macmillan, 1961: pp. 125–127.

4. Cited in the article Rivera, David. 'European Union and the Bilderberg Group, Final Warning: A History of the New World Order' published on the right-wing website http://www.the7thfire.com/new_world_order/final_warning/EU_and_Bilderberg_Group.html (02/04/06).

5. See Robin, Mowat. *Creating the European Community*. London: Blandford Press, 1973.

6. See Anderson, Benedict. *Imagined Communities*. London, New York: Verso, 1991.

7. Woolf, Stuart. 'Risorgimento e fascismo: il senso della continuità nella storiografia italiana'. *Belfagor*, Vol. 20 (1965).

8. Grand, Alexander de. *The Italian Nationalist Association and the Rise of Fascism in Italy*. Lincoln: University of Nebraska Press, 1978.

9. Gentile, Emilio. *Il culto del littorio*. Rome-Bari: Laterza, 1993.

10. Roberts, David. *The Syndicalist Tradition in Italian Fascism*. Manchester: Manchester University Press, 1979.

11. Griffin, Roger. *The Nature of Fascism*. London: Printer, 1991, pp. 56–63.

12. Sznajder, Mario. 'The "Carta del Carnaro" and Modernization'. *Tel Aviv Jahrbuch für Deutsche Geschichte*, Vol. 18 (1989).

13. Ledeen, Michael. *Universal Fascism*. New York: Howard Fertig, 1972.
14. Gentile. *Il mito dello stato nuovo*, pp. 103–134.
15. Simonini, Augusto. 'Il linguaggio di Mussolini'. Milano: Bompiani, 1978: pp. 99–101, 113–115.
16. Zunino, Pier-Giorgio. *I'Ideologia del fascismo*. Bologna: Il Mulino, 1985.
17. Quoted in Barnes, James Strachey. *The Universal Aspects of Fascism*. London: Williams and Norgate, 1929: p. xxviii.
18. Ibid., pp. xxvi–xxvii.
19. Ledeen, Michael. *Universal Fascism*. New York: Howard Fertig, 1972: p. 63.
20. Quoted in Lyttleton, Adrian. *Italian Fascism from Pareto to Gentile*. London: Jonathan Cape, 1973.
21. Quoted in Cannistraro, Phillip (ed.). *Historical Dictionary of Fascist Italy*. Westport, CT: Greenwood Press, 1982: p. 361.
22. The duce's character weaknesses are relentlessly exposed in Mack Smith, Denis. *Mussolini*. London: Weidenfeld & Nicolson, 1981.
23. De Felice, Renzo. *Mussolini il Duce*: Vol. 2, Lo stato totalitario, 1936–1940. Turin: Einaudi, 1981: p. 290.
24. Zunino. *I'ideologia del fascismo*, p. 135; cf. pp. 131–144.
25. Ibid., 'Tra americanismo e bolscevismo', [Between Americanism and Bolshevism], pp. 322–344.
26. Gregor, A. James. *The Ideology of Fascism: The Rationale of Totalitarianism*. New York: Free Press, 1969: p. 356.
27. Gentile, Giovanni. *Origini e dottrine del fascismo*. Rome: Istituto nazionale del fascismo, 1934: p. 55.
28. Gentile. *Il mito dello stato nuovo*, p. 26.
29. Malgieri, Gennaro. *Carlo Costamagna*. Vibo Valentia: Edizioni Sette Colori, 1981: p. 134.
30. Quoted in Ledeen. *Universal Fascism,* p. 20.
31. Ibid., p. 35.
32. *Antieuropa*, Vol. 1, No. 1 (1929): pp. 1–13, summarised in a later declaration published in *Antieuropa*, Vol. 2, No. 5 (1930).
33. Ibid., Vol. 2, No. 9 (1930): pp. 1468–1486.
34. Ibid., Vol. 3, No. 3 (1931): pp. 1727–1734.
35. For example, Ibid., Vol. 2, No. 9 (1930).
36. Ibid., Vols 7–9 (1930).
37. Quoted in Gregor. *The Ideology of Fascism*, pp. 388–389.
38. See Griffin. *The Nature of Fascism*, pp. 213–216.
39. For example, in Sternhell, Ze'ev. 'Fascist Ideology', in Laqueur, Walter (ed.). *Fascism: A Reader's Guide*. Harmondsworth: The Penguin Press, 1969: p. 333.
40. For example, Stern, Fritz. *The Politics of Cultural Despair*. Berkeley: University of California Press, 1961.
41. See Swart, Koenraad. *The Sense of Decadence in Nineteenth-Century France*. The Hague: Nijhoff, 1964.
42. See Hughes, Stuart. *Consciousness and Society*. New York: Vintage, 1958.
43. See Weber, Eugen. 'Decadence on a Private Income'. *Journal of Contemporary History*, Vol. 17, No.1 (1982): p. 19.
44. Thurlow, Richard. *Fascism in Britain: A History, 1918–1985*. Oxford: Blackwell, 1987: Chs 5–8.

45. Conway, Martin. 'Le Rexisme de 1940 à 1944: Degrelle et les autres'. *Centre de Recherches et d'Études Historiques de la Seconde Guerre Mondiale*, 10 (1986)
46. Brugmans, Henri. *L'Idée Européenne, 1918–1965*. Bruges: De Tempel, 1965, Ch. 3.
47. See Griffin. *The Nature of Fascism*, pp. 148–160.
48. Szálasi, quoted in Szollosi-Janze, Margit. *Die Pfeilkreuzerbewegung in Ungarn*. Munich: R. Oldenbourg, 1989: pp. 221–250.
49. Sternhell, Ze'ev. *Neither Right nor Left: Fascist Ideology in France*. Berkeley, CA: Princeton UP, 1986: p. 15.
50. Plumyène, Jean and Lasierre, Raymond. *Les Fascismes Français*. Paris: Seuil, 1963.
51. Bucard quoted in Algazy, Joseph. *La Tentation néo-fasciste en France, 1944–65*. Paris: Fayard, 1984: p. 34.
52. Ibid., p. 42.
53. Doriot quoted in ibid., p. 51.
54. Brasillach quoted in ibid., p. 54.
55. See Soucy, Robert. *Fascist Intellectual: Drieu la Rochelle*. Berkeley: University of California Press, 1979.
56. Drieu la Rochelle quoted in Romualdi, Adriano, Giannetti, Guido, and Prisco, Mario. *Drieu la Rochelle: Il Mito d'Europa*. Rome: Edizioni della Salamandra, 1981: p. 73.
57. Drieu la Rochelle quoted in ibid., p. 9.
58. See Griffin. *The Nature of Fascism*, pp. 134–136.
59. De Brion quoted in Algazy. *La Tentation néofasciste en France*, p. 56.
60. Ibid., p. 55.
61. See Hauner, Milan. 'Did Hitler Want World Dominion?' *Journal of Contemporary History*, Vol. 13, No. 1 (1978).
62. Kluke, Paul. 'Nationsozialistische Europaideologie'. *Vierteljahreshefte für Zeitgeschichte*, Vol. 3, No. 3 (1955).
63. Lane, Barbara and Rupp, Leila. *Nazi Ideology before 1933*. Manchester: Manchester UP, 1978: p. 84.
64. Rosenberg quoted in ibid., pp. 64, 71.
65. Cited in Herzstein, Robert. *When Nazi Dreams Come True*. London: Abacus, 1982: p. 91.
66. See Griffin. *The Nature of Fascism*, pp. 219–221.
67. Notable exceptions are Sheehan, Thomas. 'Myth and Violence: The Fascism of Julius Evola and Alain de Benoist'. *Social Research*, Vol. 48, No. 1 (1981); Ferraresi, Franco. 'Julius Evola: Tradition, Reaction and the Radical Right', in *European Journal of Sociology*, Vol. 28 (1987): pp. 107–151.
68. Evola, Julius. *La rivolta contro il mondo moderno*. 5th Edn, Rome: Edizioni Mediterranee, 1976 (1934): p. 367.
69. Evola. *L'Arco e la clava*. Milan: Scheiwiller, 1971: p. 258.
70. Evola. *Saggi di Dottrina Politica*. Genoa: I Dioscuri, 1989: pp. 53–61.
71. Quoted in *The Scorpion*, Vol. 9, No. 19 (1986).
72. Evola. *Gli uomini e le rovine*. Rome: Edizioni dell'Ascia, 1954, Ch. 16.
73. A doctrine expounded in Evola, Julius. *Cavalcare la tigre*. Milan: Scheiwiller, 1961.
74. See Sheehan. 'Myth and Violence'.
75. See Harris, Geoffrey. *The Dark Side of Europe: The Extreme Right Today*. Edinburgh: Edinburgh UP, 1990: p. 29.
76. See Algazy. *La Tentation néofasciste*, p. 75.
77. Binet quoted in ibid., p. 100.

78. Binet quoted in ibid., p. 105.
79. Binet quoted in ibid., pp. 297–301.
80. See Ó Maoláin, Ciarán. *The Radical Right: A World Directory.* London: Longman, 1987: pp. 141–143.
81. Algazy. *La Tentation néofasciste*, p. 76.
82. Ibid., p. 317.
83. Stichting, Anne Frank. *The Extreme Right in Europe and the United States.* Amsterdam: Anne Frank Foundation, 1984.
84. Cited in Algazy. *La Tentation néofasciste*, p. 289.
85. Nolte, Ernst. *Three Faces of Fascism Action Française, Italian Fascism, National Socialism.* New York, Holt, Rinehart and Winston, 1965: p. 401.
86. De Benoist, Alain. *Vu de Droite.* Paris: Copernic, 1977: p. 32.
87. Ibid., pp. 31–32.
88. De Benoist. *Le Idee a posto.* Naples: Akropolis, 1983 (Original French edition *Les Idées à l'endroit.* Paris: Albin Michel, 1980): p. 271.
89. Ibid., p. 273.
90. Ibid., p. 290.
91. Krebs quoted in Benz, Wolfgang (ed.). *Rechtsextremismus in der Bundesrepublik.* Frankfurt am Main: Fischer, 1989: p. 218.
92. Krebs, Pierre. *Die europäische Wiedergeburt.* Tübingen: Grabert-Verlag, 1982: pp. 94–95.
93. Krebs, Pierre. (ed.). *Mut zur Identität: Alternativen zum Prinzip Gleichheit.* Struckum: Verlag für ganzheitliche Forschung und Kultur, 1988: pp. 192–204.
94. Ibid., p. 260.
95. Faye quoted in ibid., De Benoist. *Les Idées à l'endroit*, pp. 119–126.
96. See Ferraresi, Franco (ed.). *La destra radicale.* Milan: Feltrinelli, 1984; Galli, Giorgio. *La destra in Italia.* Milan: Gammalibri, 1983; Griffin, Roger. 'Revolts against the Modern World: The Blend of Literary and Historical Fantasy in the Italian New Right'. *Literature and History*, Vol. 11, No. 1 (1985); Bologna, Piermario and Emma Mana (eds). *Fascismo oggi: Nuova destra e cultura reazionaria negli anni Ottanta.*
97. Freda, F.. *La disintegrazione del sistema.* Padua: Edizioni di Ar, 1980: pp. 25–28.
98. Romualdi and Prisco. *Drieu la Rochelle*, p. 15.
99. Ibid., p. 17.
100. *Nation Europa.* Vol. 39.5/6. May/June 1989: pp. 72–73.
101. Wolek quoted in Vago, Raphael. 'The East European Radical Right and European Integration', unpublished paper presented to the Conference *The Radical Right in Western Europe*, held at Minnesota University, November 1991, p. 8.
102. Ibid., p. 13.
103. Ibid., p. 15.
104. Walker quoted in ibid., p. 28.
105. Autant-Lara quoted in *Debates of the European Parliament*, 28 July 1989.
106. *Nation Europa*, Vol. 39, No. 7 (July 1989).
107. Havel, Vaclev. 'On Home'. *The New York Review of Books*, 5 December 1991.

8 Fascism's new faces (and new facelessness) in the 'post-fascist' epoch

1. Nolte, Ernst. *Three Faces of Fascism.* New York: Mentor, 1969: p. 24.
2. As this article makes clear, for Nolte, as for Wolfgang Wippermann and most historians *outside* Germany, 'fascism' embraces Nazism and hence the history of the

Third Reich. (See Wippermann, Wolfgang. 'Was ist Faschismus? – Geschichte und Theoriegeschichte', in Loh Werner and Wolfgang Wippermann (eds). *'Faschismus' – kontrovers*. Stuttgart: Lucius und Lucius, 2000: p. 150.) It has thus acquired the deep associations in the English-speaking world with elemental forces of mass mobilisation and mass destruction alluded to in this metaphor. Most German readers, however, will need to be convinced of the appropriateness of such cataclysmic connotations.

3. Felice. *Interpretations of Fascism*. Cambridge, MA: Cambridge UP, 1977: p. 10.
4. See, for example, Kitschelt, Herbert. *The Radical Right in Western Europe: A Comparative Analysis*. Michigan: University of Michigan Press, 1995.
5. For a recent theory of fascism that demonstrates how little the Marxist analysis of fascism has progressed in sophistication (in this case written in the Trotskyite dialect), see Renton, David. *Fascism: Theory and Practice*. London: Pluto Press, 1999.
6. See, for example, Loh, Werner (ed.). *Erwägungsorientierung in Philosophie und Sozialwissenschaften*. Stuttgart: Lucius und Lucius, 2001.
7. For a systemised version of Weber's methodological theory, see Burger, Thomas. *Max Weber's Theory of Concept Formation*. Durham, NC: Duke University Press, 1976. In terms of Weberian methodological theory, even attempts to define fascism on the basis of the 'role model' or 'real type' provided by Italian Fascism is, at bottom, an exercise in ideal type formation, one which 'abstracts' from a concrete example of the phenomenon. See my critique of Wolfgang Wippermann's attempt to produce a satisfactory theory of generic fascism using this procedure: Griffin, Roger. ' "Racism" or "rebirth"? The Case for Granting German Citizenship to the Alien Concept "generic fascism." ' *Ethik und Sozialwissenschaften*, Vol. 11, No. 2 (2000): pp. 300–303.
8. Freeden, Michael. 'Political Concepts and Ideological Morphology'. *The Journal of Political Philosophy*, Vol. 2, No. 2 (1994): pp. 140–164.
9. For example, Linz, Juan. 'Some notes toward a Comparative Study of Fascism in Sociological Historical Perspective', in Laqueur, Walter (ed.). *Fascism: A Reader's Guide: Analyses Interpretations, Bibliography*. London: Wildwood House, 1976: pp. 1–23; Mosse, George L. 'Towards a General Theory of Fascism', in Mosse, George L. (ed.). *Interpretations of Fascism*. London: Sage, 1979; Payne, Stanley. *Fascism: Comparison and Definition*. Madison: U of Wisconsin P, 1980.
10. For example, Allardyce, Gilbert. 'What Fascism is Not: Thoughts on the Deflation of a Concept'. *American Historical Review*, Vol. 84, No. 2 (April 1979): pp. 367–398. The publication in this issue of Allardyce's article, immediately followed by responses from Ernst Nolte and Stanley Payne, make it an early example of an attempt to create the sort of discussion forum that *EWE* now offers to social scientists on a regular basis.
11. For example, Roger Scruton's definition of fascism includes the observation that fascism has 'the form of an ideology without the content' in Scruton, Roger. *A Dictionary of Political Thought*. London: Pan Books, 1982.
12. For example, Alan Bullock and Stephen Trombley's article 'fascism' attributes to fascism traits found in Nazism but not in Fascism, such as the systematic use of terror in Bullock, Alan and Trombley, Stephen [eds]. *The New Fontana Dictionary of Modern Thought*. London: HarperCollins, 1999: pp. 310–311.
13. Griffin, Roger. 'The Primacy of Culture: The Current Growth (or Manufacture) of Consensus within Fascist Studies'. *The Journal of Contemporary History*, Vol. 37, No. 1 (2002): pp. 21–43.
14. Notable expressions of grave doubt about the existence of any sort of consensus are to be found in Renton, *Fascism: Theory and Practice*; Knox, MacGregor.

Common Destiny: Dictatorship, Foreign Policy, and War in Fascist Italy and Nazi Germany. Cambridge: Cambridge UP, 2000; Larsen, Stein. 'Was there Fascism Outside Europe? Diffusion from Europe and Domestic Impulses', in Larsen, Stein (ed.). *Fascism Outside Europe*. New York: Columbia UP (Boulder Social Sciences Monographs), 2001; Gregor, James. 'Fascism, Marxism and Some Considerations Concerning Classification'. *Totalitarian Movements and Political Religions*, Vol. 3, No. 2 (2002): pp. 61–82. For four academic reactions to my 'Primacy of culture' article written in the spirit of *EWE's* 'forum', see *The Journal of Contemporary History*, Vol. 37, No. 2 (2002).

15. Griffin, Roger. *The Nature of Fascism*. London: Pinter, 1991: p. 26. See my 'The Primacy of Culture' for examples of its application by other academics; two examples of university textbooks which apply the new consensus are Blinkhorn. *Fascism and the Far Right in Europe: 1914–1945* and Morgan, Philip. *Fascism in Europe: 1919–1945*. London: Routledge, 2002.

16. For example, Mosley, Oswald. *Fascism in Britain*. London: BUF Press, 1933; Bardèche, Maurice. *Qu'est-ce que le fascisme?* Paris: Les Sept Couleurs, 1961; Locchi, Giorgio. *L'essenza del fascismo*. La Spezia: Il Tridente, 1981. Mosley's pamphlet, for example, opens with the declaration that '[f]ascism has come to Great Britain. It comes to each nation in turn as it reaches the crisis which is inevitable in the modern age. That crisis is inevitable because an epoch of civilisation has come to an end. It is our task to bring to birth a new civilisation and to organise its system' (p. 3).

17. See Griffin, Roger. *International Fascism: Theories, Causes and the New Consensus*. Section 5: 'The Rebirth of Fascism?' pp. 286–324.

18. Gentile, Emilio. *Le religioni politiche*. Rome-Bari: Laterza, 2000. The definitional chapter of his book appeared in English as 'The Sacralisation of Politics: Definition, Interpretations and Reflections on the Question of Secular Religion and Totalitarianism'. *Totalitarian Movements and Political Religions*, Vol. 1, No. 1 (2000): pp. 18–55.

19. Martin Blinkhorn's 'author's response' to Toby Abse's review of his *'Fascism and the Far Right in History'*. Electronic Reviews in History, 24 September 2001, ashepher@ihr.sas.ac.uk, website www.ukoln.ac.uk/services/elib/projects/history-reviews/.

20. Blinkhorn, Martin. *Fascism and the Right in Europe 1919–1945*. Harlow: Longman, 2000: pp. 115–116.

21. Ibid., p. 112.

22. See Nolte. 'Part Five: Fascism as a Metapolitical Phenomenon' *Three Faces of Fascism*, pp. 537–567.

23. Gregor. *Italian Fascism and Developmental Dictatorship*. Princeton, NJ: Princeton UP, 1979.

24. Sternhell, Ze'ev. *Ni Droite, ni Gauche*. Paris: Éditions du Seuil, 1973.

25. See Wippermann's contributions to the discussion in Loh and Wippermann, *'Faschismus' kontrovers*, pp. 1–70, pp. 163–174. For a fuller version of my critique of Wipperman, see my two essays published in the same volume: pp. 81–88: ' "Racism" or "rebirth"? The Case for Granting German Citizenship to the Alien Concept 'generic fascism" ', pp. 179–190: 'Nazism's "Cleansing Hurricane" and the Metamorphosis of Fascist Studies'.

26. See the introduction to Payne. *A History of Fascism 1914–1945*, pp. 3–19.

27. Contrast Griffin. *The Nature of Fascism*, p. 26 and p. 44 with my more recent article 'Interregnum or endgame? Radical Right Thought in the "Post-fascist" Era'. *The Journal of Political Ideologies*, Vol. 5, No. 2 (2000): pp. 163–178.

28. Taguieff, Pierre-André. 'Discussion or Inquisition: The Case of Alain de Benoist'. *Telos*, Vol. 98–99 (1993/1994): p. 54.

29. See Griffin, Roger. 'The Palingenetic Political Community: Rethinking the Legitimation of Totalitarian Regimes in Inter-War Europe'. *Totalitarian Movements and Political Religions*, Vol. 3, No. 3 (2000): pp. 24–43.

30. I have called this simulation of fascism 'parafascism' in Griffin. *The Nature of Fascism*, Chapter 5 'Abortive Fascist Movements in Inter-war Europe', pp. 116–145.

31. On the spurious nature of the community forged by Nazism in the context of a generalised 'sense-making crisis' see Platt, Gerald. 'Thoughts on a Theory of Collective Action: Language, Affect, and Ideology in Revolution', in Albin, Mel (ed.). *New Directions in Psychohistory*. Lexington, MA: Lexington Books, 1980: pp. 69–94.

32. On the 'rhizome' see Deleuze, Gilles and Felix Guattari. *A Thousand Plateaus: Capitalism and Schizophrenia*. Minneapolis: U of Minnesota P, 1987. See also the web articles www.socio.demon.co.uk/rhizome.html and http://cs.art.rmit.edu.au/ deleuzeguattarionary/r/r.html (viewed: 30/08/02). For a sophisticated Web article that goes into the theory of the rhizome see Wray, Stephan, 'Rhizomes, Nomads, and Resistant Internet Use', at: www.nyu.edu/projects/wray/RhizNom.html (viewed: 14/11/02). In addition to explicating the concept 'rhizome', Wray shows how both Hakim Bey's Temporary Autonomous Zones and the Zapatista National Liberation Army utilise a rhizomic organisational structure in their struggle to overthrow the 'system' which has direct relevance to this article.

33. 'Slime mould is one of a group of single- to multi-celled organisms traditionally classified as fungi but having characteristics of both plants and animals. They reproduce by spores, but their cells can move like an amoeba and they feed by taking in particles of food. Some types of slime mould are the bane of gardeners, forming a jelly-like surface on grass' (Cited from: http://www. nifg.org.uk/facts_a.htm. Viewed: 03/09/02).

34. Betz, Hans-Georg. 'Against Globalisation: Xenophobia, Identity Politics and Exclusionary populism in Western Europe', in Panitch, Leo and Colin Leys (eds). *Socialist Register 2003*. New York: Monthly Review Press, pp. 195–213.

35. Griffin, Roger. 'Afterword: Last Rights?' in Sabrina Ramet (ed.). *The Radical Right in Central and Eastern Europe*. Pennsylvania: Penn State Press, 1999: pp. 297–321.

36. For an overview, see Griffin. 'Europe for the Europeans: The Fascist Vision of the New Europe', published as Chapter 8 of this book.

37. See Griffin, Roger. 'Plus ça change!: The Fascist Mindset Behind the Nouvelle Droite's Struggle for Cultural Renewal', in Arnold, Edward (ed.). *The Development of the Radical Right in France 1890–1995*. London: Routledge, 2000: pp. 217–252.

38. For a fascinating personal testimony of the development form activist in a fairly traditional ultra-nationalist, partly neo-Nazified political party the head of a Third Positionist groupuscule with national-Bolshevik tendencies, see Southgate, Troy. 'Transcending the Beyond: From Third Position to National-Anarchism'. *Pravda* Web-newspaper (http://english.pravda.ru/main/2002/01/17/25828.html) (viewed: 03/04/06).

39. Krebs. *Die europäische Wiedergeburt*, pp. 82–86.

40. Lipstadt, Deborah. *Denying the Holocaust*. New York: The Free Press, 1993.

41. Goodrick-Clarke, Nicholas. *Black Sun. Aryan Cults, Esoteric Nazism and the Politics of Identity*. New York and London: New York UP, 2002.

42. Griffin, Roger. 'Revolts Against the Modern World'. *Literature and History*, Vol. 11, No. 1 (1985): pp. 101–124.

43. Biehl, Janet and Staudenmaier, Peter. *Ecofascism: Lessons from the German Experience.* Oakland, CA: AK Press, 1996.
44. Kaplan, Jeffrey. *Radical Religion in America. Millenarian Movements from the Far Right to the Children of Noah (Religion and Politics).* New York: Syracuse University Press, 1997.
45. Lowles, Nick and Silver, Steve (eds). *White Noise.* London: Searchlight, 1998.
46. *Skrewdriver.* 'Hail and Thunder'. *The Strong Survive.* Germany: Rock-O-Rama Records, 1990. The lyrics are cited in the excellent article by Cotter, John M. 'Sounds of Hate: White Power Rock and Roll and the Neo-Nazi Skinhead Subculture'. *Terrorism and Political Violence*, Vol. 11, No. 2 (1999): pp. 111–140.
47. Drake, Richard. *The Revolutionary Mystique and Terrorism in Contemporary Italy.* Bloomington and Indianapolis: Indiana UP, 1989.
48. Herbeck, Dan and Herbeck, Michael. *American Terrorist – Timothy McVeigh & the Tragedy at Oklahoma City.* New York: Avon, 2001.
49. Lowles, Nick and McLagan, Graeme. *Mr Evil: The Secret Life of the Racist Bomber and Killer David Copeland.* London: John Blake, 2000.
50. Both McVeigh and Copeland lived out a psychological syndrome remarkably similar in some respects to the one enacted by Robert DeNiro in Martin Scorsesi's film *Taxi Driver.*
51. See Griffin. 'Net Gains and GUD Reactions: Patterns of Prejudice in a Neo-Fascist Groupuscule'. *Patterns of Prejudice*, Vol. 33, No. 2 (1999): pp. 31–50.
52. See Pedahzur, Ami and Weinberg, Leonard. ‚Modern European Democracies and Its Enemies: The Threat of the Extreme Right'. *Totalitarian Movements and Political Religions*, Vol. 2, No. 1 (2001): pp. 52–72; Umland, Andreas. 'Towards an Uncivil Society?: Contextualising the Decline of Post-Soviet Russian Extremely Right-Wing Parties'. *Weatherhead Center for International Affairs Working Paper Series*, No. 02–03, 2002. Available at: www.wcfia.harvard.edu/papers/555_Toward_An_Uncivil_Society.pdf (viewed: 03/04/06).
53. Quote taken from the web article on the rhizome: http://cs.art.rmit.edu.au/deleuzeguattarionary/r/pages/rhizomic.html (viewed: 30/08/02).
54. For more on the groupuscular right, see *Patterns of Prejudice*, Vol. 36, No. 3 (2002); Griffin, Roger. 'From Slime Mould to Rhizome: An Introduction to the Groupuscular Right'. *Patterns of Prejudice*, Vol. 37, No. 1 (2003): pp. 27–50.
55. Arctogaia's website has changed from http://web.redline.ru/~arctogai/eng2.htm to www.arctogaia.com, and Jonny Rotten has apparently disappeared from the pantheon, though he is still included in the Manifesto of Arctogaia at http://www.arcto.ru/modules.php?name=News&file=print&sid=1133 (viewed: 03/04/06).
56. See Mathyl, Markus. 'The National-Bolshevik Party and Arctogaia: Two Neo-Fascist Groupuscules in the Post-Soviet Political Space'. *Patterns of Prejudice*, Vol. 36, No. 3 (2002): pp. 62–76; Griffin. 'From Slime Mould to Rhizome.'
57. See Reynolds, Michael. 'Virtual Reich'. *Playboy* (US edition), Vol. 49, No. 2 (2002): pp. 62–64, pp. 146–152. Reprinted in Griffin with Feldman (eds). *Fascism*, Vol. 5: pp. 339–351.

The fascination of fascism

1. The papers were published in *Totalitarian Movements and Political Religions*, Vol. 8, No. 2 (2007), in a special issue entitled '"Clerical Fascism" in Interwar Europe', edited by Matthew Feldman and Marius Turda.

2. Griffin. 'Notes Towards the Definition of Fascist Culture: The Prospects for Synergy between Marxist and Liberal Heuristics.' *Renaissance and Modern Studies*, Vol. 42 Autumn 2001: pp. 95–115.
3. Bardèche, Maurice. *Qu'est-ce que le fascisme?* Paris: Les Sept Couleurs, 1961.
4. Tooze, Adam. *The Wages of Destruction: The Making and Breaking of the Nazi Economy.* Harmondsworth: Penguin, 2006: p. xx.
5. Griffin, Roger. 'Cloister or Cluster? The Implications of Emilio Gentile's Ecumenical Theory of Political Religion for the Study of Extremism.' *Totalitarian Movements and Political Religions*, Vol. 6, No. 1 (2005), pp. 33–52.

Bibliography

(I) Printed Sources

Abelshauser, Werner and Anselm Faust. *Eine nationalsozialistische Sozialrevolution? Teil 4: Wirtschafts- und Sozialpolitik*. Tübingen: DIFF, 1983.

Adam, Peter. *Art in the Third Reich*. London: Thames and Hudson, England, 1992.

Adamson, Walter. *Hegemony and Revolution: A Study of Antonio Gramsci's Political and Cultural Theory*. Berkeley: University of California Press, 1980.

———. 'Gramsci's Interpretation of Fascism'. *Journal of the History of Ideas* 41.4 (1980): pp. 615–633.

———. 'Modernism and Fascism: The Politics of Culture in Italy, 1903–1922'. *The American Historical Review* 95.2 (1990): pp. 359–390.

———. 'The Language of Opposition in Early Twentieth-Century Italy: Rhetorical Continuities Between Prewar Florentine Avant-Gardism and Mussolini's Fascism'. *Journal of Modern History* 64 (1992): pp. 22–51.

———. *Avant-Garde Florence: From Modernism to Fascism*. Cambridge, MA: Harvard University Press, 1993.

Affron, Matthew and Mark Antliff (eds). *Fascist Visions: Art and Ideology in France and Italy*. Princeton: Princeton University Press, 1997.

Algazy, Joseph. *La Tentation néo-fasciste en France, 1944–65*. Paris: Fayard, 1984.

Allardyce, Gilbert. 'What Fascism is Not: Thoughts on the Deflation of a Concept'. *American Historical Review* 84.2 (1979): pp. 367–398.

Althusser, Louis. *Essays on Ideology*. London, New York: Verso, 1971.

Aly, Götz and Karl Roth. *Die restlose Erfassung: Volkszählung, Identifizieren, Aussondern im Nationalsozialismus*. Frankfurt am Main: Fischer Taschenbuchverlag, 2000.

Anderson, Benedict. *Imagined Communities Reflections on the Origin and Spread of Nationalism*. London, New York: Verso, 1991.

Antliff, Mark. 'Fascism, Modernism, and Modernity'. *The Art Bulletin* 84.1 (2002): pp. 148–169.

Apthorpe, Raymond. 'Modernization'. Adam Kuper and Jessica Kuper (eds). *The Social Science Encyclopedia*. London: Routledge & Kegan Paul, 1985.

Arendt, Hannah. *The Origins of Totalitarianism*. New York: Harcourt Brace, 1951.

Bardèche, Maurice. *Qu'est-ce que le fascisme?* Paris: Les Sept Couleurs, 1961.

Barnes, James Strachey. *Fascism*. London: Thornton Butterworth, 1931.

———. *The Universal Aspects of Fascism*. London: Williams and Norgate, 1929.

Bauman, Zygmunt. *Modernity and the Holocaust*. Cambridge: Polity, 1989.

———. *Modernity and Ambivalence*. Cambridge: Polity Press, 1991.

Beetham, David. *Marxists in Face of Fascism*. Manchester: Manchester University Press, 1983.

Ben-Ghiat, Ruth. 'Italian Fascism and the Aesthetics of the "Third Way"'. *Journal of Contemporary History* 31.2 (1996): pp. 293–316.

———. *Fascist Modernities*. Berkeley and Los Angeles: University of California Press, 2001.

Benjamin, Walter. 'Theses on the Philosophy of History'. (1940). *Illuminations*. London: Fontana Press, 1992: pp. 245–255

Benn, Gottfried. 'Züchtung I'. Gottfried Benn (ed.). *Der neue Staat und die Intellektuellen.* Stuttgart and Berlin: Deutsche Verlags Anstalt, 1933.

———. 'Züchtung I'. Gottfried Benn (ed.). *Essays, Reden, Vorträge.* Wiesbaden: Limes Verlag, 1959: pp. 214–222.

Benoist, Alain de. *Vu de Droite.* Paris: Copernic, 1977.

———. *Les Idées à l'endroit.* Paris: Albin Michel, 1980.

———. *Le Idee a posto.* Naples: Akropolis, 1983.

———. 'Introduction'. *Krisis* 1 (1988).

———. 'The Idea of Empire'. *Telos* 98–99 (Winter 1993–Fall 1994): pp. 81–98.

———. 'Three Interviews with Alain de Benoist'. *Telos* 98–99 (1993/1994): pp. 173–180.

———. *L'Empire intérieur.* Fontfroide le Haut: Fata Morgana, 1995.

———. 'Confronting Globalization'. *Telos* 108 (1996): pp. 117–138.

Berezin, Mabel. *Making the Fascist Self: The Political Culture of Interwar Italy.* Ithaca: Cornell University Press, 1997.

Berghaus, Günter. *Futurism and Politics.* Oxford: Berghahn Books, 1996.

Bergier, Jacques and Louis Pauwels. *Le Matin des Magiciens.* Paris: Gallimard, 1960.

Berlet, Chip and Matthew N. Lyons. *Right-Wing Populism in America: Too Close for Comfort.* New York: Guilford, 2000.

Biehl, Janet and Peter Staudenmaier. *Ecofascism: Lessons from the German Experience.* Oakland, CA: AK Press, 1996.

Black, Edwin. *IBM and the Holocaust: The Strategic Alliance Between Nazi Germany and America.* London: Time Warner Paperbacks, 2002.

Blackbourn, David and Geoff Eley. *The Peculiarities of German History.* New York: Oxford University Press, 1984.

Blinkhorn, Martin. *Fascists and Conservatives.* London: Unwin Hyman, 1990.

———. *Mussolini and Fascist Italy.* London: Routledge (Lancaster Pamphlets), 1994.

———. *Fascism and the Right in Europe 1919–1945.* Harlow: Longman, 2000.

Bloch, Jean-Richard. 'La democrazia e la festa'. *La Voce* 28 July 1914.

Bloch, Ernst. *The Principle of Hope.* Cambridge, MA: MIT Press, 1986.

———. 'Inventory of Revolutionary Appearance'. Ernst Bloch (ed.). *The Heritage of Our Time.* Cambridge: Polity, 1991: pp. 64–69.

Blum, George P. *The Rise of Fascism in Europe.* Westport and Connecticut: Greenwood Press, 1998.

Bologna, Piermario and Emma Mana (eds). *Fascismo oggi: Nuova destra e cultura reazionaria negli anni Ottanta.* Cuneo: Isr, 1983.

Bonadeo, Alfredo. *D'Annunzio and the Great War.* Madison and Teaneck: Associated University Press, 1995.

Bosworth, Richard J. B. *The Italian Dictatorship: Problems and Perspectives in the Interpretation of Mussolini and Fascism.* London: Arnold, 1998.

———. *Mussolini.* London: Arnold, 2002.

Bracher, Karl. *The Nazi Dictatorship.* Harmondsworth: Penguin, 1978.

———. *The German Dictatorship.* London: Penguin, 1988.

Braun, Emily. *Mario Sironi and Italian Modernism: Art and Politics Under Fascism.* Cambridge, MA: Harvard University Press, 1993.

Brender, Reinhold. *Kollaboration im Zweiten Weltkrieg.* Munich: Oldenbourg, 1993.

Broch, Hermann. *The Sleepwalkers.* New York: Grosset and Dunlap, 1964.

Brooker, Paul. *The Faces of Fraternalism: Nazi Germany, Fascist Italy, and Imperial Japan.* Oxford: Oxford University Press, 1991.

Broszat, Martin. *German National Socialism.* Santa Barbara: Clio, 1966.

Browning, Christopher. *Nazi Policy, Jewish Workers, German Killers*. Cambridge: Cambridge University Press, 2000.

Brugmans, Henri. *L'Idée Européenne, 1918–1965*. Bruges: De Tempel, 1965.

Bullock, Alan and Stephen Trombley (eds). *The New Fontana Dictionary of Modern Thought*. London: HarperCollins, 1999.

Burger, Thomas. *Max Weber's Theory of Concept Formation*. Durham, NC: Duke University Press, 1976.

Burleigh, Michael and Wolfgang Wippermann. *The Racial State*. Cambridge: Cambridge University Press, 1991.

Burleigh, Michael. *The Third Reich*. London: Macmillan, 2000.

———. 'National Socialism as a Political Religion'. *Totalitarian Movements and Political Religions* 1.2 (2002): pp. 1–26.

Callinicos, Alex. *Social Theory: A Historical Introduction*. Cambridge: Polity, 1999.

Campbell, Joseph. *The Hero's Journey*. New York: Harper and Row, 1990.

Cannistraro, Phillip (ed.). *Historical Dictionary of Fascist Italy* Westport, Conn: Greenwood Press, 1982.

Cardini, Franco. 'Alle radici di una concezione del mondo dell'avvenire: La comunità che si ritrova: il mito, il rito, la liturgia, il gioco, la festa'. Cison di Valmarino (ed.). *Al di là della destra e la sinistra*. Rome: Libreria editrice Europa, 1983.

Carsten, Francis. *The Rise of Fascism*. London: Methuen, 1967.

Cassels, Alan. *Fascism*. New York: Thomas Y. Cromwell, 1974.

Cheles, Luciano. ' "Nostalgia dell'avvenire": The Propaganda of the Italian Far Right Between Tradition and Innovation'. Luciano Cheles *et al.* (ed.). *The Far Right in Western and Eastern Europe*. London: Longman, 1995: pp. 41–90.

Clark, Martin. *A History of Italy 1871–1982*. London: Longman, 1984.

Cohn, Norman. *The Pursuit of the Millennium*. London: Palladin, 1970.

Conway, Martin. *Le Rexisme de 1940 à 1944: Degrelle et les autres*. Brussels: Centre de Recherches et d'Études Historiques de la Seconde Guerre Mondiale, 1986.

———. *Collaboration in Belgium: Léon Degrelle and the Rexist Movement in Belgium*. New Haven: Yale University Press, 1993.

Copsey, Nigel and David Renton (eds). *British Fascism, the Labour Movement and the State*. London: Palgrave Macmillan, 2005.

Costa-Pinto, Antonio. *Salazar's Dictatorship and European Fascism: Problems of Interpretation*. New York: Columbia University Press, 1995.

———. *The Blue Shirts: Portuguese Fascists and the New State*. New York: Columbia University Press, 2000.

Cotter, John M. 'Sounds of Hate: White Power Rock and Roll and the Neo-Nazi Skinhead Subculture'. *Terrorism and Political Violence* 11.2 (1999): pp. 111–140.

Council of Europe (ed.). *Art and Power*. London: Hayward Gallery, 1995.

Courtois, Stéphane, Nicolas Werth, Jean-Louis Panné, Andrzej Paczkowski, Karel Bartosek, and Jean-Louis Margolin. *The Black Book of Communism: Crimes, Terror, Repression*. Harvard: Harvard University Press, 1999.

Cronin, Mike. *The Blueshirts and Irish Politics*. Dublin: Four Courts Press, 1997.

Currey, Muriel and Harold Goad. *The Workings of the Corporate State*. London: Nicholson and Watson, 1933.

Dahrendorf, Ralph. *Society and Democracy in Germany*. New York: Doubleday, 1968.

Dawidowicz, Lucy. *The War Against the Jews*. Harmondsworth: Penguin, 1977.

Debord, Guy. *The Society of the Spectacle*. Detroit: Black & Red, 1983, 1st edition 1967.

Derrida, Jacques. *Specters of Marx, the State of the Debt, the Work of Mourning, & the New International*. London: Routledge, 1994.

Deutscher, Isaac. *The Non-Jewish Jew*. London: The Merlin Press, 1981.

Deleuze, Gilles and Felix Guattari. *A Thousand Plateaus: Capitalism and Schizophrenia*. Minneapolis: University of Minnesota Press, 1987.

Dimitrov, Georgi. 'The Fascist Offensive and the Tasks of the Communist International'. Georgi Dimitrov (ed.). *Georgi Dimitrov: Selected Speeches and Articles*. London: Lawrence & Wishart, 1951: pp. 99–102.

Drake, Richard. *The Revolutionary Mystique and Terrorism in Contemporary Italy*. Bloomington and Indianapolis: Indiana University Press, 1989.

Dupeux, Louis. '"Rivoluzione conservatrice" e modernità'. *Diorama letterario* 79 (1985): pp. 3–16.

Eatwell, Roger. 'Towards a New Model of Generic Fascism'. *Journal of Theoretical Politics* 4.2 (1992): pp. 161–194.

———. *Fascism*. London: Chatto & Windus, 1996.

Eisenstadt, Shmuel. *Patterns of Modernity: Vol. 2, Beyond the West*. New York: New York University Press, 1987.

Eliade, Mircea. *The Myth of Eternal Return (or Cosmos and History)*. New York: Harper Torchbooks, 1954.

Evola, Julius. *Cavalcare la tigre*. Milan: Scheiwiller, 1961.

———. *L'arco e la clava*. Milan: Scheiwiller, 1971.

———. *La rivolta contro il mondo moderno*. Rome: Edizioni Mediterranee, 1976.

———. *Cavalcare la tigre*. Milan: Il Falco, 1981.

———. *Saggi di Dottrina Politica*. Genoa: I Dioscuri, 1989.

——— 'United Europe: The Spiritual Pre-Requisite'. *The Scorpion* 9.19 (1986): pp. 18–19.

Falasca-Zamponi, Simonetta. *Fascist Spectacle: The Aesthetics of Power in Mussolini's Italy*. Berkeley: University of California Press, 1997.

Favell, Adrian. 'Multi-Ethnic Britain: An Exception in Europe?' *Patterns of Prejudice* 35.1 (2000): pp. 35–58.

Feder, Gottfried. *Das Programm der NSDAP*. Franz Eher: Munich, 1933.

Feldman, Matthew. 'Between *Geist* and *Zeitgeist*: Martin Heidegger as Ideologue of a "Metapolitical Fascism"'. *Totalitarian Movements and Political Religions* 6.2 (2005): pp. 175–198.

Felice, Renzo de. *Mussolini: vols. 1–7*. Turin: Einaudi, 1965–1997.

———. *Mussolini il rivoluzionario*. Turin: Einaudi, 1965.

———, Michael Ledeen. *Fascism: An Informal Introduction to its Theory and Practice*. Princeton: Transaction, 1976.

———. *Interpretations of Fascism*. Cambridge, MA: Cambridge University Press, 1977.

———. *Mussolini il Duce: vol. 2, Lo stato totalitario, 1936–1940*. Turin: Einaudi, 1981.

Fenn, Richard. *The End of Time: Religion, Ritual, and the Forging of the Soul*. London: SPCK, 1997.

Ferraresi, Franco (ed.). *La destra radicale*. Milan: Feltrinelli, 1984.

———. 'Julius Evola: Tradition, Reaction, and the Radical Right'. *European Journal of Sociology* 28 (1987): pp. 105–151.

Fest, Joachim. *Hitler*. London: Weidenfeld & Nicolson, 1974.

———. *Der zerstörte Traum: Vom Ende des utopistischen Zeitalters*. Berlin: Siedler, 1991.

Freda, F. *La disintegrazione del sistema*. Padua: Edizioni di Ar, 1980.

Freeden, Michael. 'Political Concepts and Ideological Morphology'. *The Journal of Political Philosophy* 2.2 (1994): pp. 140–164.

———. *Ideologies and Political Theory: A Conceptual Approach*. Oxford: Clarendon Press, 1998.

Frei, Norbert. 'Wie modern war der Nationalsozialismus?' *Geschichte und Gesellschaft* 19.3 (1993): pp. 367–387.

Friedländer, Saul. *Kitsch und Tod: Der Widerschein des Nazismus*. Munich: Hanser, 1984.

Fritzsche, Peter. 'Nazi Modern'. *Modernism/Modernity* 3.1 (1996): pp. 1–21.

Fromm, Erich. *The Anatomy of Human Destruction*. New York: Holt, Rinehart and Winston, 1973.

Fukuyama, Francis. 'The End of History?' *The National Interest* 16 (1989): pp. 3–18.

Galli, Giorgio. *La destra in Italia*. Milan: Gammalibri, 1983.

Gasman, Daniel. *Haeckel's Monism and the Birth of Fascist Ideology*. New York: Peter Lang, 1998.

Geiss, Imanuel (ed.). *Meyers Enzyklopädisches Lexikon: Vol. 8*. Munich: Bibliographisches Institut, 1973.

Gentile, Emilio. *Le origini dell'ideologia fascista*. Bari: Laterza, 1975.

———. *Il mito dello Stato Nuovo dall'antigiolittismo al fascismo*. Bari: Laterza, 1982.

———. 'Il fascismo'. Gentile Emilio *et al*. (ed.). *L'Europa del XX secolo fra totalitarismo e democrazia*. Faenza: Itaca, 1991.

———. *Il culto del littorio*. Rome-Bari: Laterza, 1993.

———. 'Impending Modernity: Fascism and the Ambivalent Image of the United States'. *Journal of Contemporary History* 28 (1993): pp. 7–29.

———. *The Sacralisation of Politics in Fascist Italy*. Cambridge, MA: Harvard University Press, 1996.

———. *Le religioni politiche*. Rome-Bari: Laterza, 2000. English translation *Religion as Politics* Princeton, N.J.: Princeton University Press, 2006.

———. 'The Sacralisation of Politics: Definitions, Interpretations and Reflections on the Question of Secular Religion and Totalitarianism'. *Totalitarian Movements and Political Religion* 1.1 (2000): pp. 18–55.

———. *The Struggle for Modernity: Nationalism, Futurism, and Fascism*. New York: Praeger Books, 2003.

Gentile, Giovanni. *Fascismo e cultura*. Milan: Fratelli Treves, 1928.

———. 'The Doctrine of Fascism'. Giovanni Gentile (ed.). *Enciclopedia Italiana*. Rome: Istituto della enciclopedia italiana, 1932.

———. *Origini e dottrina del fascismo*. Rome: Istituto nazionale del fascismo, 1929.

Giannetti, Guido, Adriano Romualdi, and Mario Prisco. *Drieu la Rochelle: Il Mito d'Europa*. Rome: Edizioni della Salamandra, 1981.

Giddens, Anthony. *Modernity and Self-Identity*. Cambridge: Polity Press, 1991.

Gilbhard, Hermann and Holger Goblirsch. 'Rückkehr des Rassenwahns? Die Ideologie der "Neuen Rechte"'. Wolfgang Benz (ed.). *Rechtsextremismus in der Bundesrepublik*. Frankfurt am Main: Fischer, 1989: pp. 213–223.

Giuliano, Balbino. 'Il fascismo e l'avvenire della coltura'. Giuseppe Pomba (ed.). *La civiltà fascista*. Turin: Torinese Unione Tipografica Editoriale, 1928.

Goebbels, Joseph. *Michael: Ein deutsches Schicksal in Tagebuchblättern*. Munich: Eher, 1929.

Goldhagen, Daniel. *Hitler's Willing Executioners*. London: Abacus, 1997.

Goodrick-Clarke, Nicholas. *The Occult Roots of Nazism*. Wellington: The Aquarian Press, 1985.

———. *Black Sun: Aryan Cults, Esoteric Nazism and the Politics of Identity*. New York and London: New York University Press, 2002.

Gorce, Paul-Marie de la. 'Le XXIe siècle sera-t-il américain'. *Krisis* 20–21 (1997): pp. 150–164.

Gottlieb, Julie and Tom Linehan (eds). *Cultural Expressions of the Far Right in Britain*. London: Macmillan, 2002.

Grand, Alexander de. *The Italian Nationalist Association and the Rise of Fascism in Italy*. Lincoln: University of Nebraska Press, 1978.

———. *Fascist Italy and Nazi Germany: The Fascist Style of Rule*. New York and London: Routledge, 1995.

———. *Italian Fascism*. Lincoln: University of Nebraska Press, 2000.

Gravelli, Asvero (ed.). 'Editorial introduction'. *Antieuropa* 1.1 (1929): pp. 1–13.

———. 'Pour une internationale Fasciste'. [0] *Antieuropa* 7–9 (1930).

Gregor, A. James. *The Ideology of Fascism: The Rationale of Totalitarianism*. New York: Free Press, 1969.

———. 'Fascism and Modernization, Some Addenda'. *World Politics* 26 (1972): pp. 547–564.

———. *Italian Fascism and Developmental Dictatorship*. Princeton, NJ: Princeton University Press, 1979.

———. *The Young Mussolini and the Intellectual Origins of Fascism*. Berkeley: University of Chicago Press, 1979.

———. *Phoenix. Fascism in Our Time*. New Brunswick, NJ: Transaction, 1999.

———. 'Fascism, Marxism and Some Considerations Concerning Classification'. *Totalitarian Movements and Political Religions* 3.2 (2002): pp. 61–82.

Grenville, John A. S. *The Collins History of the World in the Twentieth Century*. London: HarperCollins, 1994.

Griffin, Roger. 'Revolts Against the Modern World: The Blend of Literary and Historical Fantasy in the Italian New Right'. *Literature and History* 11.1 (1985): pp. 101–124.

——— . *The Nature of Fascism*. London: Routledge, 1993.

——— (ed.). *Fascism*. Oxford: Oxford University Press, 1995.

——— (ed.). *International Fascism: Theories, Causes and the New Consensus*. London: Arnold, 1998.

———. 'The Sacred Synthesis: The Ideological Cohesion of Fascist Culture'. *Modern Italy* 3.1 (1998): pp. 5–23.

———. 'Afterword: Last Rights?' Sabrina Ramet (ed.). *The Radical Right in Central and Eastern Europe*. Pennsylvania: Penn State Press, 1999: pp. 297–321.

———. 'GUD Reactions: The Patterns of Prejudice in a Neo-Fascist Groupuscule'. *Patterns of Prejudice* 33.2 (1999): pp. 31–50.

———. 'Interregnum or endgame? Radical Right Thought in the "Post-fascist" Era'. *The Journal of Political Ideologies* 5.2 (2000): pp. 163–178.

———. 'Nazism's "Cleansing Hurricane" and the Metamorphosis of Fascist Studies'. Werner Loh and Wolfgang Wippermann (eds). *'Faschismus' – kontrovers*. Stuttgart: Lucius und Lucius, 2000: pp. 179–190.

———. 'Plus ça change!: The Fascist Mindset Behind the Nouvelle Droite's Struggle for Cultural Renewal'. Edward Arnold (ed.). *The Development of the Radical Right in France 1890–1995*. London: Routledge, 2000: pp. 217–252.

———. '"Racism" or "rebirth"? The Case for Granting German Citizenship to the Alien Concept "generic fascism"'. *Ethik und Sozialwissenschaften* 11.2 (2000): pp. 300–303. Reprinted in Loh Werner and Wolfgang Wippermann (eds). *'Faschismus' – kontrovers*. Stuttgart: Lucius und Lucius, 2000: pp. 81–88.

———. 'Revolution from the Right: Fascism'. David Parker (ed.). *Revolutions and the Revolutionary Tradition in the West: 1560–1991*. London: Routledge, 2000: pp. 185–201.

————. 'The Palingenetic Political Community: Rethinking the Legitimation of Totalitarian Regimes in Inter-War Europe'. *Totalitarian Movements and Political Religions* 3.3 (2000): pp. 24–43.

————. 'Interregnum or endgame? Radical Right Thought in the "Post-fascist" Era'. Michael Freeden (ed.). *Reassessing Political Ideologies*. London: Routledge, 2001: pp. 116–131.

————. 'Notes Towards the Definition of Fascist Culture: The Prospects for Synergy Between Marxist and Liberal Heuristics'. *Renaissance and Modern Studies* 42 (2001): pp. 95–115.

————. 'The Reclamation of Fascist Culture'. *European History Quarterly* 31.4 (2001): pp. 609–620.

————. 'The Primacy of Culture: The Current Growth (or Manufacture) of Consensus within Fascist Studies'. *The Journal of Contemporary History* 37.1 (2002): pp. 21–43.

————. 'From Slime Mould to Rhizome: An Introduction to the Groupuscular Right'. *Patterns of Prejudice* 37.1 (2003): pp. 27–50.

————. '"This Fortress Built Against Infection" The BUF Vision of Britain's Theatrical and Musical Renaissance'. Tom Linehan and Julie Gottlieb (eds). *Cultural Expressions of the Far Right*. London: Macmillan, 2003.

———— with Matthew Feldman (eds.). *Fascism: Critical Concepts, 5 Vols*. London: Routledge, 2005.

Hagtvet, Bernt and Stein Larsen. 'Contemporary Approaches to Fascism: A Survey of Paradigms'. Bernt Hagtvet and Stein Larsen (eds). *Who Were the Fascists*. Bergen, Oslo: Universitetforlaget, 1980: pp. 38–41.

Harris, Geoffrey. *The Dark Side of Europe: The Extreme Right Today*. Edinburgh: Edinburgh University Press, 1990.

Hauner, Mlan. 'Did Hitler Want World Dominion?' *Journal of Contemporary History* 13.1 (1978): pp. 15–32.

Havel, Vaclev. 'On Home'. *The New York Review of Books* 38.20 (5 December 1991).

Herbeck, Dan and Michael Herbeck. *American Terrorist – Timothy McVeigh & the Tragedy at Oklahoma City*. New York: Avon, 2001.

Herf, Jeffrey. *Reactionary Modernism: Technology, Culture and Politics in Weimar and the Third Reich*. Cambridge: Cambridge University Press, 1984.

————. 'The Engineer as Ideologue: Reactionary Modernists in Weimar and the Third Reich'. *Journal of Contemporary History*. 19 (1984): pp. 631–648.

Herzstein, Robert. *When Nazi Dreams Come True*. London: Abacus, 1982.

Hewitt, Adrian. *Fascist Modernism*. Stanford: Stanford University Press, 1993.

Hoare, Quintin and Smith Nowell (eds). *Antonio Gramsci: Selections from the Prison Note Books*. New York: International Publishers, 1971.

Hobsawm, Eric and Terence Ranger. *The Invention of Tradition*. Oxford: Oxford University Press, Oxford, 1983.

————. *Age of Extremes: The Short Twentieth Century 1914–1991*. London: Abacus, 1994.

Hitler, Adolf. *Liberty, Art, Nationhood: Three Addresses Delivered at the Seventh National Socialist Congress, Nuremberg, 1935*. Berlin: Müller and Sons, 1936.

————. *My New Order*. Sydney and London: Angus and Robertson, 1942.

————. *Mein Kampf: Vol. 2*. London: Pimlico, 1992.

Huber, Hartwig. 'Menschenrecht auf Heimat und Identität'. *Nation Europa* 39.7 (July 1989): pp. 5–6.

Hughes, Arnold and Martin Kolinsky. '"Paradigmatic Fascism" and Modernization: A Critique'. *Political Studies* 24.4 (1976): pp. 371–396.

Hughes, Robert. *The Shock of the New*. London: BBC, 1980.

Hughes, Stuart. *Consciousness and Society: The Reorientation of European Social Thought, 1890–1930*. London: McGibbon and Kee, 1958.

Hunt, Lynn. *Politics, Culture and Class in the French Revolution*. Berkeley and Los Angeles: University of California Press, 1981.

Jaspers, Karl. *Philosophische Autobiographie*. Munich: Piper, 1984.

Jellamo, Anna. 'Julius Evola: il pensatore della tradizione'. Franco Ferraresi (ed.). *La destra radicale*. Milan: Feltrinelli, 1984.

Jesi, Furio. *Cultura di destra*. Milan: Garzanti, 1979.

Jünger, Ernst. ,Nationalismus und modernes Leben'. *Arminius* 8.8 (1927): pp. 3–6.

Kafka, Franz. ,In the Gallery'. Malcolm Pasley (ed.). *The Transformation and Other Stories*. Harmondsworth: Penguin, 1995.

Kallis, Aristotle (ed.). *The Fascism Reader*. London: Routledge, 2002.

Kaplan, Jeffrey. *Radical Religion in America. Millenarian Movements from the Far Right to the Children of Noah (Religion and Politics)*. New York: Syracuse University Press, 1997.

Karnoouh, Claude. 'La fin des avant-gardes et le triomphe du marché'. *Krisis* 20–21 (1997): pp. 198–208.

Kater, Michael. *Different Drummers: Jazz in the Culture of Nazi Germany*. Oxford: Oxford University Press, 1992.

Kautsky, Karl. *Ethics and the Materialist Conception of History*. Chicago: Charles H. Kerr & Sons, 1906.

———. *The Twisted Muse: Musicians and their Music in the Third Reich*. Oxford: Oxford University Press, 1997.

Kern, Stephen. *The Culture of Time and Space 1880–1918*. Cambridge, MA: University of Harvard Press, 1983.

Kershaw, Ian. 'Hitler: Ideologe und Propagandist'. *Vierteljahrshefte für Zeitgeschichte* 40.2 (1992): pp. 263–271.

———. *Hitler: Hubris (Vol. 1) and Nemesis (Vol. 2)*. New York and London: Norton, 1998–1999.

———. *The Nazi Dictatorship*. London: Arnold, 2000.

———. 'Hitler and the Uniqueness of Nazism'. *The Journal of Contemporary History* 39.2 (2004): pp. 239–254.

King, Martin Luther. *The Trumpet of Conscience*. London: Hodder & Stoughton, 1968.

Kitschelt, Herbert. *The Radical Right in Western Europe: A Comparative Analysis*. Michigan: University of Michigan Press, 1995.

Klemperer, Victor. *The Language of the Third Reich: LTI, Lingua Tertii Imperii, a Philologist's Notebook*. London: Athlone, 2000.

Klingemann, Carsten. 'Sociology and Social Research in the Third Reich'. Dirk Käsler and Stephen Turner (ed.). *Sociology Responds to Fascism*. London: Routledge, 1992.

Kluke, Paul. 'Nationalsozialistische Europaideologie'. *Vierteljahreshefte für Zeitgeschichte* 3.3 (1955): pp. 240–275.

Knopp, Guido. *Hitler: Eine Bilanz*. Berlin: Siedler, 1995.

———. 'Conquest, Foreign and Domestic in Fascist Italy and Nazi Germany'. MacGregor Knox (ed.). *Common Destiny: Dictatorship, Foreign Policy, and War in Fascist Italy and Nazi Germany*. Cambridge: Cambridge University Press, 2000.

Kocka, Jürgen. 'Ursachen des Nationalsozialismus'. *Aus Politik und Zeitgeschichte (APZ)* (21 June 1980): pp. 3–15.

Koestler, Arthur. 'Epilogue'. *The Sleepwalkers. A History of Man's Changing Vision of the Universe*. London: Arkana, 1989 (1st edition London: Hutchinson, 1959): pp. 521–553.

Krasin, Yurii. 'Determinism or Voluntarism'. Yurii Kraisn (ed.). *Lenin and Revolution: A Reply to Critics*. Moscow: Novosti Press Agency Publishing House, 1969, [ch. 6, note 21].

Krebs, Pierre. *Die europäische Wiedergeburt.* Tübingen: Grabert-Verlag, 1982.

———. (ed.). *Mut zur Identität: Alternativen zum Prinzip Gleichheit.* Struckum: Verlag für ganzheitliche Forschung und Kultur, 1988.

Kroll, Frank-Lothar. *Utopie als Ideologie: Geschichtsdenken im Dritten Reich.* Paderborn: Schöningh, 1998.

Kühnl, Reinhard. 'The German *Sonderweg* Reconsidered: Continuities and Discontinuities in Modern German History'. Reinhard Alter and Peter Monteath (eds). *Rewriting the German Past: History and Identity in the New Germany.* Atlantic Highlands: NJ Humanities Press, 1997: pp. 115–128.

Laclau, Ernesto. 'Fascism and Ideology'. Ernesto Laclau (ed.). *Politics and Ideology in Marxist Theory: Capitalism, Fascism, Populism.* London: Verso, 1982.

Lane, Barbara and Leila Rupp. *Nazi Ideology Before 1933.* Austin: University of Texas Press, 1978.

Laqueur, Walter (ed.). *Fascism: A Reader's Guide.* Harmondsworth: The Penguin Press, 1969.

Larsen, Stein. 'Was there Fascism Outside Europe? Diffusion from Europe and Domestic Impulses'. Stein Larsen (ed.). *Fascism Outside Europe.* New York: Columbia University Press and Boulder Social Sciences Monographs, 2001: pp. 491–528.

Lasky, Melvin. *Utopia and Revolution.* London: Macmillan, 1976.

Le Pen, Jean-Marie. 'Für ein Europa der Europäer'. *Nation Europa* 39.5/6 (1989): pp. 72–73.

Leach, Edmund. *Claude Lévi-Strauss.* Chicago: The University of Chicago Press, 1989.

Ledeen, Michael. *Universal Fascism.* New York: Howard Fertig, 1972.

———. *The First Duce: D'Annunzio at Fiume.* Baltimore: John Hopkins University Press, 1977.

Levi, Primo. *If This is a Man. The Truce.* Harmondsworth: Penguin, 1987.

Linehan, Tom. *British Fascism 1918–39: Parties, Ideology and Culture.* Manchester: Manchester University Press, 2000.

Linz, Juan. 'Some Notes Toward a Comparative Study of Fascism in Sociological Historical Perspective'. Walter Laqueur (ed.). *Fascism: A Reader's Guide: Analyses Interpretations, Bibliography.* London: Wildwood House, 1976: pp. 1–23.

Lipstadt, Deborah. *Denying the Holocaust.* New York: The Free Press, 1993.

Locchi, Giorgio. *L'essenza del fascismo.* La Spezia: Il Tridente, 1981.

Loh, Werner (ed.). *Erwägungsorientierung in Philosophie und Sozialwissenschaften.* Stuttgart: Lucius und Lucius, 2001.

——— and Wolfgang Wippermann (eds). *'Faschismus' kontrovers.* Paderborn: Lucius und Lucius, 2003.

London, John (ed.). *Theatre Under the Nazis.* Manchester: Manchester University Press, 2000.

Lowles, Nick and Steve Silver (eds). *White Noise.* London: Searchlight, 1998.

———, Graeme McLagan. *Mr Evil: The Secret Life of the Racist Bomber and Killer David Copeland.* London: John Blake, 2000.

Lukács, Georg. *The Destruction of Reason.* New Jersey: Atlantic Highlands, 1952.

Luzzatto, Sergio. 'The Political Culture of Fascist Italy'. *Contemporary European History* 8.2 (1999): pp. 317–334.

Lyttleton, Adrian. *Italian Fascism from Pareto to Gentile.* London: Jonathan Cape, 1973.

———. *The Seizure of Power: Fascism in Italy 1919–1929.* New York: Charles Scribner's Sons, 1973.

——— (ed.). *Italian Fascisms from Pareto to Gentile.* London: Jonathan Cape, 1979.

Mack Smith, Denis. *Mussolini.* London: Weidenfeld & Nicolson, 1981.

Malgieri, Gennaro. *Carlo Costamagna.* Vibo Valentia: Edizioni Sette Colori, 1981.

Mann, Michael. *Fascists*. New York: Cambridge University Press, 2004.

Marinetti, Filippo. 'The Founding Manifesto of Futurism'. Umbro Apollionio (ed.). *Futurist Manifestos*. London: Thames and Hudson, 1973.

Marx, Karl. *The Eighteenth Brumaire of Louis Bonaparte: With Explanatory Notes*. New York: International Publications, 1963.

Mason, Tim. 'Whatever Happened to Fascism?' *Radical History Review* 49 (1991): pp. 89–98. Reprinted in Jane Caplan (ed.). *Nazism, Fascism and the Working Class: Essays by Tim Mason*. Cambridge: Cambridge University Press, 1995: pp. 323–331.

———. 'Primacy of Politics: Politics and Economics in National Socialist Germany'. Jane Caplan (ed.). *Nazism, Fascism and the Working Class*. Cambridge: Cambridge University Press, 1995: pp. 53–72.

Mathyl, Markus. 'The National-Bolshevik Party and Arctogaia: Two Neo-Fascist Groupuscules in the Post-Soviet Political Space'. *Patterns of Prejudice* 36.3 (2002): pp. 62–76.

Mavrakis, Kostas. 'Crise de l'art, crise de la société'. *Krisis* 20–21 (1997): pp. 184–197.

Mayer, Arno. *The Furies: Violence and Terror in the French and Russian Revolutions*. Princeton, NJ: Princeton University Press, 2000.

Mazgaj, Paul. *The Action Française and Revolutionary Syndicalism*. Chapel Hill, NC: University of North Carolina Press, 1979.

McGovern, William. *From Luther to Hitler: The History of Fascist-Nazi Political Philosophy*. Boston: Harrap, 1941.

Möller, Horst. 'Die nationalsozialistische Machtergreifung: Konterrevolution oder Revolution?' *Vierteljahresschrift für Zeitgeschichte* 31.1 (1983): pp. 25–51.

Mohler, Armin. *Die Konservative Revolution in Deutschland 1918–1932*. Stuttgart: Friedrich Vorwerk, 1950 Reprinted Darmstadt: Wissenschaftliche Buchgesellschaft, 1972.

———. 'German Nihilism'. Roger Griffin (ed.). *Fascism*. Oxford: Oxford University Press, 1995: pp. 351–354.

Molnar, Thomas. 'Fin de millénaire aux États Unis'. *Krisis* 20–21 (1997): pp. 139–149.

Moore, Barrington. *Social Origins of Dictatorship and Democracy*. Harmondsworth: Penguin, 1966.

Morgan, Philip. *Italian Fascism: 1919*–1945. London: Macmillan, 1995.

———. *Fascism in Europe: 1918–1945*. London: Routledge, 2002.

Mosley, Oswald. *The Greater Britain*. London: BUF Publications, 1932.

———. *Fascism in Britain*. London: BUF Press, 1933.

Mosse, George L. *The Crisis of German Ideology*. New York: Howard Fertig, 1964.

———. 'The Genesis of Fascism'. *Journal of Contemporary History* 1.1 (1966): pp. 14–26.

———. *The Nationalisation of the Masses*. New York: Howard Fertig, 1975.

——— (ed.). *International Fascism*. London: Sage, 1979.

———. 'Towards a General Theory of Fascism'. G. L. Mosse (ed.). *The Fascist Revolution: Towards a General Theory of Fascism*. New York: Howard Fertig, 1999: pp. 1–44.

———. 'The Political Culture of Political Futurism: A General Perspective'. *Journal of Contemporary History* 21.2–3 (1990): pp. 253–268.

———. 'Fascism and the French Revolution'. George L. Mosse. *The Fascist Revolution*. New York: Howard Fertig, 1999: pp. 69–93.

——— (ed.). *The Fascist Revolution*. New York: Howard Fertig, 1999.

Mowat, Robin. *Creating the European Community*. London: Blandford Press, 1973.

Mühlberger, Detlef (ed.). *Hitler's Voice: The Völkischer Beobachter, Vol. 1 (The Organization of the Party); Vol. 2 (Propaganda)*. Bern: Peter Lang Verlag, 2004.

Müller, Klaus-Jürgen. 'French Fascism and Modernization'. *Journal of Contemporary History* 11 (1976): pp. 269–283.

Mussolini, Benito. *Fascism: Doctrine and Institutions*. Rome: Arditi, 1935. Reprinted in Roger Griffin (ed.). *International Fascism: Theories, Causes, and the New Consensus*. London: Arnold, 1998: pp. 249–250.

Nagy-Talavera, Nicholas. *The Greenshirts and Others: A History of Fascism in Hungary and Romania*. Stanford, CA: Institution Press, 1970.

Neocleous, Mark. *Fascism*. Maidenhead: Open University Press, 1997.

Nolte, Ernst. *Der Faschismus in seiner Epoche*. Munich: Piper, 1963.

———. 'Part Five: Fascism as a Metapolitical Phenomenon'. Ernst Nolte (ed.). *Three Faces of Fascism: Action Française, Italian Fascism and German Nazism*. London: Weidenfeldt & Nicholson, 1965: pp. 537–567.

Ó Maoláin, Ciarán. *The Radical Right: A World Directory*. London: Longman, 1987.

Organski, Kenneth. 'Fascism and Modernization'. Stuart Woolf (ed.). *The Nature of Fascism*. London: Weidenfeld & Nicolson, 1968.

Orlow, Dietrich. *The History of the Nazi Party: Vol. 2, 1933–1945*. London: David and Charles, 1973.

Osborne, Peter. *The Politics of Time*. London: Verso, 1995.

Ozouf, Mona. *Festivals and the French Revolution*. Cambridge, MA: Harvard, 1988.

Panitch, Leo and Colin Leys (eds). *Socialist Register 2003*. New York: Monthly Review Press, 2003.

Passmore, Kevin. *From Liberalism to Fascism: The Right in a French Province 1928–1939*. Cambridge: Cambridge University Press, 1997.

Pauwels, Louis and Jacques Bergier. *The Dawn of Magic*. London: A. Gibbs & Phillips, 1963.

Paxton, Robert. *Vichy France: Old Guard and New Order*. New York: Knopf, 1972.

———. 'The Five Stages of Fascism'. *The Journal of Modern History* 70 (1998): pp. 1–23.

———. *The Anatomy of Fascism*. New York: Alfred A. Knopf, 2004.

Payne, Stanley. *Falange: A History of Spanish Fascism*. Oxford: Oxford University Press, 1962.

———. *Fascism: Comparison and Definition*. Madison: University of Wisconsin Press, 1980.

———. *A History of Fascism: 1914–1945*. London: UCL Press, 1995.

———. *Fascism in Spain: 1923–1977*. Madison: University of Wisconsin Press, 1999.

———. 'Historical Fascism and the Radical Right'. *Journal of Contemporary History* 35 (2000): pp. 109–118.

Pedahzur, Ami and Leonard Weinberg. 'Modern European Democracies and Its Enemies: The Threat of the Extreme Right'. *Totalitarian Movements and Political Religions* 2.1 (2001): pp. 52–72.

Piccone, Paul. 'Confronting the French New Right'. *Telos* 98–99 (1993–1994): pp. 3–22.

Pickering, W. S. F. *Durkheim's Sociology of Religion*. London: Routledge & Kegan Paul, 1984.

Platt, Gerald. 'Thoughts on a Theory of Collective Action: Language, Affect, and Ideology in Revolution'. Mel Albin (ed.). *New Directions in Psychohistory*. Lexington, MA: Lexington Books, 1980: pp. 69–94.

Plumyène, Jean and Raymond Lasierre. *Les Fascismes Français*. Paris: Seuil, 1963.

Pois, Robert. *National Socialism and the Religion of Nature*. London: Croom Helm, 1986.

Pollard, John. *The Fascist Experience in Italy*. London: Routledge, 1998.

Popper, Karl. *The Poverty of Historicism*. London: Routledge & Kegan Paul, 1957.

Proctor, Robert. *The Nazi War on Cancer*. Princeton: Princeton University Press, 1999.

Pulzer, Peter. *The Rise of Political Anti-Semitism in Germany and Austria*. London: Peter Halban, 1988.

Puschner, Uwe. *Handbuch zur völkischen Bewegung 1871–1918*. Munich: Saur, 1996.

Pynsent, Robert. *Decadence and Innovation*. London: Weidenfeld & Nicolson, 1989.

Quinn, Malcolm. *The Swastika*. London: Routledge, 1994.

Rabinbach, Anson. 'The Aesthetics of Production in the Third Reich'. *Journal of Contemporary History* 11 (1976): pp. 43–74.

Rauschning, Hermann. *Die Revolution des Nihilismus: Kulisse und Wirkilichkeit im Dritten Reich*. Zurich and New York: Europa Verlag, 1938.

———. *Hitler Speaks*. London: Thornton Butterworth, 1939.

Reichardt, Sven. *Faschistische Kampfbünde*. Cologne: Böhlau, 2002.

Renton, David. *Fascism: Theory and Practice*. London: Pluto Press, 1999.

Reynolds, Michael. 'Virtual Reich'. *Playboy* [US edition] 49.2 (2002): pp. 62–64, 146–152. Reprinted in Matthew Feldman and Roger Griffin (eds). *Critical Concepts in Political Science: Fascism*. London: Routledge, 2003: pp. 339–351.

Rhodes, James. *The Hitler Movement: A Modern Millenarian Revolution*. Stanford: Hoover International Press, 1980.

Roberts, David. *The Syndicalist Tradition in Italian Fascism*. Manchester: Manchester University Press, 1979.

———. 'How Not to Think About Fascism and Ideology, Intellectual Antecedents and Historical Meaning'. *Journal of Contemporary History* 35.2 (2000): pp. 185–211.

Robinson, Richard A. H. *Fascism in Europe*. London: The Historical Association, 1981.

Robson, Mark. *Italy: Liberalism and Fascism 1870–1945*. London: Hodder & Stoughton, 1992.

Röhr, Werner. 'Faschismusforschung in der DDR: Ein Problemskizze'. *Bulletin für Faschismus- und Weltkriegforschung* 16 (2001). GOOGLE

Rogger, Hans and Eugen Weber. *The European Right*. Berkeley: University of California Press, 1965.

Rosenberg, Alfred. *Letzte Aufzeichnungen: Ideale und Idole der nationalsozialistischen Revolution*. Göttingen: Plesse, 1955.

Rushdie, Salman. *Imaginary Homelands*. London: Penguin, 1992.

Sacchi, Franco. 'The Italian New Right'. *Telos* 98–99 (1993–1994): pp. 71–80.

Safranski, Rüdiger. *Martin Heidegger: Between Good and Evil*. Cambridge, MA: Harvard University Press, 1999.

Sarti, Roland. 'Fascist Modernization in Italy: Traditional or Revolutionary'. *American Historical Review* 75 (1970): pp. 1029–1045.

Schleifer, Ronald. *Modernism and Time: The Logic of Abundance in Literature, Science, and Culture 1880–1920*. Cambridge: Cambridge University Press, 2000.

Schnapp, Jeffrey. 'Forwarding Address'. *Stanford Italian Review* 8.1–2 (1990): pp. 53–80.

———. 'Epic Demonstrations: Fascist Modernity and the 1932 Exhibition of the Fascist Revolution'. Richard Golsan (ed.). *Fascism, Aesthetics, and Culture*. Hanover and London: University Press of New England, 1992.

——— (ed.). *A Primer of Italian Fascism*. Lincoln and London: University of Nebraska Press, 2000.

Schneider, Herbert. *Making the Fascist State*. New York: Howard Fertig, 1968.

Schoenbaum, David. *Hitler's Social Revolution*. New York: Norton, 1966.

Schulte-Sass, Linda. *Entertaining the Third Reich: Illusions of Wholeness in Nazi Cinema*. Durham and London: Duke University Press, 1996.

Scruton, Roger. *Dictionary of Political Thought*. London: Pan Books, 1982.

Seliger, Martin. 'Fundamental and Operative Ideology: The Two Principal Dimensions of Political Argumentation'. *Policy Sciences* 1 (1970): pp. 325–327.

Serra, Maurizio. *Al di là della decadenza*. Bologna: Il Mulino, 1994.

Shakespeare, William. *Macbeth*, Act V. Scene 5: line 20.

Shand, James. 'The Reichsautobahn: Symbol for the Third Reich'. *Journal of Contemporary History* 19 (1984): pp. 99–134.

Shandy, Robert. *Unwilling Germans?: The Goldhagen Debate*. Minneapolis: University of Minnesota Press, 1998.

Sheehan, Thomas. 'Myth and Violence: The Fascism of Julius Evola and Alain de Benoist'. *Social Research* 48.1 (1981): pp. 107–151.

Shenfield, Stephen D. *Russian Fascism: Traditions, Tendencies, and Movements*. New York: M. E. Sharpe, 2001.

Simonini, Augusto. *Il linguaggio di Mussolini*. Milano: Bompiani, 1978.

Snyder, Timothy. *Nationalism, Marxism, and Modern Central Europe: A Biography of Kazimierz Kelles-Krauz (1872–1905)*. Cambridge, MA: Harvard University Press, 1997.

Sorel, Georges. *Reflections on Violence*. London: Collier-Macmillan, 1961.

Soucy, Robert. *Fascist Intellectual: Drieu la Rochelle*. Berkeley: University of California Press, 1979.

Spackmann, Barbara. *Fascist Virilities: Rhetoric, Ideology, and Social Fantasy in Italy*. Minneapolis: University of Minnesota Press, 1996.

Speer, Albert. *Inside the Third Reich. Memoirs*. New York: Macmillan, 1970.

Stackelberg, Roderick. *Hitler's Germany*. London: Routledge, 1999.

Staub, Ervin. *The Roots of Evil: The Origins of Genocide and Other Group Violence*. Cambridge: Cambridge University Press, 1992.

Steding, Christoph. *Das Reich und die Krankheit Europas*. Hamburg: Hanseatische Verlagsanstalt, 1938.

Steigmann-Gall, Richard. *Holy Reich: Nazi Conceptions of Christianity, 1919–1945*. Cambridge: Cambridge University Press, 2003.

Stern, Fritz. *The Politics of Cultural Despair*. Berkeley: University of California Press, 1961.

Sternhell, Ze'ev. *Ni Droite, ni Gauche*. Paris: Éditions du Seuil, 1973.

———. 'Fascist Ideology'. Walter Laqueur (ed.). *Fascism: A Reader's Guide: Analyses Interpretations, Bibliography*. Harmondsworth: Penguin, 1979: pp. 325–406.

———. *Neither Right nor Left: Fascist Ideology in France*. Berkeley, CA: Princeton University Press, 1986.

———. 'Fascism'. David Miller (ed.). *The Blackwell Encyclopedia of Political Thought*. Oxford: Blackwell, 1987: pp. 148–151.

———. *The Birth of Fascist Ideology*. New Jersey: Princeton University Press, 1993.

Stichting, Anne Frank. *The Extreme Right in Europe and the United States*. Amsterdam: Anne Frank Foundation, 1984.

Stites, Richard. *Revolutionary Dreams: Utopian Dreams and Experimental Life in the Russian Revolution*. Oxford: Oxford University Press, 1992.

Stone, Marla. 'The State as Patron: Making Official Culture in Fascist Italy'. Matthew Affron and Mark Antliff (ed.). *Fascist Visions: Art and Ideology in France and Italy*. Princeton: Princeton University Press, 1997: pp. 205–238.

———. *The Patron State: Culture and Politics in Fascist Italy*. Princeton: Princeton University Press, 1998.

Strachey, John. *The Menace of Fascism*. London: Victor Gollanz, 1933.

Swart, Koenraad. *The Sense of Decadence in Nineteenth-Century France*. The Hague: International Archives of the History of Ideas, 1964.

Sznajder, Mario. 'The "Carta del Carnaro" and Modernization'. *Tel Aviv Jahrbuch für deutsche Geschichte* 18 (1989).

Szollosi-Janze, Margit. *Die Pfeilkreuzerbewegung in Ungarn*. Munich: R. Oldenbourg, 1989.

Taguieff, Pierre-André. 'Discussion or Inquisition? The Case of Alain de Benoist'. *Telos* 98–99 (1993–1994): pp. 60–71.

———. 'From Race to Culture: The New Right's View of European Identity'. *Telos* 9899 (1993/1994): pp. 99–126.

———. *Sur la Nouvelle Droite: Jalons d'une analyse critique.* Paris: Descartes & Cie, 1994.

Tal, Uriel. *Religion, Politics and Ideology in the Third Reich: Selected Essays.* London and New York: Routledge, 2004.

Tannenbaum, Edward. 'The Goals of Italian Fascism'. *American Historical Review* 74 (1969): pp. 1183–1204.

———. *Fascist in Italy: Society and Culture 1922–45.* London: Methuen, 1975.

Tarchi, Marco. 'Tra festa e rivoluzione'. *Intervento* 31 (1978): pp. 113–132.

———. *La 'rivoluzione legale'.* Bologna: Il Mulino, 1993.

Taylor, Brandon and Wilfried van der Will (eds). *The Nazification of Art.* Winchester: The Winchester Press, 1990.

Teed, Peter. *Dictionary of Twentieth Century History: 1914–1990.* Oxford: Oxford University Press, 1992.

Theweleit, Klaus. *Male Fantasies: Vols. 1 and 2.* Cambridge: Polity Press, 1989.

Thomson, Alexander Raven. *Motorways for Britain.* London: Abbey Supplies Ltd., 1938.

Thurlow, Richard. *Fascism in Britain: A History, 1918–1985.* Oxford: Basil Blackwell, 1987.

Todorov, Tzvetan. *Hope and Memory: Lessons from the Twentieth Century.* Princeton: Princeton University Press, 2003.

Toller, Ernst. *Eine deutsche Jugend.* Hamburg: Rowohlt, 1996.

Tormey, Simon. *Making Sense of Tyranny.* Manchester: Manchester University Press, 1995.

Trevor-Roper, Hugh. 'The Phenomenon of Fascism'. Stuart Joseph Woolf (ed.). *European Fascism.* London: Weidenfeld & Nicolson, 1968: pp. 18–38.

Trindade, Helgio. 'Fascism and Authoritarianism in Brazil Under Vargas (1930–1945)'. Larsen Stein (ed.). *Fascism Outside Europe.* New York: Columbia UP and Boulder Social Sciences Monographs, 2001: pp. 491–528.

Turner, Henry Jnr. 'Fascism and Modernization'. *World Politics* 24 (1972): pp. 547–564.

Turner, Victor and Edith Turner. 'Religious Celebrations'. Victor Turner (ed.). *Celebration: Studies in Festivity and Ritual.* Washington DC: Smithsonian Institution Press, 1982: pp. 211–212.

Vernon, Richard. *Commitment and Change: Georges Sorel and the Idea of Revolution.* Toronto: University of Toronto Press, 1978.

Vondung, Klaus. *Magie und Manipulation: Ideologischer Kult und politische Religion des Nationalsozialismus.* Göttingen: Vandenhoeck & Ruprecht, 1971.

———. 'Spiritual Revolution and Magic: Speculation and Political Action in National Socialism'. *The Modern Age* 23.4 (1979): pp. 391–402.

Walker, Mark. *Nazi Science: Myth, Truth, and the German Atomic Bomb.* New York: Plenum Press, 1995.

Weber, Eugen. 'Decadence on a Private Income'. *Journal of Contemporary History* 17.1 (1982): pp. 1–20.

Wegierski, Mark. 'The New Right in Europe'. *Telos* 98–99 (1993–1994): pp. 55–69.

Weigall, David and Murphy Michael. *Modern History: Letts Study Aids.* London: Charles Letts & Co, 1991.

Weigert, Hans. *Die Kunst von heute als Spiegel der Zeit.* Leipzig: Seemann, 1934.

Whittam, John. *Fascist Italy.* Manchester: Manchester University Press, 1995.

Whyte, Iain Boyd. 'Berlin, 1 May 1936'. Council of Europe (ed.). *Art and Power.* London: Hayward Gallery, 1995: pp. 41–48.

Wilde, Lawrence. *Ethical Marxism and its Radical Critics.* London: MacMillan Press, 1998.

Williams, Howard. 'Metamorphosis or Palingenesis? – Political Change in Kant'. *Review of Politics* 63.4 (2001): pp. 693–722.

Williamson, David Graham. *The Third Reich*. London and New York: Longman, 1995.

Winkler, Heinrich August. *Revolution, Staat, Faschismus*. Göttingen: Vandenhoeck & Ruprecht, 1978.

Wippermann, Wolfgang. *Wessen Schuld?* Berlin: Elefanten Press, 1997.

———. 'Hat es Faschismus überhaupt gegeben? Der generische Begriff zwischen Kritik und Autokritik'. *Ethik und Sozialwissenschaft* 11.2 (2000): pp. 289–334.

———. 'Was ist Faschismus? Geschichte und Theoriegeschichte'. Werner Loh and Wolfgang Wippermann (eds). *'Faschismus' – kontrovers*. Stuttgart: Lucius und Lucius, 2000: pp. 1–51.

Woolf, Stuart. 'Risorgimento e fascismo: il senso della continuità nella storiografia italiana'. *Belfagor* 20 (1965): pp. 71–91.

——— (ed.). *European Fascism*. London: Weidenfeld & Nicolson, revised edition 1981.

Wordsworth, William. 'Discourse of the Wanderer, and an Evening Visit to the Lake', *The Excursion*, Book Ninth (1795–1814). http://www.bartleby.com/145/ww406.html (09/05/2006).

Yasusuke, Murakami. 'Modernization in Terms of Integration: The Case of Japan'. Shmuel Eisenstadt (ed.). *Patterns of Modernity: Vol. II: Beyond the West*. New York: New York University Press, 1987: pp. 65–88.

Zitelmann, Rainer. 'Die totalitäre Seite der Moderne'. Michael Prinz and Rainer Zitelmann (eds). *Nationalsozialismus und Modernisierung*. Darmstadt: Wissenschaftliche Buchgesellschaft, 1991.

Zunino, Pier-Giorgio. *l'Ideologia del fascismo*. Bologna: Il Mulino, 1985.

(II)   Other Media Sources

II.A: Audio and Video Sources

Crossing the Lives: The History of the International Red Cross Committee (Episodes 1–3). Prod. Beth Holgate, Pres. John Simpson. BBC, 1998.

Hitler: The Rise of Evil. Dir. Christian Duguay. CBS, 2003.

Mussolini and Italian Fascism. Produced by John A. Davies, Denis Mack Smith. University of Warwick Teaching Videos, 1991.

Skrewdriver. 'Hail and Thunder'. *The Strong Survive*. Germany: Rock-O-Rama Records, 1990.

The Most Evil Men in History. Uden Associates Production, 2001.

The Occult History of the Third Reich. Dir. Dave Flitton. Lamancha Productions, 1993.

II.B: Online Publications

Blinkhorn, Martin. 'Author's response' to Toby Abse's review of his *Fascism and the Right in Europe*, Electronic Reviews in History, 24 September 2001, http://www.history.ac.uk/reviews/paper/blinkhornMartin.html (04/05/2006).

Craske, Oliver. 'Women and Children First'. *Central Europe Review* 2.12 (2000). http://www.ce-review.org/00/12/craske12.html (02/04/06).

Ingram, Mike. 'Britain's Conservative Party Exposes its Racist Underbelly'. *World Socialist Web Site* 2 April 2001. http://www.wsws.org/articles/2001/apr2001/hag-a03.shtml/ (02/04/06).

Pastel, Danny. 'The Metamorphosis of *Telos*: A Splintered Journal Pokes into its Own Contradictions'. *In These Times* 24–30 April 1991. http://info.interactivist.net/article.pl?sid=04/04/20/1213200&tid=(04/04/06).

Rivera, David. 'European Union and the Bilderberg Group, Final Warning: A History of the New World Order'. http://www.the7thfire.com/new_world_order/final_warning/EU_and_Bilderberg_Group.html [08/05/06].

Southgate, Troy. 'Transcending the Beyond: From Third Position to National-Anarchism'. *Pravda*. http://english.pravda.ru/main/2002/01/17/25828.html (03/04/06).

Wray, Stephan. 'Rhizomes, Nomads, and Resistant Internet Use'. www.nyu.edu/projects/wray/RhizNom.html (14/11/02).

Toynbee, Polly. 'Old-Fashioned Racism and a Britain that Never Was'. *The Guardian* 20 April 2001. http://www.guardian.co.uk/racism/Story/0,2763,475548,00.html(02/04/06).

Umland, Andreas. 'Towards an Uncivil Society?: Contextualising the Decline of Post-Soviet Russian Extremely Right-Wing Parties'. *Weatherhead Center for International Affairs Working Paper Series* No. 02–03 2002. www.wcfia.harvard.edu/papers/555_Toward_An_Uncivil_Society.pdf (03/04/06).

II.C: Websites accessible on 09/05/06

http://www.ainonline.com/issues/ 11_01/11_01_securitytrainingpg24.html
http://www.alphalink.com.au/~radnat/debenoist/alain15.html
http://www.arcto.ru/modules.php?name=News&file=print&sid=1133
http://www.awayuq.typepad.com/awayuq/2005/06/ram_dass_and_kn.html
http://www.bnp.net
http://www.calvin.edu/academic/cas/gpa/ww2era.html
http://www.cre.gov.uk/
http://www.fordham.edu/HALSALL/mod/1814wordsworth.html
http://cs.art.rmit.edu.au/deleuzeguattarionary/r/pages/rhizomic.html
http://www.omrlp.com/
http://www.religiologiques.uqam.ca/recen/benoist.html
http://www.runnymedetrust.org/
http://www.stormfront.org/
http://www.searchlightmagazine.com
http://www.socio.demon.co.uk/rhizome.html
http://www.cs.art.rmit.edu.au/ deleuzeguattarionary/r/r.html
http://www. nifg.org.uk/facts_a.htm

Index

Note: Locators in bold refers to discussions in detail